FROMMER'S
EasyGuide
TO
HAWAII 2017

By
Jeanette Foster

Easy Guides are ✦ Quick To Read ✦ Light To Carry
✦ For Expert Advice ✦ In All Price Ranges

FrommerMedia LLC

Published by

FROMMER MEDIA LLC

Copyright © 2017 by Frommer Media LLC. All rights reserved. No part of this publication may be repro-
duced, stored in a retrieval system, or transmitted in any form or by any means, electronic, mechanical,
photocopying, recording, scanning or otherwise, except as permitted under Sections 107 or 108 of the
1976 United States Copyright Act, without the prior written permission of the Publisher. Requests to the
Publisher for permission should be addressed to the support@frommermedia.com.

Frommer's is a registered trademark of Arthur Frommer. Frommer Media LLC is not associated with any
product or vendor mentioned in this book.

ISBN 978-1-62887-266-8 (paper), 978-1-62887-267-5 (e-book)
Editorial Director: Pauline Frommer
Editor: Melissa Klurman
Production Editor: Heather Wilcox
Editorial Assistant: Ali Arminio
Cartographer: Elizabeth Puhl
Cover Design: Howard Grossman

For information on our other products or services, see www.frommers.com.

Frommer Media LLC also publishes its books in a variety of electronic formats. Some content that
appears in print may not be available in electronic formats.

Manufactured in the United States of America

5 4 3 2 1

FROMMER'S STAR RATINGS SYSTEM

Every hotel, restaurant and attraction listed in this guide has been ranked for quality and value. Here's
what the stars mean:

★ Recommended
★★ Highly Recommended
★★★ A must! Don't miss!

AN IMPORTANT NOTE

The world is a dynamic place. Hotels change ownership, restaurants hike their prices, museums
alter their opening hours, and buses and trains change their routings. And all of this can occur
in the several months after our authors have visited, inspected, and written about these hotels,
restaurants, museums, and transportation services. Though we have made valiant efforts to keep
all our information fresh and up-to-date, some few changes can inevitably occur in the periods
before a revised edition of this guidebook is published. So please bear with us if a tiny number
of the details in this book have changed. Please also note that we have no responsibility or liabil-
ity for any inaccuracy or errors or omissions, or for inconvenience, loss, damage, or expenses suf-
fered by anyone as a result of assertions in this guide.

CONTENTS

ABOUT THE AUTHOR

Jeanette Foster is the author of more than four dozen travel books for Frommer's as well as the editor of *Zagat's Survey to Hawaiian Restaurants* since 1997. In 2010, she was awarded the Bronze Award by the Society of American Travel Writers for *Frommer's Hawaii Day by Day*. She resides on the Big Island in Hawaii.

ABOUT THE FROMMER TRAVEL GUIDES

For most of the past 50 years, Frommer's has been the leading series of travel guides in North America, accounting for as many as 24% of all guidebooks sold. I think I know why.

Although we hope our books are entertaining, we nevertheless deal with travel in a serious fashion. Our guidebooks have never looked on such journeys as a mere recreation, but as a far more important human function, a time of learning and introspection, an essential part of a civilized life. We stress the culture, lifestyle, history, and beliefs of the destinations we cover and urge our readers to seek out people and new ideas as the chief rewards of travel.

We have never shied from controversy. We have, from the beginning, encouraged our authors to be intensely judgmental, critical—both pro and con—in their comments, and wholly independent. Our only clients are our readers, and we have triggered the ire of countless prominent sorts, from a tourist newspaper we called "practically worthless" (it unsuccessfully sued us) to the many rip-offs we've condemned.

And because we believe that travel should be available to everyone regardless of their incomes, we have always been cost-conscious at every level of expenditure. Although we have broadened our recommendations beyond the budget category, we insist that every lodging we include be sensibly priced. We use every form of media to assist our readers and are particularly proud of our feisty daily website, the award-winning Frommers.com.

I have high hopes for the future of Frommer's. May these guidebooks, in all the years ahead, continue to reflect the joy of travel and the freedom that travel represents. May they always pursue a cost-conscious path, so that people of all incomes can enjoy the rewards of travel. And may they create, for both the traveler and the persons among whom we travel, a community of friends, where all human beings live in harmony and peace.

Arthur Frommer

THE BEST OF HAWAII

There's no place on Earth quite like this handful of sun-drenched, mid-Pacific islands. The Hawaii of South Seas literature and Hollywood films really does exist. Here you'll find palm-fringed blue lagoons, lush rainforests, hidden gardens, cascading waterfalls, wild rivers running through rugged canyons, and soaring volcanoes. And oh, those beaches—gold, red, black, and even green sands caressed by endless surf. The possibilities for adventure—and relaxation—are endless. Each of the six main islands is separate, distinct, and infinitely complex. There's far too much to see and do on any 2-week vacation, which is why so many people return to the "Aloha State" year after year.

Unfortunately, even paradise has its share of stifling crowds and tourist schlock. If you're not careful, your trip to Hawaii could turn into a nightmare of tourist traps selling shells from the Philippines, hokey faux culture like cellophane-skirted hula dancers, overpriced exotic drinks, and a 4-hour timeshare lecture before you get on that "free" snorkeling trip. That's where this guide comes in. As a Hawaii resident, I can tell the extraordinary from the merely ordinary. This book steers you away from the crowded, the overrated, and the overpriced—and toward the best Hawaii has to offer. No matter what your budget, this guide helps ensure that every dollar is well spent.

HAWAII'S best ISLAND EXPERIENCES

- **Hitting the Beach:** A beach is a beach is a beach, right? Not in Hawaii. With 132 islets, shoals, and reefs, plus a general coastline of 750 miles, Hawaii has beaches in all different shapes, sizes, and colors, including black. The variety on the six major islands is astonishing; you could go to a different beach every day for years and still not see them all. For the best of the best, see "The Best Beaches," below.
- **Taking the Plunge:** Don mask, fin, and snorkel to explore Hawaii's magical underwater world, where exotic corals and

The Hawaiian Islands

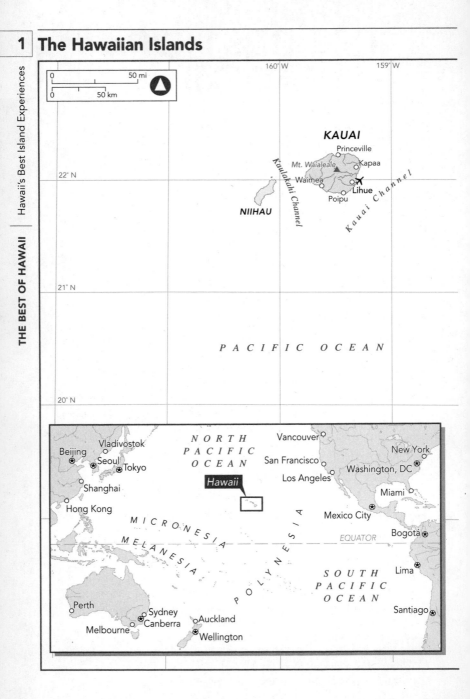

160° W   159° W

KAUAI

0   50 mi
0   50 km

Princeville
Mt. Waialeale   Kapaa
22° N   Waimea   Lihue
Poipu

Kaulakahi Channel
Kauai Channel

NIIHAU

21° N

PACIFIC OCEAN

20° N

NORTH PACIFIC OCEAN   Vancouver

Beijing   Vladivostok   San Francisco   New York
Seoul   Tokyo   Los Angeles   Washington, DC
Shanghai   Hawaii   Miami
Hong Kong   Mexico City   Bogotá

MICRONESIA
MELANESIA   EQUATOR

POLYNESIA   Lima
SOUTH PACIFIC OCEAN

Perth   Sydney   Auckland   Santiago
Melbourne   Canberra   Wellington

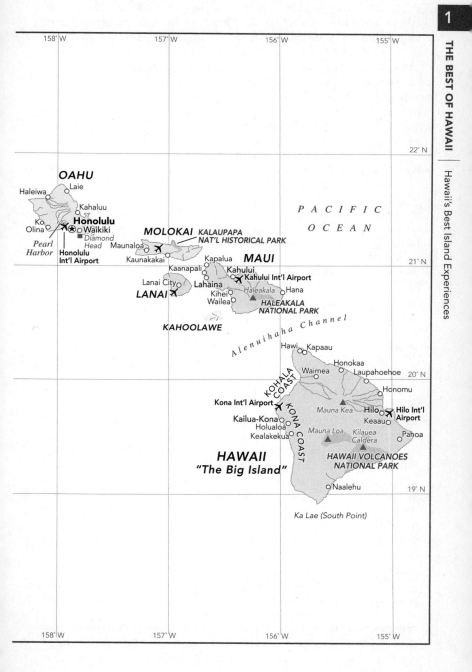

OAHU
Haleiwa
Laie
Kahaluu
Ko
Olina
Honolulu
Waikiki
Pearl
Harbor
Diamond
Head
Honolulu
Int'l Airport

MOLOKAI
Maunaloa
Kaunakakai
KALAUPAPA
NAT'L HISTORICAL PARK
Kapalua
Kaanapali
Lanai City
Lahaina
Kihei
Wailea

LANAI

KAHOOLAWE

MAUI
Kahului
Kahului Int'l Airport
Haleakala
Hana
HALEAKALA
NATIONAL PARK

PACIFIC
OCEAN

Alenuihaha Channel

Hawi
Kapaau
Honokaa
Waimea
Laupahoehoe
Honomu
Kona Int'l Airport
KOHALA
COAST
Mauna Kea
Hilo
Hilo Int'l
Airport
Kailua-Kona
Holualoa
Kealakekua
KONA
COAST
Mauna Loa
Keaau
Kilauea
Caldera
Pahoa

HAWAII
"The Big Island"
HAWAII VOLCANOES
NATIONAL PARK
Naalehu

Ka Lae (South Point)

158° W   157° W   156° W   155° W

22° N
21° N
20° N
19° N

kaleidoscopic clouds of tropical fish await you—a sea turtle may even come over to check you out. Can't swim? Then take one of the many submarine tours offered by **Atlantis Submarines** (www.go-atlantis.com; ☏ **800/548-6262**) on Oahu, the Big Island, and Maui. Check out the "Watersports" section in each island chapter for more information on all these underwater adventures.

o **Meeting Local Folks:** If you go to Hawaii and see only people like the ones back home, you might as well not have come. Extend yourself—leave your hotel, go out and meet the locals, and learn about Hawaii and its people. Just smile and say "Owzit?"—which means "How is it?" ("It's good" is the usual response)—and you're on your way to making a new friend.

o **Feeling History Come Alive at Pearl Harbor** (Oahu): The United States could no longer turn its back on World War II after December 7, 1941, when Japanese warplanes bombed Pearl Harbor. Standing on the deck of the **USS *Arizona* Memorial** (www.nps.gov/usar; ☏ **808/422-3300**)—the eternal tomb for the 1,177 sailors and Marines trapped below when the battleship sank in just 9 minutes—is a moving experience you'll never forget. See p. 52.

o **Watching for Whales:** If you happen to be in Hawaii during hump-back-whale season (roughly Dec–Apr), don't miss the opportunity to see these gentle giants. A host of boats—from small inflatables to high-tech, high-speed sailing catamarans—provide a range of whale-watching cruises on every island. One of my favorites is along the Big Island's Kona Coast, where **Captain Dan McSweeney's Whale Watch Learning Adventures** (www.ilovewhales.com; ☏ **808/322-0028**) takes you right to the whales year-round (pilot, sperm, false killer, melon-headed, pygmy killer, and beaked whales call Hawaii home even when humpbacks aren't in residence). See p. 125.

o **Creeping up to the Ooze** (Big Island): Kilauea volcano has been adding land to the Big Island continuously since 1983. The volcano goddess Pele continues to blow smoke and plumage into the air from the main crater of Halemaumau. If conditions are right, you can walk up to the red-hot lava and see it ooze along, or you can stand at the shoreline and watch with awe as 2,000°F (1,092°C) molten fire pours into the ocean. Or, you can also take to the air in a helicopter and see the volcano goddess's work from above. See p. 117.

o **Going Big-Game Fishing off the Kona Coast** (Big Island): Don't pass up the opportunity to try your luck in the sport-fishing capital of the world, where 1,000-pound marlin are taken from the sea just about every month of the year. Not looking to set a world record? Kona's charter-boat captains specialize in conservation and will be glad to tag any fish you angle and then let it go so someone else can have the fun of fighting a big-game fish tomorrow. See p. 127.

o **Greeting the Rising Sun from atop Haleakala** (Maui): Bundle up in warm clothing, fill a thermos full of hot java, and drive up to the summit to watch the sky turn from inky black to muted charcoal as a small sliver of orange light forms on the horizon. There's something magical about standing at 10,000 feet, breathing in the rarefied air, and watching the first rays of sun streak across the sky. See p. 173.

o **Soaring over the Na Pali Coast** (Kauai): A helicopter flight is the only way to see the spectacular, surreal beauty of Kauai. Your chopper will dip low over razor-thin cliffs, fluttering past sparkling waterfalls and swooping down into the canyons and valleys of the fabled Na Pali Coast. See p. 233.

HAWAII'S best BEACHES

o **Lanikai Beach** (Oahu): Too gorgeous to be real, this stretch along the Windward Coast is one of Hawaii's postcard-perfect beaches—a mile of golden sand as soft as powdered sugar bordering translucent turquoise waters. The waters are calm year-round and excellent for swimming, snorkeling, and kayaking. Two tiny offshore islands complete the picture. See p. 70.

o **Hapuna Beach** (Big Island): This half-mile-long crescent regularly wins kudos in the world's top travel magazines as the most beautiful beach in Hawaii—some consider it one of the most beautiful beaches in the world. One look and you'll see why: Perfect cream-colored sand slopes down to crystal-clear water that's great for swimming, snorkeling, and bodysurfing in summer; come winter, waves thunder in like stampeding horses. The facilities for picnicking and camping are top-notch, and there's plenty of parking. See p. 124.

o **Kapalua Beach** (Maui): On an island with many great beaches, Kapalua takes the prize. This golden crescent with swaying palms is protected from strong winds and currents by two outstretched lava-rock promontories. Its calm waters are perfect for snorkeling, swimming, and kayaking. Facilities include showers, restrooms, and lifeguards. See p. 183.

o **Haena Beach** (Kauai): Backed by verdant cliffs, this curvaceous North Shore beach has starred as Paradise in many a movie. It's easy to see why Hollywood loves Haena Beach, with its grainy golden sand and translucent turquoise waters. Summer months bring calm waters for swimming and snorkeling; winter brings mighty waves for surfers. Numerous facilities include picnic tables, restrooms, and showers. See p. 243.

HAWAII'S best OUTDOORS

o **Volcanoes:** The entire island chain is made of volcanoes; don't miss the opportunity to see one. On Oahu, the entire family can hike to the top of ancient, world-famous **Diamond Head** (p. 74). At the other end of the spectrum is fire-breathing Kilauea at **Hawaii Volcanoes National Park,** on the Big Island, where you can get an up-close-and-personal experience with the red-hot lava ooze (p. 117). On Maui, **Haleakala National Park** provides a bird's-eye view into a long-dormant volcanic crater (p. 173).

o **Waterfalls:** Rushing waterfalls thundering downward into sparkling fresh-water pools are some of Hawaii's most beautiful natural wonders. If you're on the Big Island, stop by **Rainbow Falls** (p. 117) in Hilo, or the spectacular 442-foot **Akaka Falls** (p. 113) just outside Hilo. On Maui, the Road to Hana offers numerous viewing opportunities; at the end of the drive, you'll find **Oheo Gulch** (also known as the Seven Sacred Pools), with some of the most dramatic and accessible waterfalls on the islands (p. 181). Kauai is loaded with waterfalls, especially along the North Shore and in the Wailua area, where you'll find 40-foot **Opaekaa Falls** (p. 235), probably the best-looking drive-up waterfall on Kauai.

o **Gardens:** The islands are redolent with the sweet scent of flowers. For a glimpse of the full breadth and beauty of Hawaii's spectacular range of tropical flora, I suggest spending an afternoon at a lush garden. On Oahu, amid the high-rises of downtown Honolulu, the leafy oasis of **Foster Botanical Garden** (p. 53) showcases 26 native Hawaiian trees and the last stand of several rare trees, including an East African, whose white flowers bloom only at night. On the Big Island, **Liliuokalani Gardens** (p. 115), the largest formal Japanese garden this side of Tokyo, resembles a postcard from Asia, with bonsai, carp ponds, pagodas, and even a moon-gate bridge. At Maui's **Iao Valley Botanic Garden** (p. 170), you can take a leisurely self-guided stroll through more than 700 native and exotic plants, including orchids, proteas, and bromeliads. On lush Kauai, **Na Aina Kai Botanical Gardens** (p. 238), on some 240 acres, is sprinkled with around 70 life-size (some larger-than-life-size) whimsical bronze statues, hidden off the beaten path of the North Shore.

o **Marine Life Conservation Areas:** Nine underwater parks are spread across Hawaii, most notably **Waikiki Beach** (p. 68) and **Hanauma Bay** (p. 68), on Oahu; **Kealakekua Bay** (p. 126), on the Big Island; and **Molokini,** just off the coast of Maui (see "Watersports" in chapter 6). Be sure to bring snorkel gear.

o **Waimea Canyon** (Kauai): This valley, known for its reddish lava beds, reminds many people who see it of Arizona's Grand Canyon. Kauai's version is bursting with ever-changing color, just like Arizona's, but it's smaller—only a mile wide, 3,567 feet deep, and 12 miles long. All this grandeur was caused by a massive earthquake that sent all the streams flowing into a single river, which then carved this picturesque canyon. You can stop by the road and look at it, hike down into it, or swoop through it by helicopter. See p. 232.

HAWAII'S best CULTURAL EXPERIENCES

o **Experiencing the Hula:** For a real, authentic hula experience on Oahu, check out the **Bishop Museum** (p. 47), which stages excellent performances on weekdays, or head to Halekulani's **House Without a Key**

(p. 82) at sunset to watch the enchanting Kanoelehua Miller dance beautiful hula under a century-old kiawe tree. The first week after Easter is Hawaii's biggest and most prestigious hula extravaganza, the **Merrie Monarch Hula Festival** (p. 88), in Hilo on the Big Island; tickets sell out by January 1, so reserve early.

o **Visiting the Missionary's Hawaii** (Maui): On your way to Hana, on the famous Hana Highway, take a spin into the tiny village of Huelo, and visit the 1853 historic **Kaulanapueo Church** (p. 179). Sitting in the coral and cement church will give you a feel for the New England missionaries who traveled thousands of miles from their home to spread the good word to Hawaiians.

o **Seeing How the Royalty Lived** (Kauai): Wander through the magnificent grounds of the **McBryde Garden** (p. 230) royal home of Queen Emma in the 1860s. Famous for the elaborate formal gardens, popular during that century, with waterfalls, bubbling streams, manicured plants and statues.

o **Watching the Ancient Hawaiian Sport of Canoe Paddling** (Oahu): From February to September, on weekday evenings and weekend days, hundreds of canoe paddlers gather at Ala Wai Canal and practice the Hawaiian sport of canoe paddling. Find a comfortable spot at Ala Wai Park, next to the canal, and watch this ancient sport come to life.

o **Attending a Hawaiian-Language Church Service** (Oahu): **Kawaiaha'o Church** (© **808/522-1333**) is the Westminster Abbey of Hawaii. The coral church is a perfect setting in which to experience an all-Hawaiian service, held several times a year, on Sunday at 9am, complete with Hawaiian song. Admission is free; let your conscience be your guide regarding donations. See p. 51.

o **Buying a Lei in Chinatown** (Oahu): There's a host of cultural sights and experiences to be had in Honolulu's Chinatown. Wander through this several-square-block area with its jumble of exotic shops selling herbs, Chinese groceries, and acupuncture services. Before you leave, check out the lei sellers on Maunakea Street (near N. Hotel St.), where Hawaii's finest leis go for as little as $15. If you'd like a little guidance, you can follow the walking tour described on p. 55.

o **Listening to Old-Fashioned "Talk Story" with Hawaiian Song and Dance** (Big Island): Once a month, under a full moon, **Twilight at Kala-huipua'a,** a celebration of the Hawaiian culture that includes storytelling, singing, and dancing, takes place ocean-side at Mauna Lani Resort, www. maunalani.com/events/twilight-at-kalahuipuaa (© **808/885-6622**). It hearkens back to another time in Hawaii, when family and neighbors would gather on back porches to sing, dance, and "talk story." See p. 137.

o **Visiting Ancient Hawaii's Most Sacred Temple** (Big Island): On the Kohala Coast, next to where King Kamehameha the Great was born, stands Hawaii's oldest, largest, and most sacred religious site: the 1,500-year-old **Mookini Luakini Heiau,** used by kings to pray and offer human sacrifices. This massive three-story stone temple, dedicated to Ku, the Hawaiian god

THE welcoming LEI

Nothing makes you feel more welcome than a lei. The tropical beauty of the delicate garland, the deliciously sweet fragrance of the blossoms, the sensual way the flowers curl softly around your neck—there's no doubt about it: Getting "lei'd" in Hawaii is a sensuous experience.

Leis are much more than just a decorative necklace of flowers—they're also one of the nicest ways to say "hello," "goodbye," "congratulations," "I salute you," "my sympathies are with you," or "I love you."

During ancient times, leis given to *alii* (royalty) were accompanied by a bow, because it was *kapu* (forbidden) for a commoner to raise his arms higher than the king's head. The presentation of a kiss with a lei didn't come about until World War II; it's generally attributed to an entertainer who kissed an officer on a dare and then quickly presented him with her lei, saying it was an old Hawaiian custom. It wasn't then, but it sure caught on fast.

Lei-making is a tropical art form. All leis are fashioned by hand in a variety of traditional patterns; some are sewn with hundreds of tiny blooms or shells, or bits of ferns and leaves. Some are twisted, some braided, some strung. Every island has its own special flower lei—the lei of the land, so to speak. On Oahu, the choice is *ilima*, a small orange flower. Big Islanders prefer the *lehua*, a large, delicate red puff. On Maui, it's the *lokelani*, a small rose; on Kauai, it's the *mokihana*, a fragrant green vine and berry; on Molokai, it's the *kukui*, the white blossom of a candlenut tree; and on Lanai, it's the *kaunaoa*, a bright yellow moss. Residents of Niihau use the island's abundant seashells to make leis that were once prized by royalty and are now worth a small fortune.

Leis are available at all of the islands' airports, from florists, and even at supermarkets. You can find wonderful inexpensive leis at the half-dozen lei shops on **Maunakea Street** in Honolulu's Chinatown and, on the Big Island, at **Castillo Orchids** (© **808/329-6070;** 73-4310 Laui St.), off Kaiminani Drive in the Kona Palisades subdivision, across from the Kona Airport. If you plan ahead, you can also arrange to have a lei-greeter meet you as you deplane; **Greeters of Hawaii** (www.greetersofhawaii.com; © **800/366-8559** or 808/836-3246) serves the Honolulu (Oahu), Kona (Big Island), Kahului (Maui), and Lihue (Kauai) airports.

of war, was erected in A.D. 480. It's said that each stone was passed from hand to hand from Pololu Valley, 14 miles away, by 18,000 men who worked from sunset to sunrise. For group visits contact Alexia Lum Carvalho (© 808/373-8000).

o **Hunting for Petroglyphs** (Big Island): Archaeologists are still uncertain exactly what these ancient rock carvings mean. The majority are found in the 233-acre **Puako Petroglyph Archaeological District,** near Mauna Lani Resort on the Kohala Coast. The best time to hunt for these intricate depictions of ancient life is either early in the morning or late afternoon, when the angle of the sun lets you see the forms clearly. See p. 109.

o **Exploring Puuhonua O Honaunau National Historical Park** (Big Island): This sacred site on the southern Kona Coast (www.nps.gov/puho; © **808/328-2326**) was once a place of refuge and a revered place of rejuvenation.

You can walk the same consecrated grounds where priests once conducted holy ceremonies and glimpse the ancient way of life in pre-contact Hawaii in the re-created 180-acre village. See p. 108.

HAWAII'S best FAMILY BEACHES

- **Hanauma Bay** (Oahu): It can get crowded, but for clear, warm, calm waters; an abundance of fish that are so friendly they'll swim right up to your face mask; a beautiful setting; and easy access, there's no place like Hanauma Bay. Just wade in waist-deep and look down to see more than 50 species of reef and inshore fish. Snorkelers hug the safe, shallow inner bay—it's like swimming in an outdoor aquarium. See p. 68.
- **Kahaluu Beach** (Big Island): The calm, shallow waters of Kahaluu are perfect for beginning snorkelers or those who are unsure of their swimming abilities and want the comfort of being able to stand up at any time. The sunlight through the shallow waters casts a dazzling spotlight on the colorful sea life and coral formations. See p. 122.
- **Kealakekua Bay** (Big Island): Mile-wide Kealakekua Bay, at the foot of massive U-shaped sea cliffs, is rich with marine life, snorkelers, and history. A white obelisk marks the spot where, in 1778, the great British navigator Captain James Cook, who charted most of the Pacific, was killed by Hawaiians. The bay itself is a marine sanctuary that teems with schools of polychromatic tropical fish. See p. 126.
- **Molokini** (Maui): The islet of Molokini is shaped like a crescent moon that fell from the sky. Its shallow concave side serves as a sheltering backstop against sea currents for tiny tropical fish; its opposite side is a deepwater cliff inhabited by spiny lobsters, moray eels, and white-tipped sharks. Neophyte snorkelers should report to the concave side, experienced scuba divers the other. The clear water and abundant marine life make this islet off the Makena coast one of Hawaii's most popular dive spots, so expect crowds. See "Watersports" in chapter 5.
- **Kee Beach** (Kauai): Where the road ends on the North Shore, you'll find a dandy little reddish-gold beach almost too beautiful to be real. It borders a reef-protected cove at the foot of fluted volcanic cliffs. Swimming and snorkeling are safe inside the reef, where long-nosed butterfly fish flitter about and schools of *taape* (bluestripe snapper) swarm over the coral. See p. 243.

HAWAII'S best ACTIVE ADVENTURES

- **Swimming with Sharks** (Oahu): You are out in the blue depths of the open ocean when suddenly you see a form in the distance. As it gets closer, the distinct sleek, pale gray shape of a 6-foot-long reef shark appears. Your

PAMPERING IN paradise

Hawaii's spas have raised the art of relaxation and healing to a new level. The traditional Greco-Roman-style spas have evolved into airy, open facilities that embrace the tropics. Spa-goers in Hawaii want to hear the sound of the ocean, smell the salt air, and feel the caress of the warm breeze. They want to experience Hawaiian products and traditional treatments they can get only here.

Today's spas offer a wide diversity of treatments. Massage options include Hawaiian lomilomi, Swedish, aromatherapy, *craniosacral* (massaging the head), *shiatsu* (no oil, just deep thumb pressure on acupuncture points), Thai (another oilless massage involving stretching), and hot stone. There are even side-by-side massages for couples and duo massages—two massage therapists working on you at once.

Body treatments for the entire body or just the face involve a variety of herbal wraps, masks, or scrubs using a range of ingredients from seaweed to salt to mud, with or without accompanying aromatherapy. After you have been rubbed and scrubbed, most spas offer an array of water treatments—a sort of hydromassage in a tub with jets and an assortment of colored crystals, oils, and scents.

Those are just the traditional treatments. Most spas also provide a range of alternative healthcare options, such as acupuncture, and more exotic treatments, such as Ayurvedic and "siddha" from India or "Reiki" from Japan. Some use cutting-edge treatments, such as Maui's Grand Wailea Resort's full-spectrum color-light therapy pod (based on NASA's work with astronauts).

Of course, all this pampering doesn't come cheap. Massages start at $150 for 50 minutes and start at $250 for 80 minutes; body treatments are in the $150 to $250 range; and alternative healthcare treatments can be as high as $200 to $300. But you may think it's worth the expense to banish your tension and stress.

heart beats faster—it's a moment you will never forget. But you aren't worried; you're protected by a shark cage, courtesy of **North Shore Shark Adventures** (www.sharkencountershawaii.com; ✆ **808/228-5900;** p. 73). This is a memory you'll share with your friends for years to come.

o **Experiencing Where the Gods Live** (Big Island): As the muted colors of sunset slowly fade and the brilliantly lit stars become noticeable in the sky, you breathe in the cool, crisp, rarefied air at 13,000 feet atop Hawaii's tallest mountain, Mauna Kea, for a view the ancient Hawaiians thought was only experienced by the gods. **Mauna Kea Summit Adventures** (www. maunakea.com; ✆ **888/322-2366;** p. 112) has been taking visitors up to the top for more than a decade, serving them a delicious picnic dinner, and treating them to views of the stars of Hawaii (with and without high-tech telescopes). You'll never look at the night stars again without thinking of the sweet memory of the heavens over Hawaii.

o **Venturing to the Pineapple Isle** (Maui): The best snorkel-sailing trip in all Hawaii takes place off the island of Maui—the day sail and snorkel to Lanai, provided by **Trilogy** (www.sailtrilogy.com; ✆ **888/225-MAUI** [6284]; p. 188). The journey to Lanai (complete with hot, homemade cinnamon buns) is smooth sailing. The beach picnic (with lunch) and snorkeling off Lanai's Hulopoe Beach fill a day that will linger in your memory long after your tan has faded (be sure to take the personalized tour of the island).

○ **Tubing into the Past** (Kauai): In the days when sugar was king in Hawaii, the most fun activity on a hot, hot day was to grab an old inner tube and jump into the irrigation ditches surrounding the sugar cane field. You can return to those old days with **Kauai Backcountry Adventures** (http:// kauaibackcountry.com; ℂ **888/270-0550;** p. 247). All you have to do is sit in the inner tube and gently float along the gravity-fed stream, passing by tropical forests, going through lava tunnels, and finally reaching a big mountain pool where a picnic lunch awaits.

SUGGESTED HAWAII ITINERARIES

2

What should I do in Hawaii? This is the most common question that readers ask me. The purpose of this chapter is to give you my expert advice on the best things to see and do on each island and how to do them so you can spend more time "doing" and less time "getting there."

First, here's the best advice I can give you: **Do not plan to see more than one island per week.** With the exception of the ferry between Maui and Lanai, getting from one island to another is an all-day affair once you figure in packing, checking out of and into hotels, driving to and from airports, and dealing with rental cars, not to mention time actually spent at the airport and on the flight. Don't waste a day of your vacation seeing our interisland air terminals.

Second, **don't max out your days.** This is Hawaii—allow some time to do nothing but relax. You most likely will arrive jet-lagged, so it's a good idea to ease into your vacation. In fact, exposure to sunlight can help reset your internal clock, so I include time at the beach on the first day of most of these itineraries.

Third, **if this is your first trip to Hawaii, think of it as a "scouting" trip.** Hawaii is too beautiful, too sensual, too enticing to see just once in a lifetime. You'll be back—you don't need to see and do everything on this trip.

Finally, keep in mind that the following itineraries are designed to appeal to a wide range of people. If you have a specific interest, check out chapter 1, "The Best of Hawaii," to **plan your trip around your passion.**

One last thing: **You will need a car to get around the islands.** Oahu has adequate public transportation, but even so, it's set up for residents, not tourists carrying coolers and beach toys (all carry-ons must fit under the bus seat). So plan to rent a car. But also plan to get out of the car as much as possible—to smell the sweet perfume of plumeria, to hear the sound of the wind through a bamboo forest, and to plunge into the gentle waters of the Pacific.

A WEEK ON OAHU

Oahu is so stunning that the *alii,* the kings of Hawaii, made it the capital of the island nation. Below, I've presumed that you are staying in Waikiki; if your hotel is in another location, be sure to factor in extra time for traveling.

Day 1: Arriving & Seeing Waikiki Beach ★★

After you get off the plane, lather up in sunscreen and head for the most famous beach in the world—**Waikiki Beach** (p. 68). If you have kids in tow or you can't handle a whole afternoon in the intense sun, check out Hawaii's water world at the **Waikiki Aquarium** (p. 54) or gain insight into Waikiki's past on the **Waikiki Historic Trail** (p. 46), a 2-mile trail marked with bronzed surfboards. Be sure to catch the sunset (anywhere on Waikiki Beach will do) and get an early dinner.

Day 2: Visiting Pearl Harbor ★★★ & Honolulu's Chinatown ★★★

Head to the **USS *Arizona* Memorial at Pearl Harbor** (p. 52). Get here as early as possible—by the afternoon, the lines are 2 hours long. While you're here, be sure to see the **USS *Missouri* Memorial** (p. 53) and the **USS *Bowfin* Submarine Museum & Park** (p. 52). On your way back, stop in **Chinatown** for lunch and a self-guided walking tour (p. 26). In the afternoon, take a nap or head for the beach at **Ala Moana Beach Park** (p. 68) or a shopping spree across the street at the **Ala Moana Center** (p. 80). Have dinner in Honolulu or the surrounding area.

Day 3: Exploring the North Shore ★★★ & the Polynesian Cultural Center ★

Start your day with a drive to the **North Shore** (see "Central Oahu & the North Shore" on p. 66). If you're up early, have breakfast in the quaint town of **Haleiwa;** if not, at least stop and get a picnic lunch before you beach-hop down the coast of the North Shore and choose from some of the world's most beautiful beaches, like **Waimea Beach Park** (p. 71). After lunch, head for the **Polynesian Cultural Center,** in Laie (p. 66). Allow at least 2 hours to tour this mini-glimpse of the Pacific. Continue driving down the coast road to the small town of **Kailua.** Stay for dinner here to avoid the traffic back to Waikiki.

Day 4: Snorkeling in Hanauma Bay ★★★

If it's not Tuesday (when the park is closed), head out in the morning for the spectacular snorkeling at **Hanauma Bay** (p. 68). Continue beach-hopping down the coastline—check out **Sandy Beach** (p. 70) and **Makapuu Beach Park** (p. 70) to see which one appeals to you. Then turn back to take the Pali Highway home to Waikiki, and be sure to stop at the **Pali Lookout** (p. 54).

Day 5: Hiking a Rainforest ★★, Glimpsing Historic Honolulu & Experiencing Hawaiian Culture

You could probably use a day out of the sun by now, so try a short hike into the rainforest, just a 15-minute drive from downtown Honolulu. Be sure to wear good hiking or trail shoes for the **Manoa Falls Trail,** and bring mosquito repellent. Next, head for downtown Honolulu to see some of the city's historic sites, including the **Iolani Palace, Kawaiaha'o Church,** and **Mission Houses Museum** (coverage starts on p. 50). To see where you've been, go to the top of the **Aloha Tower,** at the Aloha Tower Marketplace, for a bird's-eye view of Honolulu. Grab lunch at the Marketplace or one of the nearby restaurants. Spend the afternoon at the **Bishop Museum** (p. 47) to immerse yourself in Hawaiian culture.

Day 6: Relaxing at Kailua Beach ★★★

On your last full day on Oahu, travel over the Pali Highway to the windward side of the island and spend a day at **Kailua Beach** (p. 71)—but before you leave Waikiki, drop by **MAC 24-7** (p. 42) to pick up a picnic lunch. Kailua is the perfect beach on which to just relax or snorkel or try something different, such as kayaking or windsurfing. You can spend the entire day here, or you can take an afternoon hike at the **Hoomaluhia Botanical Garden** (p. 65).

Day 7: Shopping & Museum-Hopping

Been having too much fun to shop for gifts for your friends back home? You can find a great selection of stores in Waikiki at the **Ala Moana Center** (p. 80), the **DFS Galleria,** and the **Royal Hawaiian Shopping Center** (p. 80). If you're more interested in looking than buying, check out the **Honolulu Museum of Art** (p. 47), the **Spalding House,** or the **Hawaii State Art Museum** (p. 62). On your way to the airport, be sure to stop at one of the **Maunakea Street lei shops** (p. 58) in Chinatown to buy a sweet-smelling souvenir of your trip.

A WEEK ON THE BIG ISLAND OF HAWAII

A week is barely enough time to see the entire Big Island; 2 weeks would be better. But if your schedule doesn't allow more time, this tour lets you see the highlights of this huge island (twice the size of all the other islands combined). The itinerary is set up for those staying in Kailua-Kona or on the Kohala Coast; I suggest you also spend at least 2 nights in Volcano Village to enjoy Hawaii Volcanoes National Park.

Day 1: Arriving & Making Beach Time

After you settle into your hotel, head for the beach: Snorkelers should go to **Kahaluu Beach Park** (p. 65); beach aficionados can choose from

Anaehoomalu Bay (A-Bay), Hapuna Beach, and Kaunaoa Beach (Mauna Kea Beach), depending on whether you want to snorkel, body board, or just relax (see reviews starting on p. 122 to help you decide). When the sun starts to wane, head for old Kailua-Kona town (coverage starts on p. 105) and wander through the Hulihee Palace, Mokuaikaua Church, and Kamehameha's Compound at Kamakahonu Bay. Find a spot on the pier or along the sea wall to watch the sunset and then head for dinner in Kailua-Kona or Keauhou.

Day 2: Enjoying a Morning Sail & Afternoon Drive to Hawaii Volcanoes National Park ★★★

Because you most likely will be up early on your first day in Hawaii (and still on mainland time), take advantage of it and book a morning sail/snorkel tour with Fair Wind (p. 126) to Kealakekua Bay, a marine-life preserve. After you return to Keauhou, start driving south. Great stops along the way are Puuhonua O Honaunau National Historical Park (p. 108), South Point (p. 122), and Green Sand Beach (Papakolea Beach; p. 124). Then head up Mauna Kea to Hawaii Volcanoes National Park (p. 117) and stay at one of the quaint B&Bs in the tiny village of Volcano (a list of recommended accommodations starts on p. 97).

Day 3: Exploring an Active Volcano ★★★

The highlight of your trip most likely will be the incredible Hawaii Volcanoes National Park (p. 117). Your first stop should be the Visitor Center; then you can explore Halemaumau Crater, Thurston Lava Tube, Devastation Trail, and the other sights in the crater. Find out from the rangers how to get to the current lava flow. In the afternoon, drive down to the current flow and walk out as far as the rangers will allow. Go eat a nice dinner in Volcano and return to the flow after dark, armed with a flashlight, water bottle, and jacket. Because you were here earlier during the day, the path to the volcano after dark will be familiar to you. Seeing the ribbon of red lava snake its way down the side of the mountain and then thunder into the ocean is a sight you will never forget. You are going to be tired after this full day, so I recommend spending another night in Volcano.

Day 4: Touring Old Hawaii: Hilo Town ★★★, Akaka Falls ★★★, Waipio Valley ★★★ & Cowboy Country

It's just a 45-minute drive from Volcano to Hilo (coverage starts on p. 115), so plan to arrive early in the morning, grab a cup of joe at Bears' Coffee (p. 100), and wander through the old town, being sure to see Banyan Drive, Liliuokalani Gardens, Lyman Museum & Mission House, the Pacific Tsunami Museum, and one of the wonderful botanical gardens, such as Nani Mau Gardens. Head up the Hamakua Coast, stopping at Akaka Falls (p. 113) and Honokaa for lunch. Afterward, be sure to see Waipio Valley (p. 114), the birthplace of Hawaii's kings. Spend the night along the Kohala Coast.

Day 5: Stepping Back in Time on the Kohala Coast ★★★

Get an early start on your trip back in time. The first stop is just south of Kawaihae, at the **Puukohola Heiau National Historic Site** (p. 108), the temple Kamehameha built to the war god to ensure his success in battle. Allow at least an hour here. Keep driving up Hwy. 270 to **Lapakahi State Historical Park** for a view of a typical 14th-century Hawaiian village. Plan a lunch stop in Hawi or Kapaau at either **Bamboo** (p. 103) or **Kohala Rainbow Cafe,** and stop by the **Original King Kamehameha Statue** (p. 109) in Kapaau. The final stop on your northward journey is the **Pololu Valley Lookout** (p. 110). On your way back, in the late afternoon (the best time for viewing), be sure to stop at the **Puako Petroglyph Archaeological District** (p. 109). Make reservations at either the Fairmont Orchid's Polynesian show and luau, **Gathering of the Kings** (p. 138) or at the **Sheraton Keauhou's luau, Haleo** (p. 138) for the perfect ending to your trip back in time.

Day 6: Seeing Mauna Kea ★★★

Sleep in, have a lazy morning at the beach, and in the afternoon plan to explore Hawaii's tallest mountain (and dormant volcano), **Mauna Kea** (p. 110). You need a four-wheel-drive vehicle to climb to the top of the 13,796-foot Mauna Kea, so I recommend booking with the experts, **Mauna Kea Summit Adventures** (p. 112), for a 7- to 8-hour visit to this mountain, sacred to the Hawaiians and treasured by astronomers around the globe.

Day 7: Relaxing & Shopping

Depending on how much time you have on your final day, I recommend either relaxing on the beach or being pampered at a spa. Spa-goers can choose from a range of terrific spas among the **Kohala resorts** (reviews begin on p. 93). Shoppers have lots of options—see my recommendations starting on p. 133.

A WEEK ON MAUI

I've outlined the highlights of Maui for those who have just 7 days and want to see everything. Two suggestions: First, spend 2 nights in Hana, a decision you will not regret; and second, take the Trilogy boat trip to Lanai for the day. I've designed this itinerary assuming you'll stay in West Maui for 5 days. If you are staying elsewhere (like Wailea or Kihei), allow extra driving time.

Day 1: Arriving & Seeing Kapalua Beach ★★★

After checking into your hotel, head for **Kapalua Beach** (p. 183). After an hour or two in the sun, drive to **Lahaina** (p. 171) and spend a couple of hours walking the historic old town. Go to the **Old Lahaina Luau**

(p. 206) at sunset to experience the wonders of Hawaiian culture and dance.

Day 2: Going Up a 10,000-Foot Volcano & Down Again ★★★

You'll likely wake up early on your first day in Hawaii, so take advantage of it and head up to the 10,000-foot dormant volcano, **Haleakala.** You can **hike in the crater** (p. 193), **speed down the mountain on a bicycle** (p. 197), or just wander around the national park. You don't have to be at the top for sunrise; in fact, it has gotten so congested at sunrise that you may be too busy fighting the crowds to have an awe-inspiring experience. Instead, I'd suggest wandering up any time during the day. On your way back down, stop and tour **Upcountry Maui** (p. 177), particularly the communities of **Kula, Makawao,** and **Paia.** Plan for a sunset dinner in Paia or Kuau.

Day 3: Driving the Hana Highway ★★★

Pack a lunch and spend the entire day driving the scenic **Hana Highway** (p. 177). Pull over often and get out to take photos, smell the flowers, and jump in the mountain-stream pools. Wave to everyone, move off the road for those speeding by, and breathe in Hawaii. Plan to spend at least 2 nights in Hana (p. 177).

Day 4: Spending a Day in Heavenly Hana ★★★

Take an early morning hike along the black sands of **Waianapanapa State Park** (p. 181); then explore the tiny town of **Hana** (p. 177). Be sure to see the **Hana Museum Cultural Center, Hasegawa General Store,** and **Hana Coast Gallery.** Get a picnic lunch and drive out to the Kipahulu end of Haleakala National Park at **Oheo Gulch** (p. 181). Hike to the waterfalls and swim in the pools. Spend another night in Hana.

Day 5: Enjoying Wine, Food & (Hawaiian) Song

Check to see whether the road past Hana is open (occasionally it is closed due to road conditions); if it is, continue driving around the island, past Kaupo, and up to the **Ulupalakua Ranch** and the **Tedeschi Vineyards and Winery** (p. 177). Stop at **Grandma's Coffee House** for a cup of java and head down the mountain, with a stop for lunch at **Haliimaile General Store** (p. 166). Spend the afternoon at the **Maui Ocean Center,** in Maalaea (p. 172), checking out the sharks and other marine life. Plan a dinner in Lahaina and see the drama/dance/music show **Ulalena** (p. 204).

Day 6: Sailing to Lanai ★★★

Trilogy (p. 188) provides the best sailing/snorkeling trip in Hawaii, so don't miss it. You'll spend the day (breakfast and lunch included) sailing to Lanai, snorkeling, touring the island, and sailing back to Lahaina. Plus, you still have the afternoon free to shop or take a nap.

Day 7: Relaxing & Shopping

Depending on how much time you have on your final day, you can decide to relax on the beach, get pampered in a spa, or shop for souvenirs. Spa-goers have a range of terrific spas to choose from, and shopping aficionados should check out some of my favorite stores (recommendations start on p. 199). If you have a late flight, you might want to check out **Iao Valley** (p. 109).

A WEEK ON KAUAI

Hawaii's oldest island, ringed with white-sand beaches, is small and easy to circumnavigate in a week. But there are so many wonderful things to do and see that you may find yourself wishing you had more time.

Day 1: Arriving & Making Beach Time

After settling into your hotel, head for the beach. If you're staying on the south side, **Poipu Beach** (p. 210) is your best bet; on the east in the Coconut Coast area, go to **Lydgate State Park** (p. 242); and if you're on the North Shore, try **Anini, Haena, Hanalei,** or **Kee beaches** (p. 242).

Day 2: Touring the North Shore ★★

It rains often on the Garden Isle of Kauai, so on your first sunny day, head out for the **North Shore** (p. 236). Drive all the way to the end of the road to Kee Beach. Plan to hike a little on the famous Kalalau Trail in **Na Pali Coast State Park** (p. 252)—bring hiking shoes or closed-toe tennis shoes. A half-hour on the trail will give you an idea of the spectacular coastline. The hearty may want to hike all the way to **Hanakapiai Beach,** a 2-hour trip one-way. After your hike, take a look at **Ka Ulu O Laka Heiau** at Kee Beach. Head into **Hanalei** (p. 237) for lunch, and then drive down to **Hanalei Bay** (p. 242) for a quiet afternoon on the beach, or book a tour at **Na Aina Kai Botanical Gardens** (p. 238) to see one of Kauai's most beautiful (and whimsical) gardens. Plan to have dinner on the North Shore—my recommendations begin on p. 228.

Day 3: Seeing Kauai from the Air on a Helicopter Tour ★★★

Book a **helicopter tour** (p. 233), but not until 10 or 11am at the earliest, to avoid the bumper-to-bumper commuter traffic. After your tour, head to the **Coconut Coast** area for lunch (my dining recommendations start on p. 227). Learn about Hawaiian history at **Wailua River State Park** (p. 235).

Day 4: Hiking Kokee State Park ★★ & Waimea Canyon ★★★

Get an early start and drive up to the 4,640-acre **Kokee State Park** (p. 232), where you will find a range of trails to fit every ability. Birders, hikers, and sightseers will love wandering around this park. Be sure to stop by the **Kokee Natural History Museum** (p. 233), which is full of great information as well as trail maps. In the afternoon, stop at the "Grand Canyon of the Pacific," **Waimea Canyon** (p. 232), with more great hiking. After you've had your fill of hiking for the day, don't miss the **Kiki a Ola** (**Menehune Ditch;** p. 231) and the **Russian Fort Elizabeth State Historical Park** (p. 232) on your way out of Waimea town. *Tip:* Friday is a great day to plan this trip to Kokee and Waimea. Because you'll already be on the west side, you can attend Hanapepe's Friday **Art Night** (p. 259).

Day 5: Enjoying a Beach Day ★★

Kauai has the best beaches in Hawaii, so you should devote at least a day to them. Check out my beach recommendations, starting on p. 239. If you're not the type to just lie around, you can book a kayak or snorkel tour (watersports options begin on p. 243—I particularly recommend a tour of the Na Pali Coast). If you've had enough sun to last awhile, reserve a tour at **Allerton Garden of the National Tropical Botanical Garden** (p. 230). On your way back from the garden, stop and marvel at the very unusual **Spouting Horn** (p. 230).

Day 6: Getting out of the Rain (or Sun)

It's best to plan for at least one rainy day on Kauai, but my rainy-day suggestions are just as much fun even when it's not rainy. The **Kauai Museum,** in Lihue (p. 230), is filled with treasures. And shoppers will enjoy Kauai's many unique markets (my recommendations start on p. 256).

Day 7: Indulging in a Spa Day

A treatment at a rejuvenating spa is a great way to end your trip (see "Pampering in Paradise," p. 10). Kauai's best spa is the **ANARA Spa,** at the **Grand Hyatt Kauai Resort,** in Poipu. In addition to the fabulous menu of treatments, it has a great area in which to relax, take a steam or a sauna, or just hang out in the hot tub. On the North Shore, try the **Princeville Health Club & Spa,** which is small but very good.

OAHU, THE GATHERING PLACE

3

Rising in the middle of the Pacific Ocean, Honolulu, Oahu's main city and the capital of Hawaii, offers a fast-paced urban setting with Hawaii's hottest nightlife, best shopping, and most diverse restaurants. Next door is Waikiki, the world-famous vacation playground, complete with every imaginable visitor amenity. And the memorial at Pearl Harbor gives a glimpse into world history. The island's North Shore, however, presents a different face: miles of white-sand beaches and a slower, country way of life.

Beaches Beginner snorkelers and families should head to **Hanauma Bay,** a small, curved, 2,000-foot golden-sand beach. **Lanikai** offers excellent swimming with tropical fish and sea turtles in a crystal-clear lagoon. In the winter months, when giant waves—sometimes rising to 50 feet high—pound **Waimea Beach Park,** don't miss the opportunity to see big board surfers easily conquer these monsters. For those who don't want to stray too far from urban action, **Waikiki** is the place.

Things to Do To hear the recorded chants from yesteryear and stand before carvings of Hawaiian gods, head to the **Bishop Museum.** For more recent history, the **USS *Arizona* Memorial at Pearl Harbor** puts you on the deck of the 608-foot battleship. Wander the exotic shops of **Chinatown,** where herbs, textiles, and some of the finest leis in the state are on offer.

Eating & Drinking At the beach, the tantalizing smell of "plate lunch" floats from mobile lunch wagons, offering tasty local specialties such as teriyaki beef, shoyu chicken, or garlic shrimp, all served with a scoop of rice and a scoop of macaroni salad. Alternatively, at more upscale, chef-owned restaurants, sample regional specialties such as seared Hawaiian fish, locally grown sweet potatoes, or taro risotto with locally picked greens.

Nature Just a 5-minute drive from Waikiki is **Diamond Head.** Climb to the top of the 760-foot volcanic cone, and you'll be rewarded with a 360-degree view of the island from the top.

THE best OAHU EXPERIENCES

o **Getting a Tan on Waikiki Beach:** The best spot for catching the rays on the world-famous beach (p. 68) is in front of the big pink Royal Hawaiian Hotel—the beach here is set at the perfect angle for sunning. Get here early; by midday, it's towel-to-towel.

o **Exploring Oahu's Rainforests:** In the misty sunbeams, colorful birds flit among giant ferns and hanging vines, while towering tropical trees form a thick canopy that shelters all below in cool shadows. This emerald world is a true Eden. Just a 15-minute drive from Waikiki Nuuanu Valley (p. 54) is a 2-mile-long drive through a rainforest.

o **Snorkeling the Glistening Waters of Hanauma Bay:** This underwater park (p. 68), once a volcanic crater, is teeming with a rainbow of tropical fish. Bordered by a 2,000-foot gold-sand beach, the bay's shallow water (10 ft. in places) is perfect for neophyte snorkelers. Arrive around 8am to beat the crowds—and don't forget that the bay is closed on Tuesdays.

o **Hiking to the Top of Diamond Head Crater:** Almost everyone can make this easy hike to the top of Hawaii's most famous landmark. The 1½-mile round-trip (p. 74) goes up to the top of the 750-foot volcanic cone, where you have a 360-degree view of Oahu. Allow an hour for the trip up and back, bring a buck for the entry fee (or $5 per car), and don't forget your camera.

o **Heading to Waimea Bay When the Surf's Up:** From November to March, monstrous waves—some 50 feet tall—roll into Waimea (p. 71). When they break on the shore, the ground actually shakes, and everyone on the beach is covered with salt spray mist. The best surfers in the world paddle out to challenge these freight trains. This is an experience you'll never forget—and the show won't cost you a dime.

o **Hearing the Sounds of History:** The Royal Hawaiian Band, which has been performing since being commissioned by King Kamehameha III in 1836, plays most Fridays at noon in front of the Iolani Palace (p. 50). To find out about other free concerts, check the website www.rhb-music.com.

o **Watching the Ancient Hawaiian Sport of Canoe Paddling:** On weekends from February to September, hundreds of paddlers gather at Ala Wai Canal and practice taking traditional Hawaiian canoes out to sea. Find a comfortable spot at Ala Wai Park, next to the canal, and watch the canoe paddlers re-create this centuries-old sport.

o **Finding a Bargain at the Aloha Stadium Swap Meet:** Just a buck gets you into this all-day show at the Aloha Stadium parking lot, where more than 400 vendors sell everything from junk to jewels. Go early for the best deals. It's open Wednesday and Saturday from 8am to 3pm and Sunday from 6:30am to 3pm.

o **Attending a Hawaiian-Language Church Service:** Built in 1842, Kawaiaha'o Church (p. 51) is the Westminster Abbey of Hawaii. The vestibule is lined with portraits of the Hawaiian monarchy; many of their coronations were held in this very building. Hawaiian-language services are held eight Sundays per year at 9am (www.kawaiahao.org/about-us/alii-sunday). Admission is free (donations appreciated).

o **Visiting the Lei Sellers in Chinatown:** There's a host of cultural sights and experiences to be had in Honolulu's Chinatown. Wander through this several-square-block area with its jumble of exotic shops offering herbs, Chinese groceries, and acupuncture services. Be sure to check out the lei sellers on Maunakea Street (near N. Hotel St.), where Hawaii's finest leis go for as little as $5. See p. 79 for more on shopping for leis; see p. 55 for a Chinatown walking tour.

o **Experiencing a Turning Point in America's History, the Bombing of Pearl Harbor:** Standing on the stark white platform of the USS *Arizona* Memorial at Pearl Harbor (p. 52), with the ship submerged in the water 6 feet below, is an unforgettable experience. On that fateful day—December 7, 1941—the 608-foot Arizona sank in just 9 minutes, killing 1,177 of the men on board, after being bombed during the Japanese air raid that sent the United States to war. Go first thing in the morning; you'll wait 2 to 3 hours if you visit at midday. Reserve your tour time and tickets at www.nps.gov/valr/index.htm.

o **Ordering a Shave Ice in a Tropical Flavor You Can Hardly Pronounce:** In Haleiwa, stop at Matsumoto Shave Ice (p. 67) for a snow cone with an exotic flavor poured over the top. Get the local favorite, the fruity "li hing mui," or try one with sweet Japanese adzuki beans hidden inside. This taste of tropical paradise goes for just $2.75.

o **Listening to the Soothing Sounds of Hawaiian Music:** Sit at the ocean's edge the Waikiki's Halekulani (p. 83) as hula dancer extraordinaire Kanoelehua Miller gracefully moves to the sound of Hawaiian steel guitar and the sun slowly sinks into the Pacific.

ORIENTATION

Arriving

Honolulu International Airport sits on the south shore of Oahu, west of downtown Honolulu and Waikiki, near Pearl Harbor. Most of the major American and international carriers fly to Honolulu from the mainland.

LANDING AT HONOLULU INTERNATIONAL AIRPORT

You can walk or take the free airport shuttle from your arrival gate to the main terminal and baggage claim, on the ground level. After collecting your bags, you'll exit to the palm-lined street, where uniformed attendants can either flag down a taxi or direct you to **TheBus** (for transportation information, see below). For Waikiki shuttles and rental-car vans, cross the street to the center island and wait at the designated stop.

GETTING TO & FROM THE AIRPORT

BY RENTAL CAR   All major American rental companies have cars at the airport. Rental-agency vans will pick you up curbside at the center island outside baggage claim and take you to their off-site lots.

BY TAXI Taxis are abundant at the airport; an attendant will be happy to flag one down for you. Taxi fare is about $25 from Honolulu International to downtown Honolulu, and about $30 to $40 to Waikiki. If you need to call a taxi, see "Getting Around" for a list of cab companies.

BY AIRPORT SHUTTLE **Speedi Shuttle** (www.speedishuttle.com; ✆ **877/ 242-5777**) offers transportation in air-conditioned vans from the airport to Waikiki hotels; a one-way trip from airport to Waikiki is $16 per person, or $28 round-trip. You'll find the shuttle at street level outside baggage claim on the median. You can board with two pieces of luggage and a carry-on at no extra charge. Another option is Roberts Hawaii's airport shuttle (www.roberts hawaii.com/airport-shuttle; ✆ **800/831-5541;** or 808/441-7800 on Oahu) a one-way trip from the airport to Waikiki is $16 per person, or $30 round-trip. They'll meet you at arrival and help you with your luggage at baggage claim. The fee includes two pieces of luggage plus a carry-on.

BY BUS TheBus (www.thebus.org; ✆ **808/848-4500**) nos. 19 and 20 (Waikiki Beach and Hotels) run from the airport to downtown Honolulu and Waikiki. The first bus from Waikiki to the airport leaves at 4:46am Monday through Friday and 5:27am Saturday and Sunday; the last bus departs the airport for Waikiki at 1:22am Monday through Friday, and 1:24am Saturday and Sunday. There are two bus stops on the main terminal's upper level. You can board TheBus with a carry-on or small suitcase, as long as it fits under the seat and doesn't disturb other passengers; otherwise, you'll have to take a shuttle or taxi. The approximate travel time to Waikiki is an hour. The one-way fare is $2.50 for adults and $1.25 for children 6 to 17 (exact change only). For more information on TheBus, see "Getting Around."

Visitor Information

The **Hawaii Visitors and Convention Bureau (HVCB),** 2270 Kalakaua Ave., Ste. 801, Honolulu, 96815 (www.gohawaii.com; ✆ **800/GO-HAWAII** [46-429244] or 808/923-1811), supplies free brochures, maps, accommodations guides, and "Islands of Aloha," the official HVCB magazine. The **Oahu Visitors Bureau,** 2270 Kalakaua Ave., Ste. 801, Honolulu, 96815 (www. gohawaii.com/oahu; ✆ **877/525-OAHU** [6248] or 808/524-0722; oahu@ hvcb.org), distributes a free travel planner and map.

A number of free publications, such as *This Week Oahu,* are packed with money-saving coupons and good regional maps; look for them on racks at the airport and around town.

The Island in Brief
HONOLULU

Hawaii's largest city looks like any other big metropolitan center with tall buildings. In fact, some cynics refer to it as "Los Angeles West." But within Honolulu's boundaries, you'll find rainforests, deep canyons, valleys, waterfalls, a nearly mile-high mountain range, coral reefs, and gold-sand beaches. The city proper—where most of Honolulu's residents live—is approximately

Downtown Honolulu

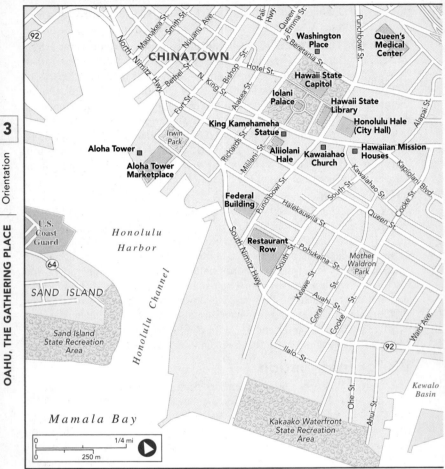

12 miles wide and 26 miles long, running east-west roughly between Diamond Head and Pearl Harbor. Within the city are seven hills laced by seven streams that run to Mamala Bay.

A plethora of neighborhoods surrounds the central area. These areas are generally quieter and more residential than Waikiki, but they're still within minutes of beaches, shopping, and all the activities Oahu has to offer.

WAIKIKI ★★★ Some say that Waikiki is past its prime—that everybody goes to Maui now. If it has fallen out of favor, you couldn't prove it by me. Waikiki is the very incarnation of Yogi Berra's comment about Toots Shor's famous New York restaurant: "Nobody goes there anymore. It's too crowded."

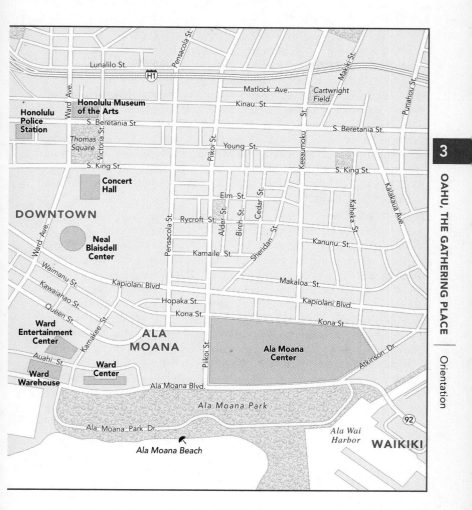

When King Kalakaua played in Waikiki, it was "a hamlet of plain cottages . . . its excitements caused by the activity of insect tribes and the occasional fall of a coconut." The Merrie Monarch, who gave his name to Waikiki's main street, would love the scene today. Some five million tourists visit Oahu every year, and 9 out of 10 of them stay in Waikiki. This urban beach is where all the action is; it's backed by 175 high-rise hotels with more than 33,000 guest rooms and hundreds of bars and restaurants, all in a 1½-square-mile beach zone. Waikiki means honeymooners and sun seekers, bikinis and bare buns, a 'round-the-clock beach party every day of the year—and it's all because of a thin crescent of sand that was shipped over from Molokai. Staying in Waikiki puts you in the heart of it all, but be aware that this is an on-the-go place with traffic noise 24 hours a day and its share of crime—it's almost always crowded.

ALA MOANA ★★ A great beach as well as a famous shopping mall, Ala Moana is the retail and transportation heart of Honolulu, a place where you can shop and suntan in the same afternoon. All bus routes lead to the open-air **Ala Moana Center,** across the street from **Ala Moana Beach Park.** This 50-acre, 200-shop behemoth attracts 56 million customers a year. Nearly every European designer from Armani to Vuitton is represented in Honolulu's answer to Beverly Hills's Rodeo Drive. For our purposes, the neighborhood called "Ala Moana" extends along Ala Moana Boulevard from Waikiki in the direction of Diamond Head to downtown Honolulu in the Ewa direction (west) and includes the **Ward Centre** and **Ward Warehouse** complexes as well as **Restaurant Row.**

DOWNTOWN ★★ A tiny cluster of high-rises west of Waikiki, downtown Honolulu is the financial, business, and government center of Hawaii. On the waterfront stands the iconic 1926 Aloha Tower, now the centerpiece of a harborfront shopping and restaurant complex known as the **Aloha Tower Marketplace.** The whole history of Honolulu can be seen in just a few short blocks: Street vendors sell papayas from trucks on skyscraper-lined concrete canyons; joggers and BMWs rush by a lacy palace where U.S. Marines overthrew Hawaii's last queen and stole her kingdom; burly bus drivers sport fragrant white ginger flowers on their dashboards; Methodist churches look like Asian temples; and businessmen wear aloha shirts to billion-dollar meetings.

On the edge of downtown is the **Chinatown Historic District,** the oldest Chinatown in America and still one of Honolulu's liveliest neighborhoods, a nonstop pageant of people, sights, sounds, smells, and tastes—not all Chinese, now that Southeast Asians, including many Vietnamese, share the old storefronts.

MANOA VALLEY ★ First inhabited by white settlers, the Manoa Valley, above Waikiki, still has vintage *kamaaina* (native-born) homes, one of Hawaii's premier botanical gardens (the Lyon Arboretum), the ever-gushing Manoa Falls, and the 320-acre campus of the University of Hawaii, where 50,000 students hit the books when they're not on the beach.

TO THE EAST: KAHALA Except for the estates of millionaires and the luxurious Kahala Hotel & Resort (home of Hoku's, an outstanding beachfront restaurant), there's not much out this way that's of interest to visitors.

EAST OAHU

Beyond Kahala lies East Honolulu and suburban bedroom communities like Aina Haina, Niu Valley, and Hawaii Kai, among others, all linked by the Kalanianaole Highway and loaded with homes, condos, fast-food joints, and shopping malls. It looks like Southern California on a good day. There are only a few reasons to come here: to have dinner at **Roy's,** the original and still-outstanding Hawaii Regional Cuisine restaurant, in Hawaii Kai; to snorkel at **Hanauma Bay** or watch daredevil surfers at **Sandy Beach;** or to just enjoy the natural splendor of the lovely coastline, which might include a hike to **Makapuu Lighthouse.**

THE WINDWARD COAST

The windward side is the opposite side of the island from Waikiki. Bed-and-breakfasts, ranging from oceanfront estates to tiny cottages on quiet residential streets, are found here. Vacations on this side are spent enjoying ocean activities and exploring the surrounding areas. Waikiki is just a 25-minute drive away.

KAILUA ★   The biggest little beach town in Hawaii, Kailua sits at the foot of the sheer green Koolau mountain range, on a great bay with two of Hawaii's best beaches. The town itself is a funky low-rise cluster of timeworn shops and homes. Kailua has become an affordable alternative to Waikiki, with rooms and vacation rentals starting at $80 a day.

KANEOHE BAY ★   Helter-skelter suburbia sprawls around the edges of Kaneohe, one of the most scenic bays in the Pacific. A handful of B&Bs dots its edge. This great bay beckons you to get out on the water; you can depart from Heeia Boat Harbor on snorkel or fishing charters.

KUALOA/LAIE ★★   The upper-northeast shore is one of Oahu's most sacred places of ancient kings, burial sites, and ghosts, who still march in the night. Thousands "explore" the South Pacific at the **Polynesian Cultural Center,** in Laie, a Mormon settlement with its own Tabernacle Choir of sweet Samoan harmony.

THE NORTH SHORE ★★★   Here's the Hawaii of Hollywood—giant waves, surfers galore, tropical jungles, waterfalls, and mysterious Hawaiian temples. If you're looking for a quieter vacation that's closer to nature and filled with swimming, snorkeling, diving, surfing, or just plain hanging out on some of the world's most beautiful beaches, the North Shore is your place. The artsy little beach town of **Haleiwa ★★** and the surrounding shoreline seem a world away from Waikiki. The North Shore boasts good restaurants,

---

Finding Your Way Around, Oahu-Style

Mainlanders sometimes find the directions given by locals a bit confusing. Seldom will you hear the terms "east," "west," "north," and "south"; instead, islanders refer to directions as either **makai** (ma-*kae*), meaning toward the sea, or **mauka** (*mow*-kah), toward the mountains. In Honolulu, people use **Diamond Head** as a direction meaning to the east (in the direction of the world-famous crater, Diamond Head) and **Ewa** as a direction meaning to the west (toward the town called Ewa, on the other side of Pearl Harbor).

So if you ask a local for directions, this is what you're likely to hear: "Drive 2 blocks makai (toward the sea), and then turn Diamond Head (east) at the stoplight. Go 1 block, and turn mauka (toward the mountains). It's on the Ewa (western) side of the street."

shopping, and cultural activities—but they come with the quiet of country living. *Be forewarned:* It's a long trip—nearly an hour's drive—to Honolulu and Waikiki.

CENTRAL OAHU: THE EWA PLAIN

Flanked by the Koolau and Waianae mountain ranges, the hot, sunbaked Ewa Plain runs up and down the center of Oahu. Once covered with sandalwood forests and later sugar cane and pineapple, Ewa today sports a new crop: suburban houses stretching to the sea. In 1914, the U.S. Army pitched a tent camp on the plain; author James Jones would later call **Schofield Barracks** "the most beautiful army post in the world." Hollywood filmed Jones's *From Here to Eternity* here.

LEEWARD OAHU: THE WAIANAE COAST

The west coast of Oahu is a hot and dry place of dramatic beauty: white-sand beaches bordering the deep-blue ocean, steep verdant green cliffs, and miles of Mother Nature's wildness. Except for the luxurious JW Marriott Ihilani Resort & Spa, Aulani: A Disney Resort & Spa, and Roy's Restaurant at the Ko Olina Resort, you'll find virtually no tourist services out here.

GETTING AROUND

BY CAR   Oahu residents own more than 686,000 registered vehicles, but they have only 1,500 miles of mostly two-lane roads to use: That's 450 cars for every mile, a fact that becomes abundantly clear during morning and evening rush hours. You can avoid the gridlock by driving between 10am and 3pm or after 6pm.

The major car-rental firms have agencies on Oahu, at the airport and in Waikiki. For tips on insurance and driving rules in Hawaii, see "Getting Around Hawaii" (p. 263).

BY BUS   One of the best deals anywhere, **TheBus** will take you around the whole island for $2.50 ($1.25 for children ages 6–17). In fact, every day more than 260,000 people use the system's 68 lines and 4,000 bus stops. TheBus goes almost everywhere almost all the time. The most popular route is **no. 8,** which arrives every 10 minutes or so to shuttle people between Waikiki and Ala Moana Center (the ride takes 15–20 min.). The **no. 19** (Airport/Hickam) and **no. 20** (Airport/Pearlridge) buses also cover the same stretch. Waikiki service begins daily at 5am and runs until midnight; most buses run about every 15 minutes during the day and every 30 minutes in the evening.

For more information on routes and schedules, call **TheBus** (© **808/848-5555** for recorded information) or check out **www.thebus.org**, which provides timetables and maps for all routes. Taking TheBus is often easier than parking your car.

BY TROLLEY   It's fun to ride the 34-seat, open-air, motorized **Waikiki Trolley** (www.waikikitrolley.com; © **800/824-8804** or 808/591-8411), which looks like a San Francisco cable car (see "Orientation Tours" on p. 77). The trolley loops around Waikiki and downtown Honolulu, stopping every 40 minutes at 12 key places, including Iolani Palace and Chinatown. The driver provides commentary along the way. A 1-day trolley pass—which costs $38 for adults and $28 for kids ages 3 to 11—allows you to jump on and off all day long (9am–9pm, depending on the line). Four-day passes cost $59 for adults and $41 for kids 3 to 11 (check website for discounts).

BY TAXI & UBER Oahu's major cab companies offer 24-hour, islandwide, radio-dispatched service, with multilingual drivers and air-conditioned cars, limos, and vans, including vehicles equipped with wheelchair lifts. Fares are standard for all taxi firms; from the airport, expect to pay about $35 to $40 to Waikiki, about $25 to $35 to downtown, about $60 and up to Kailua, about $68-plus to Hawaii Kai, and about $90 to $130 to the North Shore (plus tip). Plus there may be a $4.75 fee per piece of luggage. You can also arrange for a ride with **Uber.** First download the app; then tell them where you want to be picked up and where you're headed via your cell phone, and off you go. Pricing generally is more affordable via Uber than regulated taxi cabs and you can track your Uber ride via your cell phone.

Budget tip: For a flat fee of $30, **Star Taxi ★** (www.startaxihawaii.com; ✆ 808/942-STAR [7827] or 800/671-2999) will take up to four passengers from the airport to Waikiki (with no extra charge for baggage); however, you must book in advance by calling Star Taxi the day before your arrival with your arrival time and flight number. There is a caveat: The last time I used Star Taxi, the car was not very clean.

For a metered cab, try **Charley's Taxi** (✆ 808/531-1333), **The Cab** (✆ 808/422-2222), or **V.I.P. Transportation** (✆ 808/836-0317). **Robert's Taxi and Shuttle** (✆ 808/261-8555) serves windward Oahu, while **Hawaii Kai Hui/Koko Head Taxi** (✆ 808/396-6633) serves east Honolulu/southeast Oahu.

[FastFACTS] OAHU

Dentists If you need dental attention on Oahu, contact the **Hawaii Dental Association** (www.hawaiidentalassociation.net; ✆ 808/593-7956).

Doctors **Straub Doctors on Call,** Sheraton Waikiki, 2255 Kalakaua Ave., Honolulu (✆ 808/971-6000), can dispatch a van if you need help getting to the clinic.

Emergencies Call ✆ 911 for police, fire, and ambulance. If you need to call the **Poison Control Center** (✆ 800/222-1222), you will automatically be directed to the Poison Control Center for the area code of the phone you are calling from; they are all available 24/7 and very helpful.

Hospitals Hospitals offering 24-hour emergency care include **Queen's Medical Center,** 1301 Punchbowl St. (✆ 808/538-9011); **Kuakini Medical Center,** 347 Kuakini St. (✆ 808/536-2236);

Straub Clinic and Hospital, 888 S. King St. (✆ 808/522-4000); **Kaiser Permanente Medical Center,** 3288 Moanalua Rd. (✆ 808/432-0000); **Kapiolani Medical Center for Women and Children,** 1319 Punahou St. (✆ 808/983-8633); and **Pali Momi Medical Center,** 98–1079 Moanalua Rd. (✆ 808/486-6000). Central Oahu has **Wahiawa General Hospital,** 128 Lehua St. (✆ 808/621-8411). On the windward side is **Castle Medical Center,** 640 Ulukahiki St., Kailua (℃ 808/263-5500).

Internet Access

Hawaii State Public Library provides free Internet access, but you must have a Hawaii State library card. A 3-month nonresident library card is available for $10, and a 5-year nonresident library card is available for $25. For information on signing up for a library card, reserving a computer of

finding the closest library, go to www.librarieshawaii.org/Serials/databases.html.

Newspapers

Oahu's only daily paper is the *Honolulu Star Advertiser* (www.staradvertiser.com).

Post Office

To find the location nearest you, call ℃ **800/275-8777.** The Waikiki branch is at 330 Saratoga Ave. (Diamond Head side of Fort DeRussy; bus: 19), and in the Ala Moana Center (bus: 8, 20, or 98A).

Safety

It may be paradise, but there is no holiday from crime. Lock your car but do not leave anything of value in the car or trunk (thieves can open your trunk faster than you can open the car with the key). Park in well-lit areas. Be as cautious as you would at home.

Weather

For National Weather Service recorded forecasts for Oahu, call ℃ **808/973-4380.**

WHERE TO STAY

Before you start to book your stay, consider when you'll be visiting. The high season, when hotels are full and rates are at their peak, is mid-December to March. The secondary high season, when rates are high but rooms are somewhat easier to come by, is June to September. The low seasons—when you can expect fewer tourists and better deals—are April to June and September to mid-December. No matter when you travel, you can often get the best rate at many of Waikiki's hotels by booking a package.

Remember that hotel and room taxes of 13.96% will be added to your bill (Oahu has a .54% additional tax that the other islands do not have). And don't forget about parking charges—at up to $36 a day in Waikiki, they can add up quickly.

One more extra charge: Many hotels and resorts charge a "resort fee," an excuse to add yet another daily fee on to your room charge. Resort fees usually include a daily newspaper, use of the Internet, access to a gym, water in your room, and so forth.

BED & BREAKFASTS For a more intimate experience, try staying in a B&B. Accommodations on Oahu calling themselves bed-and-breakfasts vary from a room in a house (sometimes with a shared bathroom) to a vacation rental in a private cottage. Breakfast can be anything from coffee, pastries, and fruit to a home-cooked gourmet meal with just-caught fresh fish.

AIRPORT HOTELS If you're arriving late at night or leaving early in the morning, consider a hotel near the airport (just for a night—this is not the place to spend your whole vacation). **Best Western–The Plaza Hotel,** 3253 N. Nimitz Hwy., Honolulu (www.bestwestern.com; ℃ 800/780-7234 or 808/836-3636), has rooms from $152 (plus an additional $15–$30 per day for parking) and offers free airport shuttle service.

Waikiki

EWA WAIKIKI

All the hotels listed below are located between the ocean and Kalakaua Avenue, and between Ala Wai Terrace in the Ewa (western) direction and Olohana Street and Fort DeRussy Park in the Diamond Head (eastern) direction.

Expensive

Hilton Hawaiian Village Beach Resort & Spa ★★   Waikiki's largest resort consists of 2,860 hotel rooms spread over 20 acres (whew!). The pluses: It has everything you need for a lively, activity-packed vacation, including 20 restaurants, 6 outdoor pools, 100-plus shops, a terrific spa, great children's program, plush rooms, and a great beach out front. For a romantic night out, the resort's Bali Steak and Seafood is a spot to dress up and dine on local seafood and beef while ocean breezes waft through the open-air dining room. (Note that they don't have onsite babysitting.) The minuses: It's huge and therefore doesn't offer the sort of personal attention some visitors crave. Side note: If you watch the 2013 *Godzilla* remake, the hotel's Rainbow Tower is featured being destroyed by the beast.

2005 Kalia Rd. (at Ala Moana Blvd.). www.hiltonhawaiianvillage.com. ✆ **800/HILTONS** (445-2667) or 808/949-4321. 2,860 units. $209–$499 double; from $334 suite. Extra person (over 2 adults) $50. Children 18 and under stay free in parent's room. Resort fee $30 (includes Internet). Valet parking $36, self-parking $29. Bus: 19 or 20. **Amenities:** 20 restaurants; 3 bars; babysitting; year-round children's program; concierge; concierge-level rooms; fitness center w/high-tech equipment (for fee); 5 outdoor pools; room service; superplush Mandara Spa; watersports equipment rentals; Wi-Fi (included in resort fee).

Moderate

DoubleTree Alana Hotel Waikiki ★   Also operated by the Hilton, this boutique hotel offers a more intimate choice at more affordable prices than the Hilton Hawaiian Village Resort. The rooms are small but have everything you need and some luxuries that come as a surprise, such as very plush pillowbeds and free Wi-Fi throughout the hotel. Waikiki Beach is a 10-minute walk away; the convention center is about a 7-minute walk.

1956 Ala Moana Blvd. (on the Ewa side, near Kalakaua Ave.). www.doubletree.com. ✆ **800/222-TREE** (8733) or 808/941-7275. 317 units. $239–$275 double; from $289 suite. Extra person $40. Children 18 and under stay free in parent's room. Valet parking $30. Bus: 19 or 20. **Amenities:** Bar; concierge; poolside fitness center; outdoor heated pool; room service; Wi-Fi (complimentary).

Ramada Plaza Waikiki ★   The location makes this hotel a prime pick: 2 blocks from the beach, 2 blocks from Ala Moana Center, and a 7-minute walk from the convention center. As for the decor, it's pleasant if bland, including the chain's usual amenities and high standards for cleanliness. Kudos to the unusually helpful and friendly staff. A final perk: The property sits back from the street, so noise is at a minimum.

1830 Ala Moana Blvd. (btw. Hobron Lane and Kalia Rd.). www.ramadaplazawaikiki.com. ✆ **888/992-4545** or 808/955-1111. 199 units. $167–$200 double; from $300 suite.

Waikiki Hotels

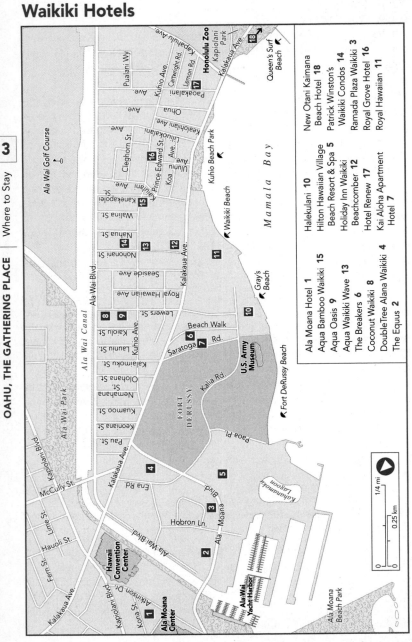

Ala Moana Hotel **1**
Aqua Bamboo Waikiki **15**
Aqua Oasis **9**
Aqua Waikiki Wave **13**
The Breakers **6**
Coconut Waikiki **8**
DoubleTree Alana Waikiki **4**
The Equus **2**

Halekulani **10**
Hilton Hawaiian Village
Beach Resort & Spa **5**
Holiday Inn Waikiki
Beachcomber **12**
Hotel Renew **17**
Kai Aloha Apartment
Hotel **7**

New Otani Kaimana
Beach Hotel **18**
Patrick Winston's
Waikiki Condos **14**
Ramada Plaza Waikiki **3**
Royal Grove Hotel **16**
Royal Hawaiian **11**

Children 19 and under stay free in parent's room using existing bedding. Parking $25. Bus: 19 or 20. **Amenities:** Restaurant; small fitness room; outdoor pool; room service; free local and toll-free phone calls; complimentary Wi-Fi.

Inexpensive

The Equus ★   This small renovated hotel (formerly the Hawaii Polo Inn) has excellent prices and is within walking distance of the Ala Moana Center, Waikiki Beach, and the Hawaii Convention Center. However, it's location on Ala Moana Boulevard is very noisy; ask for a room in the back. Also, the neighborhood can be iffy at night. One bonus: Because of the hotel's connection to the Hawaii Polo Club, all guests get free tickets to matches.

1696 Ala Moana Blvd. (btw. Hobron Lane and Ala Wai Canal). www.equushotel.com. © **800/669-7719** or 808/949-0061. 67 units (shower only). $144–$331 double; from $304 suite; from $109 studio with kitchenette in the Marina Tower next door (www.marina-towerwaikiki.com). Extra person $25. Children 18 and under stay free in parent's room. Valet parking $25. Bus: 19, 20 or 23. **Amenities:** Tiny outdoor wading pool, free Wi-Fi.

MID-WAIKIKI, MAKAI

All the hotels listed below are between Kalakaua Avenue and the ocean, and between Fort DeRussy in the Ewa (western) direction and Kaiulani Street in the Diamond Head (eastern) direction.

Expensive

Halekulani ★★★   One of Hawaii's most luxurious resorts, the Halekulani is located on 5 acres of prime Waikiki beachfront in five buildings that are connected by open courtyards and lush gardens. Even better, 90% of the lavishly furnished rooms have ocean views. Plus, the rooms are unusually large by Waikiki standards (averaging 620 sq. ft.). If you can afford it, Halekulani ("house of heaven") lives up to its name.

2199 Kalia Rd. (at the ocean end of Lewers St.). www.halekulani.com. © **800/367-2343** or 808/923-2311. 453 units. $495–$945 double; from $960 suite. Extra person $125. 1 child 16 and under stays free in parent's room using existing bedding. Maximum 3 people per room. Self-parking $35, valet $35. Bus: 19 or 20. **Amenities:** 3 superb restaurants (including La Mer, p. 40, and Orchids, p. 42); 2 bars (including Lewers Lounge, p. 83); babysitting; children's program in summer and at Christmas; 24-hr. concierge; fitness center; gorgeous outdoor pool; room service; spa; watersports equipment rentals; free Wi-Fi.

Royal Hawaiian ★★★   A symbol of Waikiki around the world, this flamingo-pink oasis is what many visitors envision when they think of Hawaii, and it actually stands where the royal summer palace once did on the best beach in Hawaii. Hidden away among blooming gardens within the concrete jungle of Waikiki, the Royal not only is a symbol of luxury, with attentive service and a full host of amenities such as complimentary cultural programming, it also recently dropped its resort fee without raising prices (in fact, they're actually lower than in years past), making the hotel a good value for all this luxury.

2259 Kalakaua Ave. (at Royal Hawaiian Ave., on the ocean side of the Royal Hawaiian Shopping Center). www.royal-hawaiian.com or www.starwoodhotelshawaii.com. © **800/325-3535** or 808/923-7311. 527 units. $283–$525 double; from $380 suite. Extra person $155 for rollaway only. Self-parking $25; valet parking $33. Bus: 19 or 20. **Amenities:** 2 restaurants; landmark bar; babysitting; year-round children's program available at the Sheraton Waikiki; multilingual concierge desk; preferential tee times at various golf courses; nearby fitness room (next door at the Sheraton Waikiki); good-size outdoor pool; room service; excellent full-service spa (Abhasa); watersports equipment rentals; free Wi-Fi.

Moderate

Aqua Oasis ★ Located on a quiet, tree-lined side street in Waikiki, this boutique hotel is a sleeper in Waikiki. New ownership has done massive room remodeling and renovations; with outstanding personal service at moderate prices, making it a great budget buy. One caveat: It's about a 10-minute walk to Waikiki Beach, although some prefer the nearby, and much less crowded, Ala Moana Beach. There's also a free shuttle to Ala Moana Center.

320 Lewers St. (btw. Kuhio and Kalakaua aves.). www.aquaoasishotel.com. © **877/997-6667** or 808/923-2300. 94 units. $123–$200 double (with continental breakfast); from $154 junior suite; from $258 1-bedroom suite. Resort fee $15. Extra person $30. Valet-only parking $30. Bus: 19 or 20. **Amenities:** Restaurant; bar; concierge; minuscule outdoor pool w/dry sauna; kitchenette in Jr. Suites; full kitchen in suites; free Wi-Fi.

Coconut Waikiki Hotel ★ Built in 1962 but remodeled in 2008 into a charming inn, the Coconut Waikiki is a real find, with spacious, high-design rooms done in aquas and teals with bubble-patterned rugs and headboards, and such niceties as flatscreen TVs. All have views of the verdant hills of Honolulu. Beachgoers, note: It's a 12- to 15-minute stroll to Waikiki Beach (carrying all your beach paraphernalia). Room rate includes continental breakfast.

450 Lewers St. (at Ala Wai Blvd.) www.coconutwaikikihotel.com. © **808/923-8828** or 866/974-2626. 80 units. $152–$269 double; from $269 suite. Extra person $36. Valet parking $30. Bus: 19 or 20. **Amenities:** Tiny outdoor pool w/sun deck; free Wi-Fi.

Inexpensive

The Breakers ★ For those looking for a deal and wanting to experience the Waikiki of yesterday, the Breakers offers old-fashioned Hawaiian aloha, comfortable budget accommodations, and family-friendly prices. This 1950s hotel has six two-story buildings set around a pool and a tropical garden. Each of the tastefully decorated, slightly oversize rooms comes with a lanai and a kitchenette. Plus it is located within easy walking distance of numerous restaurants, shopping, and Waikiki Beach.

250 Beach Walk (btw. Kalakaua Ave. and Kalia Rd.). www.breakers-hawaii.com. © **800/426-0494** or 808/923-3181. 64 units (shower only). $150 double (extra person $20 per day), $170 studio double, $220 garden suite double ($245 for 3, $265 for 4, $285 for 5). Limited free parking (just 6 stalls), additional parking across the street $40 per day. Bus: 19 or 20. **Amenities:** Restaurant; poolside bar; grill; outdoor pool; Wi-Fi in lobby.

Kai Aloha Apartment Hotel ★ Budget travelers will love this small apartment hotel just a block from the beach. After World War II, Waikiki was lined with rows of low-rise hotels and buildings with one-bedroom apartments and studios. The past lives again at Kai Aloha. The units aren't exactly

A room for everyone IN WAIKIKI: THE OUTRIGGER & OHANA HOTELS DYNASTY

Among the largest hotel chains in Waikiki, Outrigger and Ohana hotels offer excellent accommodations across the board. The Outrigger properties are more resort-oriented, with such amenities as concierge service, children's programs, and a variety of restaurants and shops. Plus, there are plenty of packages available for these properties. To ask about current offerings and to make reservations at any of the Outrigger properties throughout the islands, contact **Outrigger Hotels & Resorts** (www.outrigger.com;

© **800/OUTRIGGER** [688744437] or 866/956-4262).

The Ohana Hotels offer clean, dependable, moderately priced, and well-appointed rooms in central locations. The chain's price structure is based entirely on location, room size, and amenities. Check the website, where "best available rates" start at $111 (a true bargain in Waikiki!). Ohana also offers other deals, including air and car-rental packages; for information, contact **Ohana Hotels and Resorts** (www.ohanahotels oahu.com; © **800/462-6262**).

designer showrooms, but they do have a homey feel, are white-glove clean, and provide daily maid service.

235 Saratoga Rd. (across from Fort DeRussy and Waikiki post office, btw. Kalakaua Ave. and Kalia Rd.). www.kaialohahotel.com. © **808/923-6723.** 18 units. $100 studio double, $110 1-bedroom double. Extra person $20. 2-night minimum. Parking at separate pay lot across the street $16–$20. Bus: 19 or 20. **Amenities:** Internet access in the office.

MID-WAIKIKI, MAUKA

These mid-Waikiki hotels, on the mountain side of Kalakaua Avenue, are a little farther away from the beach than those listed above. All are between Kalakaua Avenue and Ala Wai Canal, and between Kalaimoku Street in the Ewa (western) direction and Kaiulani Street in the Diamond Head (eastern) direction.

Moderate

Holiday Inn Waikiki Beachcomber ★
Blessed with the Holiday Inn reputation for clean, comfortable rooms and located just a block from Waikiki Beach and across the street from the upscale Royal Hawaiian Shopping Center, this moderately priced hotel offers revitalized guest rooms, a new swimming pool, and a fitness room.

2300 Kalakaua Ave. (at Duke's Lane). www.holidayinn.com or www.waikikibeachcomber resort.com. © **877/317-5756** or 808/922-4646. 492 units (shower only). $180–$326 double; from $385 suite. Extra person from $50. Resort fee $20. Valet parking $35. Bus: 19 or 20. **Amenities:** Poolside coffee shop; restaurant; outdoor pool; free Internet and local calls; Wi-Fi in lobby.

Inexpensive

Patrick Winston's Waikiki Condos ★
For travelers on a budget, these well-outfitted condo units (sofa beds, separate bedrooms, lanais with breakfast table and chairs, ceiling fans, and full kitchens) and their prices are a

welcome find. An added bonus is Patrick Winston, a Waikiki veteran, who acts as your personal concierge regarding what to do in Waikiki. The beach is just a 10- to 15-minute walk away. Beware of the caveats: There is no maid service (you are the maid), the minimum stay is 7 nights, and there is a check-out cleaning fee.

Hawaiian King Bldg., 417 Nohonani St., Ste. 409 (btw. Kuhio Ave. and Ala Wai Blvd.). www.winstonswaikikicondos.com. ☏ **800/545-1948** or 808/924-3332. 9 units (shower only). 1-bedroom unit $135–$155. Extra person $10. Ask for the Frommer's discount. Cleaning fee $85. 7-night minimum. Limited parking $15–$18/day. Bus: 19 or 20. **Amenities:** Bar; small outdoor pool surrounded by tropical courtyard; free Wi-Fi.

DIAMOND HEAD WAIKIKI

You'll find all these hotels between Ala Wai Boulevard and the ocean, and between Kaiulani Street (1 block east of the International Market Place) and world-famous Diamond Head itself.

Moderate

Aqua Bamboo Waikiki ★   Once upon a time, this was a hotel. When it became old and outdated, it was converted into condominium units. Now—voila!—it's a contemporary "condotel" (a condominium/hotel) decorated with an Asian flair. It's great for families, as some of the units also feature kitchenettes or kitchens, and it's located close to the Honolulu Zoo. As for Waikiki Beach, it's about a 5-minute walk from the property. When booking, be sure to reserve a parking space if you need one—the lot has a limited number of spaces.

2425 Kuhio Ave. (at Kaiulani Ave.). www.aquaresorts.com. ☏ **866/406-2782** or 808/922-7777. 90 units. $159–$189 double, $179–$199 studio double with kitchenette; from $299 1-bedroom unit; from $499 luxury 2-bedroom suite. Extra person $30. Resort fee $15. Valet parking $25. Bus: 8 or 19. **Amenities:** Concierge; Jacuzzi; outdoor pool; sauna; spa; free Wi-Fi and local calls.

Hotel Renew ★★   Tucked away on a quiet side street, this boutique hotel just a block from the beach is one of Waikiki's hidden gems. A massive renovation in 2007 transformed this formerly forgotten, aged property into a modern, up-to-date Cinderella hotel offering good deals and aloha-spirit service. Rooms are small, but stylishly furnished with plenty of outlets and hi-tech amenities. The location's good, too: just 1 block from the beach, 2 blocks from the Honolulu Zoo, and a couple of miles from the Convention Center and Ala Moana Shopping Center.

129 Paoakalani Ave. (at Lemon Rd.). www.hotelrenew.com. ☏ **888/485-7639** or 808/687-7700. 72 units. $144–$200 double, includes continental breakfast. Extra person $50. Resort fee of $25. Valet parking $25. Bus: 8 or 19. **Amenities:** Lounge; concierge; fitness center; free Wi-Fi.

New Otani Kaimana Beach Hotel ★   For those who love Waikiki at a distance, try this small hotel at the foot of Diamond Head, with Kapiolani Park just across the street. If you want to avoid the crowds of Waikiki yet be close enough to take advantages of dining and shopping, this is your place. A good budget buy is the park-view studio with kitchen (you can stock up on provisions from the onsite mini-mart, open until 11pm). *Tip:* Check the website for special deals.

2863 Kalakaua Ave. (ocean side of the street just Diamond Head of the Waikiki Aquarium, across from Kapiolani Park). www.kaimana.com. © **800/356-8264** or 808/923-1555. 124 units. $171–$344 double; from $171 studio; from $233 1-bedroom; from $395 suite. Extra person $60. Children 12 and under stay free in parent's room using existing bedding. Check website for special packages. Valet parking $28. Bus: 8 or 19. **Amenities:** 2 restaurants (including Hau Tree Lanai); beachfront bar; babysitting; concierge; fitness room (fee); room service; watersports equipment rentals; free Wi-Fi.

Inexpensive

Royal Grove Hotel ★ Budget travelers alert: Here's one of the best frugal deals in Waikiki, a small, family-owned hotel offering old-fashioned aloha in cozy accommodations, basic and clean. Although prices start at $70 a night, I suggest spending a few dollars more on an air-conditioned room ($90) to help drown out the street noise. At these rates, you won't mind that maid service is only twice a week. The hotel is built around a courtyard pool, and the beach is just a 3-minute walk away. All of Waikiki's attractions are within walking distance. *Tip:* If you book 7 nights or more, you'll get a discount off the already-low rates.

151 Uluniu Ave. (btw. Prince Edward and Kuhio aves.). www.royalgrovehotel.com. © **808/923-7691.** 85 units. $70 double (no A/C); $90 standard double; $125–$145 standard 1-bedroom. Extra person $10. Children 5 and under stay free in parent's room. Nearby parking $20. Bus: 8 or 19. **Amenities:** Pool; Wi-Fi at office.

Honolulu Beyond Waikiki

ALA MOANA

Ala Moana Hotel ★ Convenience is the main reason to book this condominium/hotel (sometimes called a condotel), where the units are individually owned, but most are put back into the rental pool for guests. It's close to Waikiki, the downtown financial and business district, the convention center, and Hawaii's largest mall, the Ala Moana Center. The rooms vary in price according to size: The cheaper rooms are small, but all come with two double beds and all the amenities you'll need for a comfortable stay.

410 Atkinson Dr. (at Kona St., next to Ala Moana Center). www.outrigger.com. © **866/956-4262** or 808/955-4811. 1,152 units. $189–$269 double; from $319 suite. Extra person $50. Children 17 and under stay free in parent's room. Valet parking $25, self-parking $20. **Amenities:** 3 restaurants; 2 bars (including Rumours Nightclub); concierge; small fitness room; large outdoor pool; limited room service; free Wi-Fi.

The Windward Coast

KAILUA

Pat O'Malley of **Kailua Beach Properties,** 204 S. Kalaheo Ave. (www.pats kailua.com; © **808/261-1653** or 808/262-4128), books a wide range of houses and cottages on or near Kailua Beach. Rates start at $120 a day for a studio cottage 33 feet from the beach and go up to $700 per day for a multimillion-dollar home right on the sand with room to sleep eight. All units are fully furnished, with everything from cooking utensils to telephone and TV, even washer/dryers.

Lanikai Bed & Breakfast ★★ For a taste of the accommodations of a "kamaaina" (native) home, which reflects the Hawaii of yesteryear, book the garden studio or upstairs apartment. The owners also operate a booking service for several other bed-and-breakfast units on the Windward side. Note the high cleaning fee, which only makes this economical for longer stays.

1277 Mokulua Dr. (btw. Onekea and Aala Dr. in Lanikai). www.lanikaibeachrentals.com/vacationrentalsoahu.htm. ✆ **808/261-7895** or 808/261-1059. 2 units. $225 studio double; $250 apt. double or $325 for 3 or 4. Cleaning fee $100–$157. Rates include starter breakfast items in fridge. 5-night minimum. Free parking. Bus: 57A transfer to 70. **Amenities:** Free Wi-Fi.

Leeward Oahu

THE WAIANAE COAST

Aulani, a Disney Resort & Spa, Ko Olina, Hawaii ★★★ Aulani has plenty of Mickey Mouse and friends to entertain kids, such as character meals with photo ops, but it's also a celebration of authentic Hawaiian culture. Disney's "Imagineers" (including the project lead who was born on Oahu) worked with locals to get the details just right, from murals and wood carvings throughout the property that tell the story of Hawaii, to the **Olelo Room,** one of the resort bars, where you can learn the Hawaiian language from bartenders fluent in Hawaiian. Hawaiiana theme dominates in the luxurious guestrooms with bright, tropical colors and everything you need (especially if you have kids in tow) is available. A 900-foot-long lazy river threads the resort, which along with programs like storytelling nights under the stars, Hawaiian craft classes, and Disney movies on the lawn make the Aulani, perhaps unsurprisingly, one of the best lodging choices for families. Extra bonus: no resort fee.

92–1185 Ali'inui Dr., Kapolei, HI. http://resorts.disney.go.com/aulani-hawaii-resort. ✆ **866/443-4763** (reservations) or 808/674-6200 (hotel). 359 units in hotel, $449–$791 hotel room, from $1,109 suite. Villas from $563. Parking $37. No bus service. Take H-1 west toward Pearl City/Ewa Beach; stay on H-1 until it becomes Hwy. 93 (Farrington Hwy.); look for the exit sign for Ko Olina Resort; turn left on Ali'inui Dr. **Amenities:** 3 restaurants; 3 bars; babysitting; championship 18-hole Ko Olina Golf Course; 3 pools plus snorkeling lagoon, water play areas, and lazy river; 4 whirlpools spas; room service; spa; watersports equipment rentals; Wi-Fi (free).

The North Shore

The North Shore doesn't have many accommodations or an abundance of tourist facilities—but some say that's its charm. **Team Real Estate,** 66–250 Kamehameha Hwy., Ste. D-103 (www.teamrealestate.com; ✆ **800/982-8602** or 808/637-3507), manages North Shore vacation rentals ranging from affordable cottages to condos to oceanfront homes, at nightly rates from $57 for a condo unit, $100 for a one-bedroom Turtle Bay condo, and $400 for a 3-bedroom oceanfront home. Cleaning fees vary. A minimum stay of 1 week to 30 days is required for some properties.

VERY EXPENSIVE

Turtle Bay Resort ★★   The North Shore's only resort completed property-wide renovations a few years ago, updating everything in a beachy, laid-back-luxurious style befitting the less-developed, unhurried North Shore. The lobby and gym now have ocean views, the spa has doubled in size, the restaurants' menus have been revamped to highlight locally grown ingredients, and revamped rooms have a calming, neutral palette and walk-in stone showers. What hasn't changed: Every room still has an ocean view. Turtle Bay has also embraced its role as a surf-scene hub, especially in the wintertime, when the surfing season is in full swing. All the pros come to **Lei Lei's Bar and Grill** for a drink, and the new **Surfer, The Bar,** a collaboration between the resort and *Surfer* magazine, offers Talk Story nights, bringing in pro surfers and watermen to share their stories. There are also two destination golf courses here as well as a popular horseback-riding program. All in all, Turtle Bay's renovations really make the resort feel a part of the North Shore landscape.

57–091 Kamehameha Hwy. (Hwy. 83), Kahuku. www.turtlebayresort.com. ℂ **800/203-3650** or 808/293-6000. 477 units. $301–$547 double; from $627 cottage; from $501 suite; from $900 villa. Daily $40 resort fee includes self-parking. Extra person $50. Children 17 and under stay free in parent's room. **Amenities:** 4 restaurants; 2 bars; concierge; 36 holes of golf; 2 pools (w/80-ft. water slide); room service; spa w/fitness center; 4 tennis courts; watersports equipment rentals; stable w/horseback riding; free Wi-Fi.

INEXPENSIVE

Ke Iki Beach Bungalows ★★   If your dreams include staying on a beach, but you can't afford pricey Waikiki, this collection of studio, one- and two-bedroom cottages located on a beautiful white-sand beach on the North Shore could be just the ticket. Situated on a large lot with its own 200-foot stretch of beach between two legendary surf spots (Waimea Bay and Banzai Pipeline), the units are reasonably priced—and if you can live without being right on the ocean, the garden units are very affordable for the location. All units have full kitchens and their own barbecue areas. Most units are compact, with very small bedrooms. But, hey, with the ocean right outside, just how much time are you going to spend indoors?

59–579 Ke Iki Rd. (off Kamehameha Hwy.). www.keikibeach.com. ℂ **866/638-8229** or 808/638-8229. 11 units. $150–$160 double gardenview studio; $145–$155 double gardenview 1-bedroom; $195–$225 double beachfront 1-bedroom; $170–$190 double gardenview 2-bedroom; $220–$245 double beachfront 2-bedroom. Extra person stays free. Cleaning fee $75–$140 per week or per visit (if less than a week). Free parking. Bus: 52 or 55. **Amenities:** Complimentary bikes; complimentary watersports equipment; complimentary Wi-Fi.

WHERE TO EAT

On Oahu, the full range of dining choices includes chef-owned glamour restaurants, neighborhood eateries, fast-food joints, ethnic spots, and food courts in shopping malls. The recommendations below are organized by location, beginning with Waikiki, then neighborhoods west of Waikiki, neighborhoods east of Waikiki, and finally the Windward Coast and the North Shore.

Waikiki

VERY EXPENSIVE

La Mer ★★★ FRENCH   Here's the place for your special occasion meal: Oceanfront La Mer personifies romance and elegance. It's the only AAA Five Diamond restaurant in the state, with a second-floor, open-sided room with views of Diamond Head and the sound of trade winds rustling the nearby coconut fronds. As for the food: magnifique! Expect traditional French preparations with Hawaiian touches, such as seared foie gras with yuzu essence. You'll want to dress up—not just to be seen, but to match the ambience and food.

At the Halekulani, 2199 Kalia Rd. www.halekulani.com. © **844/288-8022** or 800/367-2343. Reservations recommended. Jackets or long-sleeved shirts required for men, evening attire for women. Prix-fixe menus $110 for 3 courses, $145 for 4 courses, $195 for the "Degustation" dinner. Daily 5:30–9:30pm.

Michel's ★★ FRENCH/HAWAII REGIONAL   Come at sunset to watch the sun disappear and the Waikiki skyline light up. Listen to the live music (beginning at 6:30pm) in anticipation of what Chef Hardy Kintscher has on tap tonight, from chateaubriand, to fresh seafood, or a vegetarian creation, all done with a light touch and a dash of creativity.

At the Colony Surf Hotel, 2895 Kalakaua Ave. www.michelshawaii.com. © **808/923-6552.** Reservations recommended. Collared shirts and long pants preferred for men; no shorts or beachwear permitted. Main courses $46–$85, Chef's 6-course tasting menu $95 ($135 with wine pairing). Daily 5:30–9pm.

Morimoto Waikiki ★★★ JAPANESE   Book in advance for the Modern Honolulu Hotel's signature restaurant, where Chef Masaharu Morimoto, the star of the TV show *Iron Chef,* blends traditional Japanese dishes with fresh Western ingredients to wild applause. Yes, there's a reason he always wins on the show! **Budget tip:** Go for the less expensive lunch also served daily (ask for a table outside on the open lanai).

At the Modern Honolulu Hotel, 1775 Ala Moana Blvd. (at Hobron Lane). www.morimoto waikiki.com. © **808/943-5900.** Reservations recommended for dinner. Lunch $15–$98; dinner $29–$98 (tasting menu $120). Daily 11am–2:30pm, and 5–10pm.

Room Service from 50 Different Restaurants

Forget the overpriced room service menu in your hotel. Call **Room Service in Paradise** (www.fooddeliveryhonolulu. com; © **808/941-DINE** [3463]), which delivers nearly a dozen different cuisines (from Pacific Rim to Italian to burgers) from numerous restaurants right to your room. All you do is select a restaurant and order what you want (see the online menu or pick up one of its magazines in various Waikiki locations). You'll be charged for the food, plus a $9 to $11 delivery fee in Waikiki (more in outlying areas) and a tip for the driver. Best of all, you can pay with your credit card. Both lunch and dinner are available. Another plus: Call in advance and have your food delivered whenever you want.

Waikiki Restaurants

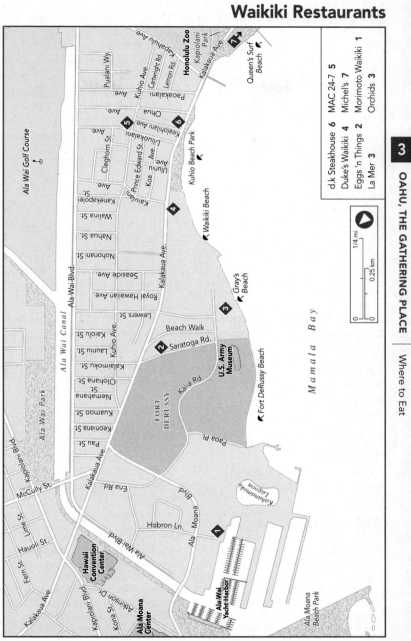

d.k Steakhouse **6**
Duke's Waikiki **4**
Eggs 'n Things **2**
La Mer **3**

MAC 24-7 **5**
Michel's **7**
Morimoto Waikiki **1**
Orchids **3**

EXPENSIVE

Orchids ★★★ INTERNATIONAL/SEAFOOD   Planning to have at least one "splurge" dinner in Waikiki? This is the place to do it: Crisp white linens plus a view of Diamond Head from the oceanfront dining room will start you off with a smile. At lunch, the seafood curry is a winner, as are the tagine of roasted vegetables and the niçoise salad with seared tuna. At dinner, *onaga* (ruby snapper) is steamed with ginger, Chinese parsley, shiitake mushrooms, and soy sauce, and then drizzled with hot sesame oil—delightful. *Tip:* Book weeks in advance for **Sunday brunch** ★★★, one of the best in Hawaii.

At the Halekulani, 2199 Kalia Rd. www.halekulani.com. (*) **808/923-2311.** Reservations recommended. Dinner main courses $29–$59; Sun brunch $69 adults ($100 holidays), $34 children 5–12. Mon–Sat 7:30–11am, 11:30am–2pm, and 5:30–9:30pm; Sun 9am–2:30pm and 5:30–9:30pm.

MODERATE

d.k Steakhouse ★★ STEAK   Well-known local celebrity chef D. K. Kodama and Hawaii's top sommelier, Chuck Furuya, have teamed up to create the ultimate steakhouse. Surprisingly, the prices are quite reasonable; try the $11 "complete meal" option, to add all the fixings to your dry-aged steak.

At the Waikiki Beach Marriott Resort, 2552 Kalakaua Ave., 3rd floor. www.dksteakhouse. com. (*) **808/931-6280.** Reservations recommended. Main courses $35–$85. Daily 5:30–10pm.

Duke's Waikiki ★★ STEAK/SEAFOOD   Named after fabled surfer Duke Kahanamoku, this casual, open-air waterfront hot spot buzzes with diners and Hawaiian-music lovers throughout the day. Come for the live entertainment daily from 4 to 6pm and 9:30pm to midnight, with no cover, but be prepared to fight the crowds if you come at sunset. Check the website for the entertainment schedule.

At the Outrigger Waikiki on the Beach, 2335 Kalakaua Ave. www.dukeswaikiki.com. (*) **808/922-2268.** Reservations recommended for dinner. Main courses $13–$33 (Barefoot Bar $11–$19); breakfast buffet $17. Daily 7am–midnight.

INEXPENSIVE

Eggs 'n Things ★★ BREAKFAST   Be prepared to stand in line for the wonderful breakfast, from fluffy omelets that come with pancakes, potatoes,

---

Dining in Waikiki 24/7

No matter what time it is, **MAC 24-7** (which stands for Modern American Cooking), is open 24 hours a day, 7 days a week, at the Hilton Waikiki Beach Hotel, 2500 Kuhio Ave., at Liliuokalani Avenue (www.mac247waikiki.com; (*) **808/921-5564**). The menu has everything from breakfast, lunch, and dinner to snacks and desserts (although the bar only pours 5–10pm). It's not just for late-night dining (although it comes in handy, as Waikiki eateries shut down by 10 or 11pm); it's also a great place to get picnic lunches during the day. The comfort food is reasonably priced for Waikiki (most entrees are $14–$30), and the portion sizes can feed two or even three hungry people.

and toast, to melt-in-your-mouth waffles, piled high with fruit and whipped cream. Prices are amazing for Waikiki. Plus, it's added a visit-worthy lunch and dinner (chicken-fried steak, calamari steak, and fresh ahi steak are the headliners).

343 Saratoga Rd.; also at 451 Piikoi St.; Waikiki and 2464 Kalakaua Ave.). www.eggsn things.com. ℂ **808/949-0820.** Breakfast/lunch entrees $11–$27; dinner entrees $13–$17. Daily 6am–2pm and 4–10pm.

Kalihi

Nico's at Pier 38 ★★ FRESH FISH   The new Nico's has expanded from a hole in the wall to a gleaming, open-air restaurant almost four times its original size. The food isn't quite as good as it used to be, but it's still one of the best places around to get fresh fish plates for less than $15. Its setting along the industrial waterfront, where Hawaii's commercial fishing fleet resides, is a real deal fisherman's pier. Popular dishes here are the furikake pan-seared ahi and the catch-of-the-day special—perhaps opah sauced with tomato beurre blanc, or swordfish topped with crab bisque (the chef, Nico Chaize, is French-born). As part of the expansion, there's also a fish market next door where you can grab fresh poke and smoked swordfish to eat on the tables outside. Renting a place with a kitchen? Pick up fresh fish to cook at home.

Pier 38, 1129 N. Nimitz Hwy. www.nicospier38.com. ℂ **808/540-1377.** Reservations not accepted, but takeout orders accepted by phone. Lunch $10–$17; dinner $10–$28. Mon–Sat 6:30am–9pm; Sun 10am–9pm.

Manoa Valley/Moiliili/Makiki
VERY EXPENSIVE

Alan Wong's Restaurant ★★★ HAWAII REGIONAL   For a splurge, try the cuisine of Alan Wong, one of Hawaii's most popular chefs. The 90-seat room has a glassed-in terrace and open exhibition kitchen. The cutting-edge menu sizzles with the Asian flavors of lemongrass, sweet-and-sour, garlic, and wasabi, highlighting the fresh seafood and produce of the Islands—the menu changes daily. Be prepared for pricey items and noise.

1857 S. King St., 3rd floor. www.alanwongs.com. ℂ **808/949-2526.** Reservations highly recommended. Main courses $33–$65; 6-course sampling menu $85 ($125 with wine). Daily 5–10pm.

Chef Mavro Restaurant ★★★ PROVENÇAL/HAWAII REGIONAL Foodie alert: If you have only a single night on Oahu, this is the restaurant to go to. Hidden in a residential area, away from the tourist path, chef/owner George Mavrothalassitis, a native of Provence (and a James Beard Award winner), specializes in Provence-cuisine-marries-Hawaii-produce. Order the prix-fixe meal of the day, with or without wine pairings (which are perfectly matched). You will not be disappointed. Bring your gold credit card for the bill.

1969 S. King St. www.chefmavro.com. ℂ **808/944-4714.** Reservations recommended. Prix-fixe menu $105–$148 ($162–$211 with wine pairings). Wed–Sun 6–9pm.

Kaimuki/Kapahulu

EXPENSIVE

3660 On the Rise ★★★ EURO-ISLAND   The cuisine of local celebrity Chef Russell Siu draws in the crowds (and *Wine Spectator* bestowing its Award of Excellence also helps), with his deft Asian touch applied to dishes ranging from potato-crusted crab cake to ahi katsu wrapped in nori.

3660 Waialae Ave. www.3660.com. ℂ **808/737-1177.** Reservations suggested. Main courses $25–$67. Tues–Sun 5:30–8:30pm.

MODERATE

12th Avenue Grill ★★ RETRO AMERICAN   People drive from all over the island for Chef Kevin Hanney's gourmet versions of American classics, such as macaroni and cheese made with a dreamy smoked Parmesan, and the restaurant's signature dish: grilled pork chops with apple chutney and potato pancakes. Make reservations in advance, as this upscale neighborhood diner is packed every night. And be sure to leave room for dessert—the flourless chocolate cake is a good bet.

1120 12th Ave. (at Waialae Ave.). www.12thavegrill.com. ℂ **808/732-9469.** Reservations recommended. Entrees $25–$36. Mon–Thurs 5:30–10pm; Fri–Sat 5:30–11pm; Sun 5–10pm.

INEXPENSIVE

The Fat Greek ★★ GREEK   I wish there were more restaurants like this: delicious food at frugal prices. Okay, it is a tiny hole-in-the-wall with just counter service (takeout is best, as the blaring television in the enclosed dining area does not make a great atmosphere for eating). But the food is terrific: "Papa Special," New Zealand rack of lamb marinated in the "special" house sauce with rosemary and garlic plus potato wedges and a Greek salad for just $20, or "shawarma" (lamb and beef in a pita with tzatziki sauce) and salad for $10. Parking is limited.

3040 Waialae Ave. (at St. Louis Ave.). www.thefatgreek.net. ℂ **808/734-0404.** Entrees $9–$20. Daily 11am–10pm. Locations also in Ala Moana Food Court; 1831 Ala Moana Blvd; and 1020 Keolu Dr. #G, Kailua.

To the East: Kahala

Hoku's ★★★ HAWAII REGIONAL   Relax in the oceanview dining room of the elegant Kahala Hotel, where Chef Wayne Hirabayashi's Hawaiian Regional cuisine blends traditional European with contemporary island (Chinese roast duck, salt crusted rack of lamb, and crispy whole fish). Sunday brunch is not to be missed. This is one of the few places in Hawaii that has a dress code—collared shirts and slacks for men and evening wear for women.

At the Kahala Hotel & Resort, 5000 Kahala Ave. www.kahalaresort.com. ℂ **808/739-8780.** Reservations recommended. Collared shirts and long pants preferred for men. Main courses $40–$128. Prix Fixe menus $70-130. Brunch $75 ($38 children 6–12). Tues–Sat 5:30–10pm; Sun brunch 10am–2pm.

East Oahu

Roy's Restaurant ★★★ EURO-ASIAN Well-known worldwide, restaurateur Chef Roy Yamaguchi got his start here at what is now his flagship restaurant, located in the suburbs of Hawaii Kai. As in most of his chain of restaurants, you'll find an open kitchen, fresh ingredients, ethnic touches, and a good dose of nostalgia mingled with European techniques. The menu changes nightly, but you can generally count on individual pizzas, a varied appetizer menu (Szechuan-spiced baby back ribs, blackened ahi), a small pasta selection, and such entrees as garlic-mustard short ribs, hibachi-style salmon in ponzu sauce, and several types of fresh catch. There's live music Wednesday through Saturday evenings from 6 to 9pm.

Other Roy's Restaurants in Hawaii are located in Ko Olina and Waikiki on Oahu; Poipu, Kauai; Waikoloa, Big Island; and Kaanapali, Maui.

6600 Kalanianaole Hwy. www.royshawaii.com. ⓒ **808/396-7697.** Reservations recommended. Main courses $20–$57; 3-course prix-fixe $50. Mon–Fri 5:30–9pm; Sat–Sun 5–9pm.

The North Shore
MODERATE

Haleiwa Joe's ★ AMERICAN/SEAFOOD The indoor and outdoor seating overlooking the ocean and sunset views beckon visitors to this harborside restaurant. The surf-and-turf menu also includes New York steak, coconut shrimp, and black-and-blue sashimi. Sandwiches and salads make it a great lunch stop, too. Haleiwa Joe's has a second location at 46-336 Haiku Rd. (ⓒ **808/247-6671**).

66–011 Kamehameha Hwy. www.haleiwajoes.com. ⓒ **808/637-8005.** Reservations not accepted. Main courses $13–$19 lunch, $17–$37 dinner. Daily 11:30am–3:30pm, Sun–Thurs 5–9:30pm; Fri–Sat 5–10pm; Aloha hour Mon–Fri 4:30–6:30pm; late-night aloha hour Fri–Sat 10pm–midnight.

INEXPENSIVE

Cafe Haleiwa ★ THAI Haleiwa's legendary breakfast joint has an all-American menu and is a big hit with surfers, urban gentry with weekend country homes, and anyone who loves generous omelets. Surf pictures line the

---

The Shrimp Trucks

Plan to have a picnic with the best, sweetest, juiciest shrimp you are ever going to eat from a shrimp truck on Oahu's North Shore. Several trucks line up around the entry to Haleiwa, just off the Kamehameha Highway, but my favorite is **Giovanni's Original White Shrimp Truck** (ⓒ **808/293-1839**), which usually arrives mid-morning and parks across the street from Haleiwa Senior Housing (or McDonald's). The menu is simple: spicy, garlic, or lemon-and-butter shrimp. Skip the lemon-and-butter (boring) and go for the garlic (my fave) or the spicy (but beware—it really packs a punch). The battered white truck has picnic tables under its awning, so you can munch away right there.

luau!

The sun is setting, the Tiki torches glow with flames, the baked pig is taken from the *imu* (the hole dug into the ground serving as an oven), the drums begin pounding—it's luau time! In ancient Hawaii when people came together to celebrate momentous occasions these gatherings were called **aha 'aina** (which translates to "gathering for a meal"). The **Royal Hawaiian Hotel** continues this tradition at their weekly luau every Monday from 5 to 9pm. Prices range from "Cocktail" seating that costs $89 for adults (children from 0–4 years $21) to "Premium" seating that costs $208 (children 5–12 years $127; 0–4 years $21). Standard seating is $187 for adults, $106 5–12 years, $21 0–4 years. Royal Hawaiian guests receive a $10 discount. Located oceanfront, 2259 Kalakaua Ave. (www.royal-hawaiian.com; *©* **808/921-4600**).

Outside Waikiki, there are two large luau companies about an hour's drive to the Leeward Coast: **Germaine's,** 91–119 Olai St. (www.germainesluau.com; *©* **800/367-5655** or 808/949-6626), and **Paradise Cove Luau,** 92–1089 Alii Nui Dr. (www.paradisecovehawaii.com; *©* **808/842-5911**). Waikiki bus pickup and return are included in the price of packages: Germaine's luau is Tuesday to Sunday at 5:30pm and costs $88 to $153 for adults, $78 to $138 for teens 13 to 20, $68 to $125 for children 4 to 12, and free for children 3 and under. Paradise Cove's luau is nightly at 5pm and costs $85 to $156 for adults, $75 to $137 for teens 13 to 20, $65 to $123 for children 4 to 12, and free for children 3 and under. Round trip transportation $14.

walls, and the ambience is Formica-style casual. Hit the espresso bar for a caffeine fix.

66–460 Kamehameha Hwy. *©* **808/637-5516.** Reservations not accepted. Breakfast $9–$13. Daily 7am–2pm.

Kua Aina ★ AMERICAN   Known island-wide for its juicy burgers and thin crunchy french fries, Kua Aina is THE place to get your burger fix.

66–160 Kamehameha Hwy. www.kuaainahawaii.com *©* **808/637-6067.** Sandwiches and burgers $5–$9. No credit cards. Daily 11am–8pm. Other locations: 1200 Ala Moana Blvd *©* 808/591-9133, and 4480 Kapolei Pkwy *©* 808/674-4031.

ATTRACTIONS IN & AROUND HONOLULU & WAIKIKI

Historic Honolulu

The Waikiki of yesteryear was a place of vast taro fields extending from the ocean to deep into Manoa Valley, dotted with numerous fish ponds and gardens tended by thousands of people. This picture of old Waikiki can be recaptured by following the **Waikiki Historic Trail** ★ (http://waikiki.com/waikiki-historic-trail.html), a meandering 2-mile walk with 20 bronze surfboard markers (standing 6 ft., 5 in. tall—you can't miss 'em), complete with descriptions and archival photos of the historic sites. The trail begins at Kuhio Beach and ends at the King Kalakaua statue, at the intersection of Kuhio and Kalakaua avenues.

Bishop Museum ★★★ MUSEUM   I never tire of the Bishop Museum. It's like the British Museum—filled with irreplaceable cultural and natural artifacts from across the Pacific (it's also one of the foremost research centers on natural history in the region).

The museum bustles with activity like a small college campus, composed of three buildings plus a planetarium, each brimming with exhibits. If you have limited time, head directly to Hawaiian Hall. Set in a dark, hushed 1890s black lava-stone building, this is where you'll find treasures collected by Hawaii's former royal family (along with other pieces collected in the last 125 years)—hundreds of Hawaiian artifacts in glass cases on three tiered levels, in the center of which hangs a model of a sperm whale, a symbol of bygone whaling days (sperm whales are rare in Hawaii waters today). The skilled (and lost) artistry of old Hawaii is seen in the royal capes of gold and red—made from hundreds of thousands of feathers (most of the birds they came from are now extinct). Another distinctive treasure are the *lei niho palaoa,* necklaces made of thin strands of finely braided human hair, that only the highest rank of *alii* (royalty) wore. Also of note are the artifacts from everyday life—stone poi pounders, the island's last grass hut, big wood bowls, and fishhooks carved from bone.

Best for families is the **Richard T. Mamiya Science Adventure Center.** A modern curvilinear building with three levels of interactive exhibits, it's the place to learn about natural Hawaii. One of the most effective exhibits is a high-tech re-creation of Kilauea's active vent called Pu'u O'o, where visitors watch staff throw cinders into a furnace to melt it into lava, which drips out glowing orange. Other displays show how waves form and feature Hawaii's indigenous wildlife. Also, be sure to pick up information on the daily oral history tours being offered, because they're always worthwhile.

1525 Bernice St., just off Kalihi St./Likelike Hwy. www.bishopmuseum.org. © **808/847-3511.** Admission $23 adults, $20 seniors, $15 children 4–12. Daily 9am–5pm. Bus: 2. Parking $5.

Honolulu Museum of Art ★   You might think a small museum in a smallish city like Honolulu wouldn't be worth a look, but there are surprising gems to be found at the Honolulu Museum of Art. It's a no-brainer that an institution in the Pacific would have one of the best Asian collections in the country. The highlight of the collection is the James Michener Collection of Japanese Ukiyo-e prints, which includes that iconic blue swell *The Great Wave off Kanagawa* by woodblock-print master Katsushika Hokusai. There are also surprising Western masterpieces to be found, like Whistler's 1881 *Arrangement in Black No. 5* and Gauguin's *Two Nudes on a Tahitian Beach.*

In 2011, the former Contemporary Museum joined the Honolulu Museum of Art, bringing its collection of almost 2,000 works by such artists as Josef

Honolulu Attractions

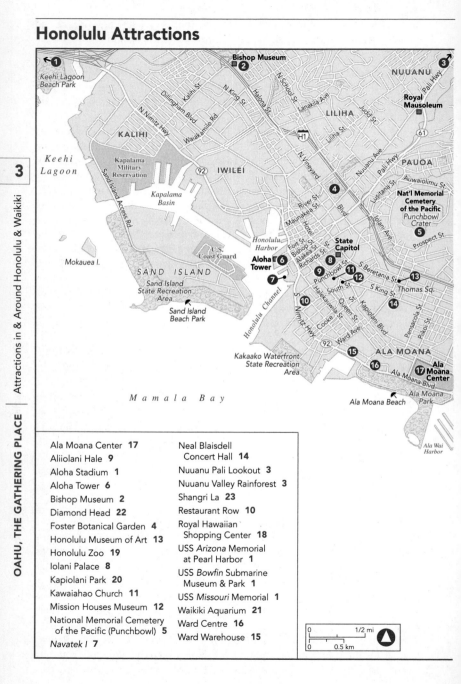

Ala Moana Center **17**
Aliiolani Hale **9**
Aloha Stadium **1**
Aloha Tower **6**
Bishop Museum **2**
Diamond Head **22**
Foster Botanical Garden **4**
Honolulu Museum of Art **13**
Honolulu Zoo **19**
Iolani Palace **8**
Kapiolani Park **20**
Kawaiahao Church **11**
Mission Houses Museum **12**
National Memorial Cemetery
  of the Pacific (Punchbowl) **5**
Navatek I **7**

Neal Blaisdell
  Concert Hall **14**
Nuuanu Pali Lookout **3**
Nuuanu Valley Rainforest **3**
Shangri La **23**
Restaurant Row **10**
Royal Hawaiian
  Shopping Center **18**
USS *Arizona* Memorial
  at Pearl Harbor **1**
USS *Bowfin* Submarine
  Museum & Park **1**
USS *Missouri* Memorial **1**
Waikiki Aquarium **21**
Ward Centre **16**
Ward Warehouse **15**

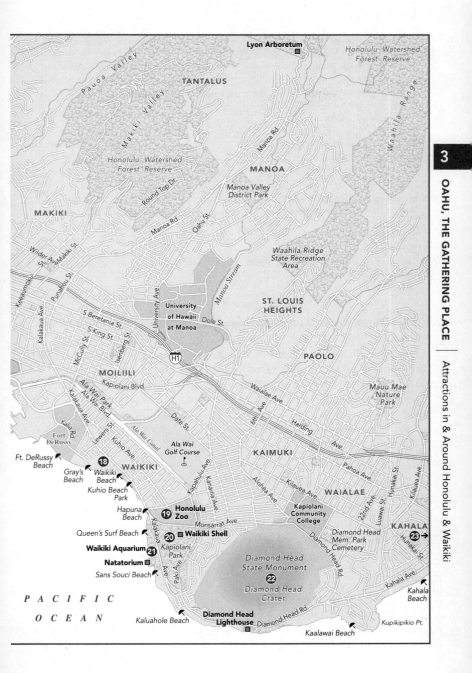

Lyon Arboretum

Honolulu Watershed
Forest Reserve

Pauoa Valley

TANTALUS

Makiki Valley

Manoa Rd.

MANOA

Waahila Range

Honolulu Watershed
Forest Reserve

Round Top Dr.

Manoa Valley
District Park

MAKIKI

Manoa Rd.

Oahu St.

Waahila Ridge
State Recreation
Area

Wilder Ave. Makiki St.

Punahou St.

Keeaumoku

University Ave.

Manoa Stream

ST. LOUIS
HEIGHTS

Kalakaua Ave.

S Beretania St

University
of Hawaii
at Manoa

Dole St.

S King St

Iseinberg St

McCully St.

H1

PAOLO

MOILIILI

Kapiolani Blvd.

Date St.

Waialae Ave.

Mauu Mae
Nature
Park

Ala Wai Park

Ala Wai Blvd.

Ala Wai Canal

Harding

6th Ave.

Ave.

Kalia Rd.

Fort
DeRussy

Ala Wai
Golf Course

KAIMUKI

Pahoa Ave.

Ft. DeRussy
Beach

Lewers St.

Kuhio Ave.

Kapahulu Ave.

Kanaina Ave.

Alohea Ave.

Kilauea Ave.

22nd Ave.

Luawai St.

Hunakai St.

Kilauea Ave.

Gray's
Beach

18

Waikiki
Beach

WAIKIKI

WAIALAE

Kuhio Beach
Park

Hapuna
Beach

19

Honolulu
Zoo

Kalakaua Ave.

Monsarrat Ave.

Kapiolani
Community
College

KAHALA

23

Queen's Surf Beach

20

Waikiki Shell

Diamond Head
Mem. Park
Cemetery

Hunakai St.

Waikiki Aquarium

21

Kapiolani
Park

Natatorium

Paki Ave.

Diamond Head Rd.

Kahala Ave.

Sans Souci Beach

Diamond Head
State Monument

Kahala
Beach

PACIFIC

22

Diamond Head
Crater

OCEAN

Kaluahole Beach

Diamond Head
Lighthouse

Diamond Head Rd.

Kupikipikio Pt.

Kaalawai Beach

ESPECIALLY FOR kids

Seeing an Erupting Volcano (p. 47) A roaring, molten-spewing, rock-launching volcano—stand back, no wait—it's inside the Bishop Museum. It's the new 16,500-square-foot Science Adventure Center, specializing in volcanology, oceanography, and biodiversity.

Visiting the Honolulu Zoo (p. 54) Right next door to Waikiki is Africa. Well, maybe not the continent, but lions, giraffes, zebras, and elephants roam the Honolulu Zoo.

Shopping the Aloha Stadium Swap Meet Most kids hate to shop. But this giant outdoor bazaar every Wednesday, Saturday, and Sunday offers more than shopping. It's an experience akin to a carnival, full of strange food, odd goods, and bold barkers. Kids under 11 get in free, for everyone else entry's just a buck.

Flying a Kite at Kapiolani Park Great open expanses of green and constant trade winds make this urban park one of Hawaii's prime locations for kite flying.

Spending a Day in Waimea Valley (p. 67) Waterfalls and pools for swimming, kayaking along a jungle river, or hiking among ancient Hawaiian ruins. Kids will love this adventure playland.

Eating Shave Ice at Haleiwa (p. 67) No visit to Hawaii is complete without an authentic shave ice. The best place to go is this funky North Shore surf town.

Beating Bamboo Drums in a Fijian Village (p. 66) Try the cultural activities at the Polynesian Cultural Center, where games played by Polynesian and Melanesian children are on tap. The activities, which range from face painting to Hawaiian bowling, go on every day from noon to 5:30pm.

Albers, Sam Francis, and Jim Dine. Highlight: David Hockney's permanent installation of his sets and costumes for the Ravel opera *L'enfant et les sortileges*—the room where it's housed cocoons you in blue, the walls alive with Hockney's whimsical red-trunked trees and flying creatures.

900 S. Beretania St. (at Ward Ave.). www.honolulumuseum.org. ℂ **808/532-8700.** Admission $10 adults, free for children. Tues–Sat 10am–4:30pm; Sun 1–5pm. Bus: 2.

Iolani Palace ★★ MUSEUM In fewer than 100 years, Hawaii's royalty went from living in thatched houses to a palace that had electricity when the White House was still in the dark. At Iolani Palace, you see the embodiment of that lavishness and a powerful symbol of a lost sovereign nation—Queen Liliuokalani was held here under house arrest after her overthrow. King Kalakaua had the four-story Italian Renaissance palace built in 1882 to the tune of $360,000, a price that almost bankrupted the government. But Hawaiian royalty didn't stay in it long; 11 years later the U.S. government overthrew the Hawaiian monarchy. A symbol of independence for today's sovereignty movement, this is where activist marches for Hawaiian issues often start. The red-and-gold throne room, holding the royal seats of King Kalakaua and Queen Kapiolani, gives an inkling of the Hawaiian nobles' taste for opulence. You can take the guided Grand Tour of the palace (be prepared to put on booties so you don't scuff the shiny wood floors), or explore the Palace Galleries on your own. In the galleries, you'll view the royal jewels, including a crown that was stolen by a guard in the 1890s but was later recovered and removed from the palace with the other jewels for safekeeping.

364 S. King St. (at Richards St.). www.iolanipalace.org. ℂ **808/522-0823** or 808/538-1471. Guided tour $22 adults, $6 children 5–12; audio tour $15 adults, $6 children 5–12; gallery tour $7 adults, $3 children 5–12. Mon–Sat 9am–4pm. Call ahead to reserve the guided tour. Children 4 and under not permitted. Extremely limited parking on palace grounds; try metered parking on the street. Bus: 20, 8 or 42.

Kawaiaha'o Church ★★ CHURCH Step inside history in this 1842 Italian Renaissance edifice, made from coral harvested from offshore reefs, which became the church of the Hawaiian royalty and remains in use today. I recommend seeing this historic place during the **Hawaiian-language services** ★★, conducted seven Sundays a year at 9am (see website for dates).

957 Punchbowl St. (at King St.). ℂ **808/522-1333.** www.kawaiahao.org. Free admission (donations appreciated). Daily 8am–4:30pm; Sun services 9am. Bus: E, 8, or 42.

Mission Houses Museum ★ MUSEUM At the Mission Houses Museum, the course of Hawaiian history was changed forever. Protestant missionaries set up their Sandwich Islands Mission here in 1820, and the small cluster of buildings remains. A "living-history" museum, houses are set up with period items—dishes on tables, wooden four-poster beds—as if the missionaries were still in residence. The centerpiece of the grounds is the 1821 Frame House, the oldest wood house in the state. The missionaries introduced the written word to Hawaii, and the Printing House is the place where the first Hawaiian-language book—the Bible, of course—was produced. In the coral-block Chamberlain House is an exhibition space where shows featuring such traditions as Hawaiian quilting are installed.

553 S. King St. (at Kawaiahao St.). www.missionhouses.org. ℂ **808/531-0481.** Admission $10 adults, $8 military personnel and seniors, $6 students and children 6 and over, free for children 5 and under. Tues–Sat 10am–4pm. Bus: 2, 13 and 42.

Shangri La ★★ HISTORIC BUILDING Tobacco heiress Doris Duke's Shangri La has quickly become one of Oahu's most popular attractions—and deservedly so. Book far in advance for this one; tours sell out, and you don't want to miss this over-the-top mansion, which will delight on a number of levels. For good ol'-fashioned lowbrow fun, it affords visitors a peephole into the privileged existence of one of the 20th century's richest and most famous heiresses, Doris Duke. And for a highbrow kick, you have one of the world's richest (and quirkiest) private collections of Islamic art housed in a stunningly beautiful complex of gardens, libraries, and dining halls, built and added to over the course of more than 60 years. Note: Tickets must be reserved in advance.

Meet at Honolulu Museum of Art for start of tour (900 S. Beretania St. at Ward Ave.). www.shangrilahawaii.org. ℂ **808/532-3853.** Admission $25. Tours Weds–Sat 9am, 10:30am, and 1:30pm. Bus: 2.

Wartime Honolulu

USS *Arizona* at Pearl Harbor ★★★ HISTORIC SITE   On December 7, 1941, Japanese planes bombed Oahu's Pearl Harbor—home to the U.S. Pacific fleet—and 2,280 military and 68 civilians were killed. Eight battleships were destroyed or badly damaged, and as a result the United States was plunged into World War II. For many Americans, that "day of infamy" is seared into their memories, but until 1962 there was no appropriate place for them to visit. In that year, an elegant, simple, and highly affecting memorial, designed by architect Alfred Preis, was built over one of the lost ships, the USS *Arizona*, and it has been Oahu's top visitor attraction since the day it opened.

Your short boat trip to the memorial is preceded by a powerful 23-minute documentary that vividly depicts the attack. Emerging from a screening of this film to the actual scene of it is highly surreal; and once you get to the *Arizona* Memorial, a visceral reminder of the attack awaits—the water above the USS *Arizona* is shiny with oil that still oozes from the ship. (And the knowledge that down below, in the ship, lie the remains of many of the 1,777 crew members only heightens emotions.)

Some practical advice: Book in advance for this popular activity at www.recreation.gov or ✆ **877/444-6777.** While you're waiting for the free shuttle to take you out to the ship, get the **audio tour ★★★**, which will make the trip even more meaningful. The tour (on an MP3 player) is about 2½ hours long, costs $7.50, and is worth every nickel; it's narrated by Ernest Borgnine and features stories told by actual Pearl Harbor survivors, both American and Japanese. Allow a total of at least 4 hours for your visit.

Due to increased security measures, visitors cannot carry purses, handbags, fanny packs, backpacks, camera bags (although you can carry your camera or video camera with you), diaper bags, or other items that offer concealment on the boat. However, there is a storage facility where you can stash carry-on-size items (no bigger than 30×30×18 in.) for a fee. **Note:** You must wear **closed-toe shoes** (no sandals allowed). **A reminder to parents:** Baby strollers, baby carriages, and baby backpacks are not allowed in the theater, on the boat, or on the USS *Arizona* Memorial. All babies must be carried. **One last note:** Most unfortunately, the USS *Arizona* Memorial is a high-theft area—so leave your valuables at the hotel.

Pearl Harbor. www.nps.gov/valr. ✆ **808/422-3300.** Free admission. Daily 7am–5pm (programs run 7:30am–3pm). Children 11 and under should be accompanied by an adult. Shirts and closed-toe shoes required; no swimsuits or flip-flops allowed (shorts are okay). Wheelchairs gladly accommodated. Drive west on H-1 past the airport; take the USS *Arizona* Memorial exit and follow the green-and-white signs; there's ample free parking. Bus: 20 or 42; or *Arizona* Memorial Shuttle Bus VIP (www.viptrans.com; ✆ **808/839-0911**), which picks up at Waikiki hotels 7–11:30am ($11 per person round-trip). No public bus route to USS *Arizona* at this time, see buses above.

USS *Bowfin* Submarine Museum & Park ★★ MUSEUM   Submarines were responsible for some of the most effective retaliations against the Japanese, and here you have the chance to crawl around one of the most successful World War II predators of the deep—the USS *Bowfin,* which was nick-named the "Pearl Harbor Avenger." Experiencing the claustrophobia of submarine life is the draw here—men were stacked like cards in a deck in the sleeping quarters, and you'll feel what that meant as you tour. You'll also have the opportunity to peer into the dark chambers of the torpedo room (kids will especially love this). The museum section of the site is less interesting, featuring the usual array of paintings, photographs, models, and things that go boom (a C-3 missile).

11 Arizona Memorial Dr. (next to the USS Arizona Memorial Visitor Center). www.bowfin. org. © **808/423-1341.** Admission $12 adults, $8 active-duty military personnel and seniors, $5 children 4–12 (children 3 and under not permitted for safety reasons). Daily 7am–5pm (last admission 4:30pm). See USS *Arizona* Memorial, above, for driving and shuttle directions.

USS *Missouri* Memorial ★★ HISTORIC SITE   The bombing of the USS *Arizona* launched the United States into World War II, and this 58,000-ton battleship was where the war came to an end with the signing of the Japanese surrender on September 2, 1945. My recommendation is to take the tour, which begins with the shuttle ride, departing from the USS *Bowfin* Submarine Museum (see above), where visitors are shuttled to Ford Island on military-style buses while listening to a 1940s-style radio program (complete with news clips, wartime commercials, and music). The USS *Missouri* has the same restrictions on bags, purses, and backpacks as the USS *Arizona* (see above).

Battleship Row, Pearl Harbor. www.ussmissouri.com. © **877/MIGHTY-MO** (644-4896) Admission $27 adults, $13 children 4–12. Mighty Mo Tour (35 min.) or Heart of the *Missouri* Tour (75 min.) $27 extra for adults, $12 for children. Daily 8am–5pm summer, 8am–4pm winter; guided tours 9am–1pm. Check in at the USS *Bowfin* Submarine Museum, next to the USS *Arizona* Memorial Visitor Center. Drive west on H-1 past the airport, take the USS *Arizona* Memorial exit, and follow the brown-and-white signs; there's ample free parking.

National Memorial Cemetery of the Pacific ★ CEMETERY   You may know this veteran's cemetery by its more popular name, Punchbowl. The 150,000-year-old crater is a burial ground for 35,000 victims of three American wars in Asia and the Pacific: World War II, Korea, and Vietnam. Among the graves, you'll find many without names with the date December 7, 1941, carved in stone.

Punchbowl Crater, 2177 Puowaina Dr. (at the end of the road). Free admission. Daily 8am–5:30pm (Mar–Sept to 6:30pm). Bus: 2, then transfer to 17, with a long walk.

Fish, Flora & Fauna

Foster Botanical Garden ★★ GARDEN   You could spend days in this unique historic garden, a leafy oasis amid the high-rises of downtown Honolulu. Combine a tour of the garden with a trip to Chinatown (just across the street) to maximize your time. This 14-acre public garden is a living museum of plants, some rare and endangered, collected from the tropical regions of the world.

50 N. Vineyard Blvd. (at Nuuanu Ave.). www.honolulu.gov/parks/hbg. © **808/522-7066.** Admission $5 adults, $1 children 6–12. Daily 9am–4pm; guided tours Mon–Sat at 1pm (reservations recommended). Bus: 2 with a short walk.

Honolulu Zoo ★★ ZOO   Even with great beaches and rolling surf, Hawaii's largest zoo gets its fair share of visitors. This 43-acre municipal zoo on the outskirts of Waikiki has an African Savannah, a 10-acre exhibit with more than 40 African critters roaming around in the open, rare Hawaiian nene goose, a Hawaiian pig, and mouflon sheep in addition to the usual monkeys, lions, and so forth. Plan to spend at least a half day here if you have kids and a couple of hours if you don't.

151 Kapahulu Ave. (btw. Paki and Kalakaua aves.), at entrance to Kapiolani Park. www. honoluluzoo.org. ✆ **808/971-7171.** Admission $14 adults, $6 children 6–12. Daily 9am–4:30pm. Zoo parking lot (entrance on Kapahulu Ave.) $1 per hour; free parking at Shell parking lot across the street on Monsarrat Ave. Bus: 8, 23, or 42 or Waikiki Trolley's Green Line.

Waikiki Aquarium ★★★ AQUARIUM   Allow at least 2 hours to explore the beauty of Hawaii's underwater world. There are oodles of magical things to see, of which my favorite is the chambered nautilus (tropical, spiral-shelled, cephalopod, mollusk—the only living one born in captivity), nature's submarine and inspiration for Jules Verne's *20,000 Leagues Under the Sea.*

2777 Kalakaua Ave. (across from Kapiolani Park). www.waikikiaquarium.org. ✆ **808/923-9741.** Admission $12 adults; $8 active military, $5 seniors, and children ages 4-12; children 3 and under free. Daily 9am–4:30pm. Bus: 20 and Waikiki Trolley's Green Line.

Other Natural Wonders & Spectacular Views

In addition to the attractions listed below, check out the hike to **Diamond Head Crater** (p. 74); almost everybody can handle it, and the 360-degree views from the top are fabulous.

Nuuanu Pali Lookout ★ NATURAL ATTRACTION   Gale-force winds sometimes howl through the mountain pass at this 1,186-foot-high perch guarded by 3,000-foot peaks, so hold on to your hat—and small children. But if you walk up from the parking lot to the precipice, you'll be rewarded with a view that'll blow you away.

Near the summit of Pali Hwy. (Hwy. 61); take the Nuuanu Pali Lookout turnoff.

Nuuanu Valley Rain Forest ★ NATURAL ATTRACTION   It's not the same as a peaceful nature walk, but if time is short and hiking isn't your thing, Honolulu has a rainforest you can drive through. It's only a few minutes from downtown Honolulu in verdant Nuuanu Valley, where it rains nearly 300 inches a year. And it's easy to reach: Take the Pali Highway to the stoplight at the Nuuanu Pali Road turnoff; turn right for a detour of about 2 miles (through a thick canopy of liana vines), past giant bamboo that creaks in the wind, and wild shell ginger. Soon the road rejoins the Pali Highway. Kailua is to the right and Honolulu to the left.

Take the Old Nuuanu Pali Rd. exit off Pali Hwy. (Hwy. 61).

Attractions in & Around Honolulu & Waikiki

OAHU, THE GATHERING PLACE

WALKING TOUR 1: **HISTORIC CHINATOWN**

GETTING THERE: **From Waikiki, take Ala Moana Boulevard and turn right on Smith Street; make a left on Beretania Street and a left again at Maunakea. The city parking garage (75¢ per half-hour; then $3 per hour) is on the Ewa (west) side of Maunakea Street, between North Hotel and North King streets. Bus: 2 or 19 toward downtown (get off on N. Hotel St., after Maunakea St.).**

START & FINISH: **North Hotel and Maunakea streets.**

TIME: **1 to 2 hours, depending on how much time you spend browsing.**

BEST TIMES: **Daylight hours.**

Chinese laborers from the Guangdong Province first came to work on Hawaii's sugar and pineapple plantations in the 1850s. They quickly figured out that they would never get rich working in the fields; once their contracts were up, some opened small shops and restaurants in the area around River Street.

Chinatown reached its peak in the 1930s. In the days before air travel, visitors arrived here by cruise ship. Just a block up the street was the pier where they disembarked—and they often headed straight for the shops and restaurants of Chinatown, which mainlanders considered an exotic treat. In the 1940s, military personnel on leave flocked here looking for different kinds of exotic treats—in the form of pool halls, tattoo joints, and brothels.

Today, Chinatown is again rising from the ashes. After deteriorating over the years into a tawdry district of seedy bars, drug dealers, and homeless squatters, the neighborhood recently underwent extensive urban renewal. There's still just enough sleaze on the fringes (a few peep shows and a couple of topless bars) to keep it from being some theme-park-style tourist attraction, but Chinatown is poised to relive its glory days. No trip to Honolulu is complete without a visit to this exotic historic district.

Start your walk on the Ewa (west) side of Maunakea Street at:

1 Hotel Street

During World War II, Hotel Street was synonymous with good times. Pool halls and beer parlors lined the blocks, and prostitutes were plentiful. Nowadays, the more nefarious establishments have been replaced with small shops, from art galleries to specialty boutiques, and urban professionals and recent immigrants look for bargains where the sailors once roamed.

Once you're finished wandering through the shops, head to the intersection with Smith Street. On the Diamond Head (east) side of Smith, you'll notice stones in the sidewalk; they were taken from the sandalwood ships, which came to Hawaii empty of cargo except for these stones, which were used as ballast on the trip over. The stones were removed, and the ships' hulls were filled with sandalwood for the return to the mainland.

Walking Tour 1: Historic Chinatown

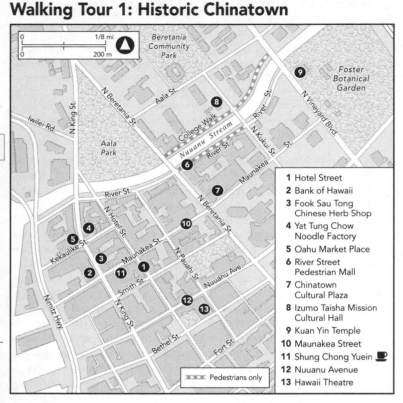

0 ——— 1/8 mi
0 ——— 200 m

Beretania Community Park

Foster Botanical Garden

N Beretania St.
Aala St.
Iwilei Rd.
N King St.
Aala Park
College Walk
Nuuanu Stream
River St.
N Kukui St.
N Vineyard Blvd
River St.
Maunakea
N Beretania St.
N Hotel St.
River St.
Kekaulike St.
Maunakea St.
N Pauahi St.
Smith St.
Nuuanu Ave.
Nimitz Hwy.
N King St.
Bethel St.
Fort St.

8 Izumo Taisha Mission
9 Kuan Yin Temple
6 River Street Pedestrian Mall
7 Chinatown Cultural Plaza
4 Yat Tung Chow Noodle Factory
10 Maunakea Street
5 Oahu Market Place
3 Fook Sau Tong
2 Bank of Hawaii
11 Shung Chong Yuein
1 Hotel Street
12 Nuuanu Avenue
13 Hawaii Theatre

1 Hotel Street
2 Bank of Hawaii
3 Fook Sau Tong Chinese Herb Shop
4 Yat Tung Chow Noodle Factory
5 Oahu Market Place
6 River Street Pedestrian Mall
7 Chinatown Cultural Plaza
8 Izumo Taisha Mission Cultural Hall
9 Kuan Yin Temple
10 Maunakea Street
11 Shung Chong Yuein ☕
12 Nuuanu Avenue
13 Hawaii Theatre

━━━ Pedestrians only

From Hotel Street, turn toward the ocean on Maunakea and proceed to the corner of King Street to the:

2 Bank of Hawaii

This unusual-looking bank is not the conservative edifice you'd expect—it's guarded by two fire-breathing-dragon statues.

Turn Ewa onto King Street, where you'll pass the shops of various Chinese herbalists. Proceed to 112 N. King St., to the:

3 Fook Sau Tong Chinese Herb Shop

Here Chinese herbalists act as both doctors and dispensers of herbs. Patients come in and tell the herbalist what ails them; the herbalist then decides which of the myriad herbs to mix together. The patient then takes the concoction home to brew into a strong tea.

Continue on King and stop at 150 N. King St., where you'll find the:

4 Yat Tung Chow Noodle Factory

The delicious, delicate noodles that star in numerous Asian dishes are made here, ranging from threadlike noodles (literally no thicker than embroidery thread) to fat udon. There aren't any tours of the factory, but you can look through the window, past the white cloud of flour that hangs in the air, and watch as dough is fed into rollers at one end of the noodle machines; perfectly cut noodles emerge at the other end.

Cross to the south side of King Street, where, just west of Kekaulike Street, you'll come to the most-visited part of Chinatown, the open-air market known as:

5 Oahu Market Place

Those interested in Asian cooking will find all the necessary ingredients here, including pigs' heads, poultry (some still squawking), fresh octopus, salted jellyfish, pungent fish sauce, fresh herbs, and thousand-year-old eggs. The friendly vendors are happy to explain their wares and give instructions on how to prepare these exotic treats. The market, which has been at this spot since 1904, is divided into meats, poultry, fish, vegetables, and fruits.

Follow King down to River Street and turn right toward the mountains. A range of inexpensive restaurants lines River Street from King to Beretania. You can get the best Vietnamese and Filipino food in town in these blocks, but go early—lines for lunch start at 11:15am. Beyond Beretania Street is the:

6 River Street Pedestrian Mall

Here River Street ends and the pedestrian mall begins with the **statue of Chinese revolutionary leader Sun Yat-sen.** The wide mall, which borders the Nuuanu Stream, is lined with shade trees, park benches, and tables where seniors gather to play mah-jongg and checkers. There are plenty of takeout restaurants nearby if you'd like to eat lunch outdoors. If you're up early (5:30am in summer and 6am in winter), you'll see seniors practicing tai chi.

Along the River Street Mall, extending nearly a block over to Maunakea Street, is the:

7 Chinatown Cultural Plaza

This modern complex is filled with shops featuring everything from tailors to calligraphers, as well as numerous restaurants—a great idea, but in reality, people seem to prefer wandering Chinatown's crowded streets to venturing into a modern mall. A couple of interesting shops here specialize in Asian magazines; there's also a small post office tucked away in a corner of the plaza, for those who want to mail cards home with the "Chinatown" postmark.

Continue up the River Street Mall and cross the Nuuanu Stream via the bridge at Kukui Street, which will bring you to the:

8 Izumo Taisha Mission Cultural Hall

This small wooden Shinto shrine, built in 1923, houses a male deity (look for the X-shaped crosses on the top). Members of the faith ring the bell out front as an act of purification when they come to pray. Inside the temple is a 100-pound sack of rice, symbolizing good health.

If temples interest you, walk a block toward the mountains to Vineyard Boulevard; cross back over Nuuanu Stream, past the entrance of Foster Botanical Garden, to:

9 Kuan Yin Temple

This Buddhist temple, painted in a brilliant red with a green ceramic-tiled roof, is dedicated to Kuan Yin Bodhisattva, the goddess of mercy. The aroma of burning incense is your clue that the temple is still a house of worship, not an exhibit, so enter with respect and leave your shoes outside. You may see people burning paper "money" for prosperity and good luck, or leaving flowers and fruits at the altar (gifts to the goddess).

Continue down Vineyard, in the Diamond Head direction, and then turn right (toward the ocean) on:

10 Maunakea Street

Between Beretania and King streets are numerous **lei shops** (with lei makers working away right on the premises). The air is heavy with the aroma of flowers being woven into beautiful treasures. This the best place in all of Hawaii to get a deal on a lei. Wander through the shops before you decide which lei you want.

bargaining: A WAY OF LIFE IN CHINATOWN

In Chinatown, nearly every purchase—from chicken feet to an 18-karat-gold necklace—is made by bargaining. It's the way of life for most Asian countries—and part of the fun and charm of shopping in Chinatown.

The main rule of thumb when negotiating a price is **respect.** The customer must have respect for the merchant and understand that he's in business to make money. This respect is coupled with the understanding that the customer does not want to be taken advantage of and would like the best deal possible.

Keep in mind two rules when bargaining: **cash** and **volume.** Don't even begin haggling if you're not planning to pay cash. The second you pull out a credit card (if the merchant or vendor will even accept it), all deals are off. And remember, the more you buy, the better the deal the merchant will extend to you.

Significant savings can be realized for high-ticket items like jewelry. The price of gold in Chinatown is based on the posted price of the tael (a unit of weight slightly more than an ounce), which is listed for 14-, 18-, and 24-karat gold, plus the value of the labor. There's no negotiating on the tael price, but the cost of the labor is where the bargaining begins.

THE aloha TOWER

One of the reasons that the word "aloha" is synonymous with Hawaii is because of the Aloha Tower. Built in 1926, this 10-story tower (until 1959, the tallest structure in Hawaii) has clocks on all four of its sides with the word "aloha" under each clock. Aloha, which has come to mean both "hello" and "farewell," was the first thing steamship passengers saw when they entered Honolulu Harbor. In the days when tourists arrived by steamer, "boat days" were a very big occasion. The Royal Hawaiian Band was on hand to play, crowds gathered, flower leis were freely given, and Honolulu came to a standstill to greet the visitors.

Go up the elevator inside the Aloha Tower to the 10th-floor **observation deck** for a bird's-eye view that encompasses Diamond Head and Waikiki, the downtown and Chinatown areas, and the harbor coastline to the airport. On the ocean side you can see the harbor mouth, Sand Island, the Honolulu reef runway, and the Pearl Harbor entrance channel. There is no charge to see the view; the Aloha Tower is open daily from 9:30am to 5pm or sunset.

Continue toward the ocean on Maunakea Street, crossing Hotel Street; on your left is a great place to take a break.

11 Shung Chong Yuein 🍵

If you have a sweet tooth, stop in at Shung Chong Yuein ★, 1027 Maunakea St. (near Hotel St.), for delicious Asian pastries such as moon cakes and almond cookies, all at very reasonable prices. The shop also has a wide selection of dried and sugared candies (such as ginger, pineapple, and lotus root) that you can eat as you stroll or give as an exotic gift to friends back home.

Walk back up Hotel Street (toward the mountains) and turn right and walk in the Diamond Head (east) direction to Nuuanu Ave and turn left (toward the mountains):

12 Nuuanu Avenue

On the corner of Nuuanu Avenue and Hotel Street is **Lai Fong Department Store,** a classic Chinatown store owned by the same family for more than 75 years. Walking into Lai Fong is like stepping back in time. The old store sells everything from precious antiques to god-awful knick-knacks to rare Hawaiian postcards from the early 1900s—but it has built its reputation on its fabulous selection of Chinese silks, brocades, and custom dresses.

Continue up Nuuanu Avenue (toward the mountains). At Pauahi Street, turn right (toward Diamond Head) and walk up to Bethel Street and the:

13 Hawaii Theatre

This restored 1920 Art Deco theater is a work of art in itself. It hosts a variety of programs, from the Hawaii International Film Festival to beauty pageants (see "Oahu After Dark" on p. 81 for more information).

From Bethel Street, walk toward the ocean and turn right again onto Hotel Street, which will lead you back to where you started.

WALKING TOUR 2: **HISTORIC HONOLULU**

GETTING THERE: **From Waikiki, take Ala Moana Boulevard in the Ewa direction. Ala Moana Boulevard ends at Nimitz Highway. Turn right on the next street on your right (Alakea St.). Park in the garage across from St. Andrews Church after you cross Beretania Street. Bus: 2, 19, 20**

START & FINISH: **St. Andrew's Church, Beretania and Alakea streets.**

TIME: **2 to 3 hours, depending on how long you linger in museums.**

BEST TIMES: **Wednesday through Saturday, daytime, when the Iolani Palace has tours.**

The 1800s were a turbulent time in Hawaii. By the end of the 1790s, Kamehameha the Great had united all the islands. Foreigners then began arriving by ship—first explorers, then merchants, and then, in 1820, missionaries. The rulers of Hawaii were hard-pressed to keep up. By 1840, it was clear that the capital had shifted from Lahaina, where the Kingdom of Hawaii was actually centered, to Honolulu, where the majority of commerce and trade was taking place. In 1848, the Great Mahele (division) enabled commoners, and eventually, foreigners to own crown land, and in two generations, more than 80% of all private lands had shifted to foreign ownership. With the introduction of sugar as a crop, the foreigners prospered, and in time they put more and more pressure on the government.

By 1872, the monarchy had run through the Kamehameha line and, in 1873, David Kalakaua was elected to the throne. By the end of the 1800s, however, the foreign sugar growers and merchants had become extremely powerful in Hawaii. With the assistance of the U.S. Marines, they orchestrated the overthrow of Queen Liliuokalani, Hawaii's last reigning monarch, in 1893. The United States declared Hawaii a territory in 1898.

You can witness the remnants of these turbulent years in just a few short blocks.

Cross the street from the garage and venture back to 1858 when you enter:

1 St. Andrew's Church

The Hawaiian monarchs were greatly influenced by the royals in Europe. When King Kamehameha IV saw the grandeur of the Church of England, he decided to build his own cathedral. He and Queen Emma founded the Anglican Church of Hawaii in 1858. Even if you aren't fond of visiting churches, you have to see the floor-to-eaves hand-blown stained-glass window that faces the setting sun.

Next, walk down Beretania Street in the Diamond Head direction to the gates of:

2 Washington Place

Once the residence of the governor of Hawaii (sorry, no tours; just peek through the iron fence), it occupies a distinguished place in Hawaii's history. The Greek Revival–style home, built in 1842 by a U.S. sea captain named John Dominis, got its name from the U.S. ambassador who

Walking Tour 2: Historic Honolulu

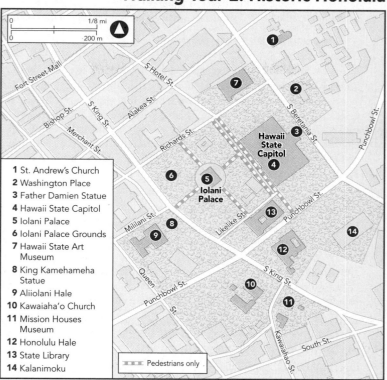

1 St. Andrew's Church
2 Washington Place
3 Father Damien Statue
4 Hawaii State Capitol
5 Iolani Palace
6 Iolani Palace Grounds
7 Hawaii State Art Museum
8 King Kamehameha Statue
9 Aliiolani Hale
10 Kawaiaha'o Church
11 Mission Houses Museum
12 Honolulu Hale
13 State Library
14 Kalanimoku

Pedestrians only

once stayed here and told so many stories about President George Washington that people starting calling the home Washington Place.

Cross the street and walk to the front of the Hawaii State Capitol, where you'll find the:

3 Father Damien Statue

The people of Hawaii have never forgotten the sacrifice this Belgian priest, recently canonized a saint, made to help the sufferers of leprosy when he volunteered to work with them in exile on the Kalaupapa Peninsula on the island of Molokai. After 16 years of service, Father Damien died of leprosy at the age of 49.

Behind the Father Damien Statue is the:

4 Hawaii State Capitol

Here's where Hawaii's state legislators work from mid-January to the end of April every year. This is not your typical white dome structure, but rather a building symbolic of Hawaii. The building's unusual design has palm tree–shaped pillars, two cone-shaped chambers (representing volcanoes) for the legislative bodies, and, in the inner courtyard, a 600,000-tile mosaic of the sea (Aquarius) created by a local artist. A reflecting pool (representing the sea) surrounds the entire structure. Open to the public, you are welcome to go into the rotunda and see the woven hangings and murals at the entrance.

Walk down Richards Street toward the ocean and stop at 364 S. King St., the:

5 Iolani Palace

Hawaii is the only state in the U.S. to have not one, but two royal palaces: one in Kona, where the royals went during the summer, and Iolani Palace (*iolani* means "royal hawk"). Don't miss the opportunity to see this grande dame of historic buildings. Basic admission is $15 for adults, $6 for children 5 to 12, and is available Monday to Saturday 9am to 4pm. Guided tours are offered Tuesday, Wednesday, and Thursday 9 to 10am, and Friday and Saturday from 9am to 11:15am. Tours cost $22 for adults, $6 for children; call © **808/522-0832** (www.iolanipalace.org) to reserve in advance, as spots are limited.

After you visit the palace, spend some time on the:

6 Iolani Palace Grounds

You can wander around the grounds at no charge. The ticket window to the palace and the gift shop are in the former barracks of the Royal Household Guards. Later it was used as a **Royal Bandstand** for concerts (King Kalakaua, along with Henri Berger, the first Royal Hawaiian Bandmaster, wrote "Hawaii Pono'i," the state anthem).

From the palace grounds, turn in the Ewa direction, cross Richards Street, and walk to the corner of Richards and Hotel streets to the:

7 Hawaii State Art Museum

Opened in 2002, the Hawaii State Art Museum is housed in the original Royal Hawaiian Hotel built in 1872, during the reign of King Kamehameha V. All of the 360 works currently displayed were created by artists who live in Hawaii.

Walk makai down Richards Street and turn left (toward Diamond Head) on South King Street to the:

8 King Kamehameha Statue

At the juncture of King, Merchant, and Mililani streets stands a replica of the man who united the Hawaiian Islands. The striking black-and-gold bronze statue is magnificent. The best day to see the statue is on June 11 (King Kamehameha Day), when it is covered with leis in honor of Hawaii's favorite son.

Right behind the King Kamehameha Statue is:

9 Aliiolani Hale

This distinctive building (the name translates to "House of Heavenly Kings") with a clock tower now houses the State Judiciary Building. King Kamehameha V originally wanted to build a palace here; however, it ended up as the first major government building for the Hawaiian monarchy. Self-guided tours are available Monday through Friday from 8am to 4:30pm.

Walk toward Diamond Head on King Street; at the corner of King and Punchbowl, stop in at the:

10 Kawaiaha'o Church

This New England–style church, built from 1837 to 1842, consists of some 14,000 giant coral slabs (some weighing more than 1,000 lb.). Hawaiian divers ravaged the reefs, digging out huge chunks of coral and causing irreparable environmental damage. The church is open Monday through Saturday from 8am to 4pm; you'll find it to be very cool in temperature. Don't sit in the pews in the back, marked with kahili feathers and velvet cushions; they are still reserved for the descendants of royalty. Sunday service is at 9am (services in the Hawaiian language take place nine Sundays per year; see www.kawaiahao.org for dates).

Cross the street, and you'll see the:

11 Mission Houses Museum

On the corner of King and Kawaiahao streets stand the original buildings of the Sandwich Islands Mission Headquarters: the **Frame House** (built in 1821), the **Chamberlain House** (1831), and the **Printing Office** (1841). The complex is open Tuesday through Saturday from 10am to 4pm; admission is $10 for adults, $8 for seniors and military personnel, and $6 for students and children 6 and older. The tours are often led by descendants of the original missionaries to Hawaii. For information, go to www.missionhouses.org.

Cross King Street and walk in the Ewa direction to the corner of Punchbowl and King to:

12 Honolulu Hale

The **Honolulu City Hall,** built in 1927, was designed by Honolulu's most famous architect, C. W. Dickey. His Spanish mission–style building has an open-air courtyard, which is used for art exhibits and concerts. It's open Monday through Friday.

Cross Punchbowl Street and walk mauka to the:

13 State Library

Anything you want to know about Hawaii and the Pacific can be found here, the main branch of the state's library system. Located in a restored historic building, it has an open garden courtyard in the middle, great for stopping for a rest on your walk.

Head mauka up Punchbowl to the corner of Punchbowl and Beretania streets, where you'll see:

14 Kalanimoku

That beautiful name, "Ship of Heaven," has been given to this dour state office building. Here you can get information from the Department of Land and Natural Resources on hiking and camping in state parks.

Retrace your steps in the Ewa direction down Beretania to Alakea back to the parking garage.

BEYOND HONOLULU: EXPLORING THE ISLAND BY CAR

The moment always arrives—usually after a couple of days at the beach, snorkeling in the warm blue-green waters of Hanauma Bay, enjoying sundown Mai Tais—when a certain curiosity kicks in about the rest of Oahu. It's time to rent a car and set out around the island. You can also explore Oahu using **TheBus** (see "Getting Around" on p. 28).

Oahu's Southeast Coast

From the high-rises of Waikiki, venture down Kalakaua Avenue through tree-lined Kapiolani Park to take a look at a different side of Oahu, the arid south shore. To get to this coast, follow Kalakaua Avenue past the multitiered Dillingham Fountain and around the bend in the road, which now becomes Poni Moi Road. Make a right on Diamond Head Road and begin the climb up the side of the old crater. At the top are several lookout points, so if the official Diamond Head Lookout is jammed with cars, try one of the other lookouts just down the road. The view of the rolling waves is spectacular; take the time to pull over.

Diamond Head Road rolls downhill into the ritzy community of **Kahala.** At the V in the road at the triangular Fort Ruger Park, veer to your right and continue on the palm tree–lined Kahala Avenue. Make a left on Hunakai Street, then a right on Kilauea Avenue, and look for the sign H-1 west—Waimanalo. Turn right at the sign, although you won't get on the H-1 freeway; instead, get on the Kalanianaole Highway, a four-lane highway interrupted every few blocks by a stoplight. This is the suburban bedroom community to Honolulu, marked by malls on the left and beach parks on the right.

One of these parks is **Hanauma Bay ★★★** (p. 68); you'll see the turnoff on the right when you're about half an hour from Waikiki. This marine preserve is a great place to stop for a swim; you'll find the friendliest fish on the island here. *A reminder:* The beach park is closed on Tuesday.

Around mile marker 11, the jagged lava coast spouts sea foam at the **Halona Blowhole.** Look out to sea from Halona over Sandy Beach and across the 26-mile gulf to neighboring Molokai and the faint triangular shadow of Lanai on the far horizon. **Sandy Beach** (p. 70) is Oahu's most dangerous beach; it's the only one with an ambulance always standing by to whisk injured wave catchers to the hospital. Body boarders just love it.

Ahead lies 647-foot-high **Makapuu Point** (p. 70), with a lighthouse that once signaled safe passage for steamship passengers arriving from San Francisco. The automated light now brightens Oahu's south coast for passing tankers, fishing boats, and sailors. You can take a short hike up here for a spectacular vista.

Turn the corner at Makapuu and you're on Oahu's windward side, where cooling trade winds propel windsurfers across turquoise bays; the waves at **Makapuu Beach Park** (p. 70) are perfect for bodysurfing.

Winding up the coast, Kalanianaole Highway (Hwy. 72) leads through rural **Waimanalo,** a country beach town of nurseries and stables, fresh-fruit stands, and some of the island's best conch- and triton-shell specimens at roadside stands. Nearly 4 miles long, **Waimanalo Beach** is Oahu's longest beach and the most popular for bodysurfing. Take a swim here or head on to **Kailua Beach ★★** (p. 71), one of Hawaii's best.

The Windward Coast

From the **Nuuanu Pali Lookout ★**, near the summit of the Pali Highway (Hwy. 61), you get the first hint of the other side of Oahu, a region so green and lovely that it could be an island sibling of Tahiti. With its many beaches and bays, the scenic 30-mile Windward Coast parallels the corduroy-ridged, nearly perpendicular cliffs of the Koolau Range, which separates the windward side of the island from Honolulu and the rest of Oahu.

From the Pali Highway, to the right is Kailua, Hawaii's biggest beach town, with more than 50,000 residents and two special beaches, **Kailua Beach** (p. 71) and **Lanikai Beach** (p. 70). Funky little Kailua is lined with million-dollar houses next to tarpaper shacks, antiques shops, and bed-and-breakfasts. If you spend a day at the beach here, stick around for sunset, when the sun sinks behind the Koolau Range and tints the clouds pink and orange. After a hard day at the beach, you'll work up an appetite, and Kailua has several great inexpensive restaurants.

If you want to skip the beaches this time, turn left on North Kalaheo Drive, which becomes Kaneohe Bay Drive as it skirts Kaneohe Bay and leads back to Kamehameha Highway (Hwy. 83). Incredibly scenic Kaneohe Bay is spiked with islets and lined with gold-sand beach parks like **Kualoa Regional Park,** a favorite picnic spot. The bay has a barrier reef and four tiny islets, one of which is known as *Moku o Loe,* or Coconut Island. Don't be surprised if it looks familiar—it appeared in *Gilligan's Island.*

Little poly-voweled beach towns like **Kahaluu, Kaaawa, Punaluu,** and **Hauula** pop up along the coast, offering passersby shell shops and art galleries to explore. Sugar, once the sole industry of this region, is gone. But **Kahuku,** the former sugar-plantation town, has found new life as a small aquaculture community with prawn farms that supply island restaurants.

From here, continue along Kamehameha Highway (Hwy. 83) to the North Shore.

ATTRACTIONS ALONG THE WINDWARD COAST

The attractions below are arranged geographically as you drive up the coast from south to north.

Hoomaluhia Botanical Garden ★ GARDEN   This 400-acre botanical garden at the foot of the steepled Koolau Range is the perfect place for a picnic, hiking and also has camping facilities. Its name means "a peaceful refuge," and that's exactly what the Army Corps of Engineers created when they installed a flood-control project here, which resulted in a 32-acre freshwater lake and garden. The park has numerous hiking trails. If you like hiking and nature, plan to spend at least a half-day here. Be prepared for rain, mud, and mosquitoes.

45–680 Luluku Rd. http://www.honolulu.gov/parks/hbg.html. © **808/233-7323.** Free admission. Daily 9am–4pm. Guided nature hikes Sat 10am and Sun 1pm. Take H-1 to the Pali Hwy. (Hwy. 61); turn left on Kamehameha Hwy. (Hwy. 83); at the 4th light, turn left onto Luluku Rd. Bus: 55 will stop on Kamehameha Hwy.; it's a 2-mile walk to the visitor center.

Polynesian Cultural Center ★★ MUSEUM   Some people dismiss this site as too "touristy." I disagree. If anything it's an authentic interactive encounter of Pacific island cultures. Not only will this "living" museum lure you in with real life depictions of the lifestyles, songs, dance, costumes, and architecture of seven Pacific islands or archipelagos—Fiji, New Zealand, Marquesas, Samoa, Tahiti, Tonga, and Hawaii—in the re-created villages scattered throughout the 42-acre lagoon park, but it is also "inhabited" by native students from those Polynesian villages who attend Hawaii's Brigham Young University. The park, which is operated by the Mormon Church, also features a variety of stage shows celebrating the music, dance, history, and culture of Polynesia. There's a luau every evening. Because a visit can take up to 8 hours, it's a good idea to arrive before 2pm.

55–370 Kamehameha Hwy. www.polynesia.com. © **800/367-7060,** 808/293-3333, or 808/923-2911. Various packages available for $60–$200 adults, $48–$160 children 5–11. Daily noon–9pm. Take H-1 to Pali Hwy. (Hwy. 61) and turn left on Kamehameha Hwy. (Hwy. 83). Parking is free. Bus: 55. Polynesian Cultural Center coaches $25–$35 round-trip; call numbers above to book.

Central Oahu & the North Shore

If you can afford the splurge, rent a bright, shiny convertible—the perfect car for Oahu because you can tan as you go—and head for the North Shore and Hawaii's surf city: **Haleiwa ★★★**, a quaint sugar-plantation town designated a historic site. A collection of faded clapboard stores with a picturesque harbor, Haleiwa has evolved into a surfer outpost and major roadside attraction with art galleries, restaurants, and shops that sell hand-decorated clothing, jewelry, and sports gear (see "Shopping A to Z," later).

Getting here is half the fun. You have two choices from Waikiki: The first is to meander north along the lush Windward Coast (attractions along that route are discussed in the previous section).

The second choice is to cruise up the H-2 through Oahu's broad and fertile central valley, past Pearl Harbor and the Schofield Barracks of *From Here to Eternity* fame, and on through the red-earthed heart of the island, where pineapple and sugar-cane fields stretch from the Koolau to the Waianae mountains, until the sea reappears on the horizon. To get here from Waikiki, take Ala Wai Boulevard out of Waikiki, turn right on to McCully St. Make a left as soon as you go under the freeway; take the ramp up to H-1 West.

Once you're on H-1, stay to the right side; the freeway tends to divide abruptly. Keep following the signs for the H-1. When you see the sign for H-2 North, turn off H-1 toward the town of Wahiawa. That's what the sign will say—not North Shore or Haleiwa, but Wahiawa.

The H-2 runs out and becomes a two-lane country road about 18 miles outside downtown Honolulu, near Schofield Barracks. The highway becomes Kamehameha Highway (Hwy. 99 and later Hwy. 83) at Wahiawa. "Kam" Highway, as everyone calls it, will be your road for most of the rest of the trip to Haleiwa, on the North Shore.

SURF CITY: HALEIWA ★★★

Only 28 miles from Waikiki is Haleiwa, the funky former sugar-plantation town that's now the world capital of big-wave surfing. This beach town really comes alive in winter, when waves rise up, and temperatures dip into the 70s (low to mid-20s Celsius); then, it seems, every surfer in the world is here to see and be seen.

Arts and crafts, boutiques, and burger stands line both sides of the town. There's also a busy fishing harbor full of charter boats and captains who hunt the Kauai Channel daily for tuna, mahimahi, and marlin. The bartenders at **Jameson's by the Sea ★**, 62–540 Kamehameha Hwy. (© **808/637-6272**), make the best Mai Tais on the North Shore; they use the original recipe by Trader Vic Bergeron.

Once in Haleiwa, the hot and thirsty traveler should report directly to the nearest shave-ice stand, like **Matsumoto Shave Ice ★★**, 66–087 Kamehameha Hwy. (© **808/637-4827**). For 40 years, this small, humble shop operated by the Matsumoto family has served a popular rendition of the Hawaii-style snow cone flavored with tropical tastes. The cooling treat is also available at neighboring stores, some of which still shave the ice with a hand-crank device.

Just down the road are some of the fabled shrines of surfing—**Waimea Beach, Banzai Pipeline, Sunset Beach**—where some of the world's largest waves, reaching 20 feet and more, rise up between November and January. They draw professional surfers as well as reckless daredevils and hordes of onlookers, who jump in their cars and head north when word goes out that "surf's up." Don't forget your binoculars. For more details on North Shore beaches, see p. 71.

WAIMEA VALLEY ★

For nearly 3 decades, this 1,875-acre park has lured visitors with activities from cliff diving and hula performances to kayaking and ATV tours. A visit here offers a lush walk into the past. The valley is packed with archaeological sites, including the 600-year-old Hale O Lono, a heiau dedicated to the Hawaiian god Lono, which you'll find to the left of the entrance. The botanical collection has 35 different gardens, including super-rare Hawaiian species such as the endangered *Kokia cookei* hibiscus. The valley is also home to fauna such as the endangered Hawaiian moorhen; look for a black bird with a red face cruising in the ponds. The 150-acre Arboretum and Botanical Garden contains more than 5,000 species of tropical plants. Walk through the gardens (take the paved paths or dirt trails) and wind up at 45-foot-high Waimea Falls—bring your bathing suit and you can dive into the cold, murky water. The public is invited to hike the trails and spend a day in this quiet oasis. There are several free walking tours all starting at 9am, plus cultural activities such as lei making, kappa demonstrations, hula lessons, Hawaiian games and crafts, and music and storytelling.

59–864 Kamehameha Hwy. www.waimeavalley.net © **808/638-7766.** Admission $16 adults, $12 seniors and $8 children 4–12. Daily 9am–5pm. Bus: 55.

BEACHES

The Waikiki Coast

ALA MOANA BEACH PARK ★★

Gold-sand Ala Moana (by the sea), on sunny Mamala Bay, stretches for more than a mile along Honolulu's coast between downtown and Waikiki. This 76-acre midtown beach park is one of the island's most popular playgrounds. It has a man-made beach, as well as its own lagoon, yacht harbor, tennis courts, music pavilion, bathhouses, picnic tables, and enough wide-open green spaces to accommodate four million visitors a year. The water is calm almost year-round, protected by black-lava rocks set offshore.

WAIKIKI BEACH ★★★

No beach anywhere is so widely known or so universally sought after as this narrow, 1½-mile-long crescent of imported sand (from Molokai) at the foot of a string of high-rise hotels. Home to the world's longest-running beach party, Waikiki attracts nearly five million visitors a year from every corner of the planet. First-timers are amazed to discover how small Waikiki Beach actually is, but there's always a place for them under the tropical sun here. Fabulous for swimming, board surfing and bodysurfing, outrigger canoeing, diving, sailing, snorkeling, and pole fishing, every imaginable type of marine equipment is available for rent here. Facilities include showers, lifeguards, restrooms, grills, picnic tables, and pavilions at the **Queen's Surf** end of the beach (at Kapiolani Park, between the zoo and the aquarium). The best place to park is at Kapiolani Park, near Sans Souci.

East Oahu

HANAUMA BAY ★★★

Oahu's most popular snorkeling spot is this volcanic crater with a curved, 2,000-foot gold-sand beach, constantly packed elbow-to-elbow with people year-round. The bay's shallow shoreline water and abundant marine life are the main attractions, but this good-looking beach is also popular for sunbathing and people-watching. You can snorkel in the safe, shallow (10-ft.) inner bay, which, along with the beach, is almost always crowded. Because Hanauma Bay is a conservation district, you cannot touch or take any marine life here. Feeding the fish is also prohibited.

A $13-million Marine Education Center features exhibits and a 7-minute video orienting visitors to this Marine Life Sanctuary. Facilities include parking, restrooms, a pavilion, a grass volleyball court, lifeguards, barbecues, picnic tables, and food concessions. Alcohol is prohibited in the park; there is no smoking past the visitor center. Expect to pay $1 per vehicle to park plus an entrance fee of $7.50 per person (free for children 12 and under and Hawaii residents). A great resource book is *Exploring Hanauma Bay* by Susan Scott (University of Hawaii Press), filled with excellent information on the Bay and terrific underwater photos identifying the fish you will encounter.

Beaches & Outdoor Activities on Oahu

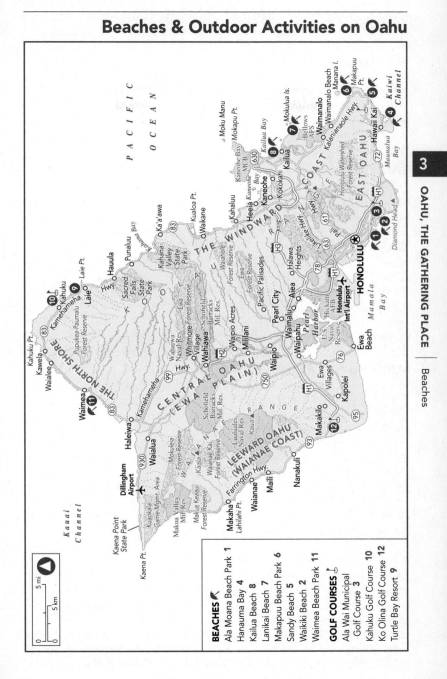

BEACHES
Ala Moana Beach Park **1**
Hanauma Bay **4**
Kailua Beach **8**
Lanikai Beach **7**
Makapuu Beach Park **6**
Sandy Beach **5**
Waikiki Beach **2**
Waimea Beach Park **11**

GOLF COURSES
Ala Wai Municipal Golf Course **3**
Kahuku Golf Course **10**
Ko Olina Golf Course **12**
Turtle Bay Resort **9**

If you're driving, take Kalanianaole Highway to Koko Head Regional Park. Avoid the crowds by going early, about 8am, on a weekday morning; once the parking lot's full, you're out of luck. Alternatively, take TheBus: 22-BEACH BUS to escape the parking problem. For a bit more money, there is a private company, The Hanauma Bay Shuttle (www.hanaumabaytours.com), which offers snorkel equipment and transportation from Waikiki to Hanauma Bay ($24–$25 adults, $22 children). Hanauma Bay is closed every Tuesday so the fish can have a day off. For information on the public park at Hanauma, go to www.hanauma-bay-hawaii.com or call (C) **808/396-4229.** Hanauma Bay is open from 6am to 7pm in the summer and 6am to 6pm in the winter.

SANDY BEACH ★★

Sandy Beach is one of the best bodysurfing beaches on Oahu; it's also one of the most dangerous. It's better to just stand and watch the daredevils literally risk their necks at this 1,200-foot-long gold-sand beach that's pounded by wild waves and haunted by a dangerous shore break and strong backwash. Weak swimmers and children should definitely stay out of the water here; Lifeguards post flags to alert beachgoers to the day's surf: Green means safe, yellow means caution, and red indicates very dangerous water conditions.

Facilities include restrooms and parking. Go weekdays to avoid the crowds or weekends to catch the bodysurfers in action. From Waikiki, drive east on the H-1, which becomes Kalanianaole Highway; proceed past Hawaii Kai, up the hill to Hanauma Bay, past the Halona Blowhole, and along the coast. The next big gold beach on the right is Sandy Beach. TheBus no. 22 or 23 will also bring you here.

MAKAPUU BEACH PARK ★★

Makapuu Beach, the most famous bodysurfing beach in Hawaii, is a beautiful 1,000-foot-long gold-sand beach cupped in the stark black Koolau cliffs on Oahu's easternmost point. Even if you never venture into the water, it's worth a visit just to enjoy the great natural beauty of this classic Hawaiian beach. (You've probably already seen it in the TV show *Hawaii Five-O.*) In summer, the ocean here is as gentle as a Jacuzzi, and swimming and diving are perfect; come winter, however, Makapuu is a hit with expert bodysurfers, who come for big, pounding waves that are too dangerous for regular swimmers.

Facilities include restrooms, lifeguards, barbecue grills, picnic tables, and parking. To get here, follow Kalanianaole Highway toward Waimanalo, or take TheBus no. 22 or 23.

The Windward Coast

LANIKAI BEACH ★★★

One of Hawaii's best spots for swimming, mile-long, golden-sand Lanikai's crystal-clear lagoon is like a giant saltwater swimming pool that you're lucky enough to be able to share with the resident tropical fish and sea turtles. Because Lanikai is in a residential neighborhood, it's less crowded than other Oahu beaches, the perfect place to enjoy a quiet day. Sun worshipers should arrive in the morning, though, as the Koolau Range blocks the afternoon rays.

There are no facilities here, just off-street parking. From Waikiki, take the H-1 to the Pali Highway (Hwy. 61) through the Nuuanu Pali Tunnel to Kailua, where the Pali Highway becomes Kailua Road as it proceeds through town. At Kalaheo Avenue, turn right and follow the coast about 2 miles to Kailua Beach Park; just past it, turn left at the T intersection and drive uphill on Aalapapa Drive, a one-way street that loops back as Mokulua Drive. Park on Mokulua Drive and walk down any of the eight public-access lanes to the shore. Or take TheBus no. 22 or 23 to Sea Life Park and transfer to Bus 57 to (Kailua) and then transfer to the shuttle bus.

KAILUA BEACH ★★★

Windward Oahu's premier beach is a 2-mile-long, wide golden strand with dunes, palm trees, panoramic views, and offshore islets that are home to seabirds. The swimming is excellent, and the azure waters are usually decorated with bright sails; this is Oahu's best windsurfing beach as well. It's also a favorite spot to sail catamarans, bodysurf the gentle waves, or paddle a kayak. Water conditions are quite safe, especially at the mouth of Kaelepulu Stream, where toddlers play in the freshwater shallows at the middle of the beach park. The 35-acre beach park is intersected by a freshwater stream and watched over by lifeguards. Facilities include picnic tables, barbecues, restrooms, a volleyball court, a public boat ramp, free parking, and an open-air cafe. Kailua's new bike path weaves through the park, and windsurfer and kayak rentals are available as well. To get here, take Pali Highway (Hwy. 61) to Kailua, drive through town, turn right on Kalaheo Avenue, and go a mile until you see the beach on your left. Or take The Bus 22 or 23 to Sea Life Park and transfer to Bus 57 to into Kailua, and then the no. 70 shuttle.

> **Impressions**
>
> *The boldness and address with which we saw them perform these difficult and dangerous maneuvers were altogether astonishing.*
> —Captain James Cook's observations of Hawaiian surfers

The North Shore

WAIMEA BEACH PARK ★★

This deep, sandy bowl has gentle summer waves that are excellent for swimming, snorkeling, and bodysurfing. To one side of the bay is a huge rock that local kids like to climb up and dive from. However, winter waves pound the narrow bay, sometimes rising to 50 feet high. When the surf's really up, very strong currents and shore breaks sweep the bay—and it seems like everyone on Oahu drives out to Waimea to get a look at the monster waves and those who ride them.

Facilities include lifeguards, restrooms, showers, parking, and nearby restaurants and shops in Haleiwa town. The beach is located on Kamehameha Highway (Hwy. 83); from Waikiki, you can take TheBus no. 55.

WATERSPORTS

If you want to rent beach toys (snorkeling equipment, boogie boards, surf-boards, kayaks, and more), check out **Snorkel Bob's,** on the way to Hanauma Bay at 700 Kapahulu Ave. (at Date St.; www.snorkelbob.com; ☏ **808/735-7944**), or **Aloha Beach Service,** in the Moana Surfrider, 2365 Kalakaua Ave. (☏ **808/922-3111,** ext. 2341). On Oahu's windward side, try **Kailua Beach Adventures,** 130 Kailua Rd., a block from Kailua Beach Park (www.kailuasail boards.com; ☏ **808/262-2555**). On the North Shore, get equipment from **Surf-N-Sea,** 62–595 Kamehameha Hwy. (www.surfnsea.com; ☏ **808/637-9887**).

Boating

Get out on the ocean, or you are missing a big part of Hawaii. You can opt for a "booze cruise," jammed with loud, rum-soaked strangers, or you can sail on one of these special yachts, all of which will take you out **whale-watching** in season (roughly Jan–Apr). For fishing charters, see "Sport Fishing," below.

Navatek I ★★★   You are guaranteed that you'll be "seasick-free," on this boat. The 140-foot-long *Navatek I* isn't even a boat; it's actually a SWATH (Small Waterplane Area Twin Hull) vessel. That means the ship's superstruc-ture—the part you ride on—rests on twin torpedo-like hulls that cut through the water so you don't bob like a cork and spill your Mai Tai.

Sunset dinner cruises leave Pier 6 nightly. If you have your heart set on seeing the city lights, take the Royal Sunset Dinner Cruise, which runs from 5:30 to 7:30pm. The best deal is the **lunch cruise** (which runs during **whale season,** roughly Jan–Apr), with a full buffet and a great view of Oahu offshore plus you get whales, to boot. The lunch cruise lasts from 11am to 1pm or 1:30 to 3pm. Royal dinner cruises include live Hawaiian music.

Aloha Tower Marketplace, Pier 6, c/o Hawaiian Cruises Ltd. www.atlantisadventures. com. ☏ **808/973-1311.** Dinner cruises $99–$164 adults, $46–$98 children 7–12; lunch cruises $47 adults, $32 children 7–12. Discount parking available. Bus: 2 and E. *Hint:* Check website for Internet deals.

Scuba Diving

Because Oahu's greatest dives are offshore, your best bet is to book a two-tank dive from a dive boat. Hawaii's oldest and largest outfitter is **Aaron's Dive Shop,** 307 Hahani St. (www.hawaii-scuba.com; ☏ **808/262-2333**), which offers boat and beach dive excursions off the coast. The two-tank boat dives start at $120 per person if you have all your gear or $130 including gear, and trans-portation from the Kailua shop is provided. Price includes pickup in Waikiki.

On the North Shore, **Surf-N-Sea,** 62–595 Kamehameha Hwy. (www.surf nsea.com; ☏ **808/637-9887**), has dive tours from the shore (starting at $75 for one tank) and from a boat ($140 for two tanks). Surf-N-Sea also rents equip-ment and can point you to the best dive sites in the area.

EXPERIENCING jaws UP CLOSE & PERSONAL

You're 4 miles out from land, surrounded by open ocean. Suddenly from out of the blue depths a shape emerges: the sleek, pale shadow of a 6-foot-long gray reef shark, followed quickly by a couple of 10-foot-long Galapagos sharks. Within moments, you are surrounded by sharks on all sides. Do you panic? No, you paid $120 to be in the midst of these jaws of the deep. And, of course, you have a 6×6×10-foot aluminum shark cage separating you from all those teeth.

It happens every day at **North Shore Shark Adventures** (www.hawaiisharkad ventures.com; ✆ **808/228-5900**), the dream of Captain Joe Pavsek, who decided after some 30 years of surfing and diving to share the experience of seeing a shark with visitors. Depending on the sea conditions and the weather, snorkelers can stay in the cage as long as they wish, with the sharks just inches away. The shark cage, connected to the boat with wire line, holds up to four snorkelers (it's comfortable with two but pretty snug at full capacity). You can also stay on the boat and view the sharks from a more respectable distance for just $70. Transportation from Waikiki and Kahala is an additional $55. Check the website for specials.

Snorkeling

Some of the best snorkeling in Oahu is at **Hanauma Bay ★★★**. It's crowded—sometimes it seems there are more people than fish—but Hanauma has clear, warm, protected waters and an abundance of friendly reef fish, including Moorish idols, scores of butterfly fish, damselfish, and wrasses. Go early: It's packed by 10am. And it's closed on Tuesdays. For details, see "Beaches," earlier in this chapter.

Sport Fishing

Kewalo Basin, located between the Honolulu International Airport and Waikiki, is the main location for charter fishing boats on Oahu. From Waikiki, take Kalakaua Avenue Ewa (west) turn left (toward the ocean) on Ala Moana continue past Ala Moana Center; Kewalo Basin is on the left, across from Ward Centre. Look for charter boats all in a row in their slips; when the fish are biting, the captains display the catch of the day in the afternoon. You can also take TheBus no. 19 or 42 (Airport).

The best sport-fishing booking desk in the state is **Sportfish Hawaii ★** (www.sportfishhawaii.com; ✆ **877/388-1376** or 808/396-2607), which books boats on all the islands. These fishing vessels have been inspected and must meet rigorous criteria to guarantee that you will have a great time. Prices range from $975 to $1,195 for a full-day exclusive charter (you, plus five friends, get the entire boat to yourself), from $775 for a half-day exclusive, or from $220 for a full-day shared charter (you share the boat with five other people).

Submarine Dives

Here's your chance to play Jules Verne and experience the underwater world from the comfort of a submarine, which will take you on an adventure below the surface in high-tech comfort. If swimming's not your thing, this is a great way to see Hawaii's spectacular sea life. Shuttle boats to the sub leave from the Hilton Hawaiian Village Pier. Call **Atlantis Submarines ★★** (www.atlantisadventures.com/hawaii.cfm; ⓒ **800/381-0237** or 808/973-9811) to reserve. The cost is $115 to $125 for adults, $48 to $55 for kids 12 and under (children must be at least 36 in. tall). *Tip:* Book online for discount rates from $105 for adults and $38 for kids. *Warning:* Skip this if you suffer from claustrophobia.

Surfing

In summer, when the water's warm and there's a soft breeze in the air, the south swell comes up. It's surf season in Waikiki, the best place on Oahu to learn how to surf. For lessons, go early to **Aloha Beach Service ★**, next to the Moana Surfrider, 2365 Kalakaua Ave. (ⓒ **808/922-3111**). The beach boys offer group lessons for $50 an hour in the water ($90 for a private lesson); board rentals are $15 for the first hour and $5 for every hour after that (everything is cash only). You must know how to swim.

More experienced surfers should drop in on any surf shop around Oahu, or call the **Surf News Network Surfline** (ⓒ **808/596-SURF** [7873]) to get the latest surf conditions. The **Cliffs,** at the base of Diamond Head, is a good spot for advanced surfers; 4- to 6-foot waves churn here, allowing for high-performance surfing.

NATURE HIKES

People are often surprised to discover that the great outdoors is less than an hour away from downtown Honolulu. The island's 33 major hiking trails traverse razor-thin ridgebacks, deep waterfall valleys, and more. The best source of hiking information on Oahu is the state's **Na Ala Hele (Trails to Go On) Program** (www.hawaiitrails.org; ⓒ **808/973-9782** or aaron.j.lowe@hawaii.gov).

The **Hawaiian Trail and Mountain Club,** P.O. Box 2238, Honolulu, HI 96804 (http://htmclub.org), offers regular hikes on Oahu. Bring $3 for the donation, your own lunch, and drinking water, and meet up with the club members at the scheduled location to join them on a hike.

Other organizations that offer regularly scheduled hikes are the **Sierra Club,** 1040 Richards St. (www.hi.sierraclub.org), and the **Hawaii Nature Center,** 2131 Makiki Heights Dr. (www.hawaiinaturecenter.org; ⓒ **888/955-0104** or 808/955-0100).

Honolulu-Area Hikes

DIAMOND HEAD CRATER ★★★

This is a moderate but steep walk to the 760-foot summit of Hawaii's most famous volcanic cone. The 1.5-mile round-trip takes about 1½ hours, and the entry fee is $5 per car load or if you walk in it is $1 per person.

GOLF & OTHER OUTDOOR ACTIVITIES

Golf

Oahu has nearly three dozen golf courses, ranging from bare-bones municipal courses to exclusive country-club courses with membership fees running to six figures a year. Below are the best of a great bunch.

As you get to know Oahu's courses, you'll see that the windward courses play much differently than the leeward courses. On the windward side, the prevailing winds blow from the ocean to shore, and the grain direction of the greens tends to run the same way—from the ocean to the mountains. Leeward golf courses have the opposite tendency: The winds usually blow from the mountains to the ocean, with the grain direction of the greens corresponding.

Tips on beating the crowds and saving money: Oahu's golf courses tend to be crowded, so go midweek if you can. Also, most island courses have twilight rates that offer substantial discounts if you're willing to tee off in the afternoon.

Transportation note: TheBus does not allow golf-club bags onboard.

WAIKIKI

Ala Wai Municipal Golf Course ★ The *Guinness Book of World Records* lists Ala Wai as the busiest golf course in the world; some 500 rounds a day are played on this 18-hole municipal course within walking distance of Waikiki's hotels. The computerized tee reservations system for all of Oahu's municipal courses allow you to book only 3 days in advance, but keep trying.

404 Kapahulu Ave., Waikiki. www.honolulu.gov/des/golf/alawai.htm. (C) **808/733-7387** for golf course, or 808/296-2000 for tee-time reservations. Greens fees $55; twilight rates $28; cart $20. From Waikiki, turn left on Kapahulu Ave.; the course is on the mauka side of Ala Wai Canal. Bus: 13 or 2.

THE NORTH SHORE

Kahuku Golf Course ★ This 9-hole budget golf course is a bit funky. There are no club rentals, no clubhouse, and no facilities other than a few pull carts that disappear with the first handful of golfers. But a round at this scenic oceanside course amid the tranquillity of the North Shore is quite an experience nonetheless. Duffers will love the ease of this recreational course, and weight watchers will be happy to walk the gently sloping greens. Don't forget to bring your camera for the views (especially at holes 3, 4, 7, and 8, which are right on the ocean). No reservations are taken; tee times

> ### Insider Tip
>
> For discount tee times, call **Stand-by Golf** (www.hawaiistandbygolf.com; (C) **888/645-BOOK** [2665]), which offers discounted tee times for same-day or future golfing. Call between 7am and 10pm for a guaranteed tee time with up to a 30% discount off greens fees.

are first-come, first-served, and with plenty of retirees happy to sit and wait, the competition is fierce for early tee times. Bring your own clubs and call ahead to check the weather.

56–501 Kamehameha Hwy., Kahuku. www.honolulu.gov/des/golf © **808/293-5842.** Greens fees $33, twilight $17, pull cart $4. Take H-1 west to H-2; follow H-2 through Wahiawa to Kamehameha Hwy. (Hwy. 99, then Hwy. 83); follow it to Kahuku.

Ko Olina Golf Club ★★★ "Golf Digest" once named this Ted Robin-son-designed course one of "America's Top 75 Resort Courses." The signature hole—the 12th, a par-3—has an elevated tee that sits on a rock garden with a cascading waterfall. At the 18th hole, you'll see and hear water all around you—seven pools begin on the right side of the fairway and slope down to a lake. Book in advance; this course is crowded all the time. Facilities include a driving range, locker rooms, a Jacuzzi, steam rooms, and a restaurant and bar. Lessons are available.

92–1220 Aliinui Dr., Kapolei. www.koolinagolf.com. © **808/676-5300.** Greens fees $210 ($185 for Ihilani Resort guests); 1pm rates drop to $145. Ask about transportation from Waikiki hotels. Collared shirts requested for men and women. Take H-1 west until it becomes Hwy. 93 (Farrington Hwy.); turn off at the Ko Olina exit; take the exit road (Aliinui Dr.) into Ko Olina Resort; turn left into the clubhouse. No bus service.

Turtle Bay Resort ★ This North Shore resort is home to two of Hawaii's top golf courses. The 18-hole **Arnold Palmer Course** (formerly the Links at Kuilima) was designed by Arnold Palmer and Ed Seay. Now that the *Casuarina* (ironwood) trees have matured, it's not as windy as it used to be, but this is still a challenging course. Another option is the par-71, 6,200-yard **George Fazio Course**—the only Fazio course in Hawaii. Facilities include a pro shop, driving range, putting and chipping greens, and a snack bar. Weekdays are best for tee times. Check on Turtle Bay's golf shuttle if you are staying in Waikiki.

57–049 Kamehameha Hwy., Kahuku. www.turtlebayresort.com. © **808/293-8574.** Greens fees: Palmer Course $185 ($155 for Turtle Bay guests), $110 after 1pm; Fazio Course $115 ($105 for Turtle Bay guests), $75 after 1pm. Take H-1 west past Pearl City; when the freeway splits, take H-2 and follow the signs to Haleiwa; at Haleiwa, take Hwy. 83 to Turtle Bay Resort. Bus: 55.

Biking

Bicycling is a great way to see Oahu; most streets here have bike lanes. For information on bikeways and maps, contact the **Honolulu City and County Bicycle Coordinator** (www.honolulu.gov/bicycle; © **808/768-8335;** csayers@honolulu.gov).

If you're in Waikiki, you can rent a bike for as little as $10 for a half-day and $20 for 24 hours at **Big Kahuna Rentals,** 407 Seaside Ave. (www.bigkahunarentals.com/sntmainbikes.htm; © **888/451-5544** or 808/924-2736).

For a bike-and-hike adventure, contact **Bike Hawaii** (www.bikehawaii.com; © **877/682-7433** or 808/734-4214), which has a variety of group tours, such as its Mountain Biking Kaaawa Valley at Kualoa. The 6-mile trip, which takes 2 to 3 hours of riding, includes van transportation from your hotel, bike, helmet, snacks, picnic lunch, water bottle, and guide; it's $119 for adults and $76 for children 14 and under.

If you'd like to join some club rides, contact the **Hawaii Bicycle League** (www.hbl.org; ✆ **808/735-5756**), which offers rides every weekend, as well as several annual events, plus great maps for bike outings. The league can also provide a schedule of upcoming rides, races, and outings.

Tennis

If you are staying in Waikiki, the tennis courts at Ala Moana Beach Park are your best (and free) bet. If you're on the North Shore, head to the **Turtle Bay Resort,** 57–091 Kamehameha Hwy. (www.turtlebayresort.com; ✆ **808/293-6024;** bus 55), which has four courts that are lit for night play. Reserve these night courts in advance, they're very popular. Court time costs $25 per hour (complimentary for guests); equipment rental and lessons are also available.

ORIENTATION TOURS
Guided Sightseeing Tours

If your time is limited, you might want to consider a guided tour. These tours are informative, can give you a good overview of Honolulu or Oahu in a limited amount of time, and are surprisingly entertaining.

E Noa Tours, 1141 Waimanu St., Ste. 105 (www.enoa.com; ✆ **800/824-8804** or 808/591-2561), offers a range of narrated tours, from island loops to explorations of Pearl Harbor, on air-conditioned, 27-passenger minibuses. The Majestic Circle Island Tour ($100 for adults, $80 for children 3–11, $61 for children under 5) stops at key Oahu landmarks, other tours go to the Pearl Harbor/USS *Arizona* Memorial and the North Shore. Note that the tour is 10 hours long and is best for kids over 8 years old.

Waikiki Trolley Tours ★, 1141 Waimanu St., Ste. 105 (www.waikiki trolley.com; ✆ **800/824-8804** or 808/593-2822), offers three fun tours of

---

A bird's-eye VIEW

To understand why Oahu was the island of kings, you need to see it from the air. **Island Seaplane Service ★★★** (www. islandseaplane.com; ✆ **808/836-6273**) operates flights departing from a floating dock in the protected waters of Keehi Lagoon in either a six-passenger DeHavilland Beaver or a four-passenger Cessna 206. There's nothing quite like feeling the slap of the waves as the plane skims across the water and then effortlessly lifts into the air.

The half-hour tour ($179) gives you aerial views of Waikiki Beach, Diamond Head Crater, Kahala's luxury estates, and the sparkling waters of Hanauma and Kaneohe bays; the 1-hour tour ($299) continues on to Chinaman's Hat, the Polynesian Cultural Center, and the rolling surf of the North Shore. The flight returns across the island, over Hawaii's historic wartime sites: Schofield Barracks and the Pearl Harbor memorials.

sightseeing, entertainment, dining, and shopping. These are a great way to get the lay of the land. You can get on and off the trolley as needed (trolleys come along every 2–20 min.). An all-day pass (8:30am–11:35pm) is $20 for adults, and $15 for children 3 to 11, per line ($38 and $28 respectively for all three lines); a 4-day pass for all three lines is $59 for adults, and $41 for children (check their website for discounts).

Waikiki & Honolulu Walking Tours

The **Hawaii Geographic Society** (hawaiigeographicsociety@gmail.com; 🕿 **800/538-3950** or 808/538-3952) presents numerous interesting and unusual tours, such as "A Temple Tour," which includes Chinese, Japanese, Christian, and Jewish houses of worship; an archaeology walking trek in and around downtown Honolulu; and others. Each is led by an expert from the Hawaii Geographic Society and must have a minimum of two people; the cost is $15 per person. The society is a wealth of information, from a hiking/camping packet to maps to a self-guided walk brochure, "Historic Downtown Honolulu Walking Trek" of the 200-year-old city center. If you'd like a copy or more information, contact **Hawaii Geographic Maps and Books,** hawaiigeographic society@gmail.com or by phone.

Guided Ecotours

Oahu isn't just high-rises in Waikiki or urban sprawl in Honolulu, but extinct craters, hidden waterfalls, lush rainforests, forgotten coastlines, and rainbow-filled valleys. To experience the other side of Oahu, contact **Oahu Nature Tours** (www.oahunaturetours.com; 🕿 **808/924-2473**). It offers a dozen different ecotours, starting at $32 per person, and provides everything: expert guides (geologists, historians, archaeologists), round-trip transportation, entrance fees, bottled water, and use of day packs, binoculars, flashlights, and rain gear.

Specialty Tours

For a really different look at Honolulu, **Oahu Ghost Tours** ★★★ (www. oahughosttours.com; 🕿 **877/597-7325**) offers a look at the supernatural side of this ancient place. The offerings include **Honolulu City Haunts,** a 2-hour walking tour of places where supernatural events are still happening today ($39 for adults, $29 for children 11 and under); **Sacred Spirits,** a 5-hour walking tour of the most sacred native Hawaiian spots on Oahu ($59 adults, $49 children); and the **Orbs of Oahu** driving tour, which circles the island, stopping at some of the "most haunted" locations ($59 adults, $49 children). New: Myths & Legends of Waikiki 2-hour walking tour ($31 adults, $23 children).

SHOPPING A TO Z

Shopping competes with golf, surfing, and sightseeing as a bona fide Honolulu activity. And why not? The proliferation of top-notch made-in-Hawaii products, the vitality of the local crafts scene, and the unquenchable thirst for mementos of the islands lend respectability to shopping here.

Oahu is also a haven for mall mavens. More than 1,000 stores occupy the 11 major shopping centers on this island. From souvenir T-shirts to high fashion, posh European to down-home local, Oahu's offerings are wide ranging indeed. But you must sometimes wade through oceans of schlock to arrive at the mother lode. Alongside the Louis Vuitton, Chanel, and Tiffany boutiques on Waikiki's Kalakaua Avenue are plenty of tacky booths hawking airbrushed T-shirts, gold by the inch, and tasteless aloha shirts.

The section that follows is not about finding cheap souvenirs or tony items from designer fashion chains; you can find these on your own. Rather, I offer a guide to finding those special treasures that lie somewhere in between.

Shopping In & Around Honolulu & Waikiki

ALOHA WEAR

One of Hawaii's lasting afflictions is the penchant tourists have for wearing loud, matching aloha shirts and muumuu. I applaud such visitors' good intentions (to act local), but no local resident would be caught dead in such a get-up. Muumuu and aloha shirts are wonderful, but the real thing is what they wear at home and to special parties where the invitation reads "Aloha Attire."

Aside from the vintage 1930s to 1950s Hawaiian wear found in collectibles shops and at swap meets, my favorite contemporary aloha-wear designer is Hawaii's **Tori Richard.** Also popular is **Kahala Sportswear,** a well-known local company established in 1936 sold in department stores, surf shops, and stylish boutiques throughout Hawaii and the mainland.

The **Hilo Hattie** store in Ala Moana (www.hilohattie.com; ✆ **808/973-3266**) is a gold mine of affordable aloha wear. You'll also find macadamia nuts, Hawaii coffees, and other souvenirs at these Hilo Hattie stores.

EDIBLES

Honolulu Chocolate Co. ★ Life's greatest pleasures are dispensed here with abandon: expensive gourmet chocolates made in Honolulu, Italian and Hawaiian biscotti, boulder-size turtles, truffles, chocolate-covered coffee beans, and jumbo apricots in white and dark chocolate, to name a few. You pay dearly for them, but the dark-chocolate-dipped macadamia-nut clusters are beyond compare. At the Ward Centre, 1200 Ala Moana Blvd. www.honoluluchocolate.com. ✆ **808/591-2997.** Sheraton Waikiki, 2255 Kalakaua Ave. ✆ **808/931-8937.**

People's Open Markets ★ Truck farmers from all over the island bring their produce to Oahu's neighborhoods in regularly scheduled, city-sponsored open markets, held Monday through Saturday at various locations. The open markets are at various sites around town; call to find the one nearest you. www.honolulu.gov/parks/dprpom.html or http://hfbf.org/markets. ✆ **808/848-2074.**

FLOWERS & LEIS

For the best prices, go to Chinatown, where lei vendors line Beretania and Maunakea streets. My top pick is **Cindy's Lei Shoppe,** 1034 Maunakea St. (✆ **808/536-6538**). "Curb service" is available with phone orders. Just give them your car's color and model, and you can pick up your lei curbside—a great convenience on this busy street.

HAWAIIANA & GIFT ITEMS

The **Museum Shop** ★★ at the Honolulu Museum of Arts, 900 S. Beretania St. (✆ **808/532-8703**), is worth a special trip whether or not you want to see the museum. (And you will want to see it.) The shop offers art books, jewelry, basketry, ethnic fabrics, native crafts from all over the world, posters and books, and fiber vessels.

Native Books & Beautiful Things ★★ This *hui* (association) of artists and craftspeople is a browser's paradise featuring a variety of Hawaiian items from musical instruments to calabashes, jewelry, leis, and books. At the Ward Warehouse, 1050 Ala Moana Blvd. www.nameahawaii.com. ✆ **808/596-8885.**

Nohea Gallery ★ A fine showcase for contemporary Hawaii art, Nohea celebrates the islands with thoughtful, attractive selections like pit-fired raku, finely turned wood vessels, jewelry, hand-blown glass, paintings, prints, fabrics (including Hawaiian-quilt cushions), and furniture. At the Ward Warehouse, 1050 Ala Moana Blvd. www.noheagallery.com. ✆ **808/596-0074.**

SHOPPING CENTERS

Ala Moana Center ★ Nearly 400 shops and restaurants sprawl over several blocks (and 1.8 million sq. ft. of store space), catering to every imaginable need, from over-the-top upscale **(Chanel)** to mainstream chains **(Gap).** But there are practical touches in the center, too, such as banks, a foreign-exchange service, a post office, several optical companies (including 1-hr. service by **LensCrafters**), a **Foodland Super Market,** and a branch of **Longs Drugs.** It's open Monday to Saturday 9:30am to 9pm, and Sunday 10am to 7pm. 1450 Ala Moana Blvd. www.alamoanacenter.com. ✆ **808/955-9517.** Bus: 8 or 13. Various shuttle services also stop here. For Waikiki Trolley info, see "Getting Around" (p. 28).

Aloha Stadium Swap Meet ★★ Just a buck (free for kids) gets you into this all-day show at the Aloha Stadium parking lot, where more than 400 vendors sell everything from junk to jewels. Go early for the best deals. It's open Wednesday and Saturday from 8am to 3pm and Sunday from 6:30am to 3pm. 99-500 Salt Lake Blvd. (about 20-min. drive from Waikiki, http://www.alohastadium swapmeet.net/). Bus: 42 (on Kuhio Ave.). Bus ride is about 1.5 hr.; get off at Kamehameha Hwy and Salt Lake Blvd. and walk ⅓ mile to the Swap Meet on Salt Lake Blvd.

Kahala Mall ★ Chic, manageable, and unfrenzied, Kahala Mall is home to some of Honolulu's best shops. Located east of Waikiki in the posh neighborhood of Kahala, the mall has everything from a small **Macy's** to chain stores such as **Banana Republic**—nearly 100 specialty shops (including dozens of eateries and eight movie theaters) in an enclosed, air-conditioned area. It's open Monday through Saturday from 10am to 9pm, Sunday from 10am to 6pm. 4211 Waialae Ave. www.kahalamallcenter.com. ✆ **808/732-7736.**

Royal Hawaiian Shopping Center ★ More than 100 stores and restaurants, located on four levels, fill this open-air mall. Although there are drugstores, lei stands, restaurants, and food kiosks, the most conspicuous stores are the designer boutiques which cater largely to visitors from Japan.

The shopping center is open daily from 10am to 10pm. 2201 Kalakaua Ave. www. royalhawaiiancenter.com. (© **808/922-2299.**

Waikele Premium Outlets ★   Just say the word "Waikele" and my eyes glaze over. So many shops, so little time! There are two sections to this sprawling discount shopping mecca: the **Waikele Premium Outlets,** some 51 retailers offering designer and name-brand merchandise, and the **Waikele Value Center** across the street, with another 25 stores more practical than fashion-oriented **(Lowe's Hardware, Sports Authority).** The 64-acre complex offers discounts in name-brand stores ranging from **Saks Fifth Avenue,** to **Banana Republic.** It's open Monday through Saturday from 9am to 9pm, Sunday from 10am to 6pm. 94–790 Lumiaina St. (about 20 miles from Waikiki). www. premiumoutlets.com/waikele. (© **808/676-5656.** Take H-1 west toward Waianae and turn off at Exit 7. Bus: 2 transfer to 81 or 13 transfer to 103, or E.

Shopping in Windward Oahu

Windward Oahu's largest shopping complex is **Windward Mall,** 46–056 Kamehameha Hwy., in Kaneohe (www.windwardmall.com; (© **808/235-1143),** open Monday through Saturday from 10am to 9pm and Sunday from 10am to 6pm. The 100 stores and services at this standard suburban mall include **Macy's,** health stores, airline counters, surf shops, **LensCrafters,** and a 10-screen theater complex.

Shopping on the North Shore: Haleiwa

Haleiwa's shops and galleries display a combination of marine art, watercolors, sculptures, and a plethora of crafts trying to masquerade (quite transparently) as fine art. This is the town for gifts, fashions, and surf stuff—mostly casual, despite some very high price tags. **Haleiwa Gallery** (www.haleiwaart gallery.com; (© **808/637-3368),** next door to the North Shore Marketplace, displays a lot of local art of the nonmarine variety. In the same building is **Oceans in Glass** ((© **808/637-3366),** with sculptures of dolphins, sea turtles, humpback whales, sharks, and colorful reef fish. You can watch local artists create these beautiful sculptures in their studios within the gallery.

OAHU AFTER DARK

"Aloha shirt to Armani" is how I describe the night scene in Honolulu—mostly casual, but with ample opportunity to part with your flip-flops and dress up.

Enjoy hula dancing and a torch-lighting ceremony on Tuesday, Thursday and Saturday from 6:30–7:30pm (6–7pm Nov–Jan), as the sun casts its golden glow on the beach, at the **Kuhio Beach Hula Mound,** close to Duke Kahanamoku's statue (Ulunui and Kalakaua sts.). This is a thoroughly delightful, free offering of hula and music by some of Hawaii's finest performers. Check the schedule, www.honolulu.gov/moca/moca-news.html and click on the month's newsletter or call (© **808/843-8002.**

The Bar Scene

ON THE BEACH   Waikiki's beachfront bars offer many possibilities, from the **Mai Tai Bar** (℃ 808/923-7311) at the Royal Hawaiian (p. 33), a few feet from the sand, to the unfailingly enchanting **House Without a Key** (℃ 808/923-2311) at the Halekulani (p. 33), where the breathtaking **Kanoelehua Miller** dances hula to the riffs of Hawaiian steel-pedal guitar (Fri and Sat evenings). The Halekulani also has light jazz by local artists in the Lewers Lounge from 7pm to 1am nightly (see "Live Jazz & Pop," below).

WAIKIKI   **Rum Fire,** in the Sheraton Waikiki, 2255 Kalakaua Ave. (http://rumfirewaikiki.com; ℃ 808/922-4422), perches on the rooftop of the hotel and offers an enchanted evening of liquid libations, which they call "Vint Edge" cocktails, small plate appetizers, entertainment by some of Hawaii's top musicians, and a view of the ocean and Waikiki that is jaw-dropping. Check the entertainment schedule on the website.

DOWNTOWN   **Hanks Cafe,** on Nuuanu Avenue between Hotel and King streets (http://hankscafehawaii.com; ℃ **808/526-1410**), is a tiny, kitschy, friendly pub with live music nightly, open-mic nights, and special events that attract great talent and a supportive crowd.

The Club Scene

The nightclub scene in Waikiki and Honolulu is just as hot as the sun-kissed beaches during the day. It's more laid-back than in big cities like New York, dress is casual (although no slippers, tank tops, or athletic wear), and there's no point to even showing up until midnight.

    Addiction, located in the Modern Honolulu Hotel, 1775 Ala Moana Blvd., at Hobron Lane (www.themodernhonolulu.com; ℃ 808/943-5800), has been voted best night club AND best dance venue by *Honolulu Weekly*. Both Honolulu-based and visiting DJs spin from 10:30pm to 3am Thursday through Sunday. Cover charge varies (expect to pay $20 per person), but dress code does not: for women, "upscale casual dress" and men "button-up shirt, long pants, and covered shoes."

Hawaiian Music

Oahu has several key spots for Hawaiian music. The **Hilton Hawaiian Village** (℃ 808/949-4321) has live music nightly at the Tapa Bar and at the Tropics Bar and Grill. And every Friday night it presents a so-called Hawaiian Rainbow Revue (a tribute to Duke Kahanamoku) at 7pm with fireworks starting at 7:45pm ($25). Its Waikiki Starlight Luau features Hawaiian entertainment with dinner 6 nights a week (Sun–Thurs) for $99 to $125.

    Nearby, the Moana Surfrider offers nightly programs of live Hawaiian music, hula, and piano in its **Beach Bar** (℃ 808/922-3111), located steps from Waikiki Beach. The Veranda at the Beach House, under the historic banyan tree so loved by Robert Louis Stevenson, serves afternoon tea and champagne.

Live Jazz & Pop

To find out what's happening in the jazz scene while you're in town, check out www.honolulujazzscene.com. **Duc's Bistro** (© 808/531-6325), downtown, often has live music on Thursday, Friday and Saturday nights.

Tops in taste and ambience are the perennially alluring **Lewers Lounge** in the Halekulani, 2199 Kalia Rd. (www.halekulani.com; © **808/923-2311**). Comfy, intimate seating makes this a great spot for contemporary jazz nightly from 7pm to 1am.

Outside Waikiki, the **Veranda** at the Kahala Hotel & Resort, 5000 Kahala Ave. (www.kahalaresort.com; © **808/739-8888**), is a popular spot for the over-40 crowd, with nightly music and a dance floor.

Showroom Acts & Revues

Showroom acts that have maintained a following include **"The Magic of Polynesia"** (www.magicofpolynesia.com; © **808/971-4321**), a show with illusionist **John Hirokawa** nightly at 6:15pm (dinner show $104–$149 adults, $69–$79 children 4–11; show only $59 adults, $39 children 4–11; see their website for discounts. This was also the home of Hawaiian entertainer Don Ho, who passed away in 2007.

The Performing Arts

Audiences have grooved to the beat of everything from off-Broadway percussion hit *Stomp* to the authentic hula of John Ka'imikaua's *Halau*—all at the **Hawaii Theatre,** 1130 Bethel St., downtown (www.hawaiitheatre.com; © **808/528-0506**).

The newly formed (after economic cutbacks) **Hawaii Symphony** (www.hawaiisymphonyorchestra.org) is being resurrected with the concert season at Neal Blaisdell Concert Hall (www.blaisdellcenter.com; © **808/946-8742**). The highly successful **Hawaii Opera Theatre** (www.hawaiiopera.org; © **808/596-7372** or 800/836-7372) has been performing opera for nearly 60 years. Hawaii's top ballet companies are **Hawaii Ballet Theatre** (www.hawaiiballettheatre.org), **Ballet Hawaii** (www.ballethawaii.org), and the **Hawaii State Ballet** (www.hawaiistateballet.com).

HAWAII, THE BIG ISLAND

This is the island of superlatives: the largest in the Hawaiian chain, with the highest volcanic peaks, the most diverse terrain. Here is a land of fiery volcanoes, sparkling waterfalls, black-lava deserts, snowcapped mountains, tropical rainforests, alpine meadows, glacial lakes, and miles of golden, black, and even green-sand beaches. Visitors flock to this larger-than-life phenomenon not only for its diversity, but also for its *mana,* or spiritual aspect, because the work of the "Volcano Goddess," Pele, can obviously be seen today as she continues to create new land.

Beaches For the island's most scenic seashore, head to **Hapuna Beach,** a ½-mile crescent of gold sand. Elsewhere, families flock to **Kahaluu Beach** on the Kona Coast, where brilliantly colored tropical fish convene in the protected reef. Then, too, **Green Sands Beach** is a spectacle to behold—tiny olivine pieces in the sand give the beach its shimmering green shade.

Things to Do Be sure to visit **Puuhonua O Honaunau National Historical Park,** a sacred site that was once a refuge for ancient Hawaiian warriors. Or discover the **Puako Petroglyph Archaeological District,** home to more than 3,000 petroglyphs. A jacket, beach mat, and binoculars are all you need to see every star and planet from **Mauna Kea.**

Eating & Drinking Good soil, creative chefs, and rich cultural tradition combine to make the Big Island a culinary destination. High-end restaurants are concentrated in the **Kohala Coast,** while those for all budgets can be found in **Kailua-Kona.** Most of the island's delicacies—including **laulau, kalua pork, lomi salmon, squid luau,** and **kulolo**—can be sampled at a luau. In **Hilo** you'll find **Japanese** and other **ethnic restaurants** that provide delicious, simple offerings in low-key settings.

Nature Take a **catamaran tour** or treat yourself to a **whale-watching adventure.** Trek through the jungle and experience **Waipio Valley.** After dark, don't miss the volcanic eruption at the **Hawaii Volcanoes National Park.**

THE best BIG ISLAND EXPERIENCES

o **Floating, Swimming, Diving, or Exploring the Most Exotic Beaches in the State:** For the island's best bodysurfing, head to **Hapuna Beach** (p. 124), a ½-mile crescent of gold sand. Unsure of your swimming ability or have small children? The protected waters inside the reef at **Kahaluu Beach** (p. 122), on the Kona Coast, are safe and filled with brilliantly colored tropical fish. Take home a memory of the most exotic beach in the state, **Green Sand Beach** (p. 124), located at the southern tip of the Big Island, where tiny olivine pieces in the sand give the beach its shimmering green shade.

o **Walking Back in Time:** Discover the ancient culture of Hawaii by walking through **Puuhonua O Honaunau National Historical Park,** a sacred site that was once a refuge for ancient Hawaiian warriors (p. 108). Or marvel over the mystery of the **Puako Petroglyph Archaeological District,** home to more than 3,000 petroglyphs (p. 109).

o **Discovering Island Cultures Through Eating & Drinking:** To really get to know a culture, you have to digest it—literally. Go to a luau (p. 138) and partake in a Hawaii feast of the island's delicacies—including **kalua pork** unearthed from its in-ground roasting pit.

o **Seeing the Island from the Ocean:** The Big Island does not end at the end of land, but extends into the ocean. Take a **catamaran tour** and learn to snorkel (p. 126), or treat yourself to a **whale-watching adventure** (p. 125). Afraid of the water? Then take a submarine ride beneath the waves (p. 127).

o **Marveling at an Erupting Volcano:** The chance of a lifetime—don't miss the volcanic eruption at the **Hawaii Volcanoes National Park** (p. 117). See the park during the day, then return at night when red rivers of molten lava flow, inching down the mountain and pouring into the Pacific. You'll never forget it.

o **Stargazing from Mauna Kea:** At 13,000 feet, the air is thin but the views are spectacular atop Hawaii's tallest volcano. Nearly a dozen nations have set up telescopes (two of them the biggest in the world) to probe deep space from here (p. 110).

o **Creeping Up to the Ooze:** Since Kilauea's ongoing eruption began in 1983, lava has been bubbling and oozing in a mild-mannered way that lets you walk right up to the creeping flow for an up-close encounter (p. 117).

o **Savoring a Cup of Kona Coffee:** It's just one of those things you have to do while you're on the Big Island. For a truly authentic cup of java, head upcountry to **Holuakoa Café,** on Mamalahoa Hwy. (Hwy. 180) in Holualoa (p. 107).

o **Hanging Out in Waipio Valley:** Pack a picnic and head for this gorgeously lush valley that time forgot. Delve deep into the jungle on foot, comb the black-sand beach, or just laze the day away by a bubbling stream, the tail end of a 1,000-foot waterfall (p. 114).

○ **Chasing Rainbows at Akaka Falls:** When the light is right, a perfect prism is formed and a rainbow leaps out of this spectacular 442-foot waterfall, about an 11-mile drive from Hilo. Take time to roam through the surrounding rainforest, where you're sure to have close encounters with exotic birds, aromatic plumeria trees, and shocking red-torch ginger (p. 113).

ESSENTIALS

Most people arrive on the Big Island at Kona International Airport, on the island's west coast. From the airport, the ritzy Kohala Coast is to the left (north) and the town of Kailua-Kona is to the right (south).

Arriving

The Big Island has two major airports for jet traffic between the islands, in Kona and Hilo.

The **Kona International Airport** receives direct flights from the U.S. Mainland, carriers include **American Airlines** (www.aa.com; ✆ 800/433-7300), with flights from Los Angeles, Phoenix and Oakland; **Delta Air Lines** (www.delta.com; ✆ 800/221-1212), with nonstop flights from Los Angeles and Seattle; **Alaska Airlines** (www.alaskaair.com; ✆ 800/252-7522) has direct flights from Anchorage, Seattle, Oakland, San Jose, San Diego and Portland; and **United Airlines** (www.united.com; ✆ 800/241-6522), with nonstop flights from Los Angeles and San Francisco. The **Hilo International Airport** has direct flights from Los Angeles via **United Airlines** (www.united.com; ✆ 800/241-6522).

If you cannot get a direct flight to the Big Island, you'll have to pick up an interisland flight in Honolulu. **Hawaiian Airlines** (www.hawaiianair.com; ✆ 800/367-5320) flies to both Kona and Hilo; **Mokulele Airlines** (www.mokulele.com; ✆ 866/260-7070) offers jet service to Kona.

All major American rental-car companies, such as Alamo, Avis, Budget, Dollar, Enterprise, Hertz, National, and Thrifty, have cars available at both airports. Also see "Getting There" and "Getting Around Hawaii" (p. 262 and p. 263) for details on interisland travel, insurance, and driving in Hawaii. For shuttle services from the Kona Airport, see "Getting Around," below.

Visitor Information

The **Big Island Visitors Bureau** (www.gohawaii.com/big-island; ✆ 800/648-2441) has two offices on the Big Island: one at 101 Aupuni St., Ste. 238, Hilo, HI 96720 (✆ 808/961-5797), and the other at the Shops at Mauna Lani, 68-1330 Mauna Lani Dr., Ste. 109B, Kohala Coast, HI 96743 (✆ 808/885-1655).

The Big Island's best free tourist publications are "This Week" (www.thisweekhawaii.com) and "101 Things to Do on Hawaii the Big Island" (www.101thingstodo.com/big-island). Both offer lots of useful information, as well as discount coupons on a variety of island adventures. Copies are easy to find all around the island.

THE ISLAND IN BRIEF

THE KONA COAST ★★   Kona is synonymous with great coffee and big fish—both of which are found in abundance along this 70-mile-long stretch of black-lava-covered coast.

A collection of tiny communities devoted to farming and fishing along the sunbaked leeward side of the island, the Kona Coast has an amazingly diverse geography and climate for such a compact area. The oceanfront town of **Kailua-Kona,** a quaint fishing village that now caters more to tourists than boat captains, is its commercial center. On the side of Hualalai Mountain, above Kailua-Kona, you'll find the funky, artsy village of **Holualoa.** About 7 miles south of Kailua-Kona, bordering the ocean, is the resort area of **Keauhou,** a suburban-like series of upscale condominiums, a shopping center, and million-dollar homes.

"Kona" means "leeward side" in Hawaiian—and that means full-on sun every day of the year. This is an affordable vacation spot: an ample selection of midpriced condo units, peppered with a few older hotels and B&Bs, lines the shore, which is mostly rocky lava reef, interrupted by an occasional pocket beach. Nestled on the shoreline is the Four Seasons at Hualalai (p. 91), one of Hawaii's luxury retreats.

Away from the bright lights of the town of Kailua lies the rural **South Kona Coast,** home to coffee farmers, macadamia-nut growers, and people escaping to the country. The serrated South Kona Coast is indented with numerous bays, from **Kealakekua,** a marine-life preserve that's the island's best diving spot, down to **Honaunau,** where a national historical park recalls the days of old Hawaii. Accommodations in this area are mainly B&Bs. This coast is a great place to stay if you want to get away from the crowds and experience peaceful country living. You'll be within driving distance of beaches and the sights of Kailua.

THE KOHALA COAST ★★   Fringes of palms and flowers, brilliant blankets of emerald green, and an occasional flash of white buildings are your only clues from the road that this black-lava coast north of Kona is more than bleak and barren. But, oh, is it! Down by the sea, pleasure domes rise like palaces no Hawaiian king ever imagined. This is where the Learjet set escapes to play in world-class beachfront hotels set like jewels in the golden sand. But you don't have to be a billionaire to visit these resorts: The fabulous beaches and abundant historic sites are open to the public, with parking and other facilities, including restaurants, golf courses, and shopping, provided by the resorts.

NORTH KOHALA ★★   Seven sugar mills once shipped enough sugar from this knob of land to sweeten all the coffee in San Francisco. **Hawi,** the region's hub and former home to the Kohala Sugar Co., was a flourishing town. Today Hawi's quaint, 3-block-long strip of sun-faded, false-fronted buildings and 1920s vintage shops lives on as a minor tourist stop in one of Hawaii's most scenic rural regions, located at the northernmost reaches of the island. North Kohala is most famous as the birthplace of King Kamehameha the Great.

WAIMEA (KAMUELA) ★★   This old upcountry cow town on the northern road between the coasts is set in lovely country: rolling green pastures, wide-open spaces dotted by *puu* (hills), and real cowpokes who ride mammoth **Parker Ranch,** Hawaii's largest working ranch. The town is also headquarters for the **Keck Telescope,** the largest and most powerful in the world. Waimea is home to several affordable B&Bs, and Merriman's restaurant is a popular foodie outpost at Opelo Plaza.

THE HAMAKUA COAST ★★   This emerald coast, a 52-mile stretch from Honokaa to Hilo on the island's windward northeast side, was once planted with sugar cane; it now blooms with flowers, macadamia nuts, papayas, and marijuana, also known as *pakalolo* (still Hawaii's number-one cash crop). Resort-free, the Hamakua Coast still has a few major destinations. Picture-perfect **Waipio Valley** has impossibly steep sides, taro patches, a green riot of wild plants, and a winding stream leading to a broad, black-sand beach.

HILO ★★   When the sun shines in Hilo, it's one of the most beautiful tropical cities in the Pacific. Being here is an entirely different kind of island experience: Hawaii's largest metropolis after Honolulu is a quaint, misty, flower-filled city of immaculately kept homes, overlooking a half-moon bay, with a restored historic downtown and a clear view of Mauna Loa's often snowcapped peak. Hilo catches everyone's eye until it rains—and it rains a lot in Hilo, and when it rains, it pours.

Hilo is one of America's wettest towns, with 128 inches of rain annually. It's ideal for growing ferns, orchids, and anthuriums, but not for catching a few rays. But there's a lot to see and do in Hilo, so grab your umbrella. The rain is warm (the temperature seldom dips below 70°F/21°C), and there's usually a rainbow afterward.

Hilo is also Hawaii's best bargain for budget travelers. It has plenty of hotel rooms—most of the year, that is. Hilo's magic moment comes in spring, the week after Easter, when hula *halau* (schools) arrive for the annual **Merrie Monarch Hula Festival** hula competition. This is a full-on Hawaiian spectacle and a wonderful cultural event. Plan ahead if you want to go: Tickets are sold out by the first week in January, and accommodations within 30 miles are usually booked solid.

Hilo is also the gateway to Hawaii Volcanoes National Park; it's just an hour's drive up-slope.

HAWAII VOLCANOES NATIONAL PARK ★★★   This is America's most exciting national park, where a live volcano called Kilauea erupts daily. If you're lucky, it will be a spectacular sight. At other times, you may not be able to see the molten lava at all, but there's always a lot to see and learn. Ideally, you should plan to spend 3 days at the park exploring the trails, watching the volcano, visiting the rainforest, and just enjoying this spectacular place. But even if you have only a day, get here—it's worth the trip. Bring your sweats or jacket (honest!); it's cool up here, especially at night.

If you plan to dally in the park, then you'll want to stay in the sleepy hamlet of **Volcano Village,** just outside the national park entrance. Several extremely cozy B&Bs, some with fireplaces, hide under tree ferns in this cool mountain hideaway. The tiny highland community (elevation 4,000 ft.) is inhabited by artists, soul-searchers, and others who like the crisp air of Hawaii's high country. It has just enough civilization to sustain a good life: a few stores, a handful of eateries, a gas station, and a golf course.

KA LAE: SOUTH POINT ★★ This is the Plymouth Rock of Hawaii, where the first Polynesians arrived in seagoing canoes (probably from the Marquesas Islands or Tahiti) around A.D. 500. You'll feel like you're at the end of the world on this lonely, windswept place, the southernmost point of the United States. Hawaii ends in a sharp, black-lava point. Bold 500-foot cliffs stand against the blue sea to the west and shelter the old fishing village of Waiahukini, which was populated from A.D. 750 until the 1860s. Ancient canoe moorings, shelter caves, and *heiau* (temples) poke through windblown pili grass. The east coast curves inland to reveal a green-sand beach, a world-famous anomaly that's accessible only by foot or four-wheel-drive. For most, the only reason to venture down to the southern tip is to experience the empty vista of land's end.

GETTING AROUND

BY TAXI Taxis are readily available at both Kona and Hilo airports. In Kailua-Kona, call **Kona Airport Taxi** (© **808/324-1234**). In Hilo, call **Ace-1** (© **808/935-8303**). Taxis will take you wherever you want to go on the Big Island, but it's prohibitively expensive to use them for long distances. As we went to press, there were no ride sharing services, like Uber or Lyft, on the Big Island.

BY CAR You'll need a rental car on the Big Island; not having one will really limit you. All major car-rental firms, including Alamo, Avis, Budget, Dollar, Enterprise, Hertz, National, and Thrifty, have agencies at the airports and at the Kohala Coast resorts. For tips on insurance and driving rules, see "Getting Around Hawaii" (p. 263).

There are more than 480 miles of paved road on the Big Island. The highway that circles the island is called the **Hawaii Belt Road.** On the Kona side of the island, you have two choices: the scenic "upper" road, **Mamalahoa Highway** (Hwy. 190), or the speedier "lower" road, **Queen Kaahumanu Highway** (Hwy. 19). The road that links east to west is called **Saddle Road** (Hwy. 200). Saddle Road looks like a shortcut from Kona to Hilo, but it usually doesn't make for a shorter trip. It's rough, narrow, and plagued by bad weather.

BY BUS & SHUTTLE Door-to-door service from the airport to your hotel is provided by **SpeediShuttle** (www.speedishuttle.com; © **808/329-5433**). Some sample per-person rates from the airport: $27 to Kailua-Kona, $27 to the Four Seasons, and $59 to the Mauna Lani Resort.

In the Keauhou Resort area, there's an open-air, 44-seat **Keauhou Resort Trolley,** with stops at Keauhou Bay, Sheraton Keauhou Bay Resort & Spa,

Keauhou Shopping Center, and Kahaluu Beach Park. In addition, three times a day the trolley travels round-trip, via Alii Drive to Kailua Village, stopping at White Sands Beach on the way. For information, contact the concierge at the Sheraton Keauhou Bay Resort & Spa or www.sheratonkona.com (℃ **808/ 930-4900**). Free to Sheraton guests, $2 per trip for non-guests.

[Fast FACTS] THE BIG ISLAND

American Express Unfortunately, there currently is no office on the Big Island. To report lost or stolen traveler's checks, call ℃ **800/221-7282**.

ATM/Banks ATMs are located everywhere on the Big Island at banks, supermarkets, Longs Drugs and at some shopping malls. Go to your bank card's website to find ATM locations on the Big Island. The major banks on the Big Island are: First Hawaiian, Bank of Hawaii, American Savings, and Central Pacific, all with branches in both Kona and Hilo.

Business Hours Most businesses on the island are open from either 8 or 9am to 5 or 6pm.

Dentists In an emergency, contact **Dr. Craig C. Kimura** at Kamuela Office Center (℃ **808/885-5947**). In Kona, call **Kona Coast Dental** at Frame 10 Center, behind Lanihau Shopping Center on Palani Road (℃ **808/329-8067**).

Doctors In Hilo, the **Hilo Medical Center** is at 1190 Waianuenue Ave. (℃ **808/ 932-3000**); on the Kona side, call **Hualalai Urgent Care,** 77-311 Sunset Dr. (℃ **808/327-HELP**). Not open Sundays.

Emergencies For ambulance, fire, and rescue

services, dial ℃ **911** (if you dial 911 from a cellphone, it will route you to the nearest 911 center) or call ℃ **808/ 326-4646**. The **Poison Control Center** hotline is ℃ **800/222-1222** (if you call from a land line, you will be routed to a center based on the area code of the phone you are calling from; if you call from a cellphone with an area code that is different from 808, tell them, and they will direct you appropriately).

Hospitals Hospitals offering 24-hour urgent-care facilities include the **Hilo Medical Center,** 1190 Waianuenue Ave. (℃ **808/ 932-3000**); **North Hawaii Community Hospital,** Waimea (℃ **808/885-4444**); and **Kona Community Hospital** on the Kona Coast in Kealakekua (℃ **808/ 322-9311**).

Internet Access Major hotels and even many small B&Bs have Internet access. Many of them offer high-speed wireless; check ahead of time and check the charges, which can be exorbitant. The best Internet deal in Hawaii is the service at the **public libraries** (to find the location nearest you, check www.libraries hawaii.org/Serials/data bases.html), which offer free

access if you get a library card, available to purchase for $10 for 3 months. For free Internet access elsewhere try **Starbucks Coffee**—to find a Starbucks near you check the website, www.starbucks.com.

Newspapers & Magazines The two daily newspapers on the Big Island are *West Hawaii Today,* serving Kona and the west side of the island (www.westhawaii today.com) and the *Hawaii Tribune Herald,* serving Hilo and the east side of the island (www.hawaiitribune-herald.com). Visitor publications include *This Week* (www.thisweekhawaii.com) and *101 Things to Do* (www.101thingstodo.com).

Pharmacies Unfortunately there are no 24-hour pharmacies on the Big Island, but the popular chain pharmacies include: **Longs Drug Stores** (in both Hilo and Kona; www.cvs. com; ℃ **808/329-1380**); and **Target** (in Kona; ℃ **808/334-4021**).

Police Dial ℃ **911** in case of emergency; otherwise, call the **Hawaii Police Department** at ℃ **808/935-3311** islandwide.

Post Office All calls to the U.S. Postal Service can be directed to

© **800/275-8777.** There
are local branches in Hilo at
1299 Kekuanaoa Ave., in

Kailua-Kona at 74–5577
Palani Rd., and in Waimea
on Lindsey Road.

Weather For weather
conditions and marine forecasts call © **808/961-5582.**

WHERE TO STAY

Before you reserve your accommodations, remember that the Big Island is really big; see "The Island in Brief," earlier in this chapter, to decide where to base yourself.

Remember to add Hawaii's 13.42% in taxes to your final bill. In the listings below, all rooms come with a full private bathroom (with tub or shower) and free parking unless otherwise noted.

If you would like to go "on the road," contact **Island RV & Safari Activities** (www.islandrv.com; © **808/960-1260**). It offers weekly rentals of 22-foot class-C motor homes, which sleeps up to four, for $2,400 plus $5 per day propane fee. Included in the package are airport pickup, linens, barbecue grill, all park registration fee permits, your last night in a local hotel, and help with planning your itinerary and booking activities.

The Kona Coast

IN & AROUND KAILUA-KONA

Very Expensive

Four Seasons Resort Hualalai at Historic Kaupulehu ★★★

Sometimes, you do get what you pay for—and that's just about anything you could desire at this serenely welcoming resort, only a 15-minute drive from the airport, but definitely worlds away from anything resembling hustle and bustle. There is an 18-hole Jack Nicklaus golf course, award-winning spa, and multi-room fitness center, and a series of renovations have only increased the sense of quiet luxury in and around the small clusters of two-story guest-room buildings and villas. Rooms start at 635 square feet, with private lanais and large bathrooms outfitted with glass-walled showers and deep soaking tubs; ask for one with an outdoor lava-rock shower. All have views of the ocean or one of seven swimming pools; the newest is the adults-only Palm Grove Pool, with a swim-up bar and daybeds, but snorkeling in Kings' Pond amid rays and tropical fish remains a top draw. Dinner at **Ulu Ocean Grill** or the **Beach Tree** is consistently excellent, if costly. Kudos to the Four Seasons for continuing to buck the resort-fee trend, for not charging for its children's or cultural programs, and for committing to numerous environmental measures, including the support of the Hawaiian Legacy Hardwoods' koa reforestation.

72–100 Kaupulehu Dr., Kailua-Kona. www.fourseasons.com/hualalai. © **888/340-5662** or 808/325-8000. 243 units. $995–$1,695 double; from $2,945 suite. Extra person $170. Children 18 and under stay free in parent's room (maximum occupancy in guest rooms is 3 people; couples with more than 1 child must get a suite or 2 rooms). Self-parking free, valet parking $20 per day. **Amenities:** 3 restaurants and lounges; 2 bars (w/nightly entertainment); babysitting; complimentary year-round children's program; concierge; cultural center; 18-hole Jack Nicklaus signature golf course, fitness center; 7 pools, including snorkeling pond; room service; award-winning spa; 8 tennis courts (4 lit for night play); watersports equipment rentals; free Wi-Fi.

Moderate

Courtyard King Kamehameha Kona Beach Hotel ★ The reputation of Marriott's Courtyard chain plus the terrific location (downtown Kailua-Kona, right on the ocean) place this moderately priced high-rise high on the list of places to stay. Ask for a room with a view of either the Kailua Pier or the sparkling Kailua Bay. The hotel's own small gold-sand beach is right out the front door. The downtown location means walking distance to shops and restaurants.

75–5660 Palani Rd. www.konabeachhotel.com. ℂ **800/367-2111** or 808/329-2911. 452 units. $159–$289 up to 4 people; from $399 suite. Check website for discounts. Parking $16. **Amenities:** 2 restaurants; outdoor bar w/Hawaiian entertainment; Jacuzzi; new outdoor infinity pool; room service; 4 tennis courts; watersports equipment rentals, free Wi-Fi.

Inexpensive

Boynton's Kona Bed & Breakfast ★★ Located on the luscious, green slopes of Mt. Hualalai, this comfy B&B has great prices in a tranquil setting that is only a 10-minute drive to Kailua Kona and beaches.

74–4920 A Palani Rd. www.konabandb.com. ℂ **808/329-4178.** 2 units. $110 1-bedroom; $140 2-bedroom. Extra person $15. 3-night minimum. No credit cards. **Amenities:** Hot tub, free Internet.

Kona Islander Inn ★ Budget traveler alert: This is the most affordable place to stay in Kailua-Kona. These plantation-style, three-story buildings are surrounded by lush palm-tree-lined gardens with torch-lit pathways that make it hard to believe you're smack-dab in the middle of downtown. The central location—in the middle of Kailua-Kona—is convenient but can be noisy. Built in 1962, the complex is showing some signs of age. The studios are small, but extras such as lanais and kitchenettes outfitted with microwaves, minifridges, and coffeemakers make up for the lack of space.

75–5776 Kuakini Hwy. (south of Hualalai Rd.). www.konahawaii.com. ℂ **800/244-4752** or 808/329-3333. 80 units. $79–$149 double. **Amenities:** Hot tub; outdoor pool; free Wi-Fi.

Kona Tiki Hotel ★★ It's hard to believe that places like this still exist. The Kona Tiki, located right on the ocean, away from the hustle and bustle of downtown Kailua-Kona, is one of the best budget deals in Hawaii. The tastefully decorated rooms feature queen-size beds, ceiling fans, and private lanais overlooking the water. Although it's called a hotel, this small, family-run operation is more like a large B&B, with lots of aloha and plenty of friendly conversation at the morning continental buffet around the pool. There are no TVs or phones in the rooms (there's a pay phone in the lobby). If a double with a kitchenette is available, grab it—the extra few bucks will save you a bundle in food costs. Book at least 2 to 3 months in advance.

75–5968 Alii Dr. (about a mile from downtown Kailua-Kona). www.konatikihotel.com. ℂ **808/329-1425.** 15 units. $89–$179 double, $119–$125 double with kitchenette. Extra person $15–$25 per adult, $7 per child 6–11. Rates include continental breakfast. 3- to 7-night minimum. **Amenities:** Outdoor pool; no phone; free Wi-Fi.

Uncle Billy's Kona Bay Hotel ★ An institution in Kona, Uncle Billy's is where visitors from the other islands stay. The rooms are modest but comfortable and come with large lanais and minifridges. This budget hotel is a good place to sleep, but don't expect new carpeting or fancy soap in the bathroom. It can be noisy at night when big groups book in; avoid Labor Day weekend, when all the canoe paddlers in the state want to stay here and rehash the race into the wee morning hours.

75–5739 Alii Dr. www.unclebilly.com. © **800/367-5102** or 808/329-1393. 139 units. $99–$132 double. Extra person $20. Children 18 and under stay free in parent's room. Check the website for specials. Parking $5. **Amenities:** Outdoor pool; watersports equipment rentals; free Wi-Fi.

SOUTH KONA
Inexpensive
Affordable Hawaii at Pomaikai (Lucky) Farm Bed & Breakfast ★
True to its name, Affordable Hawaii offers an inexpensive perch from which to explore the South Kona Coast. Away from urban areas, the century-old, 4-acre farm promises a quiet and relaxing vacation. Accommodations range from a bedroom inside the old farmhouse to a room inside the old coffee barn. Guests can use a common kitchen with a refrigerator, microwave, hot plate, and barbecue grill.

83–5465 Mamalahoa Hwy. (south of Kailua-Kona, after mile marker 107). www.luckyfarm.com. © **808/328-2112.** 4 units. $90–$150 double. Extra person $10, $5 per child 5 and under. Rates include full farm breakfast. 2-night minimum. **Amenities:** No phone; free Wi-Fi.

Manago Hotel ★ If you want to experience the history and culture of the 50th state, the Manago Hotel may be the place for you. This living relic is still operated by the third generation of the same Japanese family that opened it in 1917. It offers clean accommodations, tasty home cooking in their restaurant downstairs, and generous helpings of aloha, all at budget prices. The older rooms (with community bathrooms) are ultraspartan—strictly for desperate budget travelers. The rooms with private bathrooms in the new wing are still pretty sparse (freshly painted walls with no decoration and no TV), but they're spotlessly clean and surrounded by Japanese gardens with a koi pond. The rates increase as you go up; the third-floor units have the most spectacular views of the Kona coastline. Adventuresome travelers might want to try the Japanese rooms with tatami mats to sleep on and *furo* (deep hot tubs) in each room to soak in.

82–6151 Mamalahoa Hwy., Captain Cook, HI 96704. www.managohotel.com. © **808/323-2642.** 63 units, some with shared bathroom. $41 double with shared bathroom, $67–$72 double with private bathroom, $86 double Japanese room with small *furo* tub and private bathroom. Extra person $3. **Amenities:** Restaurant (Manago Hotel Restaurant, p. 101); bar; no phone; free Wi-Fi.

The Kohala Coast
VERY EXPENSIVE
Fairmont Orchid Hawaii ★★★
Beyond the 10,000-square-foot swimming pool here lies a cove of soft sand, where the Hui Holokai Beach

Ambassadors make guests feel at home in the water and on shore, teaching all kinds of Hawaiiana and sharing their knowledge about the area's cultural treasures. The elegant, generously proportioned rooms (starting at 510 sq. ft.) with lanais have subtle island accents such as rattan and carved wood as well as marble baths and other luxurious fittings. Golf, tennis, spa, and dining are all exceptional here, too.

At the Mauna Lani Resort, 1 N. Kaniku Dr., Waimea. www.fairmont.com/orchid-hawaii. ⓒ **800/845-9905** or 808/885-2000. 540 units. $389–$719 double; $589–$989 Gold Floor double; from $759–$3,900 suite. Check for online packages. Extra person $75. Children 17 and under stay free in parent's room. Daily resort fee $30, includes self-parking, Wi-Fi. Valet parking $22. **Amenities:** 5 restaurants; 3 bars; luau; babysitting; bike rentals; year-round children's program; concierge; concierge-level rooms; 2 championship golf courses; fitness center; pool; room service; spa; theater; 10 tennis courts (7 lit for night play); watersports equipment rentals; Wi-Fi (included in resort fee).

Hapuna Beach Prince Hotel ★★★

The larger, more low-key sibling to the Mauna Kea Beach Hotel (see below) hovers above the wide, white sands of popular Hapuna Beach. Rooms start at 600 square feet and all include balconies and an ocean view and have touches of Hawaiiana in subdued colors. The long, large pool is great for lap swimming. The sprawling, terraced grounds include an 18-hole championship golf course, several open-air restaurants, including the wonderful **Coast Grille,** and a small cafe/deli with affordable takeout options.

At the Mauna Kea Resort, 62–100 Kaunaoa Dr., Waimea. www.princeresortshawaii.com. ⓒ **800/882-6060** or 808/880-1111. 351 units. $232–$435 double; from $656 suite. Resort fee $30. Extra person $65. Children 17 and under stay free in parent's room using existing bedding. Parking $6 valet, self included in resort fee. **Amenities:** 3 restaurants; 2 bars; babysitting; cafe/gift shop; seasonal children's program; concierge; 18-hole championship golf course (at Mauna Kea Beach Hotel, below); fitness center; pool; room service; spa; tennis center (at Mauna Kea Beach Hotel); watersports equipment rentals; free Wi-Fi.

Mauna Kea Beach Hotel ★★★

This was the Big Island's first resort, built in 1965 by tycoon Laurance S. Rockefeller, who was sailing around Hawaii when he spotted a perfect crescent of gold sand and dropped anchor. Claiming he had found the most beautiful spot in all the islands, he planted his resort here. One of the most beautiful Big Island beaches sits outside; two championship golf courses are next door.

At the Mauna Kea Resort, 62–100 Mauna Kea Beach Dr. www.princeresortshawaii.com. ⓒ **866/977-4589** or 808/882-7222. 310 units. $299–$819 double; from $995 suite. Extra person $80. Valet parking $20, self-parking $15. **Amenities:** 5 restaurants; 2 bars w/live music; luau Tues & Fri; babysitting; seasonal children's program; concierge; 2 championship golf courses; excellent fitness center; Jacuzzi; large outdoor pool; room service; 13-court oceanside tennis complex; watersports equipment rentals; Wi-Fi ($15 per day).

EXPENSIVE

Hilton Waikoloa Village ★★

It's up to you how to navigate through this 62-acre oceanfront golf resort, laced with fantasy pools, lagoons, and a profusion of tropical plants in between three low-rise towers. If you're in a hurry, take the Swiss-made air-conditioned tram; for a more leisurely ride, handsome mahogany boats ply canals filled with tropical fish. Or just walk a half-mile or so through galleries of Asian and Pacific art on your way to the amply sized rooms designed for families. In 2013, the resort unveiled the new Makai section of its Lagoon Tower: 161 rooms and eight suites, all ocean view, with upgraded baths (including dual vanities), roomier closets, and high-end bedding. Kids will want to head straight to the 175-foot water slide and 1-acre pool, and will pester you to pony up for the DolphinQuest encounter. The actual beach is skimpy here, hence an enormous swimming and water sports lagoon that's home to green sea turtles and other marine life. You won't want for places to eat here, although more affordable options are available at the two nearby shopping centers.

69–425 Waikoloa Beach Dr., Waikoloa. www.hiltonwaikoloavillage.com. © **800/445-8667** or 808/886-1234. 1,241 units. $219–$379 Ocean Tower double; $269–$349 Hale Ike at Palace Tower double; $279–$399 at Makai at Lagoon Tower; from $622 suite. Daily resort fee $30, includes Wi-Fi, local/toll-free calls, cultural lessons, in-room PlayStation3 with unlimited movies and games, more. Extra person $40. Children 18 and under stay free in parent's room. Valet parking $30; self-parking $25. **Amenities:** 7 restaurants; 2 bars; luau Tues, Fri & Sun; babysitting; bike rentals; children's program; concierge; concierge-level rooms; fitness center; 2 18-hole golf courses; 3 pools (including adults-only pool); room service; spa; 6 tennis courts; watersports equipment rentals; Wi-Fi (included in resort fee).

Waikoloa Beach Marriott Resort & Spa ★

Of all the luxury resorts that line the Kohala Coast, this is the most reasonably priced (if $219 a night can be called "reasonable"). Another draw is location on Anaehoomalu Bay (or A-Bay, as the locals call it), one of the best ocean-sports bays on the Kohala Coast. The gentle sloping beach has everything: swimming, snorkeling, diving, kayaking, windsurfing, and even old royal fish ponds.

69–275 Waikoloa Beach Dr. www.marriotthawaii.com. © **888/236-2427** or 808/886-6789. 555 units. $219–$645 double; from $681 suite. Daily $30 resort fee (includes overnight self-parking, Internet, free local calls and mainland calls, discounts on luau and car rental). Extra person $45. Children 17 and under stay free in parent's room. Valet parking $3. **Amenities:** Restaurant; bar; luau Mon & Wed; babysitting; concierge; fitness center; Jacuzzi; outdoor pools (including a huge pool w/water slide and separate children's pool); room service; full-service Mandara Spa; 2 tennis courts; watersports equipment rentals; Hawaiian cultural activities, including petroglyphs tour. Wi-Fi (included in resort fee).

Waimea Garden Cottages ★★

Imagine rolling hills on pastoral ranch land. Then add a babbling stream and two cozy Hawaiian cottages. Complete the picture with mountain views, and you have Waimea Garden Cottages. It offers a quiet, relaxing vacation in your own cottage in an upcountry oasis.

65–1632 Kawaihae Rd., Waimea (off Mamalahoa Hwy., 2 miles west of Waimea town center). www.waimeagardens.com. © **808/885-8550.** 4 units. $160–$190 double. Extra person $50 for 12 years and older, $25 for children 11 years old and younger. Rates include breakfast treats in the refrigerator. 3-7 night minimum. No credit cards. **Amenities:** Free Wi-Fi.

INEXPENSIVE

Aloha Vacation Cottages ★   You'll find these two rental units in a residential area in the cool climate of Waimea. They are two small, intimate guesthouses with full kitchens, a separate bedroom, a washer/dryer, and all the comforts of home (including baby gear if you need it) on the "dry" side of Waimea, about a 15-minute drive to the beach and just a few minutes from the restaurants of Waimea.

62–1210 Puahia St., Kamuela, HI 96743. www.alohavacationcottages.com. © **808/885-6535**. 2 units. $125–$160 double. Extra person $20-$35 infant/toddler. 5- to 7-night minimum. Credit cards through PayPal. **Amenities:** Free Wi-Fi.

The Hamakua Coast

In addition to those listed below, another B&B in this area, in Ahualoa, a mountain community a short drive from Waipio, is **Mountain Meadow Ranch Bed & Breakfast,** 46–3895 Kapuna Rd., Honokaa (www.mountain meadowranch.com; © **808/775-9376**), offering both a private cottage ($150 for four) and rooms in a house ($115 double).

INEXPENSIVE

Waipio Wayside Bed & Breakfast Inn ★★   Hostess Jackie Horne's restored Hamakua Sugar supervisor's home, built in 1938, sits nestled among fruit trees, surrounded by sweet-smelling ginger, fragile orchids, and blooming birds-of-paradise. The comfortable house, done in old Hawaii style, abounds with thoughtful touches, such as the help-yourself tea-and-cookies bar with 26 different kinds of tea. A sunny lanai with hammocks overlooks a yard lush with banana, lemon, lime, tangerine, and avocado trees; the cliffside gazebo has views of the ocean 600 feet below. Jackie's friendly hospitality and excellent breakfasts round out the experience.

46–4226 Waipio Rd., Honokaa, HI 96727. www.waipiowayside.com. © **800/833-8849** or 808/775-0275. 5 units. $115–$200 double. Extra person $30. Rates include full organic tropical breakfast with coffee, fruit (sunrise papayas, mangoes, tangerines), granola, yogurt, and muffins. Located on Hwy. 240, 2 miles from the Honokaa post office; look on the right for a long white picket fence and sign on the ocean side of the road; the 2nd driveway is the parking lot. **Amenities:** Concierge; TV/VCR/DVD in living room; free Wi-Fi.

Hilo

INEXPENSIVE

Hilo Seaside Hotel ★   This family-operated hotel is located across Hilo Bay on historic Banyan Drive. Surrounded by lush tropical gardens and a spring pond filled with Japanese carp, this place isn't fancy, but it's great for those on a budget. The location is terrific for exploring East Hawaii: It's a 45-minute scenic drive to Hawaii Volcanoes National Park, a few minutes by car to downtown, and close to a 9-hole golf course and tennis courts.

126 Banyan Way (off Hwy. 19). www.hiloseasidehotel.com. © **800/560-5557** or 808/935-0821. 135 units. $99–$139 double. Extra person $20. Check website for deals. **Amenities:** Restaurant; bar; 9-hole golf course nearby; outdoor pool; free Wi-Fi.

The Old Hawaiian Bed & Breakfast ★ Bargain hunters, take note: This old plantation house from the 1930s has been renovated and offers great room rates that include breakfast. Located on the Wailuku River, the house features a large lanai, where guests have use of a phone, refrigerator, and microwave. The rooms have their own entrances and private bathrooms. Children 12 years and older only.

1492 Wailuku Dr. www.thebigislandvacation.com. ✆ **808/961-2816.** 3 units. $85–$125 double. Extra person $10. 2-night minimum. **Amenities:** Free Wi-Fi.

Pagoda Hilo Bay Hotel ★ Formerly the Uncle Billy's Hilo Bay Hotel until the management lost its lease in 2016 and Honolulu-based developer, Peter Savio took over and made it part of Castle Resorts & Hotels. The small, oceanfront budget spot boasts a dynamite location on Hilo's hotel row, but the property is in need of renovation and upgrading. The guest rooms are simple: bed, TV, phone, closet, and bathroom—that's about it. The walls seem paper thin, and it can get very noisy at night (you may want to bring earplugs), but at these rates, you're still getting your money's worth.

87 Banyan Dr. (off Hwy. 19). https://www.castleresorts.com/big-island/pagoda-hilo-bay-hotel/. ✆ **877/367-1912** or 808/935-0861. 145 units. $116-$166 double. Children 18 and under stay free in parent's room. Check the website for specials, car/room packages, and senior rates. **Amenities:** Restaurant; bar; oceanfront pool; free Wi-Fi.

Hawaii Volcanoes National Park

As a result of Hawaii Volcanoes being officially designated a national park in 1916, a village has popped up at its front door. Volcano Village isn't so much a town as a wide spot in Old Volcano Road, with two general stores, a handful of restaurants, a post office, a coffee shop, a new firehouse, and a winery.

All of the accommodations in this section are in Volcano Village. It gets cool here at night—Volcano Village is located at 3,700 feet—so a fireplace might be an attractive amenity. It also rains a lot in Volcano—100 inches a year—which makes everything grow "Jack and the Beanstalk" style.

I recommend spending at least 3 days to really see and enjoy the park.

EXPENSIVE

Volcano Village Lodge ★★ Tucked among the vivid green ferns of a rainforest are these five self-sufficient bungalows, with comfy beds, fireplaces, breakfast fixings, coffee pot, even towel warmers for chilly early mornings. Quiet, serene and private, this is the place for a romantic getaway or time to rest and relax.

19–4183 Rd. E, Volcano. www.volcanovillagelodge.com. ✆ **808/985-9500**. 5 units. Double from $280-$375; Extra person $25. **Amenities:** Hot tub; no phone; free Wi-Fi.

MODERATE

The **Volcano Teapot Cottage** (19–4041 Kilauea Rd.; www.volcanoteapot.com; ✆ **808/967-7112**) is a quaint 1914 two-bedroom cottage, decorated with one-of-a-kind antiques, and complete with hot tub in the forest out back ($195 double). Two-night minimum.

Hale Ohia Cottages ★ Take a step back in time to the 1930s. Here you'll have a choice of suites, each with private entrance. The surrounding botanical gardens contribute to the overall tranquil ambience of the estate. The lush grounds are just a mile from Hawaii Volcanoes National Park.

11–3968 Hale Ohia Rd., off Hwy. 11. www.haleohia.com. ℂ **800/455-3803** or 808/967-7986. 10 units. $105–$220 double. Extra person $20. Rates include continental breakfast (most units). 2-night minimum. **Amenities:** No phone; free Wi-Fi.

WHERE TO EAT

So many restaurants, so little time. What's a traveler to do? The Big Island's delicious dilemma is its daunting size and abundant offerings. Its gastronomic environment—the fruitful marriage of creative chefs, good soil, and rich cultural traditions—has made this island as much a culinary destination as a recreational one. And from the Kona Coffee Festival to the Aloha Festival's Poke Recipe Contest, the Big Island is host to extraordinary, world-renowned culinary events.

Kailua-Kona is teeming with restaurants for all budgets, while the haute cuisine of the island is concentrated in the Kohala Coast resorts. Waimea, also known as Kamuela, is a thriving upcountry community, a haven for yuppies, techies, and retirees who love a good bite to eat. In Hilo, in east Hawaii, you'll find pockets of trendiness among the precious old Japanese and ethnic restaurants that provide honest, tasty, and affordable meals in unpretentious surroundings.

In the listings below, reservations are not necessary unless noted. *Warning:* Big Island restaurants, especially along the Kona Coast, seem to have a chronic shortage of waitstaff. Come prepared for a leisurely meal; sit and enjoy the warm moonlit night, sip a tasty libation, and realize time is relative here.

The Kona Coast
IN & AROUND KAILUA-KONA, HOLUALOA & KEAUHOU
Expensive

Kona Inn Restaurant ★ AMERICAN/SEAFOOD This is touristy, but it can be a very pleasant experience, especially when the sun is setting. The wide-ranging menu and fresh seafood in the open-air oceanfront setting will remind you why you have come to Kailua-Kona. Also featured is a huge menu—everything from nachos and chicken Caesar salad to fresh fish.

At the Kona Inn Shopping Village, 75–5744 Alii Dr. www.konainnrestaurant.com. ℂ **808/329-4455.** Reservations recommended for dinner. Main courses $20–$70; Cafe Grill $11–$25. Dinner menu winter daily 5–9pm; summer daily 5:30–9pm. Cafe Grill menu daily 11:30am–9pm.

La Bourgogne ★★ CLASSIC FRENCH An intimate spot with 10 tables, La Bourgogne serves classic French fare with simple, skillful elegance. Classically trained chef Ron Gallaher expresses his allegiance to *la cuisine Française* down to the last morsel of flourless chocolate cake and lemon tartlet.

A tasty **TOUR**

Kona Joe Coffee Farm & Chocolate Company, 79–7346 Mamalahoa Hwy., between mile markers 113 and 114, in Kealakekua (www.konajoe.com; ℂ **808/322-2100**), home of the world's first trellised coffee farm, offers guided tours at its 20-acre estate in the "Gold Belt of Kona Coffee."

The tours begin with an excursion through the well-manicured fields of the unique coffee plants on a patented trellis technology developed by Joe Alban. In the 10,000-square-foot visitor center on the plantation, the tour continues with live demonstrations on roasting, sorting, brewing, and panning. At the end, you'll get a sample of Kona Joe Coffee in your own coffee mug. Tours are given daily from 8am to 5pm and cost $15; children under 12 are free.

77–6400 Nalani St. (3 miles south of Kailua-Kona). ℂ **808/329-6711.** Reservations recommended. Main courses $34–$42. Tues–Sat 6–10pm or time of last reservation.

Moderate

Jackie Rey's Ohana Grill ★★ ECLECTIC   This off-the-beaten-path eatery is hard to categorize: part sports bar, part family restaurant, part neighborhood cafe. No matter what you call it, you'll get great food (from burgers to bouillabaisse) at wallet-pleasing prices.

75–5995 Kuakini Hwy. www.jackiereys.com. ℂ **808/327-0209.** Reservations recommended for dinner. Main courses $13–$19 lunch, $18–$38 dinner; pupu menu $8–$18. Mon–Fri 11am–9pm; Sat–Sun 5–9pm.

Sam Choy's Kai Lanai ★★★ HAWAIIAN REGIONAL   Local celebrity chef Sam Choy (winner of a James Beard award and owner of numerous restaurants in Hawaii) is known for giant portions at moderate prices. Perched above the Keauhou Shopping Center, this open-air restaurant overlooks the shoreline and offers copious amounts of his mouthwatering cuisine (try the seafood *laulau*—fresh fish wrapped in a ti leaf), at prices most people can afford. There's also a happy hour everyday from 3 to 5pm.

78-6831 Alii Dr., Keauhou Shopping Center. ℂ **808/333-3434.** Reservations recommended for dinner. Breakfast entrees $9–$13 (Sun only), lunch entrees $9–$16, dinner entrees $17–$36. Mon–Fri 11am–9pm; Sat–Sun 8am–9pm.

Inexpensive

Ba-Le Sandwich Shop ★ FRENCH-VIETNAMESE SANDWICHES/ BAKERY   This family-run eatery is the perfect place to stop to get a picnic lunch for the beach. A statewide chain, it specializes in fast French-Vietnamese sandwiches, Vietnamese rice and noodle entrees, and bakery items. It's a nondescript place in a local shopping center, but it's worth seeking out for great deals such as sandwiches on homemade French rolls for just $5.

At the Kona Coast Shopping Center, 74–5588 Palani Rd. ℂ **808/327-1212.** Entrees $10–$15; sandwiches $5–$8. Mon–Sat 10am–9pm; Sun 10am–4pm.

KONA coffee CRAZE!

Coffeehouses are booming on the Big Island—this is, after all, the home of Kona coffee, with dozens of vendors competing for your loyalty and dollars.

Most of the farms are concentrated in the North and South Kona districts, where coffee remains a viable industry. Notable among them is the **Kona Blue Sky Coffee Company** in Holualoa (www.konablueskycoffee.com; ☏ **877/322-1700** or 808/322-1700), which handles its own beans exclusively. The Christian Twigg-Smith family and staff grow, hand-pick, sun-dry, roast, grind, and sell their coffee on a 400-acre estate. You can buy coffee on the farm itself and see the operation from field to final product. Open Monday through Friday 9am to 4pm. Tours starting hourly from 10am to 3pm.

Also in Holualoa, 10 minutes above Kailua-Kona, **Holualoa Kona Coffee Company** (www.konalea.com; ☏ **800/334-0348** or 808/322-9937) purveys organic Kona from its own farm and other growers. Not only can you buy premium, unadulterated Kona coffee here, but you can also witness the hulling, sorting, roasting, and packaging of beans on a farm tour Monday through Friday from 8am to 4pm.

A good bet in Hilo is **Bears' Coffee,** 106 Keawe St. (☏ **808/935-0708**), the quintessential sidewalk coffeehouse and a local stalwart. Regulars love to start their day here, with coffee and specialties such as souffléd eggs, cooked light and fluffy in the espresso machine and served in a croissant. It's a great lunchtime spot as well.

Big Island Grill ★ AMERICAN   One of the best-kept secrets among local residents is the Big Island Grill, where you get huge servings of home cooking at 1970s prices. The place is always packed, from the first cup of coffee at breakfast to the last bite of dessert at night. *Warning:* You'll likely have to wait (no reservations taken), and once you finally land a table, service can sometimes be slow. Relax; it's Hawaii.

75-5702 Kuakini Hwy. www.facebook.com/BigIslandGrill. ☏ **808/326-1153.** Reservations not accepted. Main courses breakfast $8–$13, lunch $12–$25, dinner $16–$28. Mon–Sat 7am–9pm; Sun 7am–noon.

Island Lava Java ★ AMERICAN   Ocean views and great prices make this inexpensive outdoor coffee shop always packed. The breakfast menu features stacks of pancakes and eggs in various preparations; the lunch menu is big on sandwiches, burgers, and salads; dinners can be small (sandwiches or salads) or big (New York steak with all the trimmings, veggie lasagna, fresh fish). Be sure to come with a laid-back attitude; service can be slow, but the price and the view more than make up for it.

75-5799 Alii Dr. www.islandlavajava.com. ☏ **808/327-2161.** Breakfast items $11–$18; lunch items $12–$24; dinner items $15–$30. Daily 6:30am–9pm.

Los Habaneros ★ MEXICAN   There's no leisurely dining at this small eatery—just great, fast Mexican food at budget prices. You order at one counter and pick up at another. Habaneros starts off the day with huevos rancheros and keeps going until after dark with tasty Mexican specialties. New location in Kona Town on Alii Dr. across from the Royal Kona Hotel ℭ 808/329-2814.

At the Keauhou Shopping Center, 78–6831 Alii Dr. ℭ **808/324-HOTT** (4688). All items under $15. Mon–Thurs 10am–8:30pm; Fri–Sat 10am–9pm; Sun 11am–8pm.

Quinn's Almost by the Sea ★ STEAK/SEAFOOD   Late-night nosh-ers, take note: This is one of the few places where you can grab a bite in Kona after 9pm. Quinn's, located at the northern gateway to town, has a nautical/sports-bar atmosphere and offers casual alfresco dining on a garden lanai, with an air-conditioned, nonsmoking area also available. The menu is surf-and-turf basic: burgers, sandwiches, and a limited dinner menu of dependably good fresh fish.

75–5655A Palani Rd. www.quinnsalmostbythesea.com. ℭ **808/329-3822.** Main courses $9–$22. Mon–Sat 11am–11pm; Sun 7-10:45am. They have the most reasonably priced breakfast in Kailua-Kona on Sunday $6-$15.

South Kona
INEXPENSIVE

Manago Hotel Restaurant ★ AMERICAN   The dining room of the decades-old Manago Hotel is a local legend, greatly loved for its unpreten-tious, tasty food at bargain prices. At breakfast, $6.50 buys you eggs, bacon, papaya, rice, and coffee. At lunch or dinner, you can dine on a 12-ounce T-bone, fried ahi, opelu, or the house specialty, pork chops—the restaurant serves nearly 1,500 pounds monthly—all under $15. This place is nothing fancy, and lots of things are fried, but the local folks would riot if anything were to change after so many years.

At the Manago Hotel, Hwy. 11. www.managohotel.com. ℭ **808/323-2642.** Reserva-tions recommended for dinner. Main courses $9–$15. Tues–Sun 7–9am, 11am–2pm, and 5–7:30pm.

Strawberry Patch ★★ ECLECTIC/AMERICAN   This nondescript building on the main highway hides one of the great gems in the area. Fresh farm produce (generally picked just hours before) is featured on the nightly specials written on the blackboard and priced at eye-popping budget deals that will make you glad you came even before your first bite. Be sure to reserve a seat inside, as the enclosed lanai is too close to the highway for polite conser-vation. The menu features individual pizza, curry dishes, and pastas; I'd sug-gest ordering something from the nightly specials, ranging from fresh fish to mouth-watering pastas and save room for desserts. No liquor license, so BYOB.

79-7491 Hwy. 11., Kealakekua. ℭ **808/322-9060.** Reservations recommended. Main Courses $15–$32. Daily 11am–8pm.

Teshima's ★ JAPANESE/AMERICAN   Wonderful home-made Japanese food at bargain prices, served with smiling aloha. The early morning crowd starts gathering for omelets or Japanese breakfasts (soup, rice, and fish) while it's still dark outside. As the day progresses, the orders pour in for shrimp tempura and sukiyaki, and *teishoku* trays—miso soup, sashimi, sukiyaki, shrimp, pickles, and other delights—stream out of the kitchen.

Hwy. 11. www.teshimarestaurant.com. © **808/322-9140.** Reservations recommended. Complete dinners $28 and under. Daily 6:30am–1:45pm and 5–9pm.

The Kohala Coast

EXPENSIVE

Napua at Mauna Lani Beach Club ★★★ PACIFIC RIM   It looks like something Hollywood would create: nestled on an isolated sandy beach cove, an open-air restaurant overlooking the ocean, and serving mouthwatering Pacific Rim cuisine. Grammy award winner Sonny Lim performs live Hawaiian music in the background. It doesn't get much better than this. *Note:* At lunch, you will have to park at the Mauna Lani Hotel and catch a shuttle; however, at dinner, you can drive straight into the restaurant's parking lot.

Mauna Lani Resort, 1292 S. Kaniku Dr. www.napuarestaurant.com. © **808/885-5910.** Reservations required. Main courses $14–$18 lunch; $36–$42 dinner. Lunch daily 11am–4pm; dinner Tues–Sun 4–9pm.

Roy's Waikoloa Bar & Grill ★★★ PACIFIC RIM/EURO-ASIAN Local chef Roy Yamaguchi has a branch restaurant on nearly every Hawaiian island, but this one is unique: large windows overlooking a 10-acre lake. Happily, there's the same award-wining East-West cuisine and signature dishes including Szechuan baby back ribs, blackened Island ahi, and hibachi-style salmon served daily. *Be warned:* Roy's is always packed (make reservations).

At Kings' Shops, Waikoloa Beach Resort, 69–250 Waikoloa Beach Dr. www.royshawaii.com. © **808/886-4321.** Reservations recommended. Main courses $14–$55; 3-course prix-fixe $58 ($78 with wine). Daily 5–9:30pm.

MODERATE

Cafe Pesto ★★ MEDITERRANEAN/ITALIAN   Fans drive miles for the gourmet pizzas, calzones, and fresh organic greens grown from Kealakekua to Kamuela. The herb-infused Italian pies are adorned with local lobster, Hamakua grown shiitake mushrooms, and fresh fish, shrimp, and crab. Also in downtown Hilo.

At the Kawaihae Shopping Center at Kawaihae Harbor (61–3665 Hwy. 270, Kawaihae) and at the S. Hata Bldg., 308 Kamehameha Ave. www.cafepesto.com. © **808/882-1071.**

Tropical Dreams of Ice Cream

Tropical Dreams ice cream has spread all over the island but got its start in North Kohala. Across the street from Bamboo, **Kohala Coffee Mill and Tropical Dreams Ice Cream,** Hwy. 270 (© **808/889-5577**), serves upscale ice cream along with sandwiches, pastries, and a selection of Island coffees. The Tahitian vanilla and litchi ice creams are local legends. Jams, jellies, herb vinegars, Hawaiian honey, herbal salts, and macadamia-nut oils are among the gift items for sale. It's open weekdays from 6am to 6pm, weekends 7am to 6pm. For other Tropical Dreams outlets, check www.tropicaldreamsicecream.com.

Main courses $11–$17 lunch, $15–$37 dinner; $10–$21 pizza. Sun–Thurs 11am–9pm; Fri–Sat 11am–10pm.

North Kohala

MODERATE

Bamboo ★★ PACIFIC RIM   Tucked into a historic building, the nostalgic interior (high-back wicker chairs, works by local artists, and old Matson liner menus accenting the bamboo-lined walls) is the perfect backdrop to the local-favorites fare (from *imu*-smoked pork quesadillas to sesame-nori-crusted shrimp) and topped off with Hawaiian music (from 6:30pm to closing on weekends).

55-3415 Akoni Pule Hwy. http://bamboorestaurant.info. ℭ **808/889-5555.** Reservations recommended. Main courses $10–$25 lunch, $15–$35 dinner. Tues–Thurs 11:30am–8pm; Fri–Sat 11:30am-2:30pm and 6-10pm; Sun brunch 11:30am–2:30pm.

Hilo

MODERATE

Hilo Bay Cafe ★★★ PACIFIC RIM   If you are craving creative, healthy cuisine in a mellow atmosphere, this is the place for you. The innovative menu ranges from spanakopita with spinach and three cheeses to macadamia nut praline scallops with capellini and beurre blanc. Lunch features salads (such as seared ahi Caesar), sandwiches (kalua pork with Swiss cheese and caramelized onions), and entrees (such as flaky-crust vegetarian potpie). Don't miss eating here.

123 Lihiwai St., overlooking Liliuokalani Gardens and Hilo Bay. www.hilobaycafe.com. ℭ **808/935-4939.** Reservations recommended for dinner. Main courses $14–$26 lunch, $13–$35 dinner. Mon–Thurs 11am–9pm; Fri–Sat 11am–9:30pm.

BET YOU CAN'T eat just one

Hawaii Island Gourmet Products, which under the brand Atebara Chips has been making potato, taro, and shrimp chips in Hilo for 70 years, recently added a couple of new products that you just cannot miss: sweet-potato chips and the delicious taro chips. You can find them at most stores and major resorts on the Big Island, or contact the company directly (the store is located at 717 Manono St.; www.hawaiichips.com; ☎ **808/969-9600**). **Warning:** As we say in Hawaii, these chips are so *ono* (delicious) that you will be mail-ordering more when you get home.

Ocean Sushi Deli ★ SUSHI   Craving sushi? This is Hilo's nexus of affordable raw fish, with a long menu of options, plus ready-to-cook sukiyaki and shabu-shabu sets, all in a non-descript atmosphere in downtown Hilo.

235 Keawe St. ☎ **808/961-6625.** Bento boxes $14–$15; family platters $16; sushi $3-$15. Mon–Sat 10:30am–2pm and 5–9pm.

INEXPENSIVE

Ken's House of Pancakes ★ AMERICAN/LOCAL   The Big Island's only 24-hour coffee shop, Ken's serves basic breakfast, lunch, and dinner simply and efficiently, with a good dose of local color. Omelets, pancakes, French toast made with Portuguese sweet bread, saimin, sandwiches, and soup stream out of the busy kitchen. Very local, very Hilo.

1730 Kamehameha Ave. www.kenshouseofpancakes-hilohi.com. ☎ **808/935-8711.** Most items under $20. Daily 24 hr.

Hawaii Volcanoes National Park
INEXPENSIVE

Lava Rock Cafe ★ ECLECTIC/LOCAL   Located in the cool air of Volcano Village, in a retro atmosphere, this cafe features a cross-cultural menu that includes everything from chow fun to fajitas. The staff will happily pack "seismic sandwiches" for hikers and picnickers. When the sun goes down, southern-fried chicken and grilled meats top the menu.

19–3972 Old Volcano Rd. (1 block off Hwy. 11, Volcano Village exit), next to Kilauea Kreations. ☎ **808/967-8526.** Main courses $8–$12 breakfast; $9–$12 lunch, $12–$26 dinner. Sun 7:30am–4pm; Mon 7:30am–5pm; Tues–Sat 7:30am–9pm.

Thai Thai Restaurant ★ THAI   Even in the outback of Volcano, you can find ethnic restaurants. Thai Thai's well-known warm curries help ward off the chill at nearly 4,000 feet. The authentic menu ranges from coconut-rich soups to sweet-and-sour stir-fries.

19–4084 Old Volcano Rd. (1 block off Hwy. 11, Volcano Village exit). ☎ **808/967-7969.** Main courses $13–$26. Daily 11:30am-8:30pm.

EXPLORING THE BIG ISLAND

The Kona Coast

WALKING TOURS The **Kona Historical Society** (www.konahistorical. org; ✆ **808/323-3222**) The self-guided **Kona Coffee Living History Tour** takes you through the everyday life of a Japanese family on the Uchida Coffee Farm during the 1920s to 1940s. The tour is offered Monday through Friday on the hour from 10am to 2pm; $15 adults, $13 seniors and $5 kids 7 to 17. Meet at the Kona Historical Society office, 81–6551 Mamalahoa Hwy. (across from mile marker 110), Kealakekua.

In & Around Kailua-Kona ★★★

Hulihee Palace ★★ HISTORIC SITE   One of two royal palaces in the US (the most famous being Oahu's Iolani Palace), this two-story New England–style mansion of lava rock and coral mortar features many 19th-century mementos and gorgeous koa furniture. You'll get lots of background and royal lore on the guided tour (note: no photography allowed).

The palace hosts 12 free **Hawaiian music and hula concerts** a year, each dedicated to a Hawaiian monarch, at noon, generally on the third Sunday of the month (except June and Dec, when the performances are held in conjunction with King Kamehameha Day and Christmas). Check the website for dates.

Across the street is **Mokuaikaua Church** (✆ **808/329-1589**), the oldest Christian church in Hawaii. It's constructed of lava stones, but its architecture is New England style all the way. The 112-foot steeple is still the tallest man-made structure in Kailua-Kona.

75–5718 Alii Dr., Kailua-Kona. www.daughtersofhawaii.org. ✆ **808/329-1877.** Admission $8 adults, $6 seniors ($2 more for docent-led tour), $1 children. Mon–Sat 9am–4pm. Tours held throughout the day (arrive at least 1 hr. before closing).

Kailua Pier ★ HISTORIC SITE   This is action central for water adventures. Fishing charters, snorkel cruises, and party boats all come and go here. It's also a great place to watch the sunset.

On the waterfront outside Honokohau Harbor.

Kamehameha's Compound at Kamakahonu Bay ★★ HISTORIC SITE   On the ocean side of the Courtyard King Kamehameha's Kona Beach Hotel is a restored area of deep spiritual meaning to Hawaiians. This was the spot that King Kamehameha the Great chose to retreat to in 1812 after conquering the Hawaiian Islands. He stayed until his death in 1819. The king built a temple, **Ahuena Heiau,** and used it as a gathering place for his *kahuna* (priests) to counsel him on governing his people in times of peace. It was on this sacred ground in 1820 that Kamehameha's son Liholiho, as king, sat down to eat with his mother, Keopuolani, and Kamehameha's principal queen, Kaahumanu, thus breaking the ancient *kapu* (taboo) against eating with women; this act established a new order in the Hawaiian kingdom. You're free to wander the grounds, envisioning the days when King Kamehameha

ESPECIALLY FOR kids

Walking Through Thurston Lava Tube at Hawaii Volcanoes National Park (p. 117) It's scary, it's spooky, and most kids love it. You hike downhill through a rainforest full of little chittering native birds to enter this huge, silent black hole full of drips, cobwebs, and tree roots that stretch underground for almost a half-mile.

Snorkeling Kahaluu Beach Park (p. 122) The shallow, calm waters off Kahaluu Beach are the perfect place to take kids snorkeling. The waters are protected by a barrier reef, and the abundance of fish will keep the kids' attention. You can pick up a fish identification card at any dive shop and make a game out of seeing how many fish the kids can find.

Riding a Submarine into the Underwater World (p. 127) The huge viewing windows on Atlantis's 48-passenger sub will have the kids enthralled as the high-tech craft leaves the surface and plunges 120 feet down through the mysterious Neptunian waters. The trip isn't too long—just an hour—and there are plenty of reef fish and prehistoric-looking corals to hold the young ones' attention.

Hunting for Petroglyphs (p. 109) There's plenty of space to run around and discover ancient stone carvings at either the Puako Petroglyph Archaeological District (at Mauna Lani Resort) or the Kings' Trail (by the Waikoloa Beach Marriott Resort). And finding the petroglyphs is only part of the game—once you find them, you have to guess what the designs mean.

Watching the Volcano (p. 117) Any kid who doesn't get a kick out of watching a live volcano set the night on fire has been watching too much television. Take snacks, bottled water, flashlights, and sturdy shoes and follow the ranger's instructions on where to view the lava safely.

appealed to the gods to help him rule with the spirit of humanity's highest nature.

On the grounds of Courtyard King Kamehameha's Kona Beach Hotel, 75–5660 Palani Rd. www.konabeachhotel.com. ✆ **808/329-2911.**

Natural Energy Laboratory of Hawaii Authority (NELHA) ★

TOUR Technology buffs should take the interesting 75-minute tour of NELHA, where the hot tropical sun, in combination with a complex pumping system that brings 42°F (6°C) ocean water from 2,000 feet deep up to land, is used to develop innovations in agriculture, aquaculture, and ocean conservation.

73–4460 Queen Kaahumanu Hwy. (at mile marker 94). www.friendsofnelha.org or www.nelha.hawaii.gov. ✆ **808/329-8073.** Public presentation 10am Mon, Tues, and Thurs. $10 adults, $8 seniors, free for children 8 and under. Call for current schedule. The 3-hour NELHA Grand Tour 10am Wed & Fri, includes a visit to 3 NELHA campus sites; $32 adults, $28 seniors (children under 8 not advised, reservations required).

Upcountry Kona: Holualoa ★★

On the slope of Hualalai volcano above Kailua-Kona sits the small village of Holualoa, which attracts travelers looking for art and culture.

This funky upcountry town, centered on two-lane Mamalahoa Highway, is nestled amid a lush, tropical landscape where avocados grow as big as footballs. Holualoa is a cluster of brightly painted, tin-roofed plantation shacks enjoying a revival as B&Bs, art galleries, and quaint shops (see "Shops & Galleries" for details). In 2 blocks, it manages to pack in two first-rate galleries, a frame shop, a potter, a glassworks, a goldsmith, an old-fashioned general store, a vintage 1930s gas station, a tiny post office, a Catholic church, and the **Kona Hotel,** a hot-pink clapboard structure that looks like a Western movie set—you're welcome to peek in, and you should.

The cool up-slope village is the best place in Hawaii for a coffee break. That's because Holualoa is in the heart of the coffee belt, a 20-mile-long strip at an elevation of between 1,000 and 1,400 feet, where all the Kona coffee in the world is grown in the rich volcanic soil of the cool uplands (see "Kona Coffee Craze!" on p. 100). Everyone's backyard seems to teem with glossy green leaves and ruby-red cherries (which contain the seeds, or beans, used to make coffee), and the air smells like an espresso bar. **Holuakoa Café,** on Mamalahoa Highway (Hwy. 180) in Holualoa (www.holuakoacafe.com; ☎ **808/322-2233**), is a great place to get a freshly brewed cup and a bite to eat.

To reach Holualoa, follow narrow, winding Hualalai Road up the hill from Hwy. 19; it's about a 15-minute drive.

South Kona ★★★

Kona Historical Society Museum ★★ HISTORIC SITE   Step back in history at former Greenwell Store, built in 1875 and filled with antiques, artifacts, and photos which tell the story of this fabled coast, complete with storekeepers dressed in period costumes, offering visitors St. Jacobs Oil to cure their arthritis or rheumatism.

Serious history buffs should sign up for one of the museum's walking tours (see "Walking Tours" on p. 105).

Hwy. 11 (btw. mile markers 111 and 112). www.konahistorical.org. ☎ **808/323-3222** or 808/323-2006. Free admission (donations accepted); admission to Greenwell Store $5. Mon and Thurs 10am–3:30pm; program Thurs 10am–1pm. Parking on grassy area next to the Museum.

Kula Kai Caverns & Lava Tubes ★★ NATURAL ATTRACTION Before you trudge up to Pele's volcanic eruption, take a look at its underground handiwork. Ric Elhard and Rose Herrera have explored and mapped out the labyrinth of lava tubes and caves, carved out over the past 1,000 years or so, that crisscross their property on the southwest rift zone on the slopes of Mauna Loa near South Point. Options range from an easy half-hour tour on a well-lit underground route to a more adventuresome 2-hour caving trip (recommended minimum age is 8). Helmets, lights, gloves, and knee pads are all included. Sturdy shoes are recommended for caving.

Off Hwy. 11 (btw. mile markers 78 and 79). www.kulakaicaverns.com. ☎ **808/929-9725.** Half-hour tour $20 adults, $10 children 6–12; 2-hour tour $95 adults, $65 children 8–12 years. Advance reservations only.

The Painted Church ★ RELIGIOUS SITE   Oh, those Belgian priests—what a talented lot. In the late 1800s, Father John Berchmans Velghe borrowed a page from Michelangelo and painted biblical scenes inside St. Benedict's Catholic Church so the illiterate Hawaiians could visualize the white man's version of creation.

84–5140 Painted Church Rd., Captain Cook. www.thepaintedchurch.org. ℰ **808/328-2227.** Turn off Hwy. 11 (toward the ocean) at about the 104 mile marker on to Rte. 160. Go on about a mile to the first turnoff to the right. Watch for the King Kamehameha sign opposite. Continue along a narrow, winding road about a quarter mile to sign and turn right.

Puuhonua O Honaunau National Historical Park ★★★ HISTORIC SITE   Walk on this sacred ground, dotted with fierce, haunting idols and bordered by black-lava on one side and a black and white peppered beach on the other. To ancient Hawaiians, Puuhonua O Honaunau served as a place of refuge, providing sanctuary for defeated warriors and *kapu* (taboo) violators. A great rock wall—1,000 feet long, 10 feet high, and 17 feet thick—defines the refuge where Hawaiians found safety. On the wall's north end is Hale O Keawe Heiau, which holds the bones of 23 Hawaiian chiefs. On a self-guided tour of the 180-acre site—which has been restored to its pre-contact state—you can see and learn about reconstructed thatched huts, canoes, and idols, and feel the *mana* (power) of old Hawaii.

Hwy. 160 (off Hwy. 11 at mile marker 104). www.nps.gov/puho. ℰ **808/328-2288.** Admission $5 per vehicle, good for 7 days. Visitor center daily 8:30am–4:30pm; park daily 7am–sunset. From Hwy. 11, it's 3½ miles to the park entrance.

The Kohala Coast ★★★

Puukohola Heiau National Historic Site ★★★ HISTORIC SITE   When ancient Hawaiian warriors approached the coast, this imposing structure greeted them. This seacoast temple, called "the hill of the whale," and built by Kamehameha I from 1790 to 1791, the *heiau* stands 224 feet long by 100 feet wide. Kamehameha built this temple after a prophet told him he would conquer and unite the islands if he did so; 4 years later, he fulfilled his kingly goal. The site also includes an interactive visitor center, the house of John Young (a trusted advisor of Kamehameha), and, offshore, the submerged ruins of Hale O Ka Puni, a shrine dedicated to the shark gods.

Hwy. 270, near Kawaihae Harbor. www.nps.gov/puho. ℰ **808/882-7218.** Free admission. Daily 7am to sunset, visitor center 8:30am-4:30pm. The visitor center is on Hwy. 270; the *heiau* is a short walk away. The trail is closed when it's too windy, so call ahead if you're in doubt.

ANCIENT HAWAIIAN FISH PONDS

Scientist today still marvel over the ancient Hawaiians' aquaculturist mastery. One of the first civilizations on the planet to use brackish ponds along the shoreline, the Hawaiians stocked these ponds and harvested fish there when needed. Generally, the Hawaiians kept and raised mullet, milkfish, and shrimp in these open ponds. Juvenile manini, papio, eels, and barracuda occasionally found their way in, too.

The **Kalahuipuaa Fish Ponds,** at Mauna Lani Resort (© **808/885-6622**), are great examples of both types of ponds in a lush tropical setting. South of the Mauna Lani Resort are **Kuualii** and **Kahapapa Fish Ponds** at the Waikoloa Beach Marriott Resort (© **808/886-6789**). Both resorts have taken great pains to restore the ponds to their original states and to preserve them for future generations; call ahead to arrange a free guided tour.

KOHALA COAST PETROGLYPHS

The Hawaiian petroglyphs are a great enigma of the Pacific—no one knows who made them or why. They appear at 135 different sites on six inhabited islands, but most of them are found on the Big Island.

At first glance, the huge slate of pahoehoe lava looks like any other smooth black slate of lava on the seacoast of the Big Island—until gradually, in slanting rays of the sun, a wonderful cast of characters leaps to life before your eyes. You might see dancers and paddlers, fishermen and chiefs, hundreds of marchers all in a row. Pictures of the tools of daily life are everywhere: fish hooks, spears, poi pounders, canoes. The largest concentration of these stone symbols in the Pacific lies within the 233-acre **Puako Petroglyph Archaeological District,** near Mauna Lani Resort. A total of 3,000 designs have been identified. The 1.5-mile **Malama Trail** starts north of Mauna Lani Resort. Take Hwy. 19 to the resort turnoff and drive toward the coast on North Kaniku Drive, which ends at a parking lot. The trail head is marked by a sign and interpretive kiosk. Go in the early morning or late afternoon, when it's cool.

The **Kings' Shops** (www.kingsshops.com; © **808/886-8811**), at the Waikoloa Beach Resort, offers a free 1-hour tour of the surrounding petroglyphs every Thursday and Friday at 9:30am. Just show up lakeside next to Island Fish & Chips a few minutes before 9:30am.

Warning: The petroglyphs are thousands of years old and easily destroyed. Do not walk on them or attempt to take a rubbing (there's a special area in the Puako Preserve for doing so). The best way to capture a petroglyph is with a photo in the late afternoon, when the shadows are long.

North Kohala ★★★

Original King Kamehameha Statue ★★ MONUMENT/MEMORIAL

A larger-than-life statue of King Kamehameha the Great stands outside Kapaau's century-old New England–style courthouse—it's the town's main attraction. There's one just like it in Honolulu, across the street from Iolani Palace, but this is the original: an 8-foot, 6-inch bronze by Thomas R. Gould, a Boston sculptor. It was cast in Europe in 1880 but was lost at sea on its way to Hawaii. A sea captain eventually recovered the statue, which was placed here, near Kamehameha's Kohala birthplace, in 1912. Kamehameha was born in a canoe off the Kohala coast in 1750, became ruler of Hawaii in 1810, and died in Kailua-Kona in 1819. His burial site remains a mystery.

Hwy. 270.

Pololu Valley Lookout ★★★ NATURAL ATTRACTION   Here's the Hawaii of travel posters. No, really, this end-of-the-road scenic lookout, which overlooks the vertical jade-green cliffs of the Hamakua Coast and two islets offshore, has appeared on numerous travel posters. Linger if you can; adventurous travelers can take a switchback trail (a good 45-min. hike—one-way) to a secluded black-sand beach at the mouth of a wild valley once planted in taro. Bring water and bug spray.

At the end of Hwy. 270.

Mauna Kea ★★★

The 13,796-foot summit of Mauna Kea, the world's tallest mountain if measured from its base on the ocean floor, is one of the best places on earth for astronomical observations, thanks to its location in the tropics, pollution-free skies, and pitch-black nights. It's home to the world's largest telescopes—and more are planned, to the dismay of some Hawaiians—but the stargazing is fantastic even with the naked eye.

SAFETY TIPS   Always check the weather and Mauna Kea road conditions before you head out (http://mkwc.ifa.hawaii.edu/forecast/mko/index.cgi; © **808/935-6268**). Dress warmly; the temperatures drop into the 30s (around 0°C) after dark. Drink as much liquid as possible, avoiding alcohol and coffee, in the 36 hours surrounding your trip to avoid dehydration. Don't go within 24 hours of scuba diving—you could get the bends. The day before you go, avoid gas-producing foods, such as beans, cabbage, onions, soft drinks, or starches. If you smoke, take a break for 48 hours before to allow the carbon monoxide in your bloodstream to dissipate—you need all the oxygen you can get. Wear dark sunglasses to avoid snow blindness, and use lots of sunscreen and lip balm. Pregnant women, children under 13, and anyone with a heart condition or lung ailment are advised to stay below. Once you're at the top, don't overexert yourself; it's bad for your heart. Take it easy up here.

SETTING OUT   You'll need a four-wheel-drive vehicle to climb to the peak, **Observatory Hill.** A standard car will get you as far as the visitor center, but check your rental agreement before you go; some agencies prohibit you from taking your car on the Saddle Road, which is narrow and rutted, and has a soft shoulder. Plus the weather up here can be wicked—strong gale winds and curtains of rain and snow.

ACCESS POINTS & VISITOR CENTERS   It's about an hour from Hilo or Waimea to the visitor center and another 30 to 45 minutes from here to the summit. Take the Saddle Road (Hwy. 200) from Hwy. 190; it's about 19 miles to Mauna Kea State Recreation Area, a good place to stop and stretch your legs. Go another 9 miles to the unmarked Summit Road turnoff, at mile marker 28 (about 9,300 ft.), across from the Hunter's Check-in Station. People usually start getting lightheaded after the 9,600-foot marker (about 6¼ miles up the Summit Rd.), the site of the last comfort zone and the **Onizuka Visitor Information Station** (www.ifa.hawaii.edu/info/vis; ✆ **808/961-2180**). Named in memory of Hawaii's fallen astronaut, a native of the Big Island and a victim of the 1986 Challenger explosion, the center is open daily from 9am to 10pm. Children under the age of 16 are recommended NOT to go higher than the Visitor Center.

TOURS & PROGRAMS   Every night from 6 to 10pm, you can do some serious **stargazing** from the Onizuka Visitor Information Station. There's a free lecture at 6pm, followed by a video, a question-and-answer session, and your chance to peer through 11-, 14-, and 16-inch telescopes. Bring a snack and, if you've got them, your own telescope or binoculars, along with a flashlight with a red filter. Dress for 30° to 40°F (–1° to 4°C) temperatures, but call ✆ **808/935-6268** for the weather report first. Families are welcome.

At the **Keck Telescope Control Center,** 65–1120 Mamalahoa Hwy. (Hwy. 19), across from the North Hawaii Community Hospital, Waimea (www.keckobservatory.org; ✆ **808/885-7887**), you can see a model of the world's largest telescope, which sits atop Mauna Kea. The center is open to the public, Monday through Friday from 10am to 2pm. A 12-minute video explains the Keck's search for objects in deep space.

The **W. M. Keck Observatory** at the summit does not offer tours, but it does provide a visitor gallery with a 12-minute video, informational panels on the observatory layout and science results, two public restrooms, and a viewing area with partial views of the Keck telescope and dome. Gallery hours are Monday through Friday from 10am to 4pm.

MAKING THE CLIMB   If you're heading up on your own, stop at the visitor center for about a half-hour to get acquainted with the altitude. Walk around, eat a banana, and drink some water before you press onward and upward in low gear, engine whining. It takes about 30 to 45 minutes to get to the top from here. The trip is a mere 6 miles, but you climb from 9,000 to nearly 14,000 feet.

AT THE SUMMIT   Up here, 11 nations, including Japan, France, and Canada, have set up peerless infrared telescopes to look into deep space. Among them sits the **Keck Telescope,** the world's largest. Developed by the University of California and the California Institute of Technology, it's eight stories

HAWAII, THE BIG ISLAND

Exploring the Big Island

EXPERIENCING WHERE THE gods live

"The ancient Hawaiians thought of the top of Mauna Kea as heaven, or at least where the gods and goddesses lived," according to Monte "Pat" Wright, owner and chief guide of **Mauna Kea Summit Adventures.** Wright was the first guide to take people up to the top of Mauna Kea. He fell in love with this often-snow-capped peak the first time he saw it.

Mauna Kea Summit Adventures offers a luxurious trip to the top of the world. The 7- to 8½-hour adventure begins midafternoon, when guests are picked up along the Kona-Kohala coasts in a custom four-wheel-drive turbo-diesel van. As the passengers make the drive up the mountain, the extensively trained guide discusses the geography, geology, natural history, and Hawaiian culture along the way.

The first stop is at the Onizuka Visitor Information Station, at 9,000 feet, where guests can stretch, get acclimatized to the altitude, and eat dinner. As they gear up with Mauna Kea Summit Adventures' heavy arctic-style hooded parkas and gloves (the average temperature on the mountain is 30°F/–1°C), the guide describes why the world's largest telescopes are located on Mauna Kea and also tells stories about the lifestyle of astronomers who live for a clear night sky.

After a hearty dinner of 3-cheese lasagna, everyone climbs back into the van for the half-hour ride to the summit. As the sun sinks into the Pacific nearly 14,000 feet below, the guide points out the various world-renowned telescopes as they rotate into position for the night viewing.

After the last trace of sunset colors has disappeared from the sky, the tour again descends down to midmountain, where the climate is more agreeable, for stargazing. Each tour has Celestron Celestar 1100 deluxe telescopes, which are capable of 30× to 175× magnification and gather up to 500 times more light than the unaided eye.

Wright advises people to book the adventure early in their vacation. "Although we do cancel about 25 trips a year due to weather, we want to be able to accommodate everyone," he says. If guests book at the beginning of their vacation and the trip is canceled due to weather, Mauna Kea Summit Adventures will attempt to reschedule another day.

Note that the summit's low oxygen level (40% less oxygen than at sea level) and the diminished air pressure (also 40% less air pressure than at sea level) can be a serious problem for people with heart or lung problems or for scuba divers who have been diving in the previous 24 hours. Pregnant women, children under 16, and obese people should not travel to the summit due to the decreased oxygen. Because the roads to the summit are bumpy, anyone with a bad back might want to opt out, too.

The cost for this celestial adventure is $212 including tax (15% off if you book online 2 weeks in advance). For more information, go to www.maunakea.com or call ✆ **888/322-2366** or 808/322-2366.

high, weighs 150 tons, and has a 33-foot-diameter mirror made of 36 perfectly attuned hexagon mirrors, like a fly's eye, rather than one conventional lens.

Also at the summit, up a narrow footpath, is a cairn of rocks; from it, you can see across the Pacific Ocean in a 360-degree view that's beyond words and pictures. When it's socked in, you get a surreal look at the summits of Mauna Loa and Maui's Haleakala poking through the puffy white cumulus clouds beneath your feet.

Inside a cinder cone just below the summit is **Lake Waiau,** the only glacial lake in the mid-Pacific and, at 13,020 feet above sea level, one of the highest lakes in the world. The lake never dries up, even though it gets only 15 inches of rain a year and sits in porous lava where there are no springs. Nobody quite knows what to make of this, but scientists suspect the lake is replenished by snowmelt and permafrost from submerged lava tubes. You can't see the lake from Summit Road; you must take a brief high-altitude hike. But it's easy: On the final approach to the summit area, upon regaining the blacktop road, go about 600 feet to the major switchback and make a hard right turn. Park on the shoulder of the road (which is at 13,200 ft.). No sign points the way, but there's an obvious .5-mile trail that goes down to the lake about 200 feet across the lava. Follow the base of the big cinder cone on your left; you should have the summit of Mauna Loa in view directly ahead as you walk.

The Hamakua Coast ★★★
NATURAL WONDERS ALONG THE COAST
Akaka Falls ★★★ NATURAL ATTRACTION   See one of Hawaii's most accessible and scenic waterfalls via an easy 1-mile paved loop through a rainforest, past bamboo and ginger, and down to an observation point. You'll have a perfect view of 442-foot Akaka and nearby Kahuna Falls, which is a mere 100-footer. Keep your eyes peeled for rainbows. The noise you hear is the sound of *coqui* frogs, an alien frog from Puerto Rico that has become a pest on the Big Island.

On Hwy. 19, Honomu (8 miles north of Hilo). Turn left at Honomu and head 3½ miles inland on Akaka Falls Rd. (Hwy. 220).

HONOKAA ★★
Honokaa is worth a visit to see the remnants of plantation life, when sugar was king. This is a real place that hasn't yet been boutiqued into a shopping mall; it looks as if someone has kept it in a bell jar since 1930. There's a real barbershop, a real Filipino store, some good shopping (see "Shops & Galleries"), and a hotel with creaky floorboards that dishes up hearty food. The town also serves as the gateway to spectacular Waipio Valley (see below).

Honokaa has no attractions, per se, but you might want to check out the **Katsu Goto Memorial,** next to the library at the Hilo end of town. Katsu

---

Co-key, Co-key: What Is That Noise?

That loud noise you hear after dark, especially on the eastern side of the Big Island, is the cry of the male coqui frog looking for a mate. A native of Puerto Rico, where the frogs are kept in check by snakes, the coqui frog came to Hawaii in some plant material, found no natural enemies, and spread across the Big Island (and Maui). A chorus of several hundred coqui frogs is deafening (up to 163 decibels, or the noise level of a jet engine from 100 ft.). In some places, like Akaka Falls, there are so many frogs that they are now chirping during daylight hours.

Goto, one of the first indentured Japanese immigrants, arrived in Honokaa in the late 1800s to work on the sugar plantations. He learned English, quit the plantation, and aided his fellow immigrants in labor disputes with American planters. On October 23, 1889, he was hanged from a lamppost in Honokaa, a victim of local-style justice.

THE END OF THE ROAD: WAIPIO VALLEY ★★★

Long ago, this lush, tropical place was the valley of kings, who called it the valley of "curving water" (which is what *waipio* means). From the black-sand bay at its mouth, Waipio sweeps 6 miles between sheer, cathedral-like walls that reach almost a mile high. Once, 40,000 Hawaiians lived here, amid taro, red bananas, and wild guavas in an area etched by streams and waterfalls. Only about 50 Hawaiians live in the valley today, tending taro, fishing, and soaking up the ambience of this old Hawaiian place.

To get to Waipio Valley, take Hwy. 19 from Hilo to Honokaa, and then Hwy. 240 to the **Waipio Valley Lookout ★★★**, a grassy park on the edge of Waipio Valley's sheer cliffs with splendid views of the wild oasis below. This is a great place for a picnic; you can sit at old redwood picnic tables and watch the peaks of the white waves roll onto the black-sand beach at the mouth of the valley. From the lookout, you can hike down into the valley.

Warning: Do not attempt to drive your rental car down into the valley (even if you see someone else doing it). The problem is not so much going down as coming back up. Every day, rental cars have to be "rescued" and towed back up to the top, at great expense to the driver. Instead, hop on the **Waipio Valley**

enlightenment FROM MUSHROOMS!

Back in the 1960's, when hippies flocked to the Big Island they proclaimed enlightenment through eating mushrooms.

Who knew they were on to something.

Today the Hamakua Mushrooms can proudly proclaim they are enlightened. Not the kind of enlightenment the 1960 hippies were talking about—these "specialty" mushrooms, raised on the slopes of Mauna Kea, above the tiny village of Laupahoehoe, are "enlightened" because they are grown in the light, instead of the dark, which is the traditional way mushrooms are cultivated.

They're also developed in an organic, sterile medium of ground-up wheat bran, corncobs, and eucalyptus sawdust, instead of the more commonly used medium, manure.

Visitors can now peek behind the scenes to see how these unique fungi are cultivated. The 70-minute Hamakua Mushrooms Factory Tour and Tasting reveals the secrets to raising delectable fungi. It starts with a video, followed by a cooking demonstration, a yummy taste testing, a tour of the 16,000 square foot facility, and ends with a spin through the retail shop (mushroom T-shirts, mushroom cookies, mushroom tea, even mushroom dog treats).

Visitors must book in advance. Cost is $20 per person, $10 for children ages 3-11 years, and $18 for seniors and military personnel. For more information: **Hamakua Mushrooms Factory Tour and Tasting**, ℂ 808/962-0305, www.hamakuamushrooms.com.

Shuttle (www.waipiovalleyshuttle.com; ☏ **808/775-7121**) for a 90- to 120-minute guided tour, offered Monday through Saturday from 9am to 3pm. Tickets are $59 for adults, $32 for kids 12 and under.

You can also explore the valley with **Waipio Valley Wagon Tours** (www. waipiovalleywagontours.com; ☏ **808/775-9518**), which offers narrated 90-minute historical rides by mule-drawn surrey. Tours are offered daily at 10:30am, 12:30pm, and 2:30pm. It costs $60 for adults, $55 for seniors, and $30 for children 3 to 11. Call for reservations.

Hilo ★★★

The **Downtown Hilo Improvement Association,** 329 Kamehameha Ave., Hilo, HI 96720, has a very informative self-guided walking tour of Hilo, which focuses on 18 historic sites dating from the 1870s to the present. For a copy, download it from their website (www.downtownhilo.com; ☏ **808/935-8850**).

ON THE WATERFRONT

Old banyan trees shade **Banyan Drive ★★**, the lane that curves along the waterfront to the Hilo Bay hotels. Most of the trees were planted in the mid-1930s by memorable visitors like Cecil B. DeMille (who was here in 1933 filming *Four Frightened People*), Babe Ruth (his tree is in front of the Hilo Hawaiian Hotel), King George V, Amelia Earhart, and other celebrities whose fleeting fame didn't last as long as the trees themselves.

It's worth a stop along Banyan Drive—especially if the coast is clear and the summit of Mauna Kea is free of clouds—to make the short walk across the concrete-arch bridge in front of the Naniloa Hotel to **Coconut Island ★**, if only to gain a panoramic sense of the place.

Also along Banyan Drive is **Liliuokalani Gardens ★★**, the largest formal Japanese garden this side of Tokyo. This 30-acre park, named for Hawaii's last monarch, Queen Liliuokalani, is as pretty as a postcard, with bonsai, carp ponds, pagodas, and a moon-gate bridge. Admission is free; open 24 hours.

OTHER HILO SIGHTS

Lyman Museum & Mission House ★ HISTORIC SITE   This is a great place to peer into Hawaii's more recent past—the oldest wood-frame house on the island, built in 1839 by David and Sarah Lyman, a missionary couple who arrived from New England in 1832 and who received such guests as Mark Twain and Hawaii's monarchs. The well-preserved house provides an insight into missionary life and times in Hawaii in the 19th century.

The **Earth Heritage Gallery,** in the complex next door, continues the story of the islands with geology and volcanology exhibits, a mineral-rock collection that's rated one of the best in the country. The **Island Heritage Gallery** features displays on Hawaiian culture, including a replica of a grass *hale* (house), as well as on other cultures transplanted to Hawaii's shores. A special gallery features changing exhibits on the history, art, and culture of Hawaii.

276 Haili St. (at Kapiolani St.). www.lymanmuseum.org. ☏ **808/935-5021.** Admission $10 adults, $8 seniors 60 and over, $3 children 6–17; $21 per family. Mon–Sat 10am–4:30pm. Tours at 11am and 2pm (call to reserve a space).

IMILOA: EXPLORING THE unknown

Absolutely do NOT miss the **Imiloa: Astronomy Center of Hawaii ★★★**. The 300 exhibits in the 12,000-square-foot gallery make the connection between the Hawaiian culture and its explorers, who "discovered" the Hawaiian Islands, and the astronomers who explore the heavens from the observatories atop Mauna Kea. *Imiloa*, which means "explorer" or "seeker of profound truth," is the perfect name for this architecturally stunning center, located on 9 landscaped acres overlooking Hilo Bay in the University of Hawaii at Hilo Science and Technology Park campus, 600 Imiloa Place (www.imiloahawaii.org; © **808/969-9700** or 808/969-9703). Plan to spend at least a couple of hours here; a half-day would be better, to allow time to browse the excellent interactive exhibits as well as take in one of the planetarium shows, which boast a state-of-the-art digital projection system. Restaurant and shop on site. Open Tuesday through Sunday from 9am to 5pm; admission is $18 for adults and $9.50 for children 4 to 12; extra planetarium shows $5 to $10.

Maunaloa Macadamia Nut Factory ★ FACTORY TOUR   There's absolutely no cost to explore this unique factory and learn how Hawaii's favorite nut is grown and processed. And, of course, you'll want to try a few free samples.

Macadamia Nut Rd., off Hwy. 11 (8 miles from Hilo). www.maunaloa.com. © **888/MAUNALOA** (628-6256) or 808/966-8618. Free admission; self-guided factory tours. Mon–Fri 8:30am–5pm (factory closed weekends). From Hwy. 11, turn on Macadamia Nut Rd.; go 3 miles down the road to the factory.

Naha Stone ★ HISTORIC SITE   According to the ancient chants, this 2½-ton stone was used as a test of royal strength: Whoever could move the stone would conquer and unite the islands. As a 14-year-old boy, King Kamehameha the Great moved the stone—and later fulfilled his destiny.

In front of the Hilo Public Library, 300 Waianuenue Ave.

Pacific Tsunami Museum ★ MUSEUM   One of Hawaii's most dreaded nature disasters, the tsunami, has a long history in the islands of destruction. Here you'll learn firsthand from the volunteers staffing this tiny museum how they survived Hawaii's most deadly "walls of water" in 1946 and 1960, both of which reshaped the town of Hilo.

130 Kamehameha Ave. www.tsunami.org/index/index.html. © **808/935-0926.** Admission $8 adults, $7 seniors, $4 children 6–17. Tues–Sat 10am–4pm.

Panaewa Rainforest Zoo ★ ZOO   This 12-acre zoo, nestled in the heart of the Panaewa Forest Reserve south of Hilo, is the only outdoor rainforest zoo in the United States and one of the few zoos anywhere with free admission. Some 50 species of animals from rainforests around the globe call Panaewa home. All of them are exhibited in a natural setting.

Stainback Hwy. (off Hwy. 11). www.hilozoo.com. © **808/959-7224.** Free admission. Daily 9am–4pm. Petting zoo Sat 1:30–2:30pm.

Papahānaumokuākea: Discovery Center for Hawaii's Remote Coral Reefs ★ MUSEUM Because you probably will not be seeing the Northwest Hawaiian Islands coral reef ecosystem, which was added to the United Nation's World Heritage sites in 2010, this 4,000-square-foot center is the next best thing. Plus, the price is right—free. Through interactive displays, three-dimensional models, and an immersion theater, you will absorb natural science, culture, and history while having a great time.

76 Kamehameha Ave. www.papahanaumokuakea.gov/education/center.html. ✆ **808/ 933-8180**. Free admission. Tues–Sat 9am–4pm.

Rainbow Falls ★ PARK/GARDEN Off the beaten path, this 80-foot waterfall, which tumbles into a giant pond, is best seen the morning, around 9 or 10am, just as the sun comes over the mango trees. According to legend, Hina, the mother of Maui, lives in the cave behind the falls. Unfortunately, swimming in the pool is no longer allowed.

West on Waianuenue Ave., past Kaumana Dr.

Hawaii Volcanoes National Park ★★★

Yellowstone, Yosemite, and other national parks are spectacular, no doubt about it. But in my opinion, they're all ho-hum compared to this one: Here, nothing less than the miracle of creation is the daily attraction.

In the 19th century, before tourism became Hawaii's middle name, the islands' singular attraction for visitors wasn't the beach, but the volcano. From the world over, curious spectators gathered on the rim of Kilauea's Halemaumau crater to see one of the greatest wonders of the globe. Nearly a century after it was named a national park (in 1916), Hawaii Volcanoes remains the state's premier natural attraction.

Hawaii Volcanoes has the only rainforest in the U.S. National Park system—and it's the only park that's home to an active volcano. Most people drive through the park (it has 50 miles of good roads, some of them often covered by lava flows) and call it a day. But it takes at least 3 days to explore the whole park, including such oddities as **Halemaumau Crater ★★★**, a still-fuming pit of steam and sulfur; the intestinal-looking **Thurston Lava Tube ★★★**; **Devastation Trail ★★★**, a short hike through a desolated area destroyed by lava; and, finally, the end of **Chain of Craters Road ★★★**, where lava regularly spills across the man-made two-lane blacktop to create its own red-hot freeway to the sea. In addition to some of the world's weirdest landscapes, the park has hiking trails, rainforests, campgrounds, a historic old hotel on the crater's rim, and that spectacular, still-erupting volcano.

NOTES ON THE ERUPTING VOLCANO Volcanologists refer to Hawaii's volcanic eruptions as "quiet" eruptions because gases escape slowly instead of building up and exploding violently all at once. Hawaii's eruptions produce slow-moving, oozing lava that provides excellent, safe viewing most of the time.

Even so, the volcano has still caused its share of destruction. Since the current eruption of Kilauea began on January 3, 1983, lava has covered some

A Volcano-Visiting Tip

Thanks to its higher elevation and windward (rainier) location, this part of the island is always colder than it is at the beach. If you're coming from the Kona side of the island in summer, expect it to be at least 10° to 20° cooler at the volcano; bring a sweater or light jacket. In the winter months, expect temperatures to be in the 40s or 50s (single digits to midteens Celsius), and dress accordingly. Always have rain gear on hand, especially in winter.

16,000 acres of lowland and rainforest, threatening rare birds, while destroying power and telephone lines and eliminating water service possibly forever. Some areas have been mantled repeatedly and are now buried underneath 80 feet of lava. At last count, the lava flow had destroyed nearly 200 homes and businesses, wiped out Kaimu Black Sand Beach (once Hawaii's most photographed beach) and Queen's Bath, obliterated entire towns and subdivisions (Kalapana, Royal Gardens, Kalapana Gardens, and Kapaahu Homesteads), and buried natural and historic landmarks (a 12th-c. *heiau,* the century-old Kalapana Mauna Kea Church, Wahaulu Visitor Center, and thousands of archaeological artifacts and sites). The cost of the destruction—so far—is estimated at $100 million. But how do you price the destruction of a 700-year-old temple or a 100-year-old church?

However, Kilauea hasn't just destroyed parts of the island; it has also added to it—more than 560 acres of new land. The volume of erupted lava over the last 3 decades measures nearly 2 billion cubic yards—enough new rock to pave a two-lane highway 1.2 million miles long, circling the earth some 50 times. Or, as a spokesperson for the park puts it: "Every 5 days, there is enough lava coming out of Kilauea volcano's eruption to place a thin veneer over Washington, D.C.—all 63 square miles."

The most prominent vent of the eruption has been Puu Oo, a 760-foot-high cinder-and-spatter cone. The most recent flow—the one you'll be able to see, if you're lucky—follows a 7-mile-long tube from the Puu Oo vent area to the sea. This lava flow has extended the Big Island's shoreline seaward and added hundreds of acres of new land along the steep southern slopes. Periodically, the new land proves unstable, falls under its own weight, and slides into the ocean. (These areas of ground gained and lost are not included in the tally of new acreage—only the land that sticks counts.)

Scientists are also keeping an eye on Mauna Loa, which has been swelling since its last eruption in 1984. If there's a new eruption, there could be a fast-moving flow down the southwest side of the island, possibly into South Kona or Kau.

WHAT YOU'RE LIKELY TO SEE   With luck, the volcano will still be streaming rivers of red lava when you visit the park, but a continuous eruption of this length (more than 3 decades) is setting new ground, so to speak.

Kilauea continues to perplex volcanologists because most major eruptions in the past have ended abruptly after only several months.

But neither Mother Nature nor Madame Pele (the volcano goddess) runs on a schedule. The volcano could be shooting fountains of lava hundreds of feet into the air on the day you arrive, or it could be completely quiet—there are no guarantees. On many days, the lava flows right by accessible roads, and you can get as close as the heat will allow; sometimes, however, the flow is in underground tubes where you can't see it, or miles away from the nearest access point, visible only in the distance. Always ask the park rangers for advice before you set out on any lava-viewing expeditions.

VOLCANO VOCABULARY The volcano has its own unique, poetic vocabulary that describes in Hawaiian what cannot be said so well in English. The lava that looks like swirls of chocolate cake frosting is called *pahoehoe* (pa-*hoy*-hoy); it results from a fast-moving flow that curls artistically as it moves. The big, blocky, jumbled lava that looks like a chopped-up parking lot is called *aa* (ah-ah); it's caused by lava that moves slowly, pulling apart as it overruns itself.

Newer words include *vog,* which is volcanic smog made of volcanic gases and smoke from forests set on fire by aa and pahoehoe, it can sting your eyes and can cause respiratory illness; don't expose yourself to either for too long. Anyone with heart or breathing trouble, as well as women who are pregnant, should avoid the vog here.

JUST THE FACTS

WHEN TO GO The best time to go is when Kilauea is really pumping. If you're lucky, you'll be in the park when the volcano is active and there's a fountain of lava. Mostly, the lava runs like a red river downslope into the sea.

ACCESS POINTS Hawaii Volcanoes National Park is 29 miles from Hilo, on Hawaii Belt Road (Hwy. 11). If you're staying in Kailua-Kona, it's 100 miles, or about a 2½-hour drive, to the park. Admission is $15 per vehicle; once you pay the fee, you can come and go as often as you want for 7 days. Hikers and bicyclists pay $8; bikes are allowed only on roads and paved trails.

VISITOR CENTERS & INFORMATION Contact **Hawaii Volcanoes National Park,** P.O. Box 52, Hawaii Volcanoes National Park, HI 96718 (www.nps.gov/havo; © **808/985-6000**). The **Kilauea Visitor Center** is at the entrance to the park, just off Hwy. 11; it's open daily from 9am to 5pm.

ERUPTION UPDATES Everything you wanted to know about Hawaii's volcanoes, from what's going on with the current eruptions to where the next eruption is likely to be, is now available on the Hawaiian Volcano Observatory's website, **http://volcanoes.usgs.gov/hvo/activity/kilaueastatus.php**. The site is divided into areas on Kilauea (the currently erupting volcano), Mauna Loa (which last erupted in 1984), and Hawaii's other volcanoes. Each section provides photos, maps, eruption summaries, and historical information.

You can also get the latest on volcanic activity in the park by calling the park's **24-hour hot line** (© **808/985-6000**). Updates on volcanic activity are posted daily on the bulletin board at the visitor center.

HIKING & CAMPING IN THE PARK   Hawaii Volcanoes National Park offers a wealth of hiking and camping possibilities. See "Hiking & Camping," p. 128, for details.

ACCOMMODATIONS IN & AROUND THE PARK   If camping isn't your thing, don't worry. There's a hotel, **Volcano House,** within the park boundary, on the rim of Halemaumau Crater. In Volcano village, there are plenty of comfortable and convenient inns, bed and breakfast and vacation rentals, plus numerous restaurants; see p. 97 for accommodation listings and p. 104 for restaurant listings.

SEEING THE HIGHLIGHTS

Your first stop should be **Kilauea Visitor Center ★★**, just inside the entrance to the park. Here you can get up-to-the-minute reports on the volcano's activity, learn how volcanoes work, see a film showing blasts from the past, get information on hiking and camping, and pick up the obligatory postcards.

Filled with a new understanding of volcanology and the volcano goddess, Pele, you should then walk across the street to **Volcano House;** go through the lobby and out the other side, where you can get a look at **Kilauea Caldera ★★★**, a 2½-mile wide, 500-foot-deep hole. The caldera used to be a bubbling pit of fountaining lava; today you can still see wisps of steam that might, while you're standing there, turn into something more.

Now get out on the road and drive by the **sulfur banks ★**, which smell like rotten eggs, and the **steam vents ★★★**, where trails of smoke, once molten lava, rise from within the inner reaches of the earth. This is one of the places where you feel that the volcano is really alive.

Stop at the **Thomas A. Jaggar Museum ★★★** (daily 10am–8pm; free admission) for a good look at Halemaumau Crater, which is a half-mile across and 1,000 feet deep. The museum shows video from days when the volcano was really spewing, explains the Pele legend in murals, and monitors earthquakes (a precursor of eruptions) on a seismograph.

Next, drive around the caldera to the south side, park your car, and take the short walk to the edge of **Halemaumau Crater ★★★**, past stinky sulfur banks and steam vents, to stand at the overlook and stare in awe at this once-fuming old fire pit, which still generates ferocious heat out of vestigial vents.

If you feel the need to cool off, go to the **Thurston Lava Tube ★★★**, the coolest place in the park. A very short hike down into a natural bowl in the earth, a forest preserve the lava didn't touch, is full of native birds and giant tree ferns. Then you'll see a black hole in the earth; step in. It's all drippy and cool here, with bare roots hanging down. You can either resurface into the bright daylight or, if you have a flashlight, poke on deeper into the tube, which goes for another .5 mile or so.

Exploring the Big Island

HAWAII, THE BIG ISLAND

If you're still game for a good hike, try **Kilauea Iki Trail** ★, a 4-mile, 2-hour hike across the floor of the crater, which became a bubbling pool of lava in 1959 and sent fountains of lava 1,900 feet in the air, completely devastating a nearby ohia forest and leaving another popular hike ominously known as **Devastation Trail ★★★**. This .5-mile walk is a startling look at the powers of a volcanic eruption on the environment. (See "Hiking & Camping," on p. 128, for details on these and other park hikes.)

Check out ancient Hawaiian art at the **Puu Loa Petroglyphs** ★, around mile marker 15 down Chain of Craters Road. Look for the stack of rocks on the road. A brief .5-mile walk will bring you to a circular boardwalk where you can see thousands of mysterious Hawaiian petroglyphs carved in stone. (***Warning:*** It's very easy to destroy these ancient works of art. Do not leave the boardwalk, and do not walk on or around the petroglyphs. Rubbings of petroglyphs will destroy them; the best way to capture them is by taking a photo.) This area, Puu Loa, was a sacred place for generations. Fathers came here to bury their newborns' umbilical cords in the numerous small holes in the lava, thus ensuring a long life for the child.

THE VOLCANO AFTER DARK   If the volcano is erupting, be sure to see it after dark. Brilliant red lava snakes down the side of the mountain and pours into the sea, creating a vivid display you'll never forget. About 1½ hours before sunset, head out of the park and back down Volcano Highway (Hwy. 11). Turn onto Hwy. 130 at Keaau; go past Pahoa to the end of the road. (The drive takes the better part of an hour.) From here (depending on the flow), it's about a mile walk over sharp crusted lava; park rangers will tell you how to get to the best viewing locations, or you can call ahead (☏ **808/985-6000**) to check where the current eruption is and how to get there. Be forewarned that the flow changes constantly and, on some days, may be too far from the road to hike, in which case you'll have to be content with seeing it from a distance. Be sure to heed the rangers: In the past, a handful of hikers who ignored these directions died en route; new lava can be unstable and break off without warning. Take water, a flashlight, and your camera, and wear sturdy shoes.

A BIRD'S-EYE VIEW   The best way to see Kilauea's bubbling caldera is from on high, in a helicopter. This bird's-eye view puts the enormity of it all into perspective. I recommend **Blue Hawaiian Helicopters ★★★** (www. bluehawaiian.com; ☏ **800/786-2583** or 808/871-1107), a professionally run, locally based company with an excellent safety record; comfortable, top-of-the-line 'copters; and pilots who are extremely knowledgeable about everything from volcanology to Hawaii lore. The company flies out of both Hilo and Waikoloa (Hilo is cheaper because it's closer). From Hilo, the 45-minute **Circle of Fire Tour ★★** takes you over the boiling volcano and then on to a bird's-eye view of the destruction the lava has caused as well as of remote beaches ($229–$282 per person, or $202–$248 online). From Waikoloa, the 2-hour **Big Island Spectacular ★★★** stars the volcano, tropical valleys, Hamakua Coast waterfalls, and the Kohala Mountains (from $464–$579, or $408–$510 online, but worth every penny).

South Point: Land's End ★★★

At the end of 11 miles of bad road that peters out at Kaulana Bay, in the lee of a jagged, black-lava point, you'll find Land's End—the tail end of the United States. From the tip (beware of the big waves that lash the shore if you walk out there), the nearest continental landfall is Antarctica, 7,500 miles away.

It's a 2½-mile four-wheel-drive trip and a hike down a cliff from South Point to the anomaly known as **Green Sand Beach ★**, described on p. 124 in the "Beaches" section of this chapter.

BEACHES

Too young geologically to have many great beaches, the Big Island instead has a collection of unusual ones: brand-new black-sand beaches, green-sand beaches, salt-and-pepper beaches, and even a rare (for this island) white-sand beach.

The Kona Coast

KAHALUU BEACH PARK ★★

This is the most popular beach on the Kona Coast; these reef-protected lagoons attract 1,000 people a day almost year-round. Kahaluu is the best all-around beach on Alii Drive, with coconut trees lining a narrow salt-and-pepper sand shore that gently slopes to turquoise pools. The schools of brilliantly colored tropical fish that weave in and out of the reef make this a great place to snorkel. In summer, it's also an ideal spot for children and beginning snorkelers; the water is so shallow that you can just stand up if you feel uncomfortable. But in winter, there's a rip current when the high surf rolls in; look for the lifeguard warnings. Kahaluu isn't the biggest beach on the island, but it's one of the best equipped, with off-road parking, beach-gear rentals, a covered pavilion, restrooms, barbecue pits, and a food concession stand.

The Kohala Coast

ANAEHOOMALU BAY (A-BAY) ★★

The Big Island makes up for its dearth of beaches with a few spectacular ones, like Anaehoomalu, or A-Bay, as the locals call it. This popular gold-sand beach, fringed by a grove of palms and backed by royal fish ponds still full of mullet, is one of Hawaii's most beautiful. It fronts the Waikoloa Beach Marriott Resort and is enjoyed by guests and locals alike (it's busier in summer but doesn't ever get truly crowded). The beach slopes gently from shallow to deep water; swimming, snorkeling, diving, kayaking, and windsurfing are all excellent here. At the far edge of the bay, snorkelers and divers can watch endangered green sea turtles line up and wait their turn to have small fish clean them. Equipment rental and snorkeling, scuba, and windsurfing instruction are available at the north end of the beach. Facilities include restrooms, showers, picnic tables, and plenty of parking.

Beaches & Outdoor Activities on the Big Island

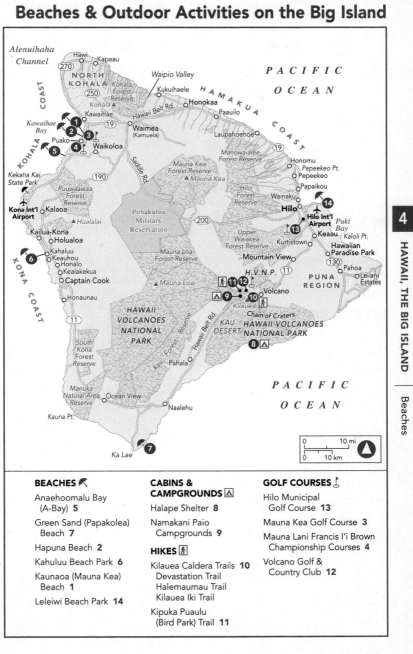

BEACHES 🏖

Anaehoomalu Bay
(A-Bay) **5**

Green Sand (Papakolea)
Beach **7**

Hapuna Beach **2**

Kahuluu Beach Park **6**

Kaunaoa (Mauna Kea)
Beach **1**

Leleiwi Beach Park **14**

CABINS & CAMPGROUNDS 🏕

Halape Shelter **8**

Namakani Paio
Campgrounds **9**

HIKES 🥾

Kilauea Caldera Trails **10**
Devastation Trail
Halemaumau Trail
Kilauea Iki Trail

Kipuka Puaulu
(Bird Park) Trail **11**

GOLF COURSES ⛳

Hilo Municipal
Golf Course **13**

Mauna Kea Golf Course **3**

Mauna Lani Francis I'i Brown
Championship Courses **4**

Volcano Golf &
Country Club **12**

HAPUNA BEACH ★★★

Just off Queen Kaahumanu Highway, south of the Hapuna Beach Prince Hotel, lies this crescent of gold sand—big, wide, and a half-mile long. In summer, when the beach is widest, the ocean calmest, and the crowds biggest, this is the island's best beach for bodysurfing. But beware of Hapuna in winter, when its thundering waves, strong rip currents, and lack of lifeguards can be dangerous. Facilities include A-frame cabins for camping, pavilions, restrooms, showers, and plenty of parking.

KAUNAOA BEACH (MAUNA KEA BEACH) ★★★

Everyone calls this gold-sand beach Mauna Kea Beach (it's at the foot of Mauna Kea Beach Hotel), but its real name is Hawaiian for "native dodder," a lacy, yellow-orange vine that once thrived on the shore. A coconut grove sweeps around this golden crescent, where the water is calm and protected by two black-lava points. The sandy bottom slopes gently into the bay, which often fills with tropical fish, sea turtles, and manta rays, especially at night, when the hotel lights flood the shore. Swimming is excellent year-round, except in rare winter storms. Snorkelers prefer the rocky points, where fish thrive in the surge. Facilities include restrooms, showers, and ample parking, but there are no lifeguards.

Hilo

LELEIWI BEACH PARK ★

Hilo's beaches may be few, but Leleiwi is one of Hawaii's most beautiful. This unusual cove of palm-fringed black-lava tide pools fed by freshwater springs and rippled by gentle waves is a photographer's delight—and the perfect place to take a plunge. In winter, big waves can splash these ponds, but the shallow pools are generally free of currents and ideal for families with children, especially in the protected inlets at the center of the park. Leleiwi often attracts endangered sea turtles, making this one of Hawaii's most popular snorkeling spots. The beach is 4 miles out of town on Kalanianaole Avenue. Facilities include restrooms, showers, lifeguards, picnic pavilions, and paved walkways. There's also a marine-life exhibit here.

South Point

GREEN SAND BEACH (PAPAKOLEA BEACH) ★

Hawaii's famous green-sand beach is located at the base of Puu o Mahana, an old cinder cone spilling into the sea. The place has its problems: It's difficult to reach; the open bay is often rough; there are no facilities, fresh water, or shade from the relentless sun; and howling winds scour the point. Nevertheless, each year the unusual green sands attract thousands of oglers, who follow a well-worn four-wheel-drive-only road for 2½ miles to the top of a cliff, which you have to climb down on foot to reach the beach. The sand is crushed olivine, a green semiprecious mineral found in eruptive rocks and meteorites. If the surf's up, check out the beach from the cliff's edge; if the water's calm, it's generally safe to swim.

To get to Green Sand Beach from the boat ramp at South Point, follow the four-wheel-drive trail. Even if you have a four-wheel-drive vehicle, you may want to walk because the trail is very, very bad in parts. Make sure you have appropriate closed-toe footwear: tennis shoes or hiking boots. The trail is relatively flat, but you're usually walking into the wind as you head toward the beach. The beginning of the trail is lava. After the first 10 to 15 minutes of walking, the lava disappears and the trail begins to cross pastureland. After about 30 to 40 minutes more, you'll see an eroded cinder cone by the water; continue to the edge, and there lie the green sands below.

The best way to reach the beach is to go over the edge from the cinder cone. (It looks like walking around the south side of the cone would be easier, but it's not.) From the cinder cone, go over the overhang of the rock, and you'll see a trail.

Going down to the beach is very difficult and treacherous, as you'll be able to see from the top. You'll have to make it over and around big lava boulders, dropping down 4 to 5 feet from boulder to boulder in certain spots. And don't forget that you'll have to climb back up. Look before you start; if you have any hesitation, don't go down (you get a pretty good view from the top, anyway).

Warning: When you get to the beach, watch the waves for about 15 minutes and make sure they don't break over the entire beach. If you walk on the beach, always keep one eye on the ocean and stick close to the rock wall. There can be strong rip currents here, and it's imperative to avoid them. Allow a minimum of 2 to 3 hours for this entire excursion.

WATERSPORTS

If you want to rent beach toys, like snorkel gear or boogie boards, the beach concessions at all the big resorts, as well as tour desks and dive shops, offer equipment rentals and sometimes lessons for beginners. The cheapest place to get great rental equipment is **Snorkel Bob's,** in the parking lot of Huggo's restaurant at 75–5831 Kahakai Rd., at Alii Drive, Kailua-Kona (www.snorkel bob.com; © **808/329-0770**), and in the Shops at Mauna Lani, 68–1330 Mauna Lani Dr. (© **808/885-9499**).

Boating

Captain Dan McSweeney's Whale Watch Learning Adventures ★★★
Hawaii's most impressive visitors—45-foot humpback whales—return to the waters off Kona every winter. Capt. Dan McSweeney, a whale researcher for more than 25 years, works daily with the whales, so he has no problem finding them. Frequently, he drops an underwater microphone into the water so you can listen to their songs, or uses an underwater video camera to show you what's going on. Cruises go year round; when the humpbacks aren't in town, you can still spot sperm whales and dolphins among other sea life.

Honokohau Harbor. www.ilovewhales.com. © **808/942-5376.** Whale-watching cruises, Dec–Apr, $110 adults, $99 children under 90 lb.

Fair Wind Snorkeling & Diving Adventures ★★★ One of the best ways to snorkel Kealakekua Bay, the marine-life preserve that's one of the top snorkel spots in Hawaii, is on Fair Wind's half-day **sail-and-snorkel cruise to Kealakekua Bay.** The *Fair Wind II,* a 60-foot catamaran that holds up to 100 passengers, offers a morning cruise that leaves from Keauhou Bay at 9am and returns at 1:30pm; it includes a light breakfast, lunch, snorkel gear, and lessons ($135 adults, $79 kids 4–12, $29 toddlers). Also on the *Fair Wind II* is a shorter (and cheaper) snack, sail-and-snorkel cruise for $79 adults and $49 children—there's no lunch, just fruit and a snack, plus snorkeling equipment.

78–7130 Kaleiopapa St. www.fair-wind.com. ℂ **800/677-9461** or 808/322-2788. Snorkel cruises $79–$149 adults, $49–$149 children 4–12; prices vary depending on cruise.

Scuba Diving

The Big Island's leeward coast offers some of the best diving in the world; the water is calm, warm, and clear. Want to swim with fast-moving game fish? Try **Ulua Cave** at the north end of the Kohala Coast. There are nearly two dozen dive operators on the west side of the Big Island, plus a couple in Hilo. They offer everything from scuba-certification courses to guided boat dives.

NIGHT DIVES WITH MANTA RAYS ★★ Something you'll never forget—swimming with manta rays on a night dive. These giant, harmless creatures, with wingspans that reach up to 14 feet, glide gracefully through the water to feed on plankton. **Jack's Diving Locker,** 75–5813 Alii Dr. (www.jacksdivinglocker.com; ℂ **800/345-4807** or 808/329-7585), offers its "Manta Ray Madness" for $155 for a two-tank dive and $125 for snorkelers. Everyone from beginners through experts will love this dive. Jack's cannot guarantee that these wild creatures will show up every night, but does boast a more than 90% sightings record.

Snorkeling

If you come to Hawaii and don't snorkel, you'll miss half the fun. The year-round calm waters along the Kona and Kohala coasts are home to spectacular marine life. Rent gear and get advice from **Snorkel Bob's,** mentioned in the intro to this section (p. 125). One of the best snorkeling areas on the Kona-Kohala coasts is **Hapuna Beach Cove,** at the foot of the Hapuna Beach Prince Hotel. But if you've never snorkeled in your life, **Kahaluu Beach Park** is the best place to start. Just wade in and look down at the schools of fish in the bay's black-lava tide pools. Other great snorkel sites include **White Sands Beach, Kekaha Kai State Park,** and **Hookena, Honaunau, Puako,** and **Spencer** beach parks.

SNORKELING CRUISES TO KEALAKEKUA BAY ★★★ Probably the best snorkeling for all levels can be found in **Kealakekua Bay.** The calm waters of this underwater preserve teem with a wealth of marine life. Coral heads, lava tubes, and underwater caves all provide an excellent habitat for Hawaii's vast array of tropical fish, making mile-wide Kealakekua the Big

Island's best accessible spot for snorkeling and diving. Kealakekua is best experienced by boat, see **Fair Wind** (p. 126).

Sport Fishing: The Hunt for Granders ★★

If you want to catch fish, it doesn't get any better than the Kona Coast, known internationally as the marlin capital of the world. Big-game fish, including gigantic blue marlin and other Pacific billfish, tuna, mahimahi, sailfish, swordfish, *ono* (also known as wahoo), and giant trevallies (*ulua*) roam the waters here. When anglers catch marlin that weigh 1,000 pounds or more, they call them "granders"; there's even a "wall of fame" on Kailua-Kona's Waterfront Row, honoring 40 anglers who've nailed more than 20 tons of fighting fish.

Nearly 100 charter boats with professional captains and crew offer fishing charters out of **Keauhou, Kawaihae, Honokohau,** and **Kailua Bay harbors.** If you're not an expert angler, the best way to arrange a charter is through a booking agency like the **Charter Desk at Honokohau Marina** (www.charter desk.com; ✆ **888/566-2487** or 808/326-1800). They will sort through the more than 40 different types of vessels, fishing specialties, and personalities to match you with the right boat. Prices range from $750 to $3,500 or so for a full-day exclusive charter (you and up to five of your friends have the entire boat to yourselves), or for $109 per person you can share a boat with others and rotate your turn at pulling in the big one.

Most big-game charter boats carry six passengers max, and the boats supply all equipment, bait, tackle, and lures. No license is required. Many captains now tag and release marlins. Other fish caught belong to the boat (not to you, but to the charter)—that's island style. If you want to eat your catch or have your trophy marlin mounted, arrange it with the captain before you go.

Submarine Dives

This is the stuff movies are made of: venturing 100 feet below the sea in a high-tech 65-foot submarine. On a 1-hour trip, you'll be able to explore a 25-acre coral reef that's teeming with schools of colorful tropical fish. Look closely and you might catch glimpses of moray eels—or even a shark—in and around the reef. On selected trips, you'll watch as divers swim among these aquatic creatures, luring them to the view ports for face-to-face observation. Call **Atlantis Submarines ★**, 75–5669 Alii Dr. (across the street from Kailua Pier), Kailua-Kona (www.atlantisadventures.com; ✆ **800/381-0237**). Trips leave daily between 10am and 2:30pm. The cost is $115 for adults and $48 for children under 12 (book on their website for a discount). *Note:* The ride is safe for everyone, but skip it if you suffer from claustrophobia.

Surfing

Most surfing off the Big Island is for the experienced only. As a general rule, the beaches on the north and west shores of the island get northern swells in winter, while those on the south and east shores get southern swells in summer. Experienced surfers should check out the waves at **Pine Trees** (north of Kailua-Kona), **Lyman's** (off Alii Dr. in Kailua-Kona), and **Banyan's** (also off Alii Dr.); reliable spots on the east side of the island include **Honolii Point** (outside Hilo), **Hilo Bay Front Park,** and **Keaukaha Beach Park.** But there are a few sites where beginners can catch a wave, too: You might want to try **Kahaluu Beach Park,** where the waves are manageable most of the year, other surfers are around to give you pointers, and there's a lifeguard on shore.

Ocean Eco Tours, 72–425 Kealakehe Pkwy. www.oceanecotours.com (✆ **808/331-2121**), owned and operated by veteran surfers, is one of the few companies on the Big Island that teaches surfing. Private lessons cost $150 per person (including all equipment) and usually last a minimum of 2 hours; 2½-hour group lessons go for $125 (also including all equipment), with a maximum of four students. The minimum age is 8, and you must be a fairly good swimmer.

Your only Big Island choice for surfboard rentals is **Pacific Vibrations,** 75–5702 Likana Lane (just off Alii Dr., across from the pier), Kailua-Kona (✆ **808/329-4140**), where short or long boards go for $15 to $20 per day.

HIKING & CAMPING

For information on camping and hiking, contact **Hawaii Volcanoes National Park,** P.O. Box 52, Hawaii National Park, HI 96718 (www.nps.gov/havo; ✆ **808/985-6000**); **Puuhonua O Honaunau National Historical Park** (www. nps.gov/puho; ✆ **808/328-2288**); the **State Division of Forestry and Wildlife,** 19 E. Kawili St. (www.hawaii.gov/dlnr/dofaw; ✆ **808/974-4221**); the **State Division of Parks,** 75 Aupuni St. (www.hawaiistateparks.org; ✆ **808/ 961-9540**); the **County Department of Parks and Recreation,** 101 Pauahi St., Ste. 6 (www.hawaiicounty.gov/parks-and-recreation; ✆ **808/961-8311**); or the **Hawaii Sierra Club's Moku Loa Group** (www.hi.sierraclub.org/ Hawaii/excomm.html).

If you are planning to camp at the Namakani Paio campground at Hawaii Volcanoes National Park (see below), a limited amount of camping equipment is available through the Volcano House. However, camping equipment is NOT available for rent for other areas on the Big Island. Plan to bring your own or buy it at the **Hilo Surplus Store,** 148 Mamo St. (www.hilosurplusstore.com; ✆ **808/935-6398**).

GUIDED DAY HIKES A guided day hike is a great way to discover natural Hawaii without having to sleep under a tree to do it. Call the following outfitters ahead of time (before you arrive) for a schedule of trips; they fill up quickly.

Naturalist and educator Rob Pacheco of **Hawaii Forest & Trail** ★★, 73–5593 A Olowalu St., across from Home Depot in Kailua-Kona (www. hawaii-forest.com; ✆ **800/464-1993** or 808/331-8505), offers fully outfitted day trips to some of the island's most remote, pristine areas, some of which he has exclusive access to visit. Rob's fully trained staff narrates the entire trip, offering extensive natural, geological, and cultural commentary (and more than a little humor). Tours are limited to 10 to 12 people and includes waterfall adventures, rainforest discovery hikes, birding tours, volcanoes, and even an off-road adventure in a 6×6 Pinzgauer Scrambler that allows you to explore hard-to-reach places. Each tour involves 2 to 4 hours of easy-to-moderate walking over terrain manageable by anyone in average physical condition. Half-day trips—including snacks, beverages, water, and gear—start at $129 for adults, and $99 for children ages 8 to 12. Full-day adventures are $179 to $249 adults, and $129 to $209 children, but keep in mind that full-day hikes are 8- to 12-hour days, which may be too strenuous for younger children.

Hawaii Volcanoes National Park ★★★

This national park is a wilderness wonderland for hikers. Miles of trails not only lace the lava, but also cross deserts, rainforests, beaches, and, in winter, snow at 13,650 feet. Trail maps (highly recommended) are sold at park headquarters. Check conditions before you head out. Come prepared for sun, rain, and hard wind any time of year. Always wear sunscreen and bring plenty of drinking water.

For complete coverage of the national park, see p. 117. *Warning:* If you have heart or respiratory problems or if you're pregnant, don't attempt any hike in the park; the fumes will bother you.

TRAILS IN THE PARK

KILAUEA IKI TRAIL   You'll experience the work of the volcano goddess, Pele, firsthand on this hike. The 4-mile trail begins at the visitor center, descends through a forest of ferns into still-fuming Kilauea Iki Crater, and then crosses the crater floor past the vent where a 1959 lava blast shot a fountain of fire 1,900 feet into the air for 36 days. Allow 2 hours for this fair-to-moderate hike.

HALEMAUMAU TRAIL   This moderate 3.5-mile hike starts at the visitor center, goes down 500 feet to the floor of Kilauea Crater, crosses the crater, and ends at Halemaumau Overlook.

DEVASTATION TRAIL   Up on the rim of Kilauea Iki Crater, you can see what an erupting volcano did to a once-flourishing ohia forest. The scorched earth with its ghostly tree skeletons stands in sharp contrast to the rest of the lush forest. Everyone can take this .5-mile hike on a paved path across the eerie bed of black cinders. The trail head is on Crater Rim Road at Puu Puai Overlook.

KIPUKA PUAULU (BIRD PARK) TRAIL   This easy, 1.5-mile, hour-long hike lets you see native Hawaiian flora and fauna in a little oasis of living nature in a field of lava. For some reason, the once red-hot lava skirted this miniforest and let it survive. At the trail head on Mauna Loa Road, there's a display of plants and birds you'll see on the walk. Go early in the morning or in the evening (or, even better, just after a rain) to see native birds like the *apapane* (a small, bright-red bird with black wings and tail) and the *iiwi* (larger and orange-vermilion colored, with a curved orange bill). Native trees along the trail include giant ohia, koa, soapberry, kolea, and mamani.

CAMPGROUNDS & WILDERNESS CABINS IN THE PARK

The only park campground accessible by car is **Namakani Paio,** which has a pavilion with picnic tables, restrooms, water, and fire pits (no wood is provided). Tent camping is $15; no reservations are required. Check to make sure campground is open ℂ **808/756-9625.** Stays are limited to 7 days per year. Backpack camping at hiker shelters and cabins is available on a first-come, shared basis, but you must register at the visitor center.

The following cabins and campgrounds are the best of what the park and surrounding area have to offer:

HALAPE SHELTER This backcountry site, about 7 miles from the nearest road, is the place for those who want to get away from it all and enjoy their own private white-sand beach. The small, three-sided stone shelter, with a roof but no floor, can accommodate two people comfortably, but four's a crowd. Go on weekdays if you're really looking for an escape. It's free to stay here, but you're limited to 3 nights. Permits are available at the visitor center on a first-come, first-served basis, no earlier than noon on the day before your trip. For more information, call ℂ **808/985-6000** or visit www.nps.gov/havo/plan yourvisit/hike_halape.htm.

NAMAKANI PAIO CAMPGROUNDS & CABINS If you are a camper, you will love the open, grassy field in a eucalyptus forest for tent camping. The trail to Kilauea Crater is just a half-mile away. Stays are limited to 7 days, at $15 per night, plus a $10 park entry fee. Facilities include pavilions with barbecues and a fireplace, picnic tables, outdoor dish-washing areas, restrooms, and drinking water. There are also 10 cabins that accommodate up to four people each. Make cabin reservations through **Volcano House** (www. hawaiivolcanohouse.com/cabins-campsites; ℂ **808/756-9625**). The cost is $80 per night for up to four people plus $10 park entry fee.

GOLF & OTHER OUTDOOR ACTIVITIES
Golf

For last-minute and discount tee times, call **Stand-by Golf** (www.hawaii standbygolf.com; ℂ **888/645-BOOK** [2665]) from 7am to 10pm. Stand-by Golf offers discounted (10–40% off), guaranteed tee times for same-day, next-day, or even future golfing.

THE KOHALA COAST
Mauna Kea Golf Course ★★★ This breathtakingly beautiful, par-72, 7,114-yard championship course, designed by Robert Trent Jones, Jr., is consistently rated one of the top golf courses in the United States. Book ahead;

the course is very popular, especially for early weekend tee times. Mauna Kea's greens, tees, fairways, and rough have recently been replaced with new hybrids of turf that can be groomed for the skill levels of both resort and professional golfers. Facilities include putting greens, driving ranges, lockers, showers, a pro shop, and restaurants.

At the Mauna Kea Beach Hotel, Mauna Kea Resort, off Hwy. 19 (near mile marker 68). www.princeresortshawaii.com. © **808/882-5400.** Greens fees $275 (resort guests $235), twilight (after 1:30pm) $165.

Mauna Lani Francis H. I'i Brown Championship Courses ★★★
The **South Course,** a 7,029-yard par-72, has an unforgettable ocean hole: the downhill, 221-yard, par-3 7th, which is bordered by the sea, a salt-and-pepper sand dune, and lush kiawe trees. The **North Course** may not have the drama of the oceanfront holes, but because it was built on older lava flows, the more extensive indigenous vegetation gives the course a Scottish feel. Facilities include two driving ranges, a golf shop (with teaching pros), a restaurant, and putting greens.

At the Mauna Lani Resort, Mauna Lani Dr., off Hwy. 19 (20 miles north of Kona Airport). www.maunalani.com. © **808/885-6655.** Greens fees $185–$225 ($150–$170 for resort guests), twilight (after noon) $160. Check website for specials. Big drop in rates

HILO
Hilo Municipal Golf Course ★
This is a great course for the casual golfer: It's flat, scenic, and often fun. *Warning:* Don't go after a heavy rain (especially in winter), when the fairways can get really soggy and play can slow way down. The rain does keep the course green and beautiful, though. Wonderful trees (monkeypods, coconuts, eucalyptus, banyans) dot the grounds, and the views—of Mauna Kea on one side and Hilo Bay on the other—are breathtaking. Getting a tee time can be a challenge; weekdays are your best bet.

340 Haihai St. (btw. Kinoole and Iwalani sts.). www.hawaiicounty.gov/pr-golf. © **808/ 959-7711.** Greens fees $35 Mon–Fri, $40 Sat–Sun and holidays; carts $20. From Hilo, take Hwy. 11 toward Volcano; turn right at Puainako St. (at Prince Kuhio Plaza), left on Kinoole, and then right on Haihai St.

VOLCANO VILLAGE
Volcano Golf & Country Club ★
Located at an altitude of 4,200 feet, this public course got its start in 1922, when the Blackshear family put in a green using old tomato cans for the holes. The course is unusually landscaped, making use of the pine and ohia trees scattered throughout. It's considered challenging by locals. Some tips from the regulars: Because the course is at such a high altitude, the ball travels farther than you're probably used to, so club down. If you hit the ball off the fairway, take the stroke—you don't want to look for your ball in the forest and undergrowth. Also, play a pitch-and-run game—the greens are slick.

Hwy. 11, on the right side, just after the entrance to Hawaii Volcanoes National Park. www.volcanogolfshop.com. © **808/967-7331.** Greens fees $60.

Biking

For mountain-bike and cross-training bike rentals in Kona, go to **Kona Beach & Sports ★**, Kona Inn Shopping Village, Alii Drive (75–5744 Alii Dr.; www.konabeachandsports.com; © **808/329-2294**), or **Bike Works,** Hale Hana Centre, 74–5583 Luhia St. (www.bikeworkskona.com; © **808/326-2453**). Both have a huge selection of bikes: cruisers ($25 a day), mountain bikes ($40 a day), hybrids ($30 a day), and racing bikes and front-suspension mountain bikes ($60 a day). Bike racks go for $5 a day, and you pay only for the days you actually use it. The folks at the shops are friendly and knowledgeable about cycling routes all over the Big Island.

GUIDED BIKE TOURS   Check out **Kona Coast Cycling** (www.orchidisle bicycling.com; © **877/592-BIKE** [2453] or 808/327-1133), which offers half-day (3–4 hr.) and full-day (4–6 hr.) bicycling tours, ranging from a casual ride to intense mountain biking at its best to 6-day bike tours of the Big Island. Most tours include round-trip transportation from hotels, van support, tour guide, helmet, gloves, water, snacks, and lunch on the full-day trips. Prices range from $125 to $145 for the day tours and $3,000 to $3,500 for the 4- to 8-day tours (includes airport pickup; accommodations; breakfast, lunch, and dinner; bicycle; helmet; and tour guide).

Contact the **Big Island Mountain Bike Association,** 318 E. Kawili St., Hilo, HI 96720 (© **808/961-4452**), for a copy of John Alford's *Mountain Biking the Hawaiian Islands* (Ohana Publishing), which includes maps and descriptions of bike rides for all of the islands.

Birding

Native Hawaiian birds are few—and dwindling. But Hawaii still offers extraordinary birding for anyone nimble enough to traverse the tough, mucky landscape. And the best birding is on the Big Island; birders the world over come here hoping to see three Hawaiian birds, in particular: the *akiapolaau,* a woodpecker wannabe with a war club–like head; the *nukupuu,* an elusive little yellow bird with a curved beak, one of the crown jewels of Hawaiian birding; and the *alala,* a critically endangered Hawaiian crow that's now almost impossible to see in the wild.

If you don't know an apapane from a nukupuu, go with someone who does. Contact the experts at **Hawaii Forest & Trail,** 73-5593 A Olowalu St., Kailua-Kona (www.hawaii-forest.com; © **800/464-1993** or 808/331-8505), to sign up for the **Rainforest & Dryforest Adventure ★★**. On this tour, you'll venture into the pristine rainforest to see rare and endangered Hawaiian birds. The full-day (12-hr.) tour costs $192 and includes a midmorning snack with coffee, lunch, beverages, daypack, binoculars, walking stick, and rain gear.

If you want to head out on your own, good spots to see native Hawaiian and other birds include the following:

HAWAII VOLCANOES NATIONAL PARK   The best places for accomplished birders to go on their own are the ohia forests of this national park, usually at sunrise or sunset, when the little forest birds seem to be most active. The Hawaiian nene goose can be spotted at the park's Kipuka Nene Campground, a favorite nesting habitat. Geese and pheasants sometimes appear on the Volcano Golf Course in the afternoon.

HILO PONDS Ducks, coots, herons (night and great blue), cattle egrets, and even Canada and snow geese fly into these popular coastal wetlands in Hilo, near the airport. Take Kalanianaole Highway about 3 miles east, past the industrial port facilities to Loko Waka Pond and Waiakea Pond.

Tennis

You can play for free at any Hawaii County tennis court. For a detailed list of all courts on the island, contact **Hawaii County Department of Parks and Recreation,** 101 Pauahi St. S̶t̶ 553 or 808/961-8311). The tadium, located next to the eservation and fees (☎ **808/** reas do not allow nonguests

ground for crops and food, to their creative endeavors. Big Island, in villages like wood-turning, handmade re sold in serene settings. in many media. Items for na, and accoutrements at gifts to go, as can locally wers, Kona coffee, and

reets in a festival atmo-'s, with Alii Drive at the Kona include the **Kona Inn Shopping** V̶i̶l̶l̶a̶g̶e̶, on Alii Drive, and, further south on the same street, **Alii Gardens Marketplace,** a pleasant, tented outdoor marketplace with fresh fruit, flowers, imports, local crafts, and a wonderful selection of orchid plants. There's cheesy stuff here, too, but somehow it's less noticeable outdoors.

Edibles & Everyday Things

The Big Island's **green markets** are notable for the quality of produce and the abundance of Island specialties at better-than-usual prices. Look for the cheerful green kiosks of the **Alii Gardens Marketplace,** 75–6129 Alii Dr. (at the south end), where local farmers and artists set up their wares Tuesday to Sunday from 10am to 5pm. This is not your garden-variety marketplace; some vendors are permanent, some drive over from Hilo, and the owners have planted shade trees and foliage to make the 5-acre plot a Kona landmark.

Java junkies jump-start their day at **Island Lava Java** (© **808/327-2161**), the magnet for coffee lovers at the Coconut Grove Market Place, on Alii Drive. At the other end of Kailua-Kona, in the New Industrial Area, between Costco and Home Depot, the handmade candies of the **Kailua Candy Company,** 73–5612 Kauhola St. (www.kailua-candy.com; © **808/329-2522,** or 800/622-2462 for orders), also beckon, especially the macadamia-nut clusters with ground ginger or the legendary macadamia-nut *honu* (turtle).

UPCOUNTRY KONA: HOLUALOA

Charming Holualoa, 1,400 feet and 10 minutes above Kailua-Kona at the top of Hualalai Road, is a place for strong espresso, leisurely gallery hopping, and nostalgic explorations across several cultural and time zones. One narrow road takes you across generations and cultures. **Paul's Place** is Holualoa's only all-purpose general store, a time warp tucked between frame shops, galleries, and studios (www.holualoahawaii.com).

All galleries listed are on the main street, Mamalahoa Highway, and all are within walking distance of one another.

Holualoa Gallery ★ Owners Matthew and Mary Lovein show their own work as well as the work of selected Hawaii artists in this roadside gallery in Holualoa. Sculptures, paintings, koa furniture, fused-glass bowls, raku ceramics, and creations in paper, bronze, metal, and glass are among the gallery's offerings. 76–5921 Mamalahoa Hwy. www.lovein.com/holualoagalleryblue. © **808/322-8484.**

Kimura Lauhala Shop ★ Everyone loves Kimura and the masterpieces of weaving that spill out of the tiny shop. It's lined with lauhala, from rolled-up mats and wide-brimmed hats to tote bags, coasters, and coin purses. The fragrant, resilient fiber—woven from the spiny leaves of the *hala* (pandanus) tree—is smooth to the touch and becomes softer with use. 77–996 Mamalahoa Hwy., at Hualalai Rd. © **808/324-0053.**

Studio 7 ★ Some of Hawaii's most respected artists, among them gallery owners Setsuko and Hiroki Morinoue, exhibit their works in this serenely beautiful studio. Smooth pebbles, stark woods, and a garden setting provide the backdrop for Hiroki's paintings and prints, as well as Setsuko's pottery, paper collages, and wall pieces. 76–5920 Mamalahoa Hwy. © **808/324-1335.**

Farmers Market, Fruit Stands & Espresso Bar

South Kona, one of the best growing regions on the Big Island, has a weekly **farmers market** every Saturday from 8am to noon at the **Keauhou Shopping Center** parking lot, near Ace Hardware. It's a true farmers market, selling only produce grown on the Big Island.

Another great vegetable and fruit stand down south is the **South Kona Fruit Stand,** 84–4770 Mamalahoa Hwy. between mile markers 103 and 104, Captain Cook (© **808/328-8547**), which sells some of the most unusual tropical produce from the Big Island.

The Kohala Coast

Harbor Gallery ★★   Next door to Cafe Pesto in this industrial harbor area of Kawaihae is a treasure trove or wonderful art from some 150 Big Island artists. The range is vast—from jewelry to basketry, ceramics to heirloom-quality koa furniture. Kawaihae Shopping Center, Hwy. 270 (just north of Hwy. 19). www.harborgallery.biz. © **808/882-1510.**

North Kohala

As Hawi Turns ★   You never know what you'll find in this whimsical, delightful shop of women's clothing and accessories. This is the perfect place to pamper yourself with such fripperies as tatami zoris and flamboyant accessories for a colorful, tropical life. Hwy. 270 (Akoni Pule Hwy.). © **808/889-5023.**

Waimea

Waimea is lei country as well as the island's breadbasket, so look for protea, vegetables, vine-ripened tomatoes, and tuberose stalks here at reasonable prices.

Two of the best farmer's markets are the **Homestead Farmers Market** (www.waimeafarmersmarket.com), 67–1229 Mamalahoa Hwy. (on the Waimea Middle School playground, behind the post office), which draws a loyal crowd from 7am to noon on Saturday. At the other end of Waimea, the **Parker School Farmers Market** (www.waimeatownmarket.com) is held Saturday from 7am to noon.

Gallery of Great Things ★   Here's an eye-popping assemblage of local art and Pacific Rim artifacts. You'll find jewelry, glassware, photographs, greeting cards, fiber baskets, and hand-turned bowls of beautifully grained woods. Parker Sq., Hwy. 19. www.galleryofgreatthingshawaii.com. © **808/885-7706.**

Waimea General Store ★   This charming, unpretentious country store offers a superb assortment of Hawaii-themed books, cookbooks, candles, linens, greeting cards, Japanese *hapi* coats, Island teas, rare kiawe honey, cookies, and countless gift items, from the practical to the whimsical. Parker Sq., Hwy. 19. www.waimeageneralstore.com. © **808/885-4479.**

The Hamakua Coast

HONOKAA

Honokaa Trading Company ★   "Rustic, tacky, rare—there's something for everyone," says owner Grace Walker, who has been in business for 3 decades. Every inch of this labyrinthine 2,200-square-foot bazaar is occupied by antiques and collectibles, new and used goods, and countless treasures. Mamane St. © **808/775-0808.**

THE END OF THE ROAD: WAIPIO VALLEY

Waipio Valley Artworks ★★   Housed in an old wooden building at the end of the road before the Waipio Valley, this gallery/boutique offers treasures for the home. The focus here is strictly local, with a strong emphasis on woodwork—one of the largest selections in the state. All the luminaries of wood-turning have works here: bowls, rocking chairs, and jewelry boxes exhibit flawless craftsmanship and richly burnished grains. 48–5416 Kukuihale Rd. www.waipiovalleyartworks.com. © **808/775-0958.**

Hilo

Shopping in Hilo is centered on the **Kaikoo Mall,** 777 Kilauea Ave., near the state and county buildings; the **Prince Kuhio Plaza,** 111 E. Puainako St., just off Hwy. 11 on the road north to Volcano, where you'll find a drugstore, Macy's, and other standards; the **Bayfront** area downtown, where the hippest new businesses have taken up residence in the historic buildings lining Kamehameha Avenue; and the new **Waiakea Plaza,** where the big-box retailers (Ross, OfficeMax, Walmart) have moved in.

Dragon Mama ★ For a dreamy stop in Hilo, head for this haven of all-natural comforters, cushions, futons, meditation pillows, antique kimonos and obi, tatami mats sold by the panel, and all manner of comforts in the elegantly spare Japanese esthetic. 266 Kamehameha Ave. © **808/934-9081.**

Sig Zane Designs ★★ My favorite stop in Hilo, Sig Zane Designs evokes such loyalty that people make special trips from the outer islands for this inspired line of authentic Hawaiian wear. The shop is awash in gleaming woods, lauhala mats, and clothing and accessories—handmade house slippers, aloha shirts, pareu, muumuu, T-shirts, and high-quality crafts. They all center on the Sig Zane fabric designs. To add to the delight, Sig and his staff take time to talk story and explain the significance of the images, or simply chat about Hilo, hula, and Hawaiian culture. 122 Kamehameha Ave. www.sigzane. com. © **808/935-7077.**

EDIBLES

Big Island Candies ★ Abandon all restraint: The chocolate-dipped shortbread and macadamia nuts, not to mention the free samples, will make it very hard to be sensible. Owner Alan Ikawa has turned cookie making into a spectator sport. Large viewing windows allow you to watch the hand-dipping from huge vats of chocolate while the aroma of butter fills the room. 585 Hinano St. www.bigislandcandies.com. © **800/935-5510** or 808/935-8890.

Hilo Farmers Market ★★ This has grown into the state's best farmers market, embodying what I love most in Hawaii: local color, good soil and weather, the mixing of cultures, and new adventures in taste. More than 150 vendors from around the island bring their flowers, produce, and baked goods to this teeming corner of Hilo every day. But the best days to go are Wednesday and Saturday from 6am to 4pm. Because many of the vendors sell out quickly, go as early as you can. Kamehameha Ave. (at Mamo St.). www.hilofarmers market.com. © **808/933-1000.**

Hawaii Volcanoes National Park

Volcano Art Center ★ Housed in the original 1877 Volcano House, VAC is a not-for-profit art-education center that offers exhibits and shows that change monthly. The fine crafts include baskets, jewelry, mixed-media pieces, stone and wood carvings. Hawaii Volcanoes National Park. www.volcanoartcenter. org. ℂ **808/967-7565.**

Volcano Winery ★ Lift a glass of Volcano Blush or Macadamia Nut Honey and toast Pele at this boutique winery, where the local wines are made from tropical honey (no grapes) and tropical fruit blends (half-grape and half-fruit). It's open daily (except Christmas) from 10am to 5:30pm; tastings are $5 to $8. Pii Mauna Dr. (off Hwy. 11 at mile marker 30, all the way to the end). http://volcanowinery.com. ℂ **808/967-7772.**

ENTERTAINMENT & NIGHTLIFE

There are a few pockets of entertainment on the Big Island, largely in the Kailua-Kona and Kohala Coast resorts. Your best bet is to check the local newspapers, *West Hawaii Today* and *Hilo Tribune,* for special shows, such as fundraisers, that are held at local venues.

Some of the island's best events are held at the **Kahilu Theatre** in Waimea (http://kahilutheatre.org; ℂ **808/885-6868**), so be on the lookout for any mention of it during your stay. The top Hawaiian music groups from all over Hawaii, hula, drama, and all aspects of the performing arts use Kahilu as a venue.

old-style HAWAIIAN ENTERTAINMENT

The plaintive drone of the conch shell pierces the air, calling all to assemble. A sizzling orange sun sinks slowly toward the cobalt waters of the Pacific. In the distance, the majestic mountain Mauna Kea reflects the waning sun's light with a fiery red that fades to a hazy purple and finally to an inky black as a voluptuous full moon dramatically rises over its shoulder.

It's **Twilight at Kalahuipua'a,** a monthly Hawaiian cultural celebration that includes storytelling, singing, and dancing on the oceanside grassy lawn at Mauna Lani Resort (ℂ **808/885-6622**; www.maunalani.com/events/twilight-at-kalahuipuaa). Scheduled on the Saturday closest to the full-moon, this one-of-a-kind event (created by Daniel Akaka Jr., Mauna Lani Resort's director of cultural affairs) hearkens back to another time in Hawaii, when family and neighbors

gathered to sing, dance, and "talk story." Best of all—it's free!

Each month, the guests—ranging from the ultra-well-known in the world of Hawaiian entertainment to the virtually unknown local *kupuna* (elder)—gather to perpetuate the traditional folk art of storytelling, with music and dance thrown in.

Twilight at Kalahuipua'a gets underway at least an hour before the 5:30pm start, when people from across the island and guests staying at the hotel begin arriving. They carry picnic baskets, mats, coolers, babies, and cameras. A sort of oceanside, pre-music tailgate party takes place with *kamaaina* (local resident) families sharing their plate lunches, sushi, and beverages with visitors, who have catered lunches, packaged sandwiches, and taro chips, in a truly old-fashioned demonstration of aloha.

Big Island Luau

Gathering of the Kings ★★★   The Fairmont Orchid's Polynesian show—a series of traditional dances and music blended with modern choreography, Island rhythms, and high-tech lighting and set design—tells the story of the Polynesians' journey across the Pacific to Hawaii. Complementing the show, the luau also highlights the cuisine of these Pacific islands. At the Fairmont Orchid, Mauna Lani Resort, 1 N. Kaniku Dr. www.fairmont.com/orchid. ℂ **808/326-4969.** Reservations required. Show and luau $109–$134 adults, $75 children 6–12, free for children 5 and under. Sat 5:30pm.

Haleo ★   The food is delicious, but you really come here for the show, created by Island Breeze Productions. Filled with lavish theatrics woven into Hawaiian chants, legends, hula, and acrobatic performing arts, this is definitely not your tired Polynesian revue. At the Sheraton Keauhou Bay Resort, 78–128 Ehukai St. www.sheratonkona.com. ℂ **808/326-4969** or 808/930-4900. Reservations required. Show and luau $99–$109 adults, $47–$57 children 6–12, free for children 4 and under. Mon & Fri 5:30pm.

Kailua-Kona

A host of bars and restaurants feature dancing and live music when the sun goes down, all of them on Alii Drive in Kailua-Kona. Starting from the south end of Alii Drive, **Huggo's on the Rocks** (www.huggosontherocks.com; ℂ **808/329-1493**) has dancing and live music weeknights starting at 6pm (3pm Fri–Sun), and next door at **Huggo's** restaurant, there's live local music Friday and Saturday (check calendar at www.huggos.com/entertainment).

The Kohala Coast

Evening entertainment here usually takes the form of a luau or indistinctive lounge music at scenic resort bars with scintillating sunset views. Waikoloa Beach Marriott's **Clipper Lounge** offers a range of live music most nights (call for schedule; ℂ **808/886-6789**) from 7 to 8:30pm.

The resort roundup includes the Hilton Waikoloa Village's **Legends of the Pacific** (ℂ **808/886-2929**) Sunday, Tuesday, and Friday dinner show ($125–$154 adults, $113–$139 seniors and teens 13–18, $68–$97 children 5–12). If you get a chance to see the **Lim Family,** don't miss them. Immensely talented in hula and song, members of the family perform in the intimate setting of the Mauna Lani Bay Hotel's **Atrium** nightly at 6pm (ℂ **808/885-6622**).

Just beyond the resorts lies a great music spot—the **Blue Dragon,** 61–3616 Kawaihae Rd. (www.bluedragonrestaurant.com; ℂ **808/882-7771**), where you can enjoy an eclectic mix of music (jazz, rock, swing, Hawaiian, even bigband music) most nights.

MAUI, THE VALLEY ISLE

Although it's only 75 miles from bustling Oahu, Maui is a very different island—a collection of mostly small towns, plus natural wonders like Haleakala National Park, that introduce visitors to a slower way of life. It's famous for its extensive beaches, tumbling waterfalls, romantic sunsets, and variety of adventures, from golf to snorkeling to scuba diving. Its climate varies greatly from region to region: The island's as lush as an equatorial rainforest in Hana, as hot and dry as Mexico in Lahaina, and as cool and misty as Oregon in Kula.

Beaches Hedonists looking for a day of lying on the soft sand head to **D. T. Fleming Beach Park.** More avid sorts, namely Jacques Cousteau types, can don a mask and fins and snorkel through rainbows of tropical fish at **Wailea Beach** or on the islet of **Molokini,** one of Hawaii's most popular dive spots. When the big waves are up, surfers and surfer-wannabes make their way to **Hookipa Beach Park.**

Things to Do For an awe-inspiring experience, drive to the highest point on Maui, the 10,000-foot volcano **Haleakala,** just before dawn, and watch the sunrise. Or take an entire day to drive along the **Hana Highway,** a barely two-lane road with the tropical jungle on one side and the churning ocean on the other. Get close to marine life at the **Maui Ocean Center,** a 5-acre facility housing sharks, reefs, and touch pools.

Eating & Drinking At the oceanfront **Old Lahaina Luau,** you're treated to a traditional feast of **kalua pig** cooked in an imu. If you want a more formal dining experience, Maui's star chefs at restaurants such as **Ka`Ana Kitchen, Morimoto,** and **Migrant** create menus with local ingredients and fresh fish. Upcountry, look for low-key ethnic spots that serve *manapua,* a bready, doughy sphere filled with sweetened pork or sweet beans.

Nature On the outskirts of **Hana,** visit the shiny black-sand **Waianapanapa Beach,** or venture to the **Seven Sacred Pools** of **Oheo Gulch.** The pools are fern-shrouded, dazzlingly beautiful, and swimmable (mostly).

THE best MAUI EXPERIENCES

- **Greeting the Rising Sun from atop Haleakala** (p. 173): Bundle up, fill a thermos with hot java, and drive up the 37 miles from sea level to 10,000 feet to witness the birth of yet another day. Breathing in the rarefied air and watching the first rays of light streak across the sky makes the Haleakala sunrise a mystical experience.

- **Watching for Whales** (p. 191): No need to head out in a boat—in winter you can see these majestic mammals breach and spy-hop from shore. One of the best viewing spots is scenic McGregor Point, at mile marker 9 along Honoapiilani Highway, just outside Maalaea in South Maui. The Majority of humpbacks travel through Maui's waters from mid-December to mid-April.

- **Snorkeling off Makena Landing:** Calm waters and an abundance of marine life make Makena Bay one of Hawaii's best places to swim with the fishes. Don a mask and snorkel to paddle with turtles, watch clouds of butterfly fish flitter past, and search for tiny damselfish in the coral.

- **Taking a Dip in the Seven Sacred Pools** (p. 181): There are actually more than seven of these fern-shrouded waterfall pools, and they're all beautiful. They spill seaward at Oheo Gulch, on the rainy eastern flanks of Haleakala.

- **Venturing Back in Time in a Historical Port Town** (p. 171): In the 1800s, when whaling was at its height, seafarers swarmed into Lahaina and missionaries fought to stem the spread of the whalers' sinful influence. It was a wild time, and this tiny town was an exciting place. The Lahaina Restoration Foundation provides a free map that will let you discover those wild whaling days for yourself.

- **Watching Windsurfers Ride the Waves at Hookipa** (p. 186): Just off the Hana Highway past Paia is Hookipa Beach, known the world over as a windsurfing mecca. Great waves and consistent wind draw top windsurfers from around the globe. Watch spellbound as these colorful sailboarders ride, sail, and pirouette over the waves, turning into the wind and flipping into the air while rotating 360 degrees. It's the best free show in town.

- **Exploring Iao Valley** (p. 169): When the sun strikes Iao Valley in the West Maui Mountains, an almost ethereal light sends rays out in all directions. This really may be Eden.

- **Walking the Shoreline Trail at Waianapanapa** (p. 187): A 6-mile trail follows the shoreline, bordered on one side by lava cliffs and a forest of lauhala trees on the other, beside the open ocean. As you go, you'll pass an ancient *heiau* (temple), some fascinating caves, a pretty cool blowhole, jungly native Hawaiian plants, and the ever-changing sea.

- **Heading to Kula to Bid the Sun Aloha:** Harold Rice Park, just off Kula Highway, is the perfect vantage point for watching the sun set over the entire island, with Molokai and Lanai in the distance. As the sun sinks in the sky, the light shifts from bright yellow to mellow red. Once the sun drops below the horizon, the sky puts on a Technicolor show in a dazzling array of colors.

o **Experiencing Art Night in Lahaina:** Every second Friday of the month, after the sun goes down, most of the town's galleries open their doors, serve pupu and refreshments, and hope you'll wander in. You may even be able to meet the artists; many are on hand to talk about their works.

ORIENTATION

Arriving

If you think of the island of Maui as the shape of a person's head and shoulders, you'll probably arrive near its neck, at **Kahului Airport.**

Try to fly directly to Maui—otherwise, you will be stuck with flying into Honolulu, with the likelihood of a 2-hour layover between flights. As of press time, these airlines fly directly from the U.S. mainland to Maui: **United Airlines** (www.united.com; © **800/241-6522**) has nonstop service from Los Angeles, Denver and San Francisco; **Hawaiian Airlines** (www.hawaiianair. com; © **800/367-5320**) offers limited direct flights from Los Angeles, Seattle, San Francisco and Oakland; **Alaska Airlines** (www.alaskaair.com; © **800/252-7522**) has nonstop flights from Seattle, San Diego, Oakland, Portland, and Sacramento; **American Airlines** (www.aa.com; © **800/433-7300**) has direct service from Los Angeles, San Jose, Phoenix and Dallas; **Delta Air Lines** (www.delta.com; © **800/221-1212**) flies direct from Los Angeles and Seattle.

Direct flights from Canada are available on **Air Canada** (www.aircanada. com; © **888/247-2262**), which flies from Vancouver and Calgary; and **West Jet** (www.westjet.com; © **888/937-8538**), which flies from Vancouver.

The other major carriers fly to Honolulu, where you'll have to pick up an interisland flight to Maui on **Hawaiian Airlines** (www.hawaiianair.com; © **800/367-5320**); **Island Air** (www.islandair.com; © **800/388-1105**); or **Mokulele Airlines** (www.mokulele.com; © **866/260-7070**), which offer jet service from Honolulu to and around the other islands.

LANDING AT KAHULUI If there's a long wait at baggage claim, step over to the state-operated **Visitor Information Center** and pick up brochures and the latest issue of *This Week Maui,* which features great regional maps of the islands. After collecting your bags, proceed to the rental-car pickup area (at the ocean end, to your right as you stand with your back to the terminal) and wait for the appropriate rental-agency shuttle van to take you a half-mile away to the rental-car checkout desk. All of the major rental companies—including Alamo, Avis, Budget, Dollar, Enterprise, Hertz, National, and Thrifty—have branches at Kahului. For tips on insurance and driving rules in Hawaii, see "Getting Around Hawaii" (p. 263).

If you're not renting a car, the cheapest way to get to your hotel is via **SpeediShuttle** (www.speedishuttle.com; © **877/242-5777**), which can take you between Kahului Airport and all the major resorts between 5am and 11pm daily. Rates vary, but figure on $42 for one person to Wailea (one-way), $67 one-way to Kaanapali, and $80 one-way to Kapalua. Be sure to call ahead to arrange pickup.

Uber (www.uber.com) is available on Maui. Costs from the airport to Wailea range from $83–$109, from the airport to Kaanapali $135–$178, and airport to Kapalua range from $156–$206. As we went to press, Uber is the only ride-sharing company available on Maui.

If possible, avoid landing between 3 and 6pm, when Maui's working stiffs are *pau work* (finished with work) and a major traffic jam occurs.

VISITOR INFORMATION The **Maui Visitors Bureau** is at 1727 Wili Pa Loop (www.gohawaii.com/maui; © **800/525-MAUI** [6284] or 808/244-3530).

The Island in Brief
CENTRAL MAUI

Maui's main airport lies in this flat, windy corridor between Maui's two volcanoes, and this is where most of the island's population lives. You'll find good shopping and dining bargains here, as well as the heart of the business community and the local government.

KAHULUI This is "Dream City," home to thousands of former sugar-cane workers whose dream in life was to own their own home away from the sugar plantation. There's oodles of shopping here (especially at discount stores), but this is not a place to spend your vacation.

WAILUKU Wailuku is like a time capsule, with its faded wooden storefronts, old plantation homes, shops straight out of the 1950s, and relaxed way of life. Although most people race through on their way to see the natural beauty of **Iao Valley,** this quaint little town is worth a brief visit, if only to see a real place where real people actually appear to be working at something other than a suntan. The town has a spectacular view of Haleakala, great budget restaurants, some interesting bungalow architecture, a wonderful historic B&B, and the always-endearing Bailey House Museum.

WEST MAUI

This is the fabled Maui you see on postcards. Jagged peaks, green velvet valleys, a wilderness full of native species—the majestic West Maui Mountains are the epitome of earthly paradise. The beaches here are some of the islands' best. And it's no secret: This stretch of coastline along Maui's "forehead," from Kapalua to the historic port of Lahaina, is the island's most bustling resort area (with South Maui close behind). Expect a few mainland-style traffic jams.

If you want to book into a resort or condo on this coast, first consider what community you'd like to base yourself in. Starting at the southern end of West Maui and moving northward, the coastal communities look like this:

LAHAINA This old seaport is a tame version of its former self, a raucous whaling town where sailors swaggered ashore in search of women and grog. Today, the village teems with restaurants, T-shirt shops, and galleries, and parts of it are downright tacky, but there's still a lot of real history to be found. Lahaina is a great place to stay. Accommodations include a few old hotels (such as the newly restored 1901 Pioneer Inn on the harbor), quaint bed-and-breakfasts, and a handful of oceanfront condos.

KAANAPALI Farther north along the West Maui coast is Hawaii's first master-planned destination resort. Pricey midrise hotels line nearly 3 miles of gold-sand beach; they're linked by a landscaped parkway and a walking path along the sand. Golf greens wrap around the slope between beachfront and hillside properties. **Whalers Village**—a seaside mall with 90 shops and restaurants, plus the best little whale museum in Hawaii—and other restaurants are easy to reach on foot along the oceanfront walkway or by resort shuttle, which also serves the small West Maui airport just to the north. Shuttles also go to Lahaina (see above), 3 miles to the south, for shopping, dining, entertainment, and boat tours.

HONOKOWAI, KAHANA & NAPILI In the building binge of the 1970s, condominiums sprouted along this gorgeous coastline like mushrooms after a rain. Today, these older oceanside units offer excellent bargains for astute travelers. The great location—along sandy beaches, within minutes of both the Kapalua and Kaanapali resort areas, and close enough to the goings-on in Lahaina town—makes this area an accommodations heaven for the budget-minded.

In **Honokowai** and **Mahinahina,** you'll find mostly older units that tend to be cheaper. There's not much shopping here (mostly convenience stores), but you'll have easy access to the shops and restaurants of Kaanapali.

Kahana is a little more upscale than Honokowai and Mahinahina. Most of its condos are big high-rise types, newer than those immediately to the south. You'll find a nice selection of shops and restaurants in the area, and Kapalua–West Maui Airport is nearby.

Napili is a much-sought-after area for condo seekers: It's quiet; has great beaches, restaurants, and shops; and is close to Kapalua. Units are generally more expensive here (although I've found a few hidden gems at affordable prices).

KAPALUA North beyond Kaanapali and the shopping centers of Napili and Kahana, the road starts to climb and the vista opens up to fields of golden-green pineapple and manicured golf fairways. A country lane lined with Pacific pines that leads toward the sea brings you to Kapalua. It's the very exclusive domain of the luxurious Ritz-Carlton hotel and expensive condos and villas, set on one of Hawaii's best white-sand beaches, next to two bays that are marine-life preserves (with fabulous surfing in winter).

SOUTH MAUI

This is the hottest, sunniest, driest, most popular coastline on Maui for sun lovers—Arizona by the sea. Rain rarely falls here, and temperatures stick around 85°F (29°C) year-round. On this former scrubland from Maalaea to Makena, where cacti once grew wild and cows grazed, there are now four distinctive areas—Maalaea, Kihei, Wailea, and Makena—and a surprising amount of traffic.

MAALAEA If West Maui is the island's head, Maalaea is just under the chin. This windy, oceanfront village centers on the small boat harbor (with a tiny general store and a handful of restaurants) and the **Maui Ocean Center,** an aquarium/ocean complex. Visitors staying here should be aware that it's almost always very windy. All the wind from the Pacific is funneled between the West Maui Mountains and Haleakala, and comes out in Maalaea.

KIHEI Kihei is less a proper town than a nearly continuous series of condos and mini-malls lining South Kihei Road. This is Maui's best vacation bargain. Budget travelers swarm like sun-seeking geckos over the eight sandy beaches along this scalloped, condo-packed, 7-mile stretch of coast. Kihei is neither charming nor quaint; what it lacks in aesthetics, though, it more than makes up for in sunshine, affordability, and convenience.

WAILEA Just 4 decades ago, this was wall-to-wall scrub kiawe trees, but now Wailea is a manicured oasis of multimillion-dollar resort hotels along 2 miles of palm-fringed gold coast. Wailea has warm, clear water full of tropical fish; year-round golden sunshine and clear blue skies; and hedonistic pleasure palaces on 1,500 acres of black-lava shore indented by five beautiful beaches. Amazing what a billion dollars can do.

This is the playground of the stretch-limo set. The planned resort development—practically a well-heeled town—has a shopping village, three prized golf courses of its own and three more in close range, and a tennis complex.

Appealing natural features include the coastal trail, a 3-mile round-trip path along the oceanfront with pleasing views everywhere you look. But the chief attractions, of course, are those five outstanding beaches (the best is Wailea).

MAKENA Suddenly, the road enters raw wilderness. After Wailea's overdone density, the thorny landscape is a welcome relief. Although beautiful, this is an end-of-the-road kind of place: It's a long drive from Makena to anywhere on Maui. If you're looking for an activity-filled vacation, you might want to try somewhere else, or you'll spend most of your vacation in the car. But if you want a quiet, relaxing respite, where the biggest trip of the day is from your bed to the beach, Makena is the place.

Beyond Makena, you'll discover Haleakala's last lava flow, which ran to the sea in 1790; the bay named for French explorer La Pérouse; and a chunky lava trail known as the King's Highway, which leads around Maui's empty south shore past ruins and fish camps. Puu Olai stands like Maui's Diamond Head on the shore, where a sunken crater shelters tropical fish, and empty golden-sand beaches stand at the end of dirt roads.

UPCOUNTRY MAUI

After a few days at the beach, you'll probably notice the 10,000-foot mountain in the middle of Maui. The slopes of *Haleakala* (House of the Sun) are home to cowboys, growers, and other country people who wave at you as you drive by. They're all up here enjoying the crisp air, emerald pastures, eucalyptus, and flower farms of this tropical Olympus—there's even a misty California redwood grove. You can see a thousand tropical sunsets reflected in the windows of houses old and new, strung along a road that runs like a loose hound from Makawao to Kula, where it leads up to the crater and **Haleakala National Park.** The rumpled, two-lane blacktop of Hwy. 37 narrows on the other side of Tedeschi Winery, where wine grapes and wild elk flourish on the Ulupalakua Ranch, the biggest on Maui. A stay upcountry is usually affordable and a nice contrast to the sizzling beaches and busy resorts below.

MAKAWAO   Until recently, this small, two-street upcountry town was little more than a post office, gas station, feed store, bakery, and restaurant/bar serving the cowboys and farmers living in the surrounding community; the hitching posts outside storefronts were really used to tie up horses. As the population of Maui started expanding in the 1970s, a health-food store sprang up, followed by boutiques, a chiropractic clinic, and a host of health-conscious restaurants. The result is an eclectic amalgam of old *paniolo* (cowboy) Hawaii and the baby-boomer trends of transplanted mainlanders. **Hui No'Eau Visual Arts Center,** Hawaii's premier arts collective, is definitely worth a peek. The only accommodations here are reasonably priced bed-and-breakfasts, perfect for those who enjoy great views and don't mind slightly chilly nights.

KULA   A feeling of pastoral remoteness prevails in this upcountry community of old flower farms, humble cottages, and new suburban ranch houses with million-dollar views that take in the ocean, the isthmus, the West Maui Mountains, and, at night, the lights that run along the gold coast like a string of pearls from Maalaea to Puu Olai. Everything flourishes at a cool 3,000 feet (bring a jacket), just below the cloud line, along a winding road on the way up to Haleakala National Park. Everyone here grows something—Maui onions, carnations, orchids, and proteas—and B&Bs cater to guests seeking cool tropic nights, panoramic views, and a rural upland escape. Here you'll find the true peace and quiet that only rural farming country can offer—yet you're still just 30 to 40 minutes away from the beach, and an hour's drive from Lahaina.

GETTING AROUND

BY CAR   The only way to really see Maui is by rental car; there's no island-wide public transit. All of the major car-rental firms—including Alamo, Avis, Budget, Dollar, Enterprise, Hertz, National, and Thrifty—have agencies on Maui. For tips on insurance and driving rules in Hawaii, see "Getting Around Hawaii" (p. 263).

Maui has only a handful of major roads, and you can expect to encounter a traffic jam or two in the major resort areas. Two of the roads follow the coastline around the two volcanoes that form the island, Haleakala and Puu Kukui (the West Maui Mountains); one road goes up to Haleakala's summit, one road goes to Hana, one goes to Wailea, and one goes to Lahaina. It sounds simple, right? Well, it isn't, because the names of the few roads change en route. Study a map before you set out.

A traffic advisory: Be alert on the Honoapiilani Highway (Hwy. 30) en route to Lahaina, because drivers who spot whales in the channel between Maui and Lanai often slam on the brakes and cause major tie-ups and accidents. Since this is the only main road connecting the west side to the rest of the island, if there is an accident, flooding, a rock slide, or any other road hazard, traffic can back up for 1 to 8 hours (no joking)—plan accordingly.

If you get into trouble on Maui's highways, look for the flashing blue strobe lights on 12-foot poles; at the base are emergency solar-powered call boxes (programmed to dial 911 as soon as you pick up the handset). There are 29 emergency call boxes on the island's busiest highways and remote areas, including along the Hana and Haleakala highways and on the north end of the island in the remote community of Kahakuloa.

BY MOTORCYCLE   Feel the wind on your face and smell the salt air as you tour the island on a Harley, available for rent from **Cycle City Maui,** 150 Dairy Rd. (www.hawaiiharleyrental.com; ☎ **808/831-2698**). Rentals start at $139 per day (9am–6pm daily). A second location is at 602 Front St. (☎ **808/831-2698**).

BY TAXI & SHUTTLE   Alii Taxi (☎ **808/661-3688**) offers 24-hour service islandwide. You can also call **Kihei Wailea Taxi** (☎ **808/877-7000**) or **CB Taxi Maui** (☎ **808/243-8294**) if you need a ride.

Maui Public Transit is a public/private partnership that has convenient, economical, and air-conditioned shuttle buses on 13 routes, all operated by Roberts Hawaii (www.mauicounty.gov/bus; ☎ **808/871-4838**). These routes are funded by the County of Maui and provide service in and between various Central, West, South, and Upcountry Maui communities (including the airport). All routes operate daily. They go from as far south as Wailea up to as far north as Kapalua. Fares are $2 for most routes.

[FastFACTS] MAUI

American Express   For lost or stolen cards, call ☎ **888/246-1076.**

Dentists   Emergency dental care is available at **Hawaii Family Dental,** 1847 S. Kihei Rd. (☎ **808/874-8401**), or at **Aloha Lahaina Dentists,** 134 Luakini St. (in the Maui Medical Group Bldg.; ☎ **808/661-4005**).

Doctors   The **Urgent Care West Maui,** Fairway Shops (2580 Kekaa Dr., Lahaina; www.westmaui doctors.com; ☎ **808/667-9721**), is open 365 days a year 8am to 9pm; no appointment is necessary. In Kihei, call **Urgent Care Maui,** 1325 S. Kihei Rd., Ste. 103 (at Lipoa St., across from Star Market; www. urgentcaremaui.com; ☎ **808/879-7781**), open every day 8am-6pm.

Emergencies   Call ☎ **911** for police, fire, and ambulance service. District stations are located in Lahaina (☎ **808/661-4441**) and in Hana (☎ **808/248-8311**).

Hospitals   In Central Maui, **Maui Memorial Medical Center** is at 221 Mahalani (☎ **808/244-9056**). East Maui's **Hana Health** is on the Hana Highway (☎ **808/**

248-8294). In Upcountry Maui, **Kula Hospital** is at 100 Keokea Pl. (📞 **808/878-1221**).

Internet Access Every major hotel and even many small B&Bs have Internet access. Many of them offer Wi-Fi (high-speed wireless); check ahead of time, and check the charges, which can be exorbitant. The best Internet deal in Hawaii is the service at the public libraries (to find the closest location near you, check www.librarieshawaii.org/Serials/databases.html), which offer free access if you have a library card, which you can purchase for $10 for 3 months. Other Internet access: Try the **Coffee Store,** 5095 Napilihau St., #108-B (📞 **808/669-4170**), open daily from 6am to 6pm; and **Blue Moon Café,** located off Kihei Road, behind the Tesoro Gas Station, at 362 Huku Lii Place (📞 **808/874-8600**), open Monday to Saturday from 7:30am to 8pm, Sunday 8am to 2pm. Also **Starbucks** (www.starbucks.com/store-locator) provides Wi-Fi in its stores in Kahului, Pukalani, Lahaina, Kahalui, Wailua, and Kihei.

Post Office To find the nearest post office, call 📞 **800/ASK-USPS** (275-8777). In Lahaina, there are branches at the Lahaina Civic Center, 1760 Honoapiilani Hwy., and at the Lahaina Shopping Center, 132 Papalaua St. In Kahului, there's a branch at 138 S. Puunene Ave., and in Kihei, there's one at 1254 S. Kihei Rd.

Weather For the current weather, the Haleakala National Park weather, or the marine weather and surf and wave conditions, www.prh.noaa.gov/hnl or call 📞 **808/944-3756.**

WHERE TO STAY

Maui has accommodations to fit every kind of vacation, from deluxe oceanfront resorts to reasonably priced condos to historic bed-and-breakfasts. Before you book, be sure to read "The Island in Brief," earlier in this chapter, which will help you settle on a location.

Remember that Hawaii's 13.42% accommodations tax will be added to your final bill. Parking is free unless otherwise noted. Also, if you're booking at an upscale hotel, be sure to ask if there is a "resort fee" ($12–$35 a day) tacked onto your bill.

Central Maui

If you're arriving late at night or you have an early morning flight out, the best choice near Kahului Airport is the **Courtyard Maui Kahului Airport,** 532 Keolani Pl. (www.marriott.com/hotels/travel/hnmmk-courtyard-maui-kahului-airport; 📞 **866/430-2692**), featuring 138 air conditioned units with small refrigerators, free Wi-Fi, and iPod docking stations, starting at $269 a night. For a cheaper airport hotel, book the **Maui Beach Hotel,** 170 Kaahumanu Ave. (www.mauibeachhotel.net; 📞 **866/970-4168** or 808/954-7421). The nondescript, motel-like rooms (the standard room is so small, you can barely walk around the queen-size bed) start at $119 and include free airport shuttle service (6am–9pm only). Both are okay for a night, but neither is the place to spend your entire vacation.

WAILUKU

Old Wailuku Inn at Ulupono ★★ This 1924 former plantation manager's home offers a genuine old Hawaii experience. The theme is Hawaii of the 1920s and 1930s, with decor, design, and landscaping to match. You'll feel right at home lounging on the living-room sofa or in an old wicker chair on the enclosed lanai, where a full gourmet breakfast is served in the morning. The inn is located in the historic area of Wailuku, just a few minutes' walk from the Maui County Seat Government Building, the courthouse, and a wonderful stretch of antiques shops.

2199 Kahookele St. (at High St., across from the Wailuku School). www.mauiinn.com. ✆ **800/305-4899** or 808/244-5897. 10 units. $165–$195 double. Rates include full breakfast. 2-night minimum. **Amenities:** Jacuzzi; free Wi-Fi.

West Maui

In addition to the following choices below, you may want to consider the oceanfront condos at **Lahaina Shores Beach Resort,** 475 Front St. (www.lahainashores.com; ✆ **844/230-3933**). Rates are $195 to $300 studio double, $355 to $415 one-bedroom double, and $355 to $405 one-bedroom penthouse double. 3-night minimum. Parking is $8. Value-priced **Old Lahaina House,** 407 Ilikahi St. (www.oldlahaina.com; ✆ **800/847-0761** or 808/667-4663), features comfy twin- and king-bedded doubles for just $109 to $159; it's about a 2-minute walk to the water just across Front Street.

LAHAINA

Moderate

Best Western Pioneer Inn ★ This historic old hotel, built in 1901 and located in the center of Lahaina, overlooks the streets of Lahaina and the harbor (just 50 ft. away). The remodeled rooms all have vintage-style (but up-to-date) bathrooms. A restaurant, good for breakfast, and a bar with live music are downstairs.

658 Wharf St. (in front of Lahaina Pier). www.pioneerinnmaui.com. ✆ **800/457-5457** or 808/661-3636. 34 units. $170–$275 double. **Amenities:** Restaurant; bar w/live music; outdoor pool; free Wi-Fi.

Inexpensive

Lahaina Inn ★ If you like old hotels that have genuine historic touches, you'll love this place. As in many older hotels, some of these antiques-stuffed rooms are small; if that's a problem for you, ask for a larger unit. All come with private bathrooms and lanais.

127 Lahainaluna Rd. (near Front St.). www.lahainainn.com. ✆ **800/222-5642** or 808/661-0577. 12 units (most shower only). $109–$189 double; from $189 suite. Next-door parking $15 per day. **Amenities:** Bar; concierge; free Wi-Fi.

Makai Inn ★ Budget travelers, take note: Here's a small apartment complex located right on the water (okay, no white-sand beach out front, but what do you want at these eye-popping prices?). You can take a 10-minute stroll from this quiet neighborhood to the closest white-sand beach, or walk 20 minutes to the center of Lahaina town. The units are small (400 sq. ft.) but clean and have full kitchens, ocean views (from most units), and separate bedrooms. There are no phones or TVs, but there's a public phone near the office.

1415 Front St. www.makaiinn.net. ✆ **808/662-3200.** 18 units. $110–$190 double. Extra person $15. **Amenities:** A/C in 3 units; free Wi-Fi.

Hotels & Restaurants in West Maui

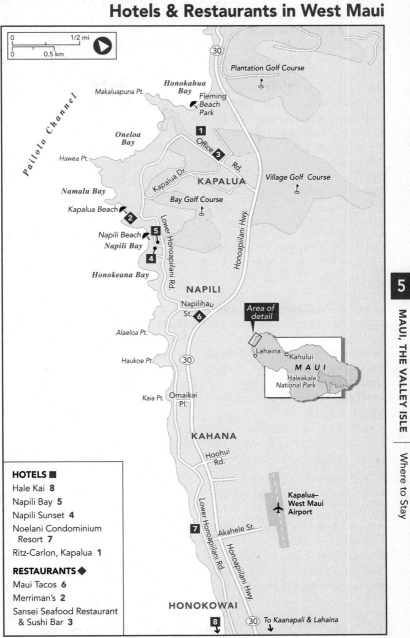

0   1/2 mi
0   0.5 km

Pailolo Channel

Plantation Golf Course

30

Honokahua Bay

Makaluapuna Pt.

Fleming Beach Park

Oneloa Bay

Office 3

Kapalua Dr.

Hawea Pt.

KAPALUA

Village Golf Course

Rd.

Namalu Bay

Bay Golf Course

Kapalua Beach 2

Napili Beach 5

Napili Bay

Honokeana Bay

Lower Honoapiilani Rd.

NAPILI

Napiliha u St. 6

Honoapiilani Hwy.

Area of detail

Alaeloa Pt.

Lahaina   Kahului

Haukoe Pt.   30

MAUI

Haleakala National Park

Kaia Pt.   Omaikai Pl.

KAHANA

Hoohui Rd.

Kapalua– West Maui Airport

Lower Honoapiilani Rd.

7

Akahele St.

Honoapiilani Hwy.

HOTELS ■
Hale Kai **8**
Napili Bay **5**
Napili Sunset **4**
Noelani Condominium Resort **7**
Ritz-Carlon, Kapalua **1**

RESTAURANTS ◆
Maui Tacos **6**
Merriman's **2**
Sansei Seafood Restaurant & Sushi Bar **3**

HONOKOWAI

8

30   To Kaanapali & Lahaina

KAANAPALI

Expensive

Sheraton Maui Resort & Spa ★★   The Sheraton occupies the nicest spot on Kaanapali Beach, built into the side of Puu Kekaa, the dramatic lava rock point at the beach's north end. The stretch of golden sand fronting the resort is widest here and the snorkeling is best around the base of the point, also known as Black Rock. Every night at sunset, cliff divers swan-dive into the sea from the torch-lit cliff—a magical sight. The resort's prime location, ample amenities, and typically great service make it an all-around great place to stay. Rooms feature Hawaiian-inspired decor, private lanais, and trademark Sweet Sleeper beds, which live up to their name. The *ohana* (family) suites accommodate all ages with two double beds plus a *punee* (sleeping chaise). A full roster of activities ranging from outrigger canoe to hula and ukulele lessons will immerse you in Hawaiian culture.

2605 Kaanapali Pkwy., Lahaina. www.sheraton-maui.com. ☏**866/716-8109** or 808/661-0031. 508 units. $296–$584 double; from $548 suite. Daily $25 resort fee. Extra person $89. Children 17 and under stay free in parent's room using existing bedding. Valet parking $30; self-parking $20. **Amenities:** 3 restaurants; 1 poolside bar; weekly luau; indoor lounge; babysitting; lobby and poolside concierge; 36-hole golf course; fitness center; day spa; Jacuzzi; lagoon-style pool; room service; 3 tennis courts; watersports equipment/rentals; shuttle service; free Wi-Fi.

Westin Maui Resort & Spa ★★   If you're looking for luxury with a healthy component, this 12-acre, ocean-front property is for you. The highrise is landscaped with lush tropical gardens, cascading waterfalls, and five outdoor pools and is completely smoke-free. Spacious mountain- or ocean-view rooms inspire sweet dreams with comfy "Heavenly Beds" and a choice of five types of pillows. The property includes a host of restaurants (with healthy choices on the menus), a luau, and a top ranked spa. There's a great kids club for ages 5 to 12, too.

2365 Kaanapali Pkwy., Lahaina. www.westinmaui.com. ☏ **888/627-8413** or 808/667-2525. 759 units. $639–$999 double; from $1,400 suite. Daily $30 resort fee. Extra person $89. Children 17 and under stay free in parent's room using existing bedding. Valet parking $25; self-parking free. **Amenities:** 2 restaurants; luau; 3 bars; babysitting; lobby and poolside concierge; 36-hole golf course; fitness center; spa; Jacuzzi; 5 pools; room service; watersports equipment/rentals; free Wi-Fi.

Moderate

Aston at the Whaler on Kaanapali Beach ★   For the best value in Kaanapali, the Whaler offers condominium living (your own kitchen!) on the beach, right next door to Whaler's Village, with oodles of restaurants to choose from. Here's the place to bring a family and spread out in these studio or one- or two-bedroom units right on the beach plus the year-round children's program

2481 Kaanapali Pkwy. www.whalerkaanapali.com. ☏ **877/997-6667.** 360 units. Studio from $239; 1-bedroom from $375; 2-bedroom from $859. Resort fee $15. 2-night minimum. Ask about package deals and AAA and senior discounts. **Amenities:** 36-hole golf course nearby; outdoor pool; access to tennis courts; watersports equipment rentals; free Wi-Fi.

Kaanapali Beach Hotel ★　A relic from a bygone era, this hotel has a humble charm and authentic Hawaiian warmth that's missing from many of its upscale neighbors. Three low-rise buildings border fabulous Kaanapali Beach; the beachfront units are mere steps from the water. The motel-like rooms are decorated with wicker and rattan furniture and Hawaiian-style bedspreads (beware the lumpy pillows, the property's only downside). As part of the hotel's extensive, and free, Hawaiiana program, you can learn to cut pineapple, weave lauhala, and even dance the hula. Children's activities, which come with myriad free treats, are complimentary as well. There are also complimentary traditional music and hula every night and a farewell lei ceremony when you depart.

2525 Kaanapali Pkwy., Lahaina. www.kbhmaui.com. (℃ **800/262-8450** or 808/661-0011. 430 units. $217–$258 double; from $535 suite. Extra person $40. Packages available, as well as senior discounts. Valet parking $13; self-parking $11. **Amenities:** 2 restaurants; poolside bar; babysitting; children's program (not supervised); concierge; outdoor pool; watersports equipment rentals; free Wi-Fi.

HONOKOWAI, KAHANA & NAPILI
Moderate

Napili Sunset ★　The location, the moderate prices, and the friendly staff are the real hidden treasures here. In addition to daily maid service, the staff makes sure each unit has the basics (paper towels, dishwasher soap, coffee filters, condiments) to get your stay off to a good start. There are restaurants within walking distance. It's true that the beach out front, one of Maui's best, can get a little crowded.

46 Hui Rd. (in Napili). www.napilisunset.com. (℃ **800/447-9229** or 808/669-8083. 26 units. $180 studio double; $340–$360 1-bedroom double (sleeps 5–6); $510 2-bedroom (sleeps up to 7). **Amenities:** Small outdoor pool; daily maid service; free Wi-Fi.

Noelani Condominium Resort ★　This oceanfront condo is a great value, whether you stay in a studio or a three-bedroom unit (ideal for large families). Everything is first class, from the furnishings to the oceanfront location. Though it's on the water, there's no white sand beach here (despite the photos posted on the website)—but right next door is a sandy cove at the county park. Guests are invited to a continental breakfast orientation on their first day and Mai Tai parties at night.

4095 Lower Honoapiilani Rd. www.noelani-condo-resort.com. (℃ **800/367-6030** or 808/669-8374. 45 units. $150–$209 studio double; $185–$247 1-bedroom (sleeps up to 4); $305–$339 2-bedroom (sleeps up to 6); $345–$403 3-bedroom (sleeps up to 8). Extra person $20. Children 17 and under stay free in parent's room. Packages for honeymooners, seniors, and AAA members available. Rates include continental breakfast on 1st morning. 3-night minimum. **Amenities:** Concierge; small fitness center; oceanfront Jacuzzi; 2 freshwater pools (1 heated for night swimming); free Wi-Fi.

Inexpensive

Hale Kai ★　This small two-story condo complex is ideally located, right on the beach and next door to a county park—a great location for those traveling with kids. Shops, restaurants, and ocean activities are all within a 6-mile radius. Lots of guests clamor for the oceanfront pool units, but I find the parkview units cooler, and they still have ocean views (upstairs units also have cathedral ceilings). This place fills up fast, so book early.

3691 Lower Honoapiilani Rd. (in Honokowai). www.halekai.com. © **800/446-7307** or 808/669-6333. 40 units. $112–$205 1-bedroom double; $158–$285 2-bedroom (sleeps up to 4); $261–$360 3-bedroom (sleeps up to 6). Extra person $10. 5-night minimum (fewer than 5 nights incurs a cleaning fee). **Amenities:** Concierge; outdoor pool; free Wi-Fi.

Napili Bay ★★   One of Maui's best secret bargains is this small two-story complex on Napili's beautiful half-mile white-sand beach. It's perfect for a romantic getaway: The beach here is one of the best on the coast, with great swimming and snorkeling There's no air-conditioning, but louvered windows and ceiling fans keep the units fairly cool during the day. Lots of restaurants and a convenience store are within walking distance, and you're about 10 to 15 minutes away from Lahaina and some great golf courses.

33 Hui Dr. (off Lower Honoapiilani Hwy., in Napili). www.alohacondos.com. © **877/877-5758.** 28 units. $69–$319 double. Cleaning fee $120. **Amenities:** Free Wi-Fi (some units).

KAPALUA
Expensive
Ritz-Carlton, Kapalua ★★★   Perched majestically on a knoll above D. T. Fleming Beach, this resort is a complete universe where you can while away your days without ever leaving the grounds. Rooms have dark wood floors, plush beds and couches, marble bathrooms, and private lanais overlooking the landscaped grounds and mostly undeveloped coast. Amenities include several superior dining options; a 10,000-square-foot, three-tiered pool; a fitness center; and the Waihua Spa, with steam rooms, saunas, and whirlpools surrounded by lava-rock walls. Another highlight is Jean-Michel Cousteau's Ambassadors of the Environment center with programs ranging from SUP lessons to snorkeling safaris and a great kids' club. A bit of a hike from the resort proper, D. T. Fleming Beach is beautiful but tends to be windier and rougher than the bays immediately south; a 5-minute shuttle ride delivers you to Kapalua.

1 Ritz-Carlton Dr., Kapalua. www.ritzcarlton.com. © **800/262-8440** or 808/669-6200. 463 units. $499–$720 double; $864–$1,050 Club Level double; from $825 suite; from $1,220 Club Level suite; residential suites from $740 1-bedroom, $1,090 2-bedroom. Extra person $100 club level only. Daily $35 resort fee; Wedding/honeymoon, golf, and other packages available. Valet parking $30; self-parking $22. **Amenities:** 5 restaurants; 4 bars; babysitting; basketball and bocce ball courts; bike rentals; children's program; club floor; concierge; cultural-history tours; 24-hr. ocean view fitness room; fitness classes; 2 championship golf courses (each w/its own pro shop) and golf academy; hiking trails; outdoor 3-tiered pool; room service; shuttle service; luxury spa with steam rooms, saunas, and whirlpools; deluxe tennis complex; watersports equipment rentals; free Wi-Fi.

South Maui
KIHEI
I recommend two booking agencies that rent a host of condominiums and vacation homes in the Kihei/Wailea/Maalaea area: **Maui Real Estate Sales &**

Hotels & Restaurants in South Maui

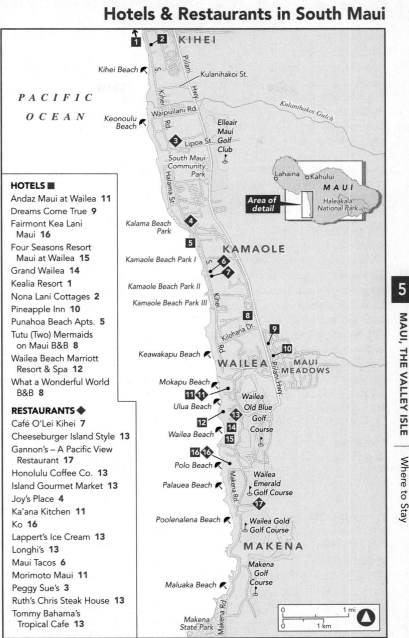

PACIFIC
OCEAN

Kihei Beach

Keonoulu
Beach

Kihei Beach

Kulanihakoi St.

Pilani Hwy.

Kihei Hwy.

Waipulani Rd.

Lipoa St.

South Maui
Community
Park

Elleair
Maui
Golf
Club

Kulanihakoi Gulch

Lahaina   Kahului

MAUI

Area of
detail

Haleakala
National Park

KIHEI

Halama St.

Kalama Beach
Park

Kamaole Beach Park I

Kamaole Beach Park II

Kamaole Beach Park III

Keawakapu Beach

Mokapu Beach

Ulua Beach

Wailea Beach

Polo Beach

Palauea Beach

Poolenalena Beach

Maluaka Beach

Makena
State Park

KAMAOLE

Kihei Rd.

Kilohana Dr.

WAILEA   MAUI
MEADOWS

Pilani Hwy.

Wailea
Old Blue
Golf
Course

Wailea
Emerald
Golf Course

Wailea Gold
Golf Course

MAKENA

Makena
Golf
Course

Makena Rd.

HOTELS ■

Andaz Maui at Wailea **11**
Dreams Come True **9**
Fairmont Kea Lani
  Maui **16**
Four Seasons Resort
  Maui at Wailea **15**
Grand Wailea **14**
Kealia Resort **1**
Nona Lani Cottages **2**
Pineapple Inn **10**
Punahoa Beach Apts. **5**
Tutu (Two) Mermaids
  on Maui B&B **8**
Wailea Beach Marriott
  Resort & Spa **12**
What a Wonderful World
  B&B **8**

RESTAURANTS ◆

Café O'Lei Kihei **7**
Cheeseburger Island Style **13**
Gannon's – A Pacific View
  Restaurant **17**
Honolulu Coffee Co. **13**
Island Gourmet Market **13**
Joy's Place **4**
Ka'ana Kitchen **11**
Ko **16**
Lappert's Ice Cream **13**
Longhi's **13**
Maui Tacos **6**
Morimoto Maui **11**
Peggy Sue's **3**
Ruth's Chris Steak House **13**
Tommy Bahama's
  Tropical Cafe **13**

0   1 mi
0   1 km

5

MAUI, THE VALLEY ISLE | Where to Stay

Vacation Rentals (www.kmvmaui.com; ✆ **808/879-4000**) and **Condominium Rentals Hawaii** (www.crhmaui.com; ✆ **800/367-5242** or 808/879-2778).

Moderate

Kealia Resort ★ This oceanfront property at the northern end of Kihei is well maintained and nicely furnished—and the prices are excellent. But as tempting as the lower-priced units may sound, don't give in: They face noisy Kihei Road and are near a major junction, so big trucks downshifting can be especially loud at night. Instead, go for one of the oceanview units, which all have full kitchens and private lanais. The grounds face a 5-mile stretch of white-sand beach.

191 N. Kihei Rd. (north of Hwy. 31, at the Maalaea end of Kihei). www.kealiaresort.com. ✆ **800/265-0686** or 808/280-1192. 51 units. $125–$140 studio double; $160–$200 1-bedroom double; $225–$260 2-bedroom (sleeps up to 4). Children 12 and under stay free in parent's room. Cleaning $75–$125. Reservation fee $25. 4–10 night minimum. **Amenities:** Outdoor pool; free Wi-Fi (some units).

Pineapple Inn Maui ★★ This charming inn (four rooms, plus a two-bedroom cottage) is not only an exquisite find, but also a terrific value. Located in the residential Maui Meadows area, with panoramic ocean views, the two-story inn is expertly landscaped, with a lily pond in the front and a giant saltwater pool and Jacuzzi overlooking the ocean. Each of the expertly decorated, soundproof rooms has a private lanai with an incredible view, plus a small kitchenette (fridge, coffeemaker, toaster, and microwave) that's stocked with juice, pastries, and drinks on your arrival. There's also a darling two-bedroom, one-bathroom cottage (wood floors, beautiful artwork) that's landscaped for maximum privacy and has a full kitchen.

3170 Akala Dr. www.pineappleinnmaui.com. ✆ **877/212-MAUI** (6284) or 808/298-4403. 5 units. $159–$189 double; from $215 cottage for 4. 3-night minimum for rooms, 6-night minimum for cottage. No credit cards. **Amenities:** Jacuzzi; large saltwater pool; no phone in rooms; free Wi-Fi.

Punahoa Beach Apartments ★ With its quiet location, on a white sand beach and moderate pricing, what else could you want? Shopping and restaurants are all within walking distance. Units go quickly in winter, so reserve early.

2142 Iliili Rd. (off S. Kihei Rd., 300 ft. from Kamaole Beach I). www.punahoabeach.com. ✆ **800/564-4380** or 808/879-2720. 13 units. $132–$224 studio double; $164–$299 1-bedroom double; $234–$315 2-bedroom double; $229–$324 1-bedroom penthouse. Extra person $15. $125–$150 cleaning fee. 5-night minimum. **Amenities:** Free Wi-Fi.

Inexpensive

Dreams Come True on Maui ★ This B&B was a dream come true for hosts Tom Croly and Denise McKinnon, who, after years of vacationing in Maui, opened this three-unit property in 2002. It's centrally located in the Maui Meadows subdivision, just a few minutes' drive to golf courses, tennis courts, white-sand beaches, shopping, and restaurants in Kihei and Wailea. The one-bedroom oceanview cottage has a gourmet kitchen, two TVs, washer/

dryer, computer with high-speed Internet access, and wraparound decks. Also available are two rooms in the house, each with TV, private entrance, kitchenette, use of washer/dryer, and lots of other amenities not usually found in B&Bs. The owners also have a one- and two-bedroom condo, across the street from the beach, which they rent for $1,045 to $1,295 per week.

3259 Akala Dr. www.dreamscometrueonmaui.com. © **877/782-9628** or 808/879-7099. 3 units. $104–$199 double (3- to 4-night minimum). Room rates include continental breakfast for the B&B guest rooms. **Amenities:** Beach equipment; A/C; free Wi-Fi.

Nona Lani Cottages ★   Old Hawaii: eight stand-alone cottages, tucked among palm, fruit, and sweet-smelling flower trees, right across the street from a white-sand beach. This is one of the great hidden deals in Kihei. The tiny cottages feature complete kitchens, twin beds that double as couches in the living room, a separate bedroom with a queen-size bed, and a lanai. The real attraction, however, is the garden setting next to the beach. There are no phones in the cabins, but there's a public one by the registration/check-in area.

455 S. Kihei Rd. (just south of Hwy. 31). www.nonalanicottages.com. © **800/733-2688** or 808/879-2497. 11 units. $140–$190 suite double; $170–$220 cottage double. Extra person $25. 3-night minimum for cottages. **Amenities:** Free Wi-Fi.

Tutu Mermaids on Maui B&B (Also Known as the Two Mermaids) ★   The two mermaids, Juddee and Miranda, both avid scuba divers, offer a friendly B&B in a quiet neighborhood, just a 10-minute walk from the beach. Continental breakfast, with some of the best homemade bread on the island, is placed on your doorstep every morning (so you can sleep in). Amenities include a range of complimentary beach equipment, microwave popcorn, and a barbecue area. Juddee is a licensed minister who can perform weddings, just in case you're in the mood.

2840 Umalu Place. www.twomermaids.com. © **808/874-8687.** 2 units. $145–$190 studio double; $175–$230 double 1- to 2-bedroom apt. Rates include continental breakfast. 3- to 5-night minimum. Credit cards through PayPal. **Amenities:** Babysitting; golf nearby; hot tub; outdoor pool; nearby tennis courts; free Wi-Fi.

What a Wonderful World B&B ★   One of Maui's finest bed-and-breakfasts, centrally located in Kihei (a half-mile from Kamaole II Beach Park; 5 min. from Wailea golf courses; convenient to shopping and restaurants) also features budget prices. Continental breakfast on the lanai, with views of white-sand beaches, the West Maui Mountains, and Haleakala, just add to the value.

2828 Umalu Place (off Keonakai St., near Hwy. 31). www.amauibedandbreakfast.com. © **800/943-5804** or 808/879-9103. 4 units. $90–$195 double. Children 11 and under stay free in parent's room. Rates include breakfast. **Amenities:** Hot tub; computer; barbecue grill; free Wi-Fi.

WAILEA-MAKENA

If money is no problem, the best pick is the **Four Seasons Resort Maui at Wailea ★★★** (www.fourseasons.com/maui; © **800/311-0630** or 808/874-8000), where rooms start at $499 a night—and go up from there. The least expensive oceanfront resort in this area is the **Wailea Beach Marriott Resort & Spa** ★★ (www.waileamarriott.com; ✆ 800/367-2960 or 808/879-1922), where room rates begin at $312 a night. For a complete selection of condo units throughout Wailea and Makena, contact **Destination Residences Hawaii** (www.drhmaui.com; ✆ 866/384-1366 or 808/891-6249). Its luxury units include studio doubles starting at $169, one-bedroom doubles from $178, two-bedrooms from $203, and three-bedrooms from $262. At most properties, those rates include free long-distance calls, Internet, and parking; one property, the Polo Beach Club, is completely nonsmoking (indoors and out). Children under 12 stay free; minimum stays vary by property.

Expensive

Andaz Maui at Wailea ★★★ The newest resort in Wailea opened to rave reviews—small wonder, considering its prime beachfront locale, chic decor, apothecary-style spa, and two phenomenal restaurants, including one by superstar chef Masaharu Morimoto. Accommodations here aren't the island's largest, but they ramp up the style quotient a notch with crisp white linens, warm wood furniture, and mid-century accents. Wrap yourself in a plush robe and nosh on the complimentary minibar snacks from the sanctuary of your private lanai. Wander past the tiered infinity pools, then hit gorgeous Mokapu Beach, and whatever you do, don't miss the Awili Spa.

3550 Wailea Ala Nui Dr. www.maui.andaz.hyatt.com/en/hotel/home.html. ✆ 808/573-1234. 297 rooms. $430–$505. Suites from $660. Resort fee $40. Extra person $50. Valet parking only, $30. **Amenities:** 5 restaurants; 4 lounges; children's program; 24-hour concierge; fitness center; 7 outdoor pools; room service; spa; watersport equipment rentals; free Wi-Fi.

The Fairmont Kea Lani Maui ★★★ For the price of a regular room at the neighboring luxury resorts, you get an entire suite here—plus some extras. Each unit in the all-suite hotel has a kitchenette with granite countertop, living room with sofa bed (great for kids), spacious bedroom, marble bathroom with deep soaking tub, and large lanai with views of the pools, lawns, and Pacific Ocean. Polo Beach is public, but feels private and secluded. Huge murals and artifacts decorate the resort's manicured property, which is home to several good restaurants, an excellent bakery and deli, and the Willow Stream Spa.

4100 Wailea Alanui Dr., Wailea. www.fairmont.com/kealani. ✆ 866/540-4456 or 808/875-4100. 450 units. $459–$1,259 suite (sleeps up to 4). $35 resort fee. Valet parking $27; free self-parking. **Amenities:** 4 restaurants, plus gourmet bakery and deli; 3 bars; babysitting; children's program; year-round concierge; 24-hr. fitness center; 2 large swimming lagoons connected by a 140-ft. water slide and swim-up bar, plus an adults-only pool; 24-hr. room service; luxury spa and salon; watersports equipment rentals and 1-hr. complimentary use of snorkel equipment; free Wi-Fi.

Grand Wailea ★★★ Built by a Japanese multi-millionaire at the pinnacle of Hawaii's fling with fantasy megaresorts, the Grand Wailea is wildly popular with families and corporate groups. No expense was spared during construction: Some $30 million worth of original artwork decorates the grounds and more than 10,000 tropical plants beautify the lobby alone. Guest rooms, too, are lavish, with oversized bathrooms and plush bedding. But for kids, all that really matters is the resort's unrivaled pool: an aquatic playground with nine separate swimming pools connected by slides, waterfalls, caves, rapids, a Tarzan swing, a swim-up bar, a baby beach, and a water elevator that shuttles swimmers back to the top. If this doesn't sate them, an actual beach of real golden sand awaits just past the resort hammocks. The Grand is also home to Hawaii's largest and most resplendent spa: a 50,000-square-foot marble paradise with mineral soaking tubs, thundering waterfall showers, Japanese furo baths, Swiss jet showers, and many other luxurious features. Dining options include the incredible **Humuhumunukunukuapua'a,** where you can fish for your lobster straight from the lagoon.

3850 Wailea Alanui Dr., Wailea. www.grandwailea.com. ℂ **800/888-6100** or 808/875-1234. 780 units. $504–$1,084 double; from $1,219 suite; from $679 Napua Club Room (in Napua Tower); from $1,195 Hoolei Villas. Extra person $50 ($100 in Napua Tower). $30 daily resort fee. Valet parking only $30. **Amenities:** 5 restaurants; 4 bars; art and garden tours; babysitting; children's program; concierge; concierge-level rooms; use of Wailea Golf Club's 3 18-hole championship golf courses; fitness center; fitness classes; 5 Jacuzzis (including one atop a man-made volcano); adults-only outdoor pool; 2,000-ft.-long Activity Pool; room service; luxury spa and salon; scuba-diving clinics; racquetball court; use of Wailea Tennis Center's 11 courts (3 lit for night play) and pro shop; shuttle service to Wailea; watersports equipment rentals; free Wi-Fi.

Upcountry Maui

You'll find it cool and peaceful up here. Be sure to bring a sweater.

MAKAWAO

Here you'll be (relatively) close to Haleakala National Park; Makawao is approximately 90 minutes from the entrance to the park at the 7,000-foot level (from there it's another 3,000 ft. and 30–45 min. to get to the top). Accommodations in Kula are the only ones closer to the park.

If you'd like your own private cottage, consider **Peace of Maui,** 1290 Haliimaile Rd. (just outside Haliimaile town, at 1290 Haliimaile Rd.; www.peaceofmaui.com; ℂ **808/572-5045**), which has a full kitchen, two bedrooms, a day bed, and a large deck. The cottage goes for $195 ($75 cleaning fee, 7-night minimum) and children are welcome. The owners also have rooms in the main house (with shared bathroom and kitchen facilities) from $95 double.

Ginger Falls Vacation Rental Cottage ★★ Honeymooners: It's worth a splurge for this cozy, romantic, intimate cottage, hidden in Miliko Gulch, overlooking a stream with a waterfall, bamboo, sweet-smelling ginger, and banana trees. The Hawaiiana-decorated cottage has a full kitchen with every possible utensil.

355 Kaluanui Rd. www.wildgingerfalls.com. ℂ **808/573-1173.** 1 unit. $185–$205 double. $75 cleaning fee. 3- to 5-night minimum. Payment through PayPal. **Amenities:** Outdoor hot tub; free Wi-Fi.

Hale Ho'okipa Inn Makawao ★ Just a 10-minute walk from the shops and restaurants of Makawao, a 15 minute-drive to beaches, and an hour's drive from the top of Haleakala, this quaint B&B allows you to step back in time at this 1924 plantation-style home. The guest rooms have separate outside entrances and private bathrooms. No children under the age of 9.

32 Pakani Place. www.maui-bed-and-breakfast.com. ✆ **877/572-6698** or 808/572-6698. 4 units (2 shower only). $125–$175 double. Rates include continental breakfast. No children 9 or under allowed. **Amenities:** Free Wi-Fi.

KULA (AT THE BASE OF HALEAKALA NATIONAL PARK)

Lodgings in Kula are the closest option to the entrance of Haleakala National Park (about 60 min. away).

Kula View Bed & Breakfast ★ Hostess and gardener extraordinaire Susan Kauai has this cute private suite (with its own deck and private entrance) upstairs in her home. The roomy studio sports a huge deck with a panoramic view of Haleakala. Inside, there's a reading area with a comfy lounge chair and an eating space with table and chairs, toaster oven, coffee-maker, and electric teakettle. Susan serves breakfast in your suite (or will pack a picnic breakfast if you are out early). She also has plenty of warm jackets, sweaters, and blankets you can borrow if you plan to make the trip to the top of Haleakala. Be sure to take a stroll through her magical garden.

600 Holopuni Rd. www.kulaview.com. ✆ **808/878-6736.** 1 suite. $130 double. Rate includes continental breakfast. 2-night minimum. Credit cards through Pay Pal.

WHERE TO EAT

You can dine well at Lahaina's open-air waterfront watering holes, where the view counts for 50% of the experience. There are still budget eateries, but not many; Maui's old-fashioned, multigenerational mom-and-pop diners are disappearing, eclipsed by the flashy newcomers, or clinging to the edge of existence in the older neighborhoods of Central Maui, like lovable Wailuku. Although you'll have to work harder to find them in the resort areas, you won't have to go far to find creative cuisine, pleasing style, and stellar dining experiences. In the listings below, reservations are not necessary unless otherwise noted.

Central Maui

The **Queen Kaahumanu Center,** the structure that looks like a white *Star Wars* umbrella in the center of Kahului, at 275 Kaahumanu Ave. (10 min. from Kahului Airport on Hwy. 32), has a very popular food court. Eateries include **Ramen Ya** for a steaming bowl of noodles and **Maui Tacos.**

MODERATE

Class Act ★ GLOBAL Serving top gourmet cuisine at budget prices, this program is run by Maui Community College. Offering 4 course lunches in a state-of-the-art, $15-million culinary facility (with floor-to-ceiling windows at one end, and an exhibition kitchen at the other), Class Act is a classroom restaurant with a huge following. Book at least a week in advance.

At Maui Community College, 310 Kaahumanu Ave. www.mauiculinary-campusdining. com. ✆ **808/984-3280.** Reservations recommended. 4-course lunch $30–$40. Wed and Fri 11am–12:30pm (last seating). Closed early May–Aug for summer vacation and parts of Dec and Jan.

A Saigon Cafe ★★ VIETNAMESE   Great Vietnamese cuisine at affordable prices. Tricky to find; call for directions.

1792 Main St., Wailuku. © **808/243-9560.** Main courses $12–$30. Daily 10am–9:30pm (Sun till 8:30pm).

INEXPENSIVE

Down to Earth ★ ORGANIC HEALTH FOOD   If you're looking for a healthy alternative to fast foods, here's your place. Fully organic ingredients, 90% vegan, appear in scrumptious salads, lasagna, chili, curries, and dozens of tasty dishes, presented at hot and cold serve-yourself stations. The food is sold by the pound, but you can buy a hearty, wholesome plate for $8 or $9. Vitamin supplements, health-food products, fresh produce, and cosmetics fill the rest of the store.

305 Dairy Rd. www.downtoearth.org. © **808/877-2661.** Self-serve hot buffet and salad bar and deli, food sold by the pound, average $7–$10 for a plate; sandwiches $6–$10. Serving hours Mon–Sat 7am–9pm; Sun 7am–8pm. Store hours Mon–Sat 7am–10pm; Sun 7am–9pm.

West Maui

LAHAINA

There's a **Maui Tacos** (p. 163) in Lahaina Square (© **808/661-8883**). Maui's branch of the **Hard Rock Cafe** is at 900 Front St. (© **808/667-7400**).

Very Expensive

The Feast at Lele ★★ POLYNESIAN   The owners of the Old Lahaina Luau (see "A Night to Remember: Luau, Maui-Style" on p. 206) have teamed up with renowned chef James McDonald (Pacific'O; see below) on a new

EAT LIKE A local

Are you the type of visitor who feels that you just haven't "experienced" a destination unless you've hit the restaurants where the local residents eat? Then **Tour da Food** ★★★ (© **808/242-8383;** www.tourdafood.com) is for you. Pastry chef (and food writer, restaurant publicist, and cookbook author) Bonnie Friedman takes foodies off the tourist path to discover the culinary treasurers—from snack shacks to restaurants to markets and manufacturers—that make up Maui's unique cuisine. You will laugh your way across the island with Bonnie's wonderful commentary about Maui's multicultural food options and its colorful history, and you'll also eat some of the island's yummiest food (which you never would have discovered on your own). Check out her website to read about the different tours. Tour prices start at $425 for two people and include transportation, bottled water, an insulated carrying bag filled with local goodies and snacks, and Bonnie's personalized up-to-the-minute guide on new restaurants you can't miss. *Tip:* Book early so you can take advantage of Bonnie's under-the-radar restaurant recommendations.

Hotels & Restaurants in Lahaina & Kaanapali

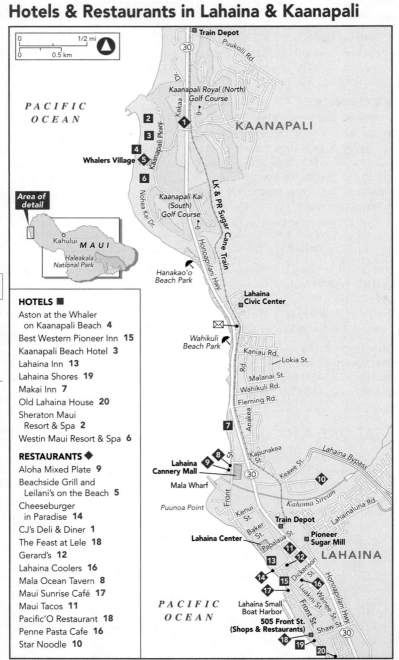

HOTELS ■
Aston at the Whaler
  on Kaanapali Beach **4**
Best Western Pioneer Inn **15**
Kaanapali Beach Hotel **3**
Lahaina Inn **13**
Lahaina Shores **19**
Makai Inn **7**
Old Lahaina House **20**
Sheraton Maui
  Resort & Spa **2**
Westin Maui Resort & Spa **6**

RESTAURANTS ◆
Aloha Mixed Plate **9**
Beachside Grill and
  Leilani's on the Beach **5**
Cheeseburger
  in Paradise **14**
CJ's Deli & Diner **1**
The Feast at Lele **18**
Gerard's **12**
Lahaina Coolers **16**
Mala Ocean Tavern **8**
Maui Sunrise Café **17**
Maui Tacos **11**
Pacific'O Restaurant **18**
Penne Pasta Cafe **16**
Star Noodle **10**

venue, placed it in a perfect outdoor oceanfront setting, and added the exquisite dancers of the Old Lahaina Luau. The result: a culinary and cultural experience that sizzles. Dances from Hawaii, New Zealand, Tahiti, and Samoa are presented, up close and personal, in full costumed splendor. Guests sit at white-clothed, candlelit tables set on the sand and dine on entrees from the islands: *imu*-roasted kalua pig and Island fish with mango sauce from Hawaii, Maori fishcake, and sea bean and duck salad from New Zealand.

505 Front St. www.feastatlele.com. © **866/244-5353** or 808/667-5353. Reservations required. Set 5-course menu (includes all beverages) $125 adults, $95 children 2–12. May–Aug daily 6:30–9:30pm; Oct–Jan daily 5:30–9pm; Feb–Apr and Sept 6–8:30pm.

Expensive

Gerard's ★★★ FRENCH Traditional French, served in a comfortable atmosphere at splurge prices. Chef Gerard Reversade has called Hawai'i home for nearly 4 decades, but his French accent hasn't lost one *cédille*. His charming residence-turned-restaurant beneath the Plantation Inn in Lahaina is equally authentic. The roasted '*opakapaka* served with fennel fondue and spiked with hints of orange and ginger is stellar, as is the grilled Hawaiian filet with salsify au gratin. For dessert don't miss the marvelous *millefeuille*.

At the Plantation Inn, 174 Lahainaluna Rd. www.gerardsmaui.com. © **808/661-8939.** Reservations recommended. Main courses $39–$59. Daily 6–9pm.

Pacific'O Restaurant ★ CONTEMPORARY PACIFIC RIM Foodie alert: Award-winning seafood dishes, with touches of India and Indonesia, are delivered to you at this oceanfront restaurant with the backdrop of Lanai across the channel. It's pricey but memorable.

505 Front St. www.pacificomaui.com. © **808/667-4341.** Reservations recommended. Main courses $15–$18 lunch, $28–$46 dinner. Daily 11:30am–4pm; Happy Hour 4–5:30pm; dinner 5:30–9pm.

Moderate

Lahaina Coolers ★ AMERICAN/INTERNATIONAL An open-air, casual eatery with big servings of American favorites with great breakfasts; good burgers at lunch; and dinners ranging from pasta (Asian-style) and pizza to steak. Everything can be prepared vegetarian-style upon request.

180 Dickenson St. www.lahainacoolers.com. © **808/661-7082.** Main courses $8–$15 breakfast, $11–$16 lunch, $17–$28 dinner. Daily 8am–midnight (bar open until 1am).

Mala Ocean Tavern ★★ LOCAL/SEAFOOD Perched right on the ocean, this tiny "tavern" is the brainchild of Mark and Judy Ellman, owners of Maui Tacos. Their culinary philosophy runs to healthy, organically grown food and fresh fish, all used to make intriguing dishes. Don't miss the weekend brunches (I recommend the "killer" French toast). This is a popular place, so avoid prime lunch and dinner hours.

1307 Front St. (across from Lahaina Cannery Mall's Safeway supermarket). www.mala oceantavern.com. © **808/667-9394.** Main courses $15–$27 lunch, $19–$46 dinner, brunch $8–$20. Tavern menu $15–$20. Mon–Fri 11am–9:30pm; Sat–Sun 9am–9pm.

Star Noodle ★★ NOODLES/FUSION   This hip noodle house at the top of Lahaina's industrial park offers a deceivingly simple menu of noodles and share plates. Each dish is a gourmet twist on a local favorite; the *hapa ramen,* with its smoky pork and spicy miso broth, is guaranteed to be unlike any you've had before. With its stylish bar, long communal table, and Shepard Fairey artwork, there's a real urban vibe here; but the laid-back locals, who often opt for takeout when the wait's too long, will remind you that you're still in surf-centric Maui.

286 Kupuohi St., Lahaina. www.starnoodle.com. ☎ **808/667-5400.** Main courses $6–$15. Daily 10:30am–10pm.

Inexpensive

Aloha Mixed Plate ★ PLATE LUNCHES/BEACHSIDE GRILL   Right on the ocean, in the middle of tourist-heavy Lahaina, this local favorite dishes out budget-friendly breakfasts and island-style plate lunches: fresh-made chow mein, teriyaki chicken, and Korean kalbi ribs with the proverbial two-scoops-rice and macaroni salad. If you have a hankering for a *loco moco* (hamburger, rice, and an egg ladled with gravy), this is your spot. It's also a sweet hideaway at happy hour (2–6pm).

1285 Front St. www.alohamixedplate.com. ☎ **808/661-3322.** Main courses $7–$17. Daily 8–10:30am and 11am–10pm.

Cheeseburger in Paradise ★ AMERICAN   The biggest, juiciest beef and chicken burgers, served on whole-wheat or fresh baked sesame buns at this oceanfront eatery make it wildly successful (good value, good grinds, and a great ocean view).

811 Front St. www.cheeseburgerland.com. ☎ **808/661-4855.** Burgers $11–$16. Daily 8am–10pm. Second location: 3750 Wailua Ala Nui Dr. ☎ **808/874-8990.**

Maui Sunrise Café ★ GOURMET DELI/CAFE   For the best budget breakfast and lunch, follow the surfers to this teeny cafe on Front Street, next door to the library. Eat in the patio garden out back or take your lunch to the beach. You'll find huge breakfasts, delicious gourmet sandwiches, and filling lunch plates all at bargain prices.

693A Front St. ☎ **808/661-8558.** Breakfast items under $14; lunch items $7–$14. No credit cards. Daily 7am–3:30pm.

Penne Pasta Cafe ★ ITALIAN/MEDITERRANEAN   Bargain hunters head for this neighborhood cafe, under the helm of chef Juan Gomez, partner of Mark Ellman's (of Maui Tacos and Mala Tavern fame) until he recently bought the cafe. It features delicious Italian and Mediterranean cuisine at takeout prices, and mamma mia!—those are big plates of pasta, pizzas, salads, and sandwiches. So, what's the catch? No waitstaff. You order at the counter and your order is delivered to your table.

180 Dickenson St. www.pennepastacafe.com. ☎ **808/661-6633.** Basic menu items $10–$16; specials up to $19. Daily 11am–9:30pm.

KAANAPALI

Whalers Village, 2435 Kaanapali Pkwy. (www.whalersvillage.com/restaurants. htm), has a food court where you can buy pizza, island food, ice cream, sandwiches, wraps, and fast-food burgers at serve-yourself counters. It's an inexpensive alternative and a quick, handy stop for shoppers and Kaanapali beachgoers.

Moderate

Beachside Grill/Leilani's on the Beach ★ STEAK/SEAFOOD   The
Beachside Grill is the informal, less-expensive room downstairs on the beach, where folks wander in off the sand for a frothy beer and a beachside burger. Leilani's is the dinner-only room, with more expensive but still not outrageously priced steak and seafood offerings. All of this, of course, comes with an ocean view. There's live music Wednesday through Sunday, from 3 to 5pm. *Budget tip:* From 3 to 5pm in the Grill, there are special prices on pupus and drinks; 5 to 5:45pm, the dining room offers a 3-course dinner for $26.

At Whalers Village, 2435 Kaanapali Pkwy. www.leilanis.com. ℭ **808/661-4495.** Reservations suggested for dinner. Beachside Grill lunch and dinner $15–$24; Leilani's dinner $26–$44. Beachside Grill daily 11am–11pm; Leilani's daily 5–9:30pm.

Inexpensive

CJ's Deli & Diner ★ AMERICAN/DELI   Comfort food at knock-your-
socks-off prices. Not much atmosphere, but at these budget prices, who cares? Big breakfasts with everything from waffles to eggs, and deli sandwiches and burgers to pot roast, ribs, and fish dishes at lunch. If you are on your way to Hana or up to the top of Haleakala, stop by and get a box lunch. CJ's even has a menu for the kids. *Tip:* Check out their "Chefs to Go" menu, comfort food you can take home and heat!

At the Fairway Shops at Kaanapali, 2580 Kekaa Dr. (just off the Honoapiilani Hwy.). www.cjsmaui.com. ℭ **808/667-0968.** Breakfast items $6–$12; lunch and dinner items $9–$19; Hana Lunch Box and Air Travel Lunch Box $12 each. Daily 7am–8pm.

HONOKOWAI, KAHANA & NAPILI

Inexpensive

Maui Tacos ★ MEXICAN   Celebrity Chef Mark Ellman put gourmet Mexican on paper plates and on the island's culinary map long before Maui became known as Hawaii's center for salsa and chimichangas. Not much more than a takeout counter with a few tables, this and the other Maui Tacos in Hawaii (six on Maui alone) are popular with hungry surfers, discerning diners, burrito buffs, and Hollywood glitterati. Expect good food but not very fast service. Ellman has sold the company, but that has not made a dent in the long lines. Other locations include Lahaina Square (ℭ **808/661-8883**); Kamaole Beach Center (ℭ **808/879-5005**); Piilani Village (ℭ **808/875-9340**); and Kaahumanu Center (ℭ **808/871-7726**).

At Napili Plaza, 5095 Napilihau St. www.mauitacos.com. ℭ **808/665-0222.** All items $8–$14. Daily 9am–9pm.

KAPALUA
Very Expensive
Merriman's ★★★ PACIFIC RIM   This is probably the most beautiful location for a restaurant in the state: jutting out on a promontory into the ocean, overlooking Kapalua Bay on one side and the island of Molokai in the distance. James Beard award–winning chef opened this spectacular oceanside restaurant to rave reviews from major food publications. This is the place for a romantic splurge dinner to sample farm-to-table cuisine such as Haleakala Ranch–raised lamb, or his well-known wok-charred ahi served with pumpkin puree and tangerine-green peppercorn jus. *Insider tip:* Book your reservation for sunset to really experience the incredible romantic views. If sunset tables are booked, come for sunset anyway and sit on the large open-air patio out on the point, and enjoy a cocktail and an appetizer. Merriman's offers a "Shared Tasting Menu," 4 courses for $75 per person.

1 Bay Club Place, Kapalua Resort. www.merrimanshawaii.com. © **808/669-6400.** Reservations recommended. Dinner $31–$62. Daily 5–9pm. Point Bar with a brief menu daily 3–9pm. Sunday brunch 9:30am–1:30pm $14–$24.

Moderate
Sansei Seafood Restaurant & Sushi Bar ★★ PACIFIC RIM/SUSHI   Perpetual award-winner Sansei offers an extensive menu of Japanese and East-West delicacies. Part fusion, part Hawaii Regional Cuisine, Sansei is tirelessly creative, with a menu that scores higher with adventurous palates than with purists. (There's karaoke Thurs–Sat nights 10pm–1am.) *Money-saving tip:* Eat early; all food is 25% off between 5:15 and 6pm (Sun and Mon 5:15–6pm is 50% off!). Also at Kihei Town Center (© **808/879-0004**).

600 Office Rd. www.sanseihawaii.com. © **808/669-6286.** Reservations recommended. Main courses $16–$65. Sat–Wed 5:15–10pm, Thurs–Fri 5:15pm–1am.

South Maui
KIHEI/MAALAEA
There's a branch of **Maui Tacos** (see review above) at Kamaole Beach Center (© **808/879-5005**).

Moderate
Cafe O'Lei Kihei ★★ STEAK/SEAFOOD   The creative dishes here are so delicious that you won't even notice the lack of view. Atmosphere is relaxing and inviting. And food is not only outstanding, but also a real bargain. You can't beat the daily plate lunch for $8 (arrive early, as the locals are well aware of this wonderful gem and will book all the tables in advance). Dinners range from fresh fish to roast Japanese eggplant & quinoa for the vegetarians.

2439 S. Kihei Rd. www.cafeoleimaui.com. © **808/891-1368.** Reservations recommended. Main courses $8–$16 lunch, $17–$27 dinner. Daily 10:30am–3:30pm and 4:30–9:30pm. Other locations: Kahalui © 808/877-0073; Makawao © 808/572-8711; and Kamaole © 808/875-7522.

Inexpensive

Joy's Place ★ HEALTHY DELI/SANDWICHES   If you're in Kihei and looking for a healthy, delicious breakfast or lunch at a rock-bottom price, it's worth hunting around for Joy's Place. This tiny hole in the wall has humongous sandwiches, fresh salads, hot items (falafel and veggie burgers), soups, and desserts. Most items are organic. There are a few places to sit inside, and the beach is just a 2-minute walk away.

In the Island Surf Bldg., 1993 S. Kihei Rd. (entrance on Auhana St.). www.joysplace mauihawaii.com ✆ **808/879-9258.** All items under $13. Mon–Sat 7:30am–4pm.

Peggy Sue's ★ AMERICAN   This 1950s-style diner has sodas, shakes, floats, egg creams, milkshakes, and scoops of made-on-Maui Roselani gourmet ice cream. Old-fashioned soda-shop stools, an Elvis Presley Boulevard sign, and jukeboxes on every Formica table serve as a backdrop for the famous burgers (and veggie burgers), brushed with teriyaki sauce and served with all the goodies. The fries are great, too.

At the Azeka Place II Shopping Center, 1279 S. Kihei Rd. http://peggysuesmaui.com. ✆ **808/214-6786.** Burgers $10–$12; plate lunches $7–$17. Daily 11am–9pm (till 10pm Sat).

WAILEA

The **Shops at Wailea,** on sprawling grounds between the Grand Wailea and Outrigger Wailea Resort, has added a spate of new shops and restaurants to this stretch of South Maui. Five restaurants and dozens of shops, most of them upscale, are among the new tenants of this complex. **Ruth's Chris Steak House** is here, as well as **Tommy Bahama's Tropical Cafe & Emporium, Honolulu Coffee Company, Kai Wailea, Longhi's, Cheeseburger Island Style,** and **Lappert's Ice Cream.**

Very Expensive

Ka'ana Kitchen ★★★ HAWAII REGIONAL CUISINE   You can hardly tell where the dining room ends and the kitchen begins in this bright, open restaurant. Ask to sit ringside where you can watch award-winning chef Isaac Bancaco action. Start off with a hand-mixed cocktail and the grilled octopus: fat chunks of tender meat tossed with frisée, watercress, and goat cheese. The *ahi tataki* is edible artwork: ruby-red tuna, heirloom tomato, and fresh burrata decorated with black salt and nasturtium petals. Don't be thrown off by Bancaco's grid menu. Treat it like a gourmet bingo card; every combo is a winner. Breakfasts here are among the island's best, with local poached eggs, Molokai sweet potatoes, and creative bento boxes.

At the Andaz Maui, 3550 Wailea Alanui Dr., Wailea. www.maui.andaz.hyatt.com. ✆ **808/573-1234.** Main courses $18–$67 breakfast, $17–$56 dinner. Daily 6:30–11am and 5:30–9pm.

Ko ★★ GOURMET PLANTATION CUISINE   *Ko* is Hawaiian for sugarcane, and this restaurant revives the true melting pot of Maui's bygone plantation days. Chef Tylun Pang takes the ethnic foods of the islands' Japanese, Filipino, Chinese, Portuguese, and Korean immigrants and presents them in gourmet fashion, in a spectacularly renovated restaurant. The "ahi on the rock" appetizer is a must-order: large squares of seasoned ruby-red tuna delivered with a hot *ishiyaki* stone. Sear the ahi on the rock, then submerge it in orange-ginger miso sauce. On Sundays, a special Hawaiian *laulau* is served: fresh fish, shellfish, and bok choy steamed in ti leaves; it's a marvelous recreation of a traditional island meal.

At the Fairmont Kea Lani, 4100 Wailea Alanui Dr., Wailea. www.korestaurant.com. © **808/875-4100.** Reservations recommended. Main courses $22–$51 lunch, $28–$58 dinner. Daily 11:30am–2:30pm and 5–9pm.

Morimoto Maui ★★★ JAPANESE/PERUVIAN   "Iron Chef" Masaharu Morimoto is a culinary force to be reckoned with. His new Maui restaurant sits beside the pool at Andaz where decor is sedate and spare, directing all of the attention to the culinary fireworks. If you can afford it, go for the *omakase*—the chef's tasting menu—it starts with his signature appetizer, the toro tartare. The chef's tribute to Maui features locally caught *opakapaka* (pink snapper) in Thai curry with pohole fern. Everything is indulgent here: A *chawanmushi* (Japanese custard) is flavored with foie gras and topped with slivered duck breast and an amazing crispy, salty, fatty seared pork is amplified by sweet poha berry. The incredibly decadent lunch features flatbreads, sushi, Asian-inspired sandwiches, and many of the items served at dinner.

At the Andaz Maui, 3550 Wailea Alanui Dr., Wailea. www.maui.andaz.hyatt.com. © **808/573-1234.** Main courses $18–$39 lunch, $36–$95 dinner. Daily 11:30am–2pm; sushi 2–5pm; dinner 5:30–9:30pm.

Moderate

Gannon's—A Pacific View Restaurant ★★ ISLAND   Formerly the Seawatch Restaurant, now under the creative hand of celebrity chef Bev Gannon (see Joe's and Haliimaile General Store, below), Gannon's is a good choice from morning to evening, and it's one of the more affordable stops in tony Wailea. You'll dine on the terrace or in a high-ceilinged room, from a menu that carries the tee-off-to-19th-hole crowd with ease. From breakfast on, it's a celebration of Island bounty with dishes like crabcake eggs Benedict; at lunch it's everything from fish burger to blackened fish tacos and salads; and dinner features such goodies as tandoori loin of lamb, venison, and grilled rib-eye steak. The ocean views are fabulous.

At the Wailea Golf Club Gold Course, 100 Wailea Golf Club Dr. www.bevgannon restaurants.com. © **808/875-8080.** Reservations recommended for dinner. Main courses $10–$30 breakfast, $9–$40 lunch, $21–$69 dinner. Daily 8:30am–3pm and 5:30–9pm; bar food 3–8pm.

Upcountry Maui
HALIIMAILE (ON THE WAY TO UPCOUNTRY MAUI)
Moderate

Haliimaile General Store ★★★ HAWAII REGIONAL/AMERICAN
For a couple of decades, Bev Gannon, one of the original Hawaii Regional Cuisine chefs, has been going strong at her foodie haven in the pineapple

fields. You'll dine at tables set on old wood floors under high ceilings, eating a blend of eclectic American with ethnic touches; even the fresh-catch sandwich on the lunch menu is anything but prosaic, sort of a bridge between Hawaii and Gannon's Texas roots.

900 Haliimaile Rd. www.bevgannonrestaurants.com. ✆ **808/572-2666.** Reservations recommended. Main courses $16–$26 lunch, $28–$46 dinner. Mon–Fri 11am–2:30pm; daily 5–9pm.

MAKAWAO & PUKALANI
Moderate
Market Fresh Bistro ★★ HAWAIIAN/MEDITERRANEAN   Attention foodies: Plan to eat dinner here at least once during your stay on Maui. Yes, it is a long drive from a resort area and yes, parking is on the street and you may have to walk a block or two, but Chef Justin Pardo (formerly of the Union Square Cafe in New York City and the Wailea Grand on Maui) is a culinary genius. He uses 90% local products and is having fun creating menus at this off-the-beaten-path restaurant, hidden in a mini-mall complex behind the Makawao Steak House. The menu changes daily—ranging from an appetizer of pan-seared sea scallops with a curried watermelon gazpacho to a pork loin wrapped in applewood-smoked bacon.

3620 Baldwin Ave. www.marketfreshbistromaui.com. ✆ **808/572-4877.** Reservations required for dinner. Breakfast $10–$15; lunch $11–$22; dinner $75 (add $45 for wine). Tues–Sat 9am–3pm; Sunday brunch 9am–2pm; Thurs prix-fixe 6–8pm.

Inexpensive
Casanova Italian Restaurant ★ ITALIAN   In the cool environs of Upcountry, in the heart of cowboy country, lies this Italian pasta heaven and center of nightlife in Makawao. From the spinach gnocchi to grilled lamb chops in an Italian mushroom marinade, you'll leave with a smile. Check their website for a live entertainment calendar.

1188 Makawao Ave. www.casanovamaui.com. ✆ **808/572-0220.** Reservations recommended for dinner. Lunch items $12–$24; dinner main courses $26–$44; 12-in. pizzas $14–$18; pastas $14–$22. Mon–Tues and Thurs–Sat 11:30am–2pm; daily 5–9pm. Dancing or entertainment Wed and Fri–Sat 9:30pm–1am. Lounge daily 5pm–1am. Deli daily 7:30am–5:30pm. Also located in Kahului 33 Lono Ave. ✆ 808/873-3650.

KULA (AT THE BASE OF HALEAKALA NATIONAL PARK)
Moderate
Kula Lodge ★ HAWAII REGIONAL/AMERICAN   The million-dollar vista here spans the flanks of Haleakala, rolling 3,200 feet down to Central Maui, the ocean, and the West Maui Mountains. The Kula Lodge has always been known for its hearty breakfasts. Lunch, especially pizza from the outdoor wood-burning oven, is a good option as well. If possible, go for sunset cocktails and watch the colors change into deep end-of-day hues. When darkness descends, a roaring fire and lodge atmosphere add to the coziness of the room.

15200 Haleakala Hwy. (Hwy. 377). www.kulalodge.com. ✆ **808/878-2517.** Reservations recommended for dinner. Breakfast $11–$22; lunch $17–$38; dinner $24–$38. Daily 7am–9pm.

Kula Sandalwoods Cafe ★ AMERICAN   This is Kula cuisine, with produce from the backyard and everything made from scratch, including French toast made from home-baked Portuguese sweet bread or hotcakes with fresh fruit; open-faced country omelets; hamburgers drenched in a special cheese sauce made with grated sharp cheddar; a killer kalua-pork sandwich; a grilled ono sandwich; and an outstanding veggie burger. Dine in the gazebo or on the terrace, with dazzling views in all directions—including, in the spring, a yard dusted with lavender jacaranda flowers and a hillside ablaze with fields of orange akulikuli blossoms.

15427 Haleakala Hwy. (Hwy. 377). www.kulasandalwoods.com. ✆ **808/878-3523.** Breakfast $9–$16; lunch $8–$17. Mon–Sat 7am–3pm; Sun 7–Noon.

East Maui

PAIA

Moderate

Charley's Restaurant ★ AMERICAN/MEXICAN   Although Charley's (named after Charley P. Woofer, a Great Dane) serves three meals a day, breakfast is really the time to come here. Located in downtown Paia, Charley's is a cross between a 1960s hippie hangout, a windsurfers' power-breakfast spot, and a honky-tonk bar that gets going after dark. Before you head out to Hana, stop at Charley's for a larger-than-life breakfast (eggs, potatoes, toast, and coffee cost about $12). You'll see all walks of life here, from visitors on their way to Hana at 7am to buff windsurfers chowing down at noon to Willie Nelson on his way to the bar to play a tune.

142 Hana Hwy. www.charleysmaui.com. ✆ **808/579-8085.** Breakfast items $10–$17; lunch items $12–$20; dinner main courses $15–$30. Daily 7am–10pm; food served at the bar until about 10:30pm, later on the weekends.

Inexpensive

Milagros Food Company ★ SOUTHWESTERN/SEAFOOD   Home-style cooking draws a crowd at this indoor/outdoor restaurant. If you want a front row seat to watch Paia's tie-dyes, beads, hippie flavor, and well-built windsurfers walk the streets, ask for a table outside. Happy hour in the bar from 3 to 6pm features cheap and fabulous margaritas.

Hana Hwy. and Baldwin Ave. www.milagrosfoodcompany.com. ✆ **808/579-8755.** Main items $9–$22. Daily 11am–10pm.

Paia Fish Market ★ SEAFOOD   Fresh-cooked, cheap, and tasty seafood, salads, pastas, fajitas, and quesadillas are served here; you can take out or enjoy at the few picnic tables inside the restaurant. It's an appealing selection: Cajun-style fresh catch, fresh-fish specials (usually ahi or salmon), fresh-fish tacos and quesadillas, and seafood and chicken pastas. Second location in Kihei. 1913 S. Kihei Rd. ✆ 808/874-8888.

110 Hana Hwy. www.paiafishmarket.com. ✆ **808/579-8030.** Lunch and dinner plates $10–$21. Daily 11am–9:30pm.

HAIKU

Inexpensive

Colleen's at the Cannery ★★★ ECLECTIC   Way, way, way off the beaten path lies this fabulous find in the rural Haiku Cannery Marketplace. Once through the doors, you'll swear you've dropped down into the middle of a hip, chic boutique restaurant in SoHo in Manhattan (only when you look around at the patrons, they are pure Haiku upcountry residents). It's worth the drive to enjoy Colleen's fabulous culinary creations, like a wild-mushroom ravioli with sautéed Portobello mushrooms, tomatoes, herbs, and a roasted-pepper coulis; pan-seared ahi; or filet mignon.

At the Haiku Cannery Marketplace, 810 Haiku Rd. www.colleensinhaiku.com. ⓒ **808/ 575-9211.** Reservations not accepted. Breakfast $7–$15; lunch $9–16; dinner entrees $11–$30. Daily 6am–10pm.

EXPLORING MAUI

Central Maui

Central Maui isn't exactly tourist central; this is where real people live. Most likely, you'll land here and head directly to the beach. However, there are a few sights worth checking out if you feel like a respite from the sun and surf.

WAILUKU & WAIKAPU

Wailuku, the historic gateway to Iao Valley, is worth a visit for a little antiquing and a visit to the **Bailey House Museum** ★, 2375-A Main St. (www. mauimuseum.org; ⓒ **808/244-3326**). Missionary and sugar planter Edward Bailey's 1833 home—an architectural hybrid of stones laid by Hawaiian craftsmen and timbers joined in a display of Yankee ingenuity—is a treasure trove of Hawaiiana. Inside you'll find an eclectic collection, from pre-contact artifacts to Duke Kahanamoku's 1919 redwood surfboard and a koa-wood table given to President Ulysses S. Grant, who had to refuse it because he couldn't accept gifts from foreign countries. It's open Monday through Saturday from 10am to 4pm; admission is $7 for adults, $5 for seniors, and $2 for children 7 to 12.

About 3 miles south of Wailuku lies the tiny one-street village of Waikapu, which has two attractions that are worth a peek. Relive Maui's past by taking a 40-minute narrated tram ride around fields of pineapple, sugar cane, and papaya trees at **Maui Tropical Plantation,** 1670 Honoapiilani Hwy. (www. mauitropicalplantation.com; ⓒ **800/451-6805** or 808/244-7643), a real working plantation open daily from 9am to 4pm. Admission is free; the tram tours, which start at 10am and leave about every hour, are $20 for adults, $10 for kids 3 to 12.

IAO VALLEY ★

A couple of miles north of Wailuku, where the little plantation houses stop and the road climbs ever higher, Maui's true nature begins to reveal itself. The transition from suburban sprawl to raw nature is so abrupt that most people who drive up into the valley don't realize they're suddenly in a rainforest. This is Iao Valley, a 6¼-acre state park whose great nature, history, and beauty have been enjoyed by millions of people from around the world for more than a century. *Iao* (Supreme Light) Valley, 10 miles long and encompassing 4,000 acres, is the eroded volcanic caldera of the West Maui Mountains. No other Hawaiian valley lets you go from seacoast to rainforest so easily. This peaceful valley, full of tropical plants, rainbows, waterfalls, swimming holes, and hiking trails, is a place of solitude, reflection, and escape for residents and visitors alike.

To get here from Wailuku, take Main Street to Iao Valley Road to the entrance to the state park. Two paved walkways loop into the massive green amphitheater, across the bridge of Iao Valley Stream, and along the stream itself. This paved .35-mile loop is Maui's easiest hike—you can take your grandmother on this one. The leisurely walk will allow you to enjoy lovely views of Iao Needle and the lush vegetation.

The feature known as **Iao Needle** is an erosional remnant consisting of basalt dikes. This phallic rock juts an impressive 2,250 feet above sea level. Youngsters play in **Iao Stream,** a peaceful brook that belies its bloody history. In 1790, King Kamehameha the Great and his men engaged in the battle of Iao Valley to gain control of Maui. When the battle ended, so many bodies blocked Iao Stream that the battle site was named *Kepaniwai,* or "Damming of the Waters." An architectural heritage park of Hawaiian, Japanese, Chinese, Filipino, and New England–style houses stands in harmony by Iao Stream at **Kepaniwai Heritage Garden.** This is a good picnic spot, with plenty of tables and benches. You can see ferns, banana trees, and other native and exotic plants in the **Iao Valley Botanic Garden** along the stream.

WHEN TO GO   The park is open daily from 7am to 5:30pm October 1 to March 31, 7am to 6pm, April 1 to September 30; entrance fee is $5 per car. Go early in the morning or late in the afternoon, when the sun's rays slant into the valley and create a mystical mood. You can bring a picnic and spend the day, but be prepared at any time for one of the frequent tropical cloudbursts that soak the valley and swell both waterfalls and streams.

INFORMATION & VISITOR CENTERS For information, contact **Iao Valley State Park,** State Parks and Recreation, 54 S. High St., Room 101 (www.hawaiistateparks.org/parks/maui; ✆ **808/984-8109**).

West Maui
HISTORIC LAHAINA

Back when "there was no God west of the Horn," Lahaina was the capital of Hawaii and the Pacific's wildest port. Today it's a milder version of its old self—mostly a hustle-bustle of whale art, timeshares, and "Just Got Lei'd" T-shirts. I'm not sure the rowdy whalers would be pleased. But if you look hard, you'll still find the historic port town they loved, filled with the kind of history that inspired James Michener to write his best-selling epic novel *Hawaii.*

Baldwin Home Museum ★ HISTORIC SITE The oldest house in Lahaina, this coral-and-rock structure was built in 1834 by Rev. Dwight Baldwin, a doctor with the fourth company of American missionaries to sail round the Horn to Hawaii. The house looks as if Baldwin has just stepped out for a minute to tend a sick neighbor down the street.

Next door is the **Master's Reading Room,** now the headquarters of the **Lahaina Restoration Foundation** (www.lahainarestoration.org; ✆ **808/661-3262**), a plucky band of historians who try to keep this town alive and antique at the same time. Stop in and pick up a self-guided walking-tour map, which will take you to Lahaina's most historic sites. Master's Reading Room is not open to the public.

120 Dickenson St. (at Front St.). www.lahainarestoration.org. ✆ **808/661-3262.** Admission $7 adults (13 years and older), $5 seniors, children 12 and under free. Daily 10am–4pm; Fri until 8:30pm.

Banyan Tree ★ NATURAL ATTRACTION Of all the banyan trees in Hawaii, this is the greatest of all—so big that you can't get it all in your camera's viewfinder. It was only 8 feet tall when it was planted in 1873 by Maui sheriff William O. Smith to mark the 50th anniversary of Lahaina's first Christian mission. Today the big old banyan from India is more than 50 feet tall, has 12 major trunks, and shades two-thirds of an acre in Courthouse Square.

Maluuluolele Park ★ HISTORIC SITE At first glance, this Front Street park appears to be only a hot, dry, dusty softball field. But under home plate is an edge of Mokuula, where a royal compound once stood more than 100 years ago, now buried under tons of red dirt and sand. Here, Prince Kauikeaolui, who ascended the throne as King Kamehameha III when he was only 10, lived with the love of his life, his sister, Princess Nahienaena. Missionaries took a dim view of incest, which was acceptable to Hawaiian nobles in order to preserve the royal bloodline. Torn between love for her brother and the new Christian morality, Nahienaena grew despondent and died at the age of 21. King Kamehameha III, who reigned for 29 years—longer than any other Hawaiian monarch—presided over Hawaii as it went from kingdom to constitutional monarchy, and as power over the islands began to shift from island nobles to missionaries, merchants, and sugar planters. Kamehameha died in 1854; he was 39. In 1918, his royal compound, containing a mausoleum and artifacts of the kingdom, was demolished and covered with dirt to create a public park.

Front and Shaw sts.

Whalers Village ★ SHOPPING CENTER/MUSEUM If you haven't seen a real whale yet, go to **Whalers Village,** 2435 Kaanapali Pkwy., an oceanfront shopping center that has adopted the whale as its mascot. You can't miss it: A huge, almost life-size metal sculpture of a mother whale and two nursing calves greets you. A few more steps, and you're met by the looming, bleached-white skeleton of a 40-foot sperm whale; it's pretty impressive.

On the second floor of the mall is the **Whalers Village Museum** (www. whalersvillage.com/museum.htm; ℂ **808/661-5992**), which celebrates the "Golden Era of Whaling" from 1825 to 1860. Harpoons and scrimshaw are on display and the museum has even re-created the cramped quarters of a whaler's seagoing vessel. It's open daily from 10am to 4pm; admission $3 adults, $2 seniors, $1 children 6-18 yrs.

South Maui

MAALAEA

Maui Ocean Center ★★★ AQUARIUM This 5-acre facility houses the largest aquarium in the state and features one of Hawaii's largest predators: the tiger shark. As you enter, the exhibits allow you to slowly descend from the "beach" to the deepest part of the ocean, without ever getting wet. Start at the surge pool, where you'll see shallow-water marine life like spiny urchins and cauliflower coral; then move on to the reef tanks, turtle pool, touch pool (with starfish and urchins), and eagle-ray pool before reaching the star of the show: the 100-foot-long, 600,000-gallon main tank featuring tiger, gray, and white-tip sharks, as well as tuna, surgeonfish, triggerfish, and numerous others.

At the Maalaea Harbor Village, 192 Maalaea Rd. (the triangle btw. Honoapiilani Hwy. and Maalaea Rd.). www.mauioceancenter.com. ℂ **808/270-7000.** Admission $28 adults, $25 seniors, $20 children 3–12). Daily 9am–5pm (until 6pm July–Aug).

KIHEI

Captain George Vancouver "discovered" Kihei in 1778, when it was only a collection of fishermen's grass shacks on the hot, dry, dusty coast (hard to believe, eh?). A **totem pole** stands today where he's believed to have landed, across from the Aston Maui Lu Resort, 575 S. Kihei Rd. Vancouver sailed on to "discover" British Columbia, where a great international city and harbor now bear his name.

West of the junction of Piilani Highway (Hwy. 31) and Mokulele Highway (Hwy. 350) is **Kealia Pond National Wildlife Preserve** (www.fws.gov/kealiapond; ℂ **808/875-1582**), a 700-acre U.S. Fish and Wildlife wetland preserve where endangered Hawaiian stilts, coots, and ducks hang out and splash. These ponds work two ways: as bird preserves and as sedimentation basins that keep the coral reefs from silting from runoff. You can take a self-guided tour along a boardwalk dotted with interpretive signs and shade shelters, through sand dunes, and around ponds to Maalaea Harbor. From July to December, the hawksbill turtle comes ashore here to lay its eggs.

WAILEA

The best way to explore this golden resort coast is to rise with the sun and head for Wailea's 1.5-mile **coastal nature trail** ★, stretching between the Fairmont Kea Lani and the kiawe thicket just beyond the new Andaz Maui Wailea Resort. It's a great morning walk on a serpentine path that meanders uphill and down past native plants, old Hawaiian habitats, and a billion dollars' worth of luxury hotels. You can pick up the trail at any of the resorts or from clearly marked shoreline access points along the coast. The best time to go is when you first wake up; by midmorning, the coastal trail is too often clogged with pushy joggers, and it grows crowded with beachgoers as the day wears on. Sunset is another good time to hit the trail.

MAKENA

A few miles south of Wailea, the manicured coast turns to wilderness; now you're in Makena. Once, cattle were driven down the slope from upland ranches, lashed to rafts, and sent into the water to swim to boats that waited to take them to market. Now **Makena Landing** ★ is the best place to launch kayaks bound for La Pérouse Bay and Ahihi-Kinau Natural Preserve.

From the landing, go south on Makena Road; on the right is **Keawalai Congregational Church** (www.keawalai.org; © 808/879-5557), built in 1855, with walls 3 feet thick. Surrounded by ti leaves, which by Hawaiian custom provide protection, and built of lava rock with coral used as mortar, this church sits on its own cove with a gold-sand beach. It always attracts a Sunday crowd for its 7:30am and 10am Hawaiian-language services.

A little farther south on the coast is **La Pérouse Monument,** a pyramid of lava rocks that marks the spot where French explorer Adm. Comte de la Pérouse set foot on Maui in 1789. He described the "burning climate" of the leeward coast, observed several fishing villages near Kihei, and sailed on into oblivion, never to be seen again; some believe he may have been eaten by cannibals in what is now Vanuatu. To get here, drive south past Puu Olai to Ahihi Bay, where the road turns to gravel. Go another 2 miles along the coast to La Pérouse Bay; the monument sits amid a clearing in black lava at the end of the dirt road.

House of the Sun: Haleakala National Park ★★★

At once forbidding and compelling, *Haleakala* (House of the Sun) National Park is Maui's main natural attraction. More than 1.3 million people a year go up the 10,023-foot-high mountain to peer down into the crater of the world's largest dormant volcano. (Haleakala is officially considered active, even though it has not rumbled since 1790.) That hole would hold Manhattan.

But there's more to do here than stare into a big black hole: Just going up the mountain is an experience. Where else on the planet can you climb from sea level to 10,000 feet in just 37 miles, or a 2-hour drive? The snaky road

> There are few enough places in the world that belong entirely to themselves. The human passion to carry all things everywhere, so that every place is home, seems well on its way to homogenizing our planet, save for the odd unreachable corner. Haleakala Crater is one of those corners.
> —Barbara Kingsolver, *The New York Times*

passes through big, puffy cumulus clouds to offer magnificent views of the isthmus of Maui, the West Maui Mountains, and the Pacific Ocean.

Many drive up to the summit in predawn darkness to watch the **sunrise over Haleakala ★★**; others coast down the 37-mile road from the summit on a bicycle with special brakes (see "Biking"). Hardy adventurers hike and camp inside the crater's wilderness (see "Hiking & Camping"). Those bound for the interior should bring appropriate gear: The terrain is raw, rugged, and punishing—not unlike the moon.

JUST THE FACTS

Haleakala National Park extends from the summit of Mount Haleakala down the volcano's southeast flank to Maui's eastern coast, beyond Hana. There are actually two separate and distinct destinations within the park: **Haleakala Summit** and **Kipahulu** (see "Tropical Haleakala: Oheo Gulch at Kipahulu" on p. 181). The summit gets all the publicity, but the Kipahulu coast draws crowds, too—it's lush, green, and tropical, and home to Oheo Gulch (also known as Seven Sacred Pools). No road links the summit and the Kipahulu coast; you have to approach them separately, and you need at least a day to see each place.

WHEN TO GO At the 10,023-foot summit, the weather changes fast. With the wind chill, temperatures can be freezing any time of year. Summer can be dry and warm; winter can be wet, windy, and cold. Before you go, get current weather conditions for the park www.prh.noaa.gov/hnl or the **National Weather Service (© 808/944-3756,** option 4). From sunrise to noon, the light is weak, but the view is usually free of clouds. The best time for photos is in the afternoon, when the sun lights the crater and clouds are few. Go on full-moon nights for spectacular viewing. *A note of caution:* This is Mother Nature, not Disneyland, so there are no guarantees or schedules. Especially in winter, some mornings may be misty or rainy, and sunrise viewing may be obscured. It's the luck of the draw.

ACCESS POINTS **Haleakala Summit** is 37 miles, or a 1½- to 2-hour drive, from Kahului. To get here, take Hwy. 37 to Hwy. 377 to Hwy. 378. For details on the drive, see "The Drive to the Summit," below. Pukalani is the last town for water, food, and gas.

The **Kipahulu** section of Haleakala National Park is on Maui's east end near Hana, 60 miles from Kahului on Hwy. 36 (Hana Hwy.). Due to traffic and rough road conditions, plan on 4 hours for the one-way drive. For complete information, see "The Road to Hana" (p. 177) and "Tropical Haleakala: Oheo Gulch at Kipahulu" (p. 181).

At both entrances to the park, the admission fee is $8 per person or $15 per car, good for 3 days of unlimited entry.

INFORMATION, VISITOR CENTERS & RANGER PROGRAMS   For information before you go, contact **Haleakala National Park,** Box 369, Makawao, HI 96768 (www.nps.gov/hale; ☎ **808/572-4400**).

One mile from the park entrance, at 7,000 feet, is **Haleakala National Park Headquarters** (☎ **808/572-4459**), open daily from 8am to 3:45pm. Stop here to pick up information on park programs and activities, get camping permits, and, occasionally, see a Hawaiian nene bird. Restrooms, a pay phone, and drinking water are available.

The **Haleakala Visitor Center,** open daily from 6am to 3pm, is near the summit, 11 miles past the park entrance. It offers a panoramic view of the volcanic landscape, with photos identifying the various features, and exhibits that explain the area's history, ecology, geology, and volcanology. Park staff members are often on hand to answer questions. Restrooms and water are available.

For information on hiking and camping possibilities, including wilderness cabins and campgrounds, see "Hiking & Camping" on p. 192.

THE DRIVE TO THE SUMMIT

If you look on a Maui map, almost in the middle of the part that resembles a torso, there's a black wiggly line that looks like this: WWWWW. That's **Hwy. 378,** also known as **Haleakala Crater Road**—one of the fastest-ascending roads in the world. This grand corniche has at least 33 switchbacks; passes through numerous climate zones; goes under, in, and out of clouds; takes you past rare silversword plants and endangered Hawaiian geese sailing through the clear, thin air; and offers a view that extends for more than 100 miles.

Going to the summit takes 1½ to 2 hours from Kahului. No matter where you start out, you'll follow Hwy. 37 (Haleakala Hwy.) to Pukalani, where you'll pick up Hwy. 377 (aka Haleakala Hwy.), which you'll take to Hwy. 378. Along the way, expect fog, rain, and wind. You may encounter stray cattle and downhill bicyclists. Fill up your gas tank before you go—the only gas available is 27 miles below the summit at Pukalani. There are no facilities beyond the ranger stations—not even a coffee urn in sight. Bring your own food and water.

Remember, you're entering a high-altitude wilderness area. Some people get dizzy due to the lack of oxygen; you might also suffer from lightheadedness, shortness of breath, nausea, severe headaches, flatulence, or dehydration. People with asthma, pregnant women, heavy smokers, and those with heart conditions should be especially careful in the rarefied air. Bring water and a jacket or a blanket, especially if you go up for sunrise. Or you might want to go up to the summit for sunset, which is also spectacular.

At the **park entrance,** you'll pay an entrance fee of $15 per car (or $8 for a bicycle). About a mile from the entrance is **park headquarters,** where an endangered *nene,* or Hawaiian goose, may greet you with its unique call. With its black face, buff cheeks, and partially webbed feet, the gray-brown bird looks like a small Canada goose with zebra stripes; it brays out "nay-nay" (thus its name), doesn't migrate, and prefers lava beds to lakes. More than 25,000 nene once inhabited Hawaii, but habitat destruction and predators (hunters, pigs, feral cats and dogs, and mongooses) nearly caused their extinction. By 1951, there were only 30 left. Now protected as Hawaii's state bird, the wild nene on Haleakala number fewer than 250—the species remains endangered.

Beyond headquarters are **two scenic overlooks** on the way to the summit; stop at Leleiwi on the way up and Kalahaku on the way back down, if only to get out, stretch, and get accustomed to the heights. Take a deep breath, look around, and pop your ears. If you feel dizzy or drowsy, or get a sudden headache, consider turning around and going back down.

Leleiwi Overlook ★ is just beyond mile marker 17. From the parking area, a short trail leads you to a panoramic view of the lunarlike crater. When the clouds are low and the sun is in the right place, usually around sunset, you may experience a phenomenon known as the "Spectre of the Brocken"—you can see a reflection of your shadow, ringed by a rainbow, in the clouds below. It's an optical illusion caused by a rare combination of sun, shadow, and fog that occurs in only three places on the planet: Haleakala, Scotland, and Germany.

Two miles farther along is **Kalahaku Overlook ★**, the best place to see a rare **silversword.** You can turn into this overlook only when you are descending from the top. The silversword is the punk of the plant world, its silvery bayonets displaying tiny purple bouquets—like a spacey artichoke with attitude. This botanical wonder proved irresistible to humans, who gathered them in gunnysacks for Chinese potions and British specimen collections, and just for the sheer thrill of having something so rare. Silverswords grow only in Hawaii, take from 4 to 50 years to bloom, and then, usually between May and October, send up a 1- to 6-foot stalk with a purple bouquet of sunflower-like blooms. They're very rare, so don't even think about taking one home.

Continue on, and you'll quickly reach the **Haleakala Visitor Center,** which offers spectacular views. You'll feel as if you're at the edge of the earth, but the actual summit's a little farther on, at **Puu Ulaula Overlook ★★★** (also known as Red Hill), the volcano's highest point, where you'll find a cluster of buildings officially known as Haleakala Observatories, but unofficially called **Science City.** If you go up for sunrise, the building at Puu Ulaula Overlook, a triangle of glass that serves as a windbreak, is the best viewing spot. After the daily miracle of sunrise—the sun seems to rise out of the vast ocean—you can see all the way across Alenuihaha Channel to the often-snowcapped summit of Mauna Kea on the Big Island.

> ### Descending from the Crater
>
> When driving down the Haleakala Crater Road, be sure to put your car in low gear so you don't destroy your brakes by riding them the whole way down.

While in the upcountry Kula region, stop by **Alii Kula Lavender,** 1100 Waipoli Rd., Kula (www.aliikulalavender.com; ☏ **808/878-3004**), which grows several different varieties of lavender, so one type of lavender will always be in bloom. Admission is $3, children 12 and under free; on the 30-minute Lavender Garden Walking Tour (daily at 9:30am, 10:30am, 11:30am, 1pm, and 2:30pm for $12 per person, $10 with advance reservation), you're given a garden and studio tour. Be sure to stop by the store and look over the culinary products (lavender seasonings, dressings, scones, honey, jelly, and teas), bath and body goodies (lotions, soaps, bubble baths), aromatherapy (oil, candles, eye pillows), and other items (T-shirts, gift baskets, and dried lavender).

Upcountry Maui

Come upcountry and discover a different side of Maui: On the slopes of Haleakala, cowboys, planters, and other country people make their homes in serene, neighborly communities like **Makawao** and **Kula,** a world away from the bustling beach resorts. Even if you can't spare a day or two in the cool, upcountry air, there are some sights that are worth a look on your way to or from the crater. Shoppers and gallery hoppers might want to spend more time here; see "Shops & Galleries," p. 199, for details.

Tedeschi Vineyards and Winery ★ VINEYARD/WINERY   In the southern shoulder of Haleakala is **Ulupalakua Ranch,** a 20,000-acre spread now home to Maui's only winery, established in 1974 by Napa vintner Emil Tedeschi, who began growing California and European grapes here and producing serious still and sparkling wines, plus a silly wine made of pineapple juice. The rustic grounds are the perfect place for a picnic. Pack a basket before you go, but don't BYOB: There's plenty of great wine to enjoy at Tedeschi. Settle in under the sprawling camphor tree, pop the cork on a blanc de blanc, and toast your good fortune in being here.

Off Hwy. 37 (Kula Hwy.). www.mauiwine.com. ☏ **808/878-6058.** Free tastings daily 10am–5:30pm. Free tours at 10:30am and 1:30pm. King's Tasting Tour, 60 min. for $50.

East Maui & Heavenly Hana

Hana is Paradise on Earth—or just about as close as you can get to it, anyway. In and around Hana, you'll find a lush tropical rainforest dotted with cascading waterfalls and sparkling blue pools, skirted by red- and black-sand beaches.

THE ROAD TO HANA ★★★

Top down, sunscreen on, radio tuned to a little Hawaiian music on a Maui morning—it's time to head out to Hana along the Hana Highway (Hwy. 36), a wiggle of a road that runs along Maui's northeastern shore. The drive takes at least 3 hours from Lahaina or Kihei—but take all day. Going to Hana is about the journey, not the destination.

There are wilder roads, steeper roads, and more dangerous roads, but in all of Hawaii, no road is more celebrated than this one. It winds 50 miles past taro patches, magnificent seascapes, waterfall pools, botanical gardens, and verdant rainforests, and ends at one of Hawaii's most beautiful tropical places.

The outside world discovered the little village of Hana in 1926, when the narrow coastal road, carved by pickax-wielding convicts, opened. The mud-and-gravel road, often subject to landslides and washouts, was paved in 1962, when tourist traffic began to increase; it now sees 1,000 cars and dozens of vans a day. That translates into half a million people a year, which is way too many. Go at the wrong time, and you'll be stuck in a bumper-to-bumper rental-car parade—peak traffic hours are midmorning and midafternoon year-round, especially on weekends.

In the rush to "do" Hana in a day, most visitors spin around town in 10 minutes and wonder what all the fuss is about. It takes time to take in Hana, play in the waterfalls, sniff the tropical flowers, hike to bamboo forests, and view the spectacular scenery. Stay overnight if you can, and meander back in a day or two. If you really must do the Hana Highway in a day, go just before sunrise and return after sunset.

Tips: Practice aloha. Give way at one-lane bridges, wave at oncoming motorists, let the big guys in 4×4s have the right of way—it's just common sense, brah. If the guy behind you blinks his lights, let him pass. And don't honk your horn—in Hawaii, it's considered rude.

THE JOURNEY BEGINS IN PAIA   Before you even start out, fill up your gas tank. Gas in Paia is expensive, and it's the last place for gas until you get to Hana, some 54 bridges and 600 hairpin turns down the road.

Paia ★★ was once a thriving sugar-mill town. The mill is still here, but the population shifted to Kahului in the 1950s when subdivisions opened there, leaving Paia to shrivel up and die. But the town refused to give up, and it has proven its ability to adapt to the times. Now chic eateries and trendy shops stand next door to the old ma-and-pa establishments. Plan to be here early, around 7am, when **Charley's** (p. 168) opens. Enjoy a big, hearty breakfast for a reasonable price.

WINDSURFING MECCA   Just before mile marker 9 is **Hookipa Beach Park ★**, where top-ranked windsurfers come to test themselves against the forces of nature: thunderous surf and forceful wind. On nearly every windy day after noon (the board surfers have the waves in the morning), you can watch dozens of windsurfers twirling and dancing in the wind like colored butterflies. To watch them, do not stop on the highway, but go past the park and turn left at the entrance on the far side of the beach. You can either park on the high grassy bluff or drive down to the sandy beach and park alongside the pavilion. Facilities include restrooms, a shower, picnic tables, and a barbecue area.

INTO THE COUNTRY   Past Hookipa Beach, the road winds down into **Maliko Gulch** at mile marker 10. There are no facilities here except a boat-launch ramp. In the 1940s, Maliko had a thriving community at the mouth of the bay, but its residents rebuilt farther inland after a strong tidal wave wiped it out.

Back on the Hana Highway, for the next few miles, you'll pass through the rural area of **Haiku,** where you'll see banana patches, forests of guavas and palms, and avocados.

At mile marker 16, the curves begin, one right after another. Slow down and enjoy the view of bucolic rolling hills, mango trees, and vibrant ferns. After mile marker 16, the road is still called the Hana Highway, but the number changes from Hwy. 36 to Hwy. 360, and the mile markers go back to 0.

HIDDEN HUELO   Just before mile marker 4 on a blind curve, look for a double row of mailboxes on the left side by the pay phone. Down the road lies a hidden Hawaii of an earlier time, where an indescribable sense of serenity prevails. Hemmed in by Waipo and Hoalua bays is the remote community of **Huelo ★.** This fertile area once supported a population of 75,000; today only a few hundred live among the scattered homes here, where a handful of B&Bs and exquisite vacation rentals cater to a trickle of travelers.

The only reason Huelo is even marked is the historic 1853 **Kaulanapueo Church.** Reminiscent of New England architecture, this coral-and-cement church, topped with a plantation-green steeple and a gray tin roof, is still in use, although services are held just once or twice a month. It still has the same austere interior of 1853: straight-backed benches, a no-nonsense platform for the minister, and no distractions on the walls to tempt you from paying attention to the sermon. Next to the church is a small graveyard, a personal history of this village in concrete and stone.

KOOLAU FOREST RESERVE   After Huelo, the vegetation seems lusher, as though Mother Nature had poured Miracle-Gro on everything. This is the edge of the **Koolau Forest Reserve.** *Koolau* means "windward," and this certainly is one of the greatest examples of a lush windward area: The coastline here gets about 60 to 80 inches of rain a year, as well as runoff from the 200 to 300 inches that falls farther up the mountain. You'll see trees laden with guavas, as well as mangoes, java plums, and avocados the size of softballs. The spiny, long-leafed plants are hala trees, which the Hawaiians used for weaving baskets, mats, and even canoe sails.

From here on out, there's a waterfall (and one-lane bridge) around nearly every turn in the road, so drive slowly and be prepared to stop and yield to oncoming cars.

DANGEROUS CURVES   About a half-mile after mile marker 6, there's a sharp U-curve in the road, going uphill. The road is practically one-lane here, with a brick wall on one side and virtually no maneuvering room. Sound your horn at the start of the U-curve to let approaching cars know you're coming. Take this curve, as well as the few more coming up in the next several miles, very slowly.

Just before mile marker 7 is a forest of waving **bamboo.** The sight is so spectacular that drivers are often tempted to take their eyes off the road. Be very cautious. Wait until just after mile marker 7, at the **Ka'aiea Bridge** and stream below, to pull over and take a closer look at the hand-hewn stone walls. Then turn around to see the vista of bamboo.

A GREAT FAMILY HIKE At mile marker 9, there's a small state wayside area with restrooms, picnic tables, and a barbecue area. The sign says KOOLAU FOREST RESERVE, but the real attraction here is the **Waikamoi Ridge Trail ★**, an easy .75-mile loop. The start of the trail is just behind the quiet trees at work sign. The well-marked trail meanders through eucalyptus, ferns, and hala trees.

SAFETY WARNING I used to recommend another waterfall, **Puohokamoa Falls,** at mile marker 11, but not anymore. Unfortunately, what was once a great thing has been overrun by hordes of not-so-polite tourists. You will see cars parking on the already dangerous, barely two-lane Hana Highway half a mile before the waterfall. Slow down after the 10-mile marker. As you get close to the 11-mile marker, the highway becomes a congested one-lane road due to visitors parking on this narrow stretch. Don't add to the congestion by trying to park: There are plenty of other great waterfalls; just drive slowly and safely through this area.

CAN'T-MISS PHOTO OPS Just past mile marker 12 is the **Kaumahina State Wayside Park ★**. This is not only a good pit stop (restrooms are available) and a wonderful place for a picnic (with tables and a barbecue area), but also a great vista point. The view of the rugged coastline makes an excellent shot—you can see all the way down to the jutting Keanae Peninsula.

Another mile and a couple of bends in the road, and you'll enter the Honomanu Valley, with its beautiful bay. To get to the **Honomanu Bay County Beach Park ★**, look for the turnoff on your left, just after mile marker 14, as you begin your ascent up the other side of the valley. The rutted dirt-and-cinder road takes you down to the rocky black-sand beach. There are no facilities here. Because of the strong rip currents offshore, swimming is best in the stream inland from the ocean. You'll consider the drive down worthwhile as you stand on the beach, well away from the ocean, and turn to look back on the steep cliffs covered with vegetation.

KEANAE PENINSULA & ARBORETUM At mile marker 17, the old Hawaiian village of **Keanae ★★** stands out against the Pacific like a place time forgot. Here, on an old lava flow graced by an 1860 stone church and swaying palms is one of the last coastal enclaves of native Hawaiians. They still grow taro in patches and pound it into *poi,* the staple of the old Hawaiian diet; and they still pluck *opihi* (limpet) from tide pools along the jagged coast and cast throw-nets at schools of fish.

At nearby **Keanae Arboretum,** Hawaii's botanical world is divided into three parts: native forest, introduced forest, and traditional Hawaiian plants, food, and medicine. You can swim in the pools of Piinaau Stream or press on along a mile-long trail into Keanae Valley, where a lovely tropical rainforest waits at the end.

WAIANAPANAPA STATE PARK ★★   On the outskirts of Hana, the shiny black-sand beach appears like a vivid dream, with bright-green jungle foliage on three sides and cobalt-blue water lapping at its feet. The 120-acre state park on an ancient lava flow includes sea cliffs, lava tubes, arches, and that beach—plus a dozen rustic cabins. See p. 187 for a review of the cabins. Also see "Beaches," below, and "Hiking & Camping," p. 192.

Hana ★★★

Green, tropical Hana, which some call heavenly, is a destination all its own, a small coastal village in a rainforest inhabited by 2,500 people, many part Hawaiian. Beautiful Hana enjoys more than 90 inches of rain a year—more than enough to keep the scenery lush. Banyans, bamboo, breadfruit trees— everything seems larger than life, especially the flowers, like wild ginger and plumeria. Several roadside stands offer exotic blooms for $1 a bunch. Just "put money in box." It's the Hana honor system.

The last unspoiled Hawaiian town on Maui is, oddly enough, the home of Maui's first resort, which opened in 1946. Paul Fagan, owner of the San Francisco Seals baseball team, bought an old inn and turned it into the **Hotel Hana-Maui** (it's now the **Travaasa Hana,** an upscale boutique hotel, with rooms starting at $400; www.travaasa.com/hana), which gave Hana its first and, as it turns out, last taste of tourism. Others have tried to open hotels and golf courses and resorts, but Hana, which is interested in remaining Hana, always politely refuses. There are a few B&Bs here, though; for a comprehensive list, visit www.hanamaui.com/lodging.

A wood-frame 1871 building that served as the old Hana District Police Station now holds the **Hana Cultural Center & Museum,** 4974 Uakea Rd. (www.hanaculturalcenter.org; ✆ **808/248-8622**), Monday through Friday 10am to 4pm. The center tells the history of the area, with some excellent artifacts, memorabilia, and photographs. Also stop in at **Hasegawa General Store,** a Maui institution.

On the green hills above Hana stands a 30-foot-high white cross made of lava rock. The cross was erected by citizens in memory of Paul Fagan, who helped keep the town alive. The 3-mile hike up to **Fagan's Cross** provides a gorgeous view of the Hana coast, especially at sunset, when Fagan himself liked to climb this hill.

Tropical Haleakala: Oheo Gulch at Kipahulu

If you're thinking about heading out to the so-called Seven Sacred Pools, out past Hana at the Kipahulu end of Haleakala National Park, let's clear this up right now: There are more than 7 pools—about 24, actually—and ALL water in Hawaii is considered sacred. It's all a PR campaign that has spun out of control. Folks here call it by its rightful name, **Oheo Gulch ★★★**, and visitors sometimes refer to it as Kipahulu, which is actually the name of the area where Oheo Gulch is located. No matter what you call it, it's beautiful. This dazzling series of pools and cataracts is so popular that it has its own roadside parking lot.

From the ranger station, it's just a short hike above the famous Oheo Gulch to two spectacular **waterfalls.** Check with park rangers before hiking up to or swimming in the pools, and always keep an eye on the water in the streams. The sky can be sunny near the coast, but floodwaters travel 6 miles down from the Kipahulu Valley, and the water level can rise 4 feet in less than 10 minutes. It's not a good idea to swim in the pools in winter.

Makahiku Falls is easily reached from the central parking area; the trail head begins near the ranger station. **Pipiwai Trail** leads up to the road and beyond for .5 miles to the overlook. If you hike another 1.5 miles up the trail across two bridges and through a bamboo forest, you reach **Waimoku Falls.** It's a hard uphill hike, but press on to avoid the pool's crowd.

ACCESS POINTS   Even though Oheo is part of Haleakala National Park, you cannot drive here from the summit. Oheo is about 30 to 50 minutes beyond Hana town, along Hwy. 31. The fee to enter is $8 per person or $15 per car. The Hwy. 31 bridge passes over some of the pools near the ocean; the others, plus magnificent 400-foot Waimoku Falls, are uphill, via an often-muddy but rewarding hour-long hike; see "Hiking & Camping at Kipahulu (Near Hana)" on p. 195. Expect showers on the Kipahulu coast.

VISITOR CENTER   The **Kipahulu Ranger Station** (℃ 808/248-7375) is staffed from 9am to 4:30pm daily. Restrooms are available, but there's no drinking water. Here you'll find park-safety information, exhibits, and books. Rangers offer a variety of walks and hikes year-round; check at the station for current activities. Tent camping is permitted in the park; see "Hiking & Camping at Kipahulu (Near Hana)" on p. 195 for details.

Beyond Oheo Gulch

A mile past Oheo Gulch on the ocean side of the road is **Lindbergh's Grave.** First to fly across the Atlantic Ocean, Charles A. Lindbergh found peace in the Pacific; he settled in Hana, where he died of cancer in 1974. The famous aviator is buried under river stones in a seaside graveyard behind the 1857 **Palapala Hoomau Congregational Church.**

Those of you who are continuing on around Maui to the fishing village of **Kaupo** and beyond should be warned that Kaupo Road, or Old Piilani Highway (Hwy. 31), is rough and unpaved, often full of potholes and ruts. There are no goods or services until you reach **Ulupalakua Ranch** (www.ulupalakua ranch.com/store.; ℃ 808/878-2561), where there's a winery, a general store, and a gas station, which is likely to be closed. Before you attempt this journey, ask around about road conditions, or call the **Maui Public Works Department** (℃ 808/248-8254) or the **Police Department** (℃ 808/248-8311). This road frequently washes out in the rain. Most rental-car companies forbid you from taking their cars on this road (they don't want to trek all the way out here to get you if your car breaks down), so you'd really be better off retracing your route back through Hana. But if conditions are good, it can be a pretty drive in the spring (it tends to be dry in summer).

BEACHES

For beach toys and equipment, head to **Snorkel Bob's** (www.snorkelbob. com), which rents snorkel gear, boogie boards, and other ocean toys at six locations: 1217 Front St. (© **808/661-4421**); Honokowai, 3350 Lower Honoapiilani Hwy. (© **808/667-9999**); Napili Village, 5425-C Lower Honoapiilani Hwy. (© **808/669-9603**); Azeka Place II, 1279 S. Kihei Rd. #310 (© **808/875-6188**); Kamaole Beach Center, 2411 S. Kihei Rd. (© **808/879-7449**); and in Wailea, 100 Wailea Ike Dr. (© **808/874-0011**). All locations are open daily from 8am to 5pm. If you're island-hopping, you can rent from a Snorkel Bob's location on one island and return to a branch on another.

West Maui

KAANAPALI BEACH ★

Four-mile-long Kaanapali is one of Maui's best beaches, with grainy gold sand as far as the eye can see. A paved walk along the shore links hotels and condos, open-air restaurants, and the Whalers Village shopping center. Summertime swimming is excellent. The best snorkeling is around Black Rock, in front of the Sheraton, where the water is clear, calm, and populated with clouds of tropical fish.

Facilities include outdoor showers. Various beach-activities vendors line up in front of the hotels. Parking is a problem, though. There are two public entrances: At the south end, turn off Honoapiilani Highway into the Kaanapali Resort and pay for parking here; or continue on Honoapiilani Highway, turn off at the last Kaanapali exit at the stoplight near the Maui Kaanapali Villas, and park next to the beach signs indicating public access.

KAPALUA BEACH ★★★

The beach cove that fronts the Coconut Grove Villas is the stuff of dreams: a golden crescent bordered by two palm-studded points. The sandy bottom slopes gently to deep water at the bay mouth; the water's so clear that you can see it turn to green and then deep blue. Protected from strong winds and currents by the lava-rock promontories, Kapalua's calm waters are ideal for swimmers of all ages and abilities, and the bay is big enough to paddle a kayak around in without getting into the more challenging channel that separates Maui from Molokai. Waves come in just right for riding, and fish hang out by the rocks, making it great for snorkeling.

Parking is limited to about 30 spaces in a small lot off Lower Honoapiilani Road, by Napili Kai Beach Resort, so arrive early. Next door is a nice but very pricey oceanfront restaurant, Merriman's (p. 164). Facilities include showers, restrooms, lifeguards, a rental shack, and plenty of shade.

South Maui

Wailea's beaches may seem off limits, hidden from plain view as they are by an intimidating wall of luxury resorts, but they're all open to the public by law.

Beaches & Outdoor Activities on Maui

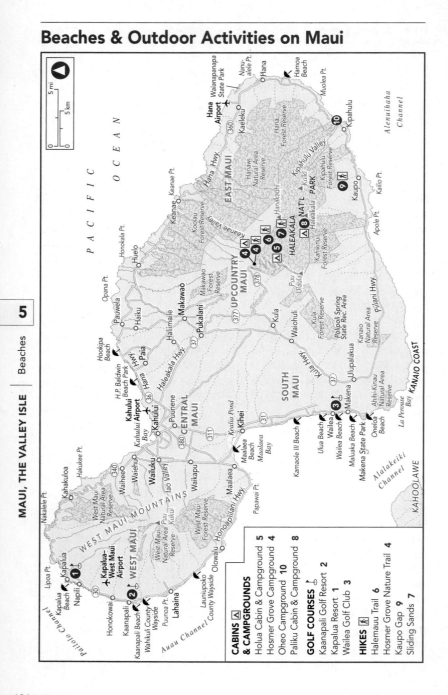

CABINS & CAMPGROUNDS

Holua Cabin & Campground **5**
Hosmer Grove Campground **4**
Oheo Campground **10**
Paliku Cabin & Campground **8**

GOLF COURSES

Kaanapali Golf Resort **1**
Kapalua Resort **2**
Wailea Golf Club **3**

HIKES

Halemauu Trail **6**
Hosmer Grove Nature Trail **4**
Kaupo Gap **9**
Sliding Sands **7**

Look for the shoreline access signs along Wailea Alanui Drive, the resort's main boulevard.

KAMAOLE III BEACH PARK ★

Three beach parks—Kamaole I, II, and III—stand like golden jewels in the front yard of the funky seaside town of Kihei, which, all of a sudden, is sprawling like suburban blight. The beaches are the best thing about Kihei; these three are popular with local residents and visitors alike because they're easily accessible. On weekends, they're jam-packed with fishermen, picnickers, swimmers, and snorkelers. The most popular is Kamaole III, or "Kam-3." It's the biggest of the three beaches, with wide pockets of gold sand, and the only one with a children's playground and a grassy lawn. Swimming is safe here, but scattered lava rocks are toe-stubbers at the water line, and parents should make sure kids don't venture too far out because the bottom slopes off quickly. Kam-3 is also a wonderful place to watch the sunset. Facilities include restrooms, showers, picnic tables, barbecue grills, and lifeguards. There's plenty of parking on South Kihei Road across from the Maui Parkshore condos.

ULUA BEACH ★

One of the most popular beaches in Wailea, Ulua is a long, wide, crescent-shaped gold-sand beach between two rocky points. When the ocean's calm, Ulua offers Wailea's best snorkeling; when it's rough, the waves are excellent for bodysurfers. The ocean bottom is shallow and gently slopes down to deeper waters, making swimming generally safe. In high season (Christmas–Mar and June–Aug), the sand is carpeted with beach towels and packed with sunbathers like sardines in cocoa butter. Facilities include showers and restrooms. Beach equipment is available for rent at the nearby Wailea Ocean Activity Center. Look for the blue shoreline access sign on South Kihei Road, near the Wailea Beach Marriott Resort & Spa; a tiny parking lot is nearby.

WAILEA BEACH ★

Wailea is the best golden-sand crescent on Maui's sunbaked southwestern coast. One of five beaches within Wailea Resort, Wailea is big, wide, and protected on both sides by black-lava points. It's the front yard of the Four Seasons Resort and the Grand Wailea, Maui's most elegant and outrageous beach hotels, respectively. From the beach, the view out to sea is magnificent, framed by neighboring Kahoolawe and Lanai and the tiny crescent of Molokini, probably the most popular snorkel spot in these parts. The clear waters tumble to shore in waves just the right size for gentle riding, with or without a board. From shore, you can see Pacific humpback whales in season (Dec–Apr) and unreal sunsets nightly. Facilities include restrooms, outdoor showers, and limited free parking at the blue shoreline access sign, which points toward Wailea Alanui Drive.

MALUAKA BEACH (MAKENA BEACH) ★

On the southern end of Maui's resort coast, development falls off dramatically, leaving a wild, dry countryside of green kiawe trees. The Makena Beach & Golf Resort sits in isolated splendor, sharing the resort's 1,800 acres with only a couple of first-rate golf courses and a necklace of perfect beaches. The strand nearest the hotel is Maluaka Beach, often called Makena, notable for its beauty and its views of Molokini Crater, the offshore islet, and Kahoolawe, the so-called target island (it was used as a bombing target from 1945 until the early 1990s). This is a short, wide, palm-fringed crescent of golden, grainy sand set between two black-lava points and bounded by big sand dunes topped by a grassy knoll. The swimming in this mostly calm bay is considered the best on Makena Bay, which is bordered on the south by Puu Olai Cinder Cone and historic Keawalai Congregational Church. The waters around Makena Landing, at the north end of the bay, are particularly good for snorkeling. Facilities include restrooms, showers, a landscaped park, lifeguards, and roadside parking. Along Makena Alanui, look for the shoreline access sign near the hotel, turn right, and head down to the shore.

ONELOA BEACH (BIG BEACH) ★★

Oneloa, whose name means "long sand" in Hawaiian, is one of the most popular beaches on Maui. Locals call it "Big Beach"—it's 3,300 feet long and more than 100 feet wide. Mauians come here to swim, fish, sunbathe, surf, and enjoy the view of Kahoolawe and Lanai. Snorkeling is good around the north end, at the foot of Puu Olai, a 360-foot cinder cone. During storms, however, big waves lash the shore, and a strong rip current sweeps the sharp drop-off, posing a danger for inexperienced open-ocean swimmers. There are no facilities except for portable toilets, but there's plenty of parking. To get here, drive past the Maui Prince Hotel to the second dirt road, which leads through a kiawe thicket to the beach.

On the other side of Puu Olai is **Little Beach,** a small pocket beach where assorted nudists work on their all-over tans, to the chagrin of uptight authorities. You can get a nasty sunburn and a lewd-conduct ticket, too.

Upcountry & East Maui
HOOKIPA BEACH PARK ★

Two miles past Paia, on the Hana Highway, is one of the most famous windsurfing sites in the world. Because of its constant wind and endless waves, Hookipa attracts top windsurfers and wave jumpers from around the globe. Surfers and fishermen also enjoy this small gold-sand beach at the foot of a grassy cliff, which provides a natural amphitheater for spectators. Except when competitions are being held, weekdays are the best times to watch the daredevils fly over the waves. When waves are flat, snorkelers and divers explore the reef. Facilities include restrooms, showers, pavilions, picnic tables, barbecues, and parking.

WAIANAPANAPA STATE PARK ★

Four miles before Hana, off the Hana Highway, is this beach park, which takes its name from the legend of the Waianapanapa Cave, where Chief Kaakea, a jealous and cruel man, suspected his wife, Popoalaea, of having an affair. Popoalaea left her husband and hid herself in a chamber of the Waianapanapa Cave. She and her attendant ventured out only at night for food. Nevertheless, a few days later, Kaakea was passing by the area and saw the shadow of the servant. Knowing he had found his wife's hiding place, Kaakea entered the cave and killed her. During certain times of the year, the water in the tide pool turns red, commemorating Popoalaea's death. (Scientists claim, less imaginatively, that the water turns red due to the presence of small red shrimp.)

Waianapanapa State Park's 120 acres contain 12 cabins, a caretaker's residence, a beach park, picnic tables, barbecue grills, restrooms, showers, a parking lot, a shoreline hiking trail, and a black-sand beach (actually, small black pebbles). This is a wonderful area for shoreline hikes (bring insect repellent—the mosquitoes are plentiful) and picnicking. Swimming is generally unsafe, though, due to strong waves and rip currents. Because Waianapanapa is crowded on weekends with local residents and their families, as well as tourists, weekdays are generally a better bet.

HAMOA BEACH ★

This half-moon-shaped, gray-sand beach (a mix of coral and lava) in a truly tropical setting is a favorite of sunbathers seeking rest and refuge. The hotel Travaasa Hana maintains the beach and acts as though it's private, which it isn't—so just march down the lava-rock steps and grab a spot on the sand. The 100-foot-wide beach is three football fields long and sits below 30-foot black-lava sea cliffs. Surf on this unprotected beach breaks offshore and rolls in, making it a popular surfing and bodysurfing area. Hamoa is often swept by powerful rip currents, so be careful. The calm left side is best for snorkeling in summer. The hotel has numerous facilities for guests; there are outdoor showers and restrooms for nonguests. Parking is limited. Look for the Hamoa Beach turnoff from Hana Highway.

WATERSPORTS

Boating

Maui is big on snorkel cruises. The crescent-shaped islet called **Molokini** is one of the best snorkel and scuba spots in Hawaii. Trips to the island of **Lanai** are also popular for a day of snorkeling. Always remember to bring a towel, a swimsuit, sunscreen, and a hat on a snorkel cruise; everything else is usually included. For fishing charters, see "Sport Fishing," later in this section, p. 190.

Pacific Whale Foundation ★ TOUR This not-for-profit foundation supports its whale research, public education, and conservation programs by offering **whale-watch cruises, wild dolphin encounters,** and **snorkel tours,** some to Molokini and Lanai. There are numerous daily trips to choose from, offered from December through May, out of both Lahaina and Maalaea harbors.

101 N. Kihei Rd. www.pacificwhale.org. ☎ **800/942-5311 x1** or 808/249-8811. Trips from $29 adults, $20 children 7–12, one free for ages 6 and under, $20 after that; snorkeling cruises from $84 adults, one free child per adult, then $42 children (book online for 10% discount).

Trilogy ★★★ TOUR   Trilogy offers my favorite **snorkel-sail trips.** Hop aboard one of the fleet of custom-built catamarans, from 54 to 64 feet long, for a 9-mile sail from Lahaina Harbor to **Lanai's Hulopoe Beach,** a terrific marine preserve, for a fun-filled day of sailing, snorkeling, swimming, and **whale-watching** (in season, of course). This is the only cruise that offers a personalized ground tour of the island and the only one with rights to take you to Hulopoe Beach. The full-day trip costs $205 for adults, $154 for teens (ages 13–18), and $103 for children 3 to 12. Ask about overnighters to Lanai, too.

Trilogy also offers **snorkel-sail trips to Molokini,** one of Hawaii's best snorkel spots. This half-day trip (5½ hr.) leaves from Maalaea Harbor and costs $129 for adults, $97 for teens, and $65 for kids 3 to 12, including breakfast and a barbecue lunch. Other options include a late-morning half-day snorkel-sail off Kaanapali Beach for the same price, plus a host of other trips.

These are the most expensive sail-snorkel cruises on Maui, but they're worth every penny. The crews are fun and knowledgeable, and the boats comfortable and well equipped. All trips include breakfast (Mom's homemade cinnamon buns) and a very good barbecue lunch (on board on the half-day trip, on land on the Lanai trip). Note, that you'll be required to wear a flotation device no matter how strong a swimmer you are; if this bothers you, go with another outfitter.

www.sailtrilogy.com. ☎ **888/225-MAUI** (6284) or 808/874-5649. Prices and departure points vary depending on cruise. Discounted prices on website.

DAY CRUISES TO MOLOKAI

You can travel across the seas by ferry from Maui's Lahaina Harbor to Molokai's Kaunakakai Wharf on the *Molokai Princess* (www.hawaiioceanproject.com; ☎ **877/500-6284** or 808/667-6165). The 100-foot yacht, certified for 149 passengers, is fitted with the latest generation of gyroscopic stabilizers, making the ride smoother. The ferry makes the 90-minute journey from Lahaina to Kaunakakai daily; the round-trip cost is $126 for adults and $63 for children 4 to 12. Or you can choose to tour the island on one of two different package options: Cruise-Drive, which includes round-trip passage and a rental car for $276 for the driver, $130 per additional adult passenger, and $65 for children; or the Alii Tour, which is a guided tour in an air-conditioned van plus lunch for $260 per adult and $160 per child. Book on website for discounts.

DAY CRUISES TO LANAI

You can also get to the island of Lanai by booking a trip with **Trilogy** (see above).

Expeditions Lahaina/Lanai Passenger Ferry ★ FERRY BOAT   The cheapest way to reach Lanai is the Maui-Lanai Ferry (www.go-lanai.com; ✆ 800/695-2624), which runs five times a day, 365 days a year. Adult round-trip fare is $60; children 2 to 11 years old $40. It leaves Lahaina at 6:45am, 9:15am, 12:45pm, 3:15pm, and 5:45pm; the return ferry from Lanai's Manele Bay leaves at 8am, 10:30am, 2pm, 4:30pm, and 6:45pm. The 9-mile channel crossing takes between 45 minutes and an hour, depending on sea conditions. Reservations are strongly recommended. Baggage is limited to two checked bags and one carry-on. Call **Dollar Rent A Car** (✆ 800/800-4000) or **Lanai City Service** (✆ 808/565-7227) to arrange a car rental or bus ride.

Scuba Diving

Everyone dives in **Molokini,** a marine-life park and one of Hawaii's top dive spots. This crescent-shaped crater has three tiers of diving: a 35-foot plateau inside the crater basin (used by beginning divers and snorkelers), a wall sloping to 70 feet just beyond the inside plateau, and a sheer wall on the outside and backside of the crater that plunges 350 feet. This underwater park is very popular, thanks to calm, clear, protected waters and an abundance of marine life, from manta rays to clouds of yellow butterfly fish.

Stop by any location of **Maui Dive Shop** ★ (www.mauidiveshop.com; ✆ 800/542-DIVE [3483]), Maui's largest diving retailer, with everything from rentals to scuba-diving instruction to dive-boat charters, for a free copy of the 64-page *Maui Dive & Surf Magazine* (you can also view it on the website). Inside are maps of and details on the 20 best shoreline and offshore dives and snorkel sites, each ranked for beginner, intermediate, or advanced snorkelers/divers. Maui Dive Shop has branches in Kihei at Azeka Place II Shopping Center, 1455 S. Kihei Rd. (✆ **808/879-3388**), and Shops at Wailea (✆ **808/875-9904**). Other locations include Maalaea Harbor Village, 300 Maalaea Rd. #225, Maalaea (✆ **808/244-5514**); and Kahana Gateway, 4405 Honoapiilani Hwy., Ste. 204, Kahana (✆ **808/669-3800**).

Snorkeling

Snorkel Bob's (www.snorkelbob.com) will rent you everything you need; see the introduction to this section for locations. Also see "Scuba Diving," above, for information on **Maui Dive Shop**'s free booklet on great snorkeling sites.

Snorkeling on Maui is easy—there are so many great spots where you can just wade in the water with a face mask look down and see tropical fish. Mornings are best; local winds kick in around noon. Maui's best snorkeling spots include **Kapalua Beach;** along the Kihei coastline, especially at **Kamaole Beach Park III;** and along the Wailea coastline, particularly at **Ulua Beach.** For an off-the-beaten-track experience, head south to **Makena Beach,** where the bay is filled with clouds of tropical fish, and, on weekdays, the waters are virtually empty.

When the whales aren't around, **Captain Steve's Rafting Excursions** (www.captainsteves.com; ✆ **808/667-5565**) offers 7-hour snorkel trips from Mala Wharf in Lahaina to the waters around **Lanai** (you don't actually land on the island). Rates of $150 for adults, $110 for children 5 to 12 years old, include breakfast, lunch, snorkel gear, and wet suits. (Discounts are listed on the website.)

A truly terrific snorkel spot, difficult to get to but worth the effort, as it is home to Hawaii's tropical marine life at its best:

Molokini ★★ NATURAL ATTRACTION   This sunken crater sits like a crescent moon fallen from the sky, almost midway between Maui and the uninhabited island of Kahoolawe. Molokini stands like a scoop against the tide and serves, on its concave side, as a natural sanctuary and marine-life preserve for tropical fish. Snorkelers commute daily in a fleet of dive boats. Molokini is accessible only by boat; see "Boating," above, for outfitters that can take you here. Expect crowds in high season.

Sport Fishing

Marlin, tuna, ono, and mahimahi await the baited hook in Maui's coastal and channel waters. No license is required; just book a sport-fishing vessel out of Lahaina or Maalaea harbors. Most charter boats that troll for big-game fish carry six passengers max.

The best way to book a sport-fishing charter is through the experts; the top booking desk in the state is **Sportfish Hawaii** ★ (www.sportfishhawaii.com; ✆ **877/388-1376** or 808/396-2607), which books boats on all the islands. These fishing vessels have been inspected and must meet rigorous criteria to guarantee that you'll have a great time. Prices range from $1,095 to $1,399 for a full-day exclusive charter (you, plus five friends, get the entire boat to yourself); it's $699 to $895 for a half-day exclusive.

Submarine Dives

Plunging 100 feet below the surface of the sea in a state-of-the-art, high-tech submarine is a great way to experience Maui's magnificent underwater world, especially if you're not a swimmer. **Atlantis Submarines** ★, 658 Front St. (www.atlantisadventures.com; ✆ **800/548-6262** or 808/667-2224), offers trips out of Lahaina Harbor every hour on the hour from 9am to 2pm; prices are $105 for adults, $115 adult and first child and $38 for additional children under 12 (children must be at least 3 ft. tall). Allow 2 hours for this underwater adventure. *Warning:* This is not a good choice if you're claustrophobic.

Surfing

Expert surfers visit Maui in winter, when the surf's really up. The best surfing beaches include **Honolua Bay,** north of the Kapalua Resort (the third bay past the Ritz-Carlton Kapalua, off the Honoapiilani Hwy., or Hwy. 30); **Lahaina Harbor** (in summer, there'll be waves just off the channel entrance with a south swell); **Maalaea Beach,** just outside the break wall of the Maalaea Harbor (a clean, world-class left); and **Hookipa Beach,** where surfers get the waves until noon (after that—in a carefully worked-out compromise to share this prized surf spot—the windsurfers take over).

Always wanted to learn to surf but didn't know whom to ask? Call the **Nancy Emerson School of Surfing,** 505 Front St., Ste. 224 (www.mauisurf clinics.com; © **808/244-SURF** [7873]). She's pioneered a new instructional technique called "Learn to Surf in One Lesson" (you can, really). It's $85 per person for a 2-hour group lesson; private 2-hour classes are $170. All instructors are lifeguard-certified.

Whale-Watching

The humpback is the star of the annual whale-watching season, which usually runs from about January to April (although it can begin as early as Dec and last until May).

WHALE-WATCHING FROM SHORE The best time to whale-watch is between mid-December and April: Just look out to sea. There's no best time of day, but it seems that when the sea is glassy and there's no wind, the whales appear. Once you see one, keep watching in the same vicinity; they may stay down for 20 minutes. Bring a book. And binoculars, if you can.

Some good whale-watching spots on Maui include:

MCGREGOR POINT On the way to Lahaina, there's a scenic lookout at mile marker 9 (just before you get to the Lahaina Tunnel); it's a good viewpoint to scan for whales.

OLOWALU REEF Along the straight part of Honoapiilani Highway, between McGregor Point and Olowalu, you'll sometimes see whales leap out of the water. Their appearance can bring traffic to a screeching halt: People abandon their cars and run down to the sea to watch, causing a major traffic jam. If you stop, pull off the road so others may pass.

WAILEA BEACH MARRIOTT RESORT In the Wailea coastal walk, stop at this resort to look for whales through the telescope installed as a public service by the Hawaii Island Humpback Whale National Marine Sanctuary.

PUU OLAI It's a tough climb up this coastal landmark near the Maui Beach & Golf Resort, but you're likely to be well rewarded: This is the island's best spot for offshore whale-watching. On the 360-foot cinder cone overlooking Makena Beach, you'll be at the right elevation to see Pacific humpbacks as they dodge Molokini and cruise up Alalakeiki Channel between Maui and Kahoolawe. If you don't see one, you'll at least have a whale of a view.

WHALE-WATCHING CRUISES For a closer look, take a whale-watching cruise. Just about all of Hawaii's snorkel and dive boats become whale-watching boats in season; some of them even carry professional naturalists onboard so you'll know what you're seeing. For the best options, see "Boating," earlier in this section.

WHALE-WATCHING BY KAYAK & RAFT Seeing a humpback whale from an ocean kayak or raft is awesome. **Captain Steve's Rafting Excursions** (www.captainsteves.com; © **808/667-5565**) offers 2-hour whale-watching excursions out of Lahaina Harbor from $55 for adults, $45 for children 3 to 12. *Tip:* Save by booking the 7:30am early-bird adventure.

Windsurfing

Maui has Hawaii's best windsurfing beaches. In winter, windsurfers from around the world flock to **Hookipa Beach, Kanaha Beach, Ohukai Park, Kihei,** and (for experienced windsurfers), in front of the **Maui Sunset** condo, 1032 S. Kihei Rd., near Waipuilani Street (a block north of McDonald's), which has great windsurfing conditions but a very shallow reef (not good for beginners).

HST Windsurfing & Kitesurfing Lessons, 425 Koloa St., Kahului (www.hstwindsurfing.com; © **800/968-5423** or 808/871-5423), offers lessons from $99.

For daily reports on wind and surf conditions, call the **Wind and Surf Report** at © **808/877-3611.**

HIKING & CAMPING

In the past 4 decades, Maui has grown from a rural island to a fast-paced resort destination, but its natural beauty remains largely inviolate; many places can be explored only on foot. Those interested in seeing the backcountry—complete with virgin waterfalls, remote wilderness trails, and quiet, meditative settings—should head for Haleakala's upcountry or the tropical Hana Coast.

Camping on Maui can be extreme (inside a volcano) or benign (by the sea in Hana). It can be wet, cold, and rainy; or hot, dry, and windy—often all on the same day. If you're heading for Haleakala, remember that U.S. astronauts trained for the moon inside the volcano; bring survival gear. You'll need your swimsuit and rain gear if you're bound for Waianapanapa. Bring your own gear, as there are no places to rent camping equipment on Maui.

For more information on Maui camping and hiking trails, and to obtain free maps, contact **Haleakala National Park,** P.O. Box 369, Makawao, HI 96768 (www.nps.gov/hale; © **808/572-4400**), or the **State Division of Forestry and Wildlife,** 1955 Main St., Wailuku (http://dlnr.hawaii.gov/dofaw/; © **808/984-8100**). Maps are available, at www.hawaiitrails.org. For information on trails, hikes, camping, and permits for state parks, contact the **Hawaii State Department of Land and Natural Resources,** State Parks Division, 54 S. High St. (http://dlnr.hawaii.gov/dsp; © **808/984-8109**); you can get information from the website as well as obtaining permits. For Maui County Parks, contact the **Department of Parks and Recreation,** 700 Halia Nakoa St. (www.co.maui.hi.us; © **808/270-7230**).

GUIDED HIKES If you'd like a knowledgeable guide to accompany you on a hike, call **Maui Hiking Safaris ★** (www.mauihikingsafaris.com; © **888/445-3963** or 808/573-0168). Owner Randy Warner takes visitors on half- and full-day hikes into valleys, rainforests, and coastal areas. His rates are $75 to $99 for a half-day and $120 to $169 for a full day, which include day packs, rain parkas, snacks, water, and, on full-day hikes, sandwiches.

For information on hikes given by the **Hawaii Sierra Club** on Maui, go to www.mauisierraclub.org.

Haleakala National Park ★★★

For complete coverage of the national park, see p. 173.

HIKING INTO THE WILDERNESS AREA: SLIDING SANDS & HALEMAUU TRAILS

Hiking into Maui's dormant volcano is the best way to see it. The terrain inside the wilderness area of the volcano, which ranges from burnt-red cinder cones to ebony-black lava flows, is simply spectacular. There are some 27 miles of hiking trails, two camping sites, and three cabins.

Entrance to Haleakala National Park is $15 per car. The rangers offer free guided hikes most days, which are a great way to learn about the unusual flora and geological formations here. Wear sturdy shoes and be prepared for wind, rain, and intense sun. Bring water and a hat. Additional options include full-moon hikes and star-program hikes. **Always call at least a month in advance:** The hikes and briefing sessions may be canceled, so check first. For details, call the park at ✆ **808/572-4400** or visit www.nps.gov/hale.

Try to arrange to stay at least 1 night in the park; 2 or 3 nights will allow you more time to explore the fascinating interior of the volcano (see below for details on the cabins and campgrounds in the wilderness area of the valley). If you want to venture out on your own, the best route takes in two trails: into the crater along **Sliding Sands Trail,** which begins on the rim at 9,800 feet and descends into the belly of the beast, to the valley floor at 6,600 feet, and back out along **Halemauu Trail.** Hardy hikers can consider making the 11-mile, one-way descent, which takes 9 hours, and the equally long return ascent in a day. The rest of us can extend this steep hike to 2 days. The descending and ascending trails aren't loops; the trail heads are miles (and several thousand feet in elevation) apart, so make transportation arrangements in advance. Before you set out, stop at park headquarters to get camping and hiking updates.

The trail head for Sliding Sands is well marked and the trail is easy to follow over lava flows and cinders. As you descend, look around: The view is

---

A Word of Warning About the Weather

The weather at nearly 10,000 feet can change suddenly and without warning. Come prepared for cold, high winds, rain, and even snow in winter. Temperatures can range from 77°F (25°C) down to 26°F (–3°C), and high winds are frequent. Daytime temperatures can be 30° colder than at sea level. Sunrise and sunset temperatures average 30° to 40°F in winter (–1° to 4°C) and 40° to 50°F (4°–10°C) in summer. Rainfall varies from 40 inches a year on the western end of the crater to more than 200 inches on the eastern side. Bring boots, waterproof gear, warm clothes, extra layers, and lots of sunscreen—the sun shines very brightly up here. For the latest weather information, call ✆ **808/944-3756 x4.**

breathtaking. In the afternoon, waves of clouds flow into the Kaupo and Koolau gaps. Vegetation is spare to nonexistent at the top, but the closer you get to the valley floor, the more growth you'll see: bracken ferns, pili grass, shrubs, even flowers. On the floor, the trail travels across rough lava flows, passing by rare silversword plants, volcanic vents, and multicolored cinder cones.

The Halemauu Trail goes over red and black lava and past vegetation, like evening primrose, as it begins its ascent up the valley wall. Occasionally, riders on horseback use this trail. The proper etiquette is to step aside and stand quietly next to the trail as the horses pass.

Some shorter and easier hiking options include the .5-mile walk down the **Hosmer Grove Nature Trail,** or just the first mile or two down **Sliding Sands Trail,** which gives you a hint of what lies ahead. (Even this short hike is exhausting at the high altitude.) A good day hike is **Halemauu Trail** to Holua Cabin and back, an 8-mile, half-day trip.

CABINS & CAMPGROUNDS IN THE WILDERNESS AREA

Most people stay at one of two tent campgrounds. For more information, contact **Haleakala National Park,** P.O. Box 369, Makawao, HI 96768 (www.nps.gov/hale; © **808/572-4400**).

CABINS　It can get really cold and windy down in the valley (see "A Word of Warning About the Weather" box, above), so try for a cabin. They're warm, protected from the elements, and reasonably priced. Each has 12 padded bunks (but no bedding; bring your own), a table, chairs, cooking utensils, a two-burner propane stove, and a wood-burning stove with firewood (you may also have a few cockroaches). The cabins are spaced so that each one is an easy walk from the other: Holua cabin is on the Halemauu Trail, Kapalaoa cabin on Sliding Sands Trail, and Paliku cabin on the eastern end by the Kaupo Gap. The rates are $75 a night for groups of one to 12.

Requests for cabins may be made up to 180 days in advance (be sure to request alternate dates). You can request all three cabins at once; you're limited to 2 nights in one cabin and 3 nights total in the wilderness each month. The rules and regulations can be found at www.nps.gov/hale; online applications are at www.recreation.gov. Click "Make Reservation," then type in Haleakala and click on "Haleakala National Park Cabin Permits" and follow the prompts.

CAMPGROUNDS　If the cabins are booked for your dates, all is not lost—there are three tent-camping sites that can accommodate you: two in the wilderness and one just outside at Hosmer Grove. There is no charge for tent camping.

Hosmer Grove, located at 6,800 feet, is a small, open, grassy area surrounded by a forest. Trees protect campers from the winds, but nights still get very cold; sometimes there's ice on the ground up here. This is the best place to spend the night in a tent if you want to see the Haleakala sunrise. Come up the day before, enjoy the park, take a day hike, and then turn in early. The enclosed-glass summit building opens at sunrise for those who come to greet the dawn—a welcome windbreak. Facilities at Hosmer Grove include a

Hiking & Camping

MAUI, THE VALLEY ISLE

covered pavilion with picnic tables and grills, chemical toilets, and drinking water. No permits are needed, and there's no charge—but you can stay for only 3 nights in a 30-day period.

The two tent-camping areas inside the volcano are **Holua,** just off Halemauu at 6,920 feet, and **Paliku,** just before the Kaupo Gap at the eastern end of the valley, at 6,380 feet. Facilities at both campgrounds are limited to pit toilets and nonpotable catchment water. Camping is free but limited to 2 consecutive nights, and no more than 3 nights a month inside the volcano. Permits are issued at park headquarters daily from 8am to 3pm, on a first-come, first-served basis on the day you plan to camp. Occupancy is limited to 25 people in each campground.

HIKING & CAMPING AT KIPAHULU (NEAR HANA)

In the East Maui section of Haleakala National Park, you can set up at **Oheo Campground,** a first-come, first-served, drive-in campground with tent sites for 100 near the ocean. It has a few tables, barbecue grills, and chemical toilets. No permit is required, but there's a 3-night limit. No food or drinking water is available, so bring your own. Bring a tent as well—it rains 75 inches a year here. Contact **Kipahulu Ranger Station,** Haleakala National Park (www.nps.gov/hale/planyourvisit/wilderness-camping.htm; © **808/248-7375**), for information.

HIKING FROM THE SUMMIT If you hike from the crater rim down **Kaupo Gap** to the ocean, more than 20 miles away, you'll pass through several climate zones. On a clear day, you can see every island except Kauai on the trip down.

APPROACHING KIPAHULU FROM HANA If you drive to Kipahulu, you'll have to approach it from the Hana Highway because it's not accessible from the summit. From the ranger station, it's a short hike above the famous **Oheo Gulch** (which was misnamed the Seven Sacred Pools in the 1940s) to two spectacular waterfalls. The first, **Makahiku Falls,** is easily reached from the central parking area; the trail head begins near the ranger station. Pipiwai Trail leads you up to the road and beyond for .5 miles to the overlook. If you hike another 1.5 miles up the trail across two bridges and through a bamboo forest, you reach **Waimoku Falls.** It's a good uphill hike, but press on to avoid the pool's crowd. In hard rain, streams swell quickly. Always be aware of your surroundings.

GOLF & OTHER OUTDOOR ACTIVITIES

Golf

For last-minute and discount tee times, call **Stand-by Golf** (www.hawaii standbygolf.com; © **888/645-2665**), which offers savings off greens fees, plus guaranteed tee times for same-day or future golfing. **Golf Club Rentals** (www.mauiclubrentals.com; ☏ **808/665-0800**) has custom-built clubs for men, women, and juniors (both right- and left-handed), which can be delivered island wide; the rates are $25 a day for steel clubs, while a full graphite set is $30 a day.

WEST MAUI

Kaanapali Golf Resort ★   Both courses at Kaanapali offer a challenge to all golfers, from high-handicappers to near-pros. The par-72, 6,305-yard **North Course** is a true Robert Trent Jones, Sr., design: an abundance of wide bunkers; several long, stretched-out tees; and the largest, most contoured greens on Maui. The par-72, 6,250-yard **South Course** is an Arthur Jack Snyder design; although shorter than the North Course, it requires more accuracy on the narrow, hilly fairways. Facilities at Kaanapali include a driving range, putting course, and clubhouse with dining. You'll have a better chance of getting a tee time on weekdays.

Off Hwy. 30, Kaanapali. www.kaanapali-golf.com. ☏ **808/661-3691.** Greens fees Royal Kaanapali Course $255 ($169 for Kaanapali guests), twilight rates $129; Kaanapali Kai Course $255 ($129 for Kaanapali guests), twilight rates $99. At the 1st stoplight in Kaanapali, turn onto Kaanapali Pkwy.; the 1st building on your right is the clubhouse.

Kapalua Resort ★★★   The views from these two championship courses are worth the greens fees alone. The par-72, 6,761-yard **Bay Course** was designed by Arnold Palmer and Ed Seay. This course is a bit forgiving, with its wide fairways; the greens, however, are difficult to read. The often-photographed 5th overlooks a small ocean cove; even the pros have trouble with this rocky par-3, 205-yard hole. The **Plantation Course,** site of the PGA Hyundai Tournament of Champions, is a Ben Crenshaw/Bill Coore design. This 6,547-yard, par-73 course, set on a rolling hillside, is excellent for developing your low shots and precise chipping. Facilities for both courses include locker rooms, a driving range, and excellent dining. Weekdays are your best bet for tee times.

Off Hwy. 30. www.golfatkapalua.com. ☏ **808/669-8044.** Greens fees Bay Course $219 ($199 for resort guests), twilight rates $159; Plantation Course $299 ($239 for guests), twilight rates $199.

SOUTH MAUI

Wailea Golf Club ★★   There are three courses to choose from at Wailea. The **Blue Course,** a par-72, 6,758-yard course designed by Arthur Jack Snyder and dotted with bunkers and water hazards, is for duffers and pros alike. A little more difficult is the par-72, 7,078-yard championship **Gold Course,** with narrow fairways, several tricky dogleg holes, and the classic Robert Trent Jones, Jr., challenges: natural hazards, such as lava-rock walls and native Hawaiian grasses. The **Emerald Course,** also designed by Robert Trent Jones, Jr., is Wailea's newest, with tropical landscaping and a player-friendly design. With 54 holes to play, getting a tee time is slightly easier on weekends than at other resorts, but weekdays are still best (the Emerald Course is

MAUI, THE VALLEY ISLE — Golf & Other Outdoor Activities

usually the toughest to book). Facilities include two pro shops, restaurants, locker rooms, and a complete golf training facility.

Wailea Alanui Dr. (off Wailea Iki Dr.). www.waileagolf.com. ℂ **888/328-MAUI** (6284) or 808/875-7450. Greens fees Blue Course $190 ($175 for resort guests), twilight rates $145 after noon; Gold Course and Emerald Course $240 ($199 for resort guests), after 1pm $160. Check for summer rates.

Biking

For information on bikeways and maps, get a copy of the "Maui County Bicycle Map," which has information on road suitability, climate, mileage, elevation changes, bike shops, safety tips, and various bicycling routes. The map is available at www.southmauibicycles.com; click on the link to "Maui County Bicycle Map."

Cruising Haleakala ★ BIKING TRAIL   It's not even close to dawn, but here you are, rubbing your eyes awake, riding in a van up the long, dark road to the top of Maui's dormant volcano. It's colder than you ever thought possible for a tropical island. The air is thin. The place is crowded, packed with people. You stomp your chilly feet while you wait, sipping hot coffee. Then comes the sun, exploding over the yawning Haleakala Crater, big enough to swallow Manhattan—a moment you won't soon forget. Now you know why Hawaiians named the crater the House of the Sun. But there's no time to linger: Decked out in your screaming-yellow parka, you mount your mechanical

ESPECIALLY FOR kids

Taking a Submarine Ride   Atlantis Submarines (p. 190) takes you and the kids down into the shallow coastal waters off Lahaina in a real sub, where you'll see plenty of fish (and maybe even a shark!). They'll love it, and you'll stay dry the entire time. Allow about 2 hours for the trip.

Riding the Sugar-Cane Train   As we went to press, the train was closed for restoration. Call or check online, ℂ **808/667-6851** or visit www.sugar canetrain.com, to make sure they are running again before you go. Small kids love this ride, as do train buffs of all ages. A steam engine pulls open-passenger cars of the Lahaina/Kaanapali and Pacific Railroad on a 30-minute, 12-mile round-trip through sugar-cane fields between Lahaina and Kaanapali while the conductor sings and calls out

the landmarks. Along the way, you can see the hidden parts of Kaanapali and the islands of Molokai and Lanai beyond.

Tour the Stars   After sunset, the stars over Kaanapali shine big and bright, because the tropical sky is almost pollut-ant-free and no big-city lights interfere with the cosmic view. Amateur astronomers can probe the Milky Way, see the rings of Saturn and Jupiter's moons, and scan the Sea of Tranquility in a 60-minute star search on the world's first recreational computer-driven telescope. It all takes place nightly at the **Hyatt Regency Maui Resort,** 200 Nohea Kai Dr. (ℂ **808/661-1234**), at 8, 9, and 10pm. The cost for hotel guests is $25 for adults and $15 for children 12 and under; nonguests pay $30 for adults and $20 for children. The 10pm show is for adults only and is $45. Reservations are a must.

steed and test its most important feature, the brakes—because you're about to coast 37 miles down a 10,000-foot volcano.

Cruising down Haleakala, from the lunarlike landscape at the top past flower farms, pineapple fields, and eucalyptus groves, is quite an experience—and just about anybody can do it. This is a safe trip that requires some stamina in the colder, wetter winter months but is fun for everyone in the warmer months—the key word being "warmer." In winter and the rainy season, conditions can be harsh, especially on the top, with below-freezing temperatures and 40-mph winds.

Maui's oldest downhill company is **Maui Downhill** ★ (201 Dairy Rd., Kahului; www.mauidownhill.com; ✆ **800/535-BIKE** [2453] or 808/871-2155), which offers a sunrise safari bike tour, including continental breakfast and a stop for lunch (not hosted), starting at $169 ($130 if booked online). **Mountain Riders Bike Tours** (www.mountainriders.com; ✆ **800/706-7700** or 808/242-9739) offers sunrise rides for $150 ($120 if booked online) and midday trips for $130 ($104 online). All rates include hotel pickup, transport to the top, coffee and pastries, bicycle, safety equipment, and a meal stop, not hosted. Wear layers of warm clothing—there may be a 30° change in temperature from the top of the mountain to the ocean. Generally, the tour groups will not take riders under 12, but younger children can ride along in the van that accompanies the groups. Pregnant women should also ride in the van.

If you want to avoid the crowds and go down the mountain at your own pace, call **Haleakala Bike Company** (www.bikemaui.com; ✆ **888/922-2453**), which will outfit you with the latest gear and take you up Haleakala.

Tennis

Maui has excellent public tennis courts; all are free and available from daylight to sunset (a few are even lit for night play until 10pm). For a complete list of public courts, call **Maui County Parks and Recreation** (www.co.maui.hi.us/facilities.aspx, and search for "tennis courts"; ✆ **808/270-7383**). The courts are available on a first-come, first-served basis. When someone is waiting, limit your play to 45 minutes. Most public courts do require a wait and are not conveniently located near the major resort areas, so most visitors are likely to play at their own hotels for a fee. The exceptions to this are in Kihei (which has courts in Kalama Park on S. Kihei Rd., and in Waipuilani Park on W. Waipuilani Rd., behind the Maui Sunset condo), in Lahaina (which has courts in Malu'uou o lele Park, at Front and Shaw sts.), and in Hana (which has courts in Hana Park, on the Hana Hwy.).

Private tennis courts are available at most resorts and hotels on the island. The **Kapalua Tennis Garden and Village Tennis Center,** Kapalua Resort (www.kapaluamaui.com; ✆ **808/662-7730**), is home to the Kapalua Open, which features the largest purse in the state, on Labor Day weekend. Court rentals are $15 per person. The staff will match you up with a partner if you need one. In Wailea, try the **Wailea Tennis Club,** 131 Wailea Iki Place (www.waileatennis.com; ✆ **808/879-1958**), with 11 Plexipave courts. Court fees are $20 per player.

SHOPS & GALLERIES

The island of Maui is a shopaholic's dream as well as an arts center, with a large number of resident artists who show their works in dozens of galleries and countless gift shops. Maui is also the queen of specialty products, an agricultural cornucopia that includes Kula onions, upcountry proteas, Kaanapali coffee, world-renowned potato chips, and many other tasty treats that are shipped worldwide.

As with any popular visitor destination, you'll have to wade through bad art and mountains of trinkets, particularly in Lahaina and Kihei, where touristy boutiques line the streets between rare pockets of treasures. If you shop in South or West Maui, expect to pay resort prices, clear down to a bottle of Evian or sunscreen.

Central Maui

KAHULUI

Kahului's best shopping is concentrated in two places. **Maui Mall,** 70 E. Kaahumanu Ave. (www.mauimall.com; © **808/877-8952**), is the place of everyday retail, from **Longs Drugs** and **Whole Foods** to **Tasaka Guri Guri** (serving icy treats that are neither ice cream nor shave ice, but something in between) and Kahului's largest movie theater, a 12-screen megaplex that features current releases as well as art-house films. **Queen Kaahumanu Center,** 275 Kaahumanu Ave. (www.queenkaahumanucenter.com; © **808/877-3369**), a 10-minute drive from the Kahului Airport on Hwy. 32, has more than 100 shops, restaurants, and theaters. It covers all the bases, from arts and crafts to a **Foodland** and everything in between: a thriving food court; the island's best beauty supply, **Lisa's Beauty Supply & Salon** (© **808/877-6463**), and its sister store for cosmetics, **Madison Avenue Day Spa and Boutique** (© **808/873-0880**); such mall standards as **Sunglass Hut, Radio Shack,** and **Local Motion** (surf wear and beachwear); and department stores likes **Macy's** and **Sears.**

Maui Swap Meet ★ Held every Saturday from 7am to 1pm, some 200 vendors and plenty of parking make this a bargain shopper's paradise. The colorful Maui specialties include vegetables from Kula and Keanae, homemade ethnic foods, and baked goods (including some fabulous fruit breads). Now students at the community college also sell artwork and ceramics, and the culinary-arts program has prepared food for sale. Between the cheap Balinese imports and New Age crystals and incense, you may find some vintage John Kelly prints and 1930s collectibles. Admission is 50¢, children under 12 are free, and if you go early while the vendors are setting up, no one will turn you away. At Maui Community College, in an area bounded by Kahului Beach Rd. and Wahine Pio Ave. (access via Wahine Pio Ave.). http://www.mauiexposition.com/MAUISWAPMEET.html © **808/244-3100.**

WAILUKU

Wailuku's attractive vintage architecture, numerous antiques shops, and mom-and-pop eateries imbue the town with a charm noticeably absent in the resort areas of West, South, and Upcountry Maui. There is no plastic aloha in Wailuku. Of course, there's junk, but a stroll along Main and Market streets usually turns up a treasure or two. It's a mixed bag, but a treasure hunt, too.

Bailey House Museum Shop ★ For made-in-Hawaii items, Bailey House is a must-stop. The shop, a small space of discriminating taste, packs a wallop with its selection of remarkable gift items, from Hawaiian music to exquisite woods, traditional Hawaiian games to pareu and books. Prints by the Hawaii artist Joelle Purse, lauhala hats hanging in midair, hand-sewn pheasant hatbands, jams and jellies, Maui cookbooks, and an occasional Hawaiian quilt are some of the treasures to be found here. At the Bailey House Museum, 2375-A Main St. www.mauimuseum.org. ℂ **808/244-3326.**

Central Maui Edibles

Maui's produce has long been a source of pride for islanders. On Tuesday, Wednesday, and Friday from 8am to 4pm, the **Ohana Farmers Market** at Queen Kaahumanu Shopping Center (ℂ **808/877-3369**) is where you'll find a fresh, inexpensive selection of Maui-grown fruit, vegetables, flowers, and plants. Crafts and gourmet foods add to the event, and the large monkeypod trees provide welcome shade.

West Maui

LAHAINA

Lahaina's merchants and art galleries go all out from 5:30 to 8pm every second Friday of the month, when **Art Night** ★ brings an extra measure of hospitality and community spirit. The Art Night openings are usually marked with live entertainment and refreshments, plus a livelier-than-usual street scene.

What was formerly a big, belching pineapple cannery is now a maze of shops and restaurants at the northern end of Lahaina town, known as the **Lahaina Cannery Mall,** 1221 Honoapiilani Hwy. (www.lahainacannerymall.com; ℂ **808/661-5304**). From footwear to aloha wear, Lahaina Cannery is a wealth of shops; a large food court serves bites ranging from Vietnamese *banh* *mi* sandwiches to Japanese sushi. There's also a **Longs Drugs** and a 24-hour **Safeway** for groceries.

A welcome touch of Hawaiiana at the **Lahaina Center** (900 Front St.; ℂ **808/667-9216**) is the conversion of 10,000 square feet of parking space into the re-creation of a traditional Hawaiian village, called **Hale Kahiko.** With the commercialization of modern Lahaina, it's easy to forget that it was once the capital of the Hawaiian kingdom and a significant historic site. Free, guided tours are offered daily between 9am and 6pm.

Lahaina Arts Society Galleries ★   With its membership of nearly 200 Maui artists, the nonprofit Lahaina Arts Society is an excellent community resource. Changing monthly exhibits in the Banyan Tree and Old Jail galleries offer a good look at the island's artistic well: two-dimensional art, fiber art, ceramics, sculpture, prints, jewelry, and more. In the shade of the humongous banyan tree in the square across from Pioneer Inn, "Art in the Park" fairs are offered several times each month (check the website for dates). 648 Wharf St. www.lahainaarts.com. ℂ **808/661-3228.**

Village Galleries in Lahaina ★   The 30-year-old-plus Village Galleries is the oldest continuously running gallery on Maui, and it's esteemed as one of the few galleries with consistently high standards. The newer contemporary gallery offers colorful gift items and jewelry. An additional location is at the Ritz-Carlton Kapalua, 1 Ritz-Carlton Dr. (ℂ **808/669-1800**). 120 Dickenson St. www.villagegalleriesmaui.com. ℂ **800/346-0585** or 808/661-4402.

KAANAPALI

On a recent trip, I was somewhat disappointed with upscale **Whalers Village,** 2435 Kaanapali Pkwy. (www.whalersvillage.com; ℂ **808/661-4567**). Although it offers everything from Pacific Regional cuisine to Tommy Bahama and Sephora, it's short on local shops, and parking at the nearby lot is expensive. The complex is home to the **Whalers Village Museum,** with its interactive exhibits, 40-foot sperm-whale skeleton, and sand castles on perpetual display, but shoppers come for the designer thrills and beachfront dining.

Sandal Tree ★   It's unusual for a resort shop to draw local customers on a regular basis, but the Sandal Tree attracts a flock of footwear fanatics who come here from throughout the islands for rubber thongs and Top-Siders, sandals and dressy pumps, athletic shoes and hats, designer footwear, and much more. Prices are realistic, too. Also at the Shops at Wailea, 3750 Wailea Alanui Dr., Kihei. At Whalers Village, 2435 Kaanapali Pkwy. www.sandaltree.com. ℂ **808/667-5330.**

Totally Hawaiian Gift Gallery ★   This gallery makes a good browse for its selection of Niihau shell jewelry, excellent Hawaiian CDs, Norfolk pine bowls, and Hawaiian quilt kits. At Whalers Village, 2435 Kaanapali Pkwy. www.totally hawaiian.com. ℂ **808/667-4070.**

HONOKOWAI, KAHANA & NAPILI

Those driving north of Kaanapali toward Kapalua will notice the **Honokowai Marketplace,** on Lower Honoapiilani Road, only minutes before the Kapalua

Airport. It houses restaurants and coffee shops, a dry cleaner, the flagship **Star Market,** and a few clothing stores.

KAPALUA

Honolua Store ★ Walk on the old wood floors peppered with holes from golf shoes and find your everyday essentials, from bottled water to suntan lotion, plus snacks and souvenirs. With picnic tables on the veranda and a takeout counter offering deli items—more than a dozen types of sandwiches, salads, and budget-friendly breakfasts—there are always long lines of customers. 502 Office Rd. (next to the Ritz-Carlton Kapalua). ✆ **808/665-9105.**

South Maui

KIHEI

Kihei is one long strip of strip malls. Most of the shopping here is concentrated in the **Azeka Place Shopping Center** on South Kihei Road. Across the street, **Azeka Place II** houses several prominent attractions, including the **Coffee Store** (p. 147) and a cluster of specialty shops with everything from children's clothes to shoes, sunglasses, and swimwear.

Hawaiian Moons Natural Foods ★ Hawaiian Moons is an exceptional health-food store, as well as a mini-supermarket with one of the best selections of Maui products on the island. The salad bar is one of the most popular food stops on the coast. 2411 S. Kihei Rd. www.hawaiianmoons.com. ✆ **808/875-4356.**

WAILEA

Ki'i Gallery ★★ Some of the works are large and lavish, such as the Toland Sand prisms for just under $5,000 and the John Stokes handblown glass. Those who love glass in all forms, from handblown vessels to jewelry, will love a browse through Ki'i. The gallery is devoted to glass and original paintings and drawings; roughly half of the artists are from Hawaii. An additional location is at the Shops at Wailea (✆ **808/874-1181**). 3850 Wailea Alanui Dr., Grand Wailea. www.kiigallery.com. ✆ **808/874-3059.**

Shops at Wailea ★ The high-end shops sell expensive souvenirs, gifts, clothing, and accessories for a life of perpetual vacations. Chains still rule (Gap, Louis Vuitton, Banana Republic, Tiffany, Crazy Shirts, Honolua Surf Co.), but there is fertile ground for the inveterate shopper in the nearly 60 shops in the complex. **Martin & MacArthur** (furniture and gift gallery; ✆ **808/891-8844**) has landed in Wailea as part of a retail mix that is similar to Whalers Village. A couple of stores of note are **Blue Ginger** (✆ **808/891-0772**) and **Tori Richard** (✆ **808/891-8633**). 3750 Wailea Alanui. www.theshopsatwailea.com. ✆ **808/891-6770.**

Upcountry Maui

MAKAWAO

Besides being a shopper's paradise, Makawao is the home of the island's most prominent arts organization, the **Hui No'eau Visual Arts Center,** 2841 Baldwin Ave. (www.huinoeau.com; ✆ **808/572-6560**). Designed in 1917 by C. W.

Dickey, one of Hawaii's most prominent architects, the two-story, Mediterranean-style stucco home that houses the center is located on a sprawling 9-acre estate called Kaluanui. Its tree-lined driveway features two of Maui's largest hybrid Cook and Norfolk Island pines. A legacy of Maui's prominent *kamaaina* (old-timers) Harry and Ethel Baldwin, the estate became an arts center in 1976. The exhibits here are drawn from a wide range of disciplines and multicultural sources, and include both contemporary and traditional art from established and emerging artists. The gift shop, featuring many one-of-a-kind works by local artists and artisans, is worth a stop. Hours are Monday through Sunday from 9am to 4pm.

Collections ★   You'll find everything from sportswear to soaps to jewelry here, with marvelous miscellany items. A Makawao must-stop. 3677 Baldwin Ave. www.collectionsmauiinc.com. ✆ **808/572-0781.**

Holiday & Co. ★   Attractive women's clothing in natural fibers hangs from racks, while jewelry to go with it beckons from the counter. Recent finds include elegant fiber evening bags, luxurious bath gels, easygoing dresses and separates, Dansko clogs, shawls, soaps, aloha shirts, books, picture frames, and jewelry. 3681 Baldwin Ave. ✆ **808/572-1470.**

Hot Island Glassblowing Studio & Gallery ★   You can watch the artist transform molten glass into works of art and utility in this studio at the Makawao Courtyard, where an award-winning family of glass blowers built its own furnaces. It's fascinating to watch the shapes emerge from glass melted at 2,300°F (1,260°C). The colorful works displayed range from small paperweights to large vessels. 3620 Baldwin Ave. www.hotislandglass.com. ✆ **808/572-4527.**

Fresh Flowers in Kula
Like anthuriums on the Big Island, proteas are a Maui trademark and an abundant crop on Haleakala's rich volcanic slopes. They also travel well, dry beautifully, and can be shipped worldwide with ease. Check out **Proteas of Hawaii** (15200 Haleakala Hwy., next to Kula Lodge; www.proteasofhawaii.com; ✆ **808/878-2536**).

Upcountry Edibles
Working folks in Makawao pick up spaghetti and lasagna, sandwiches, salads, and changing specials from the **Rodeo General Store,** 3661 Baldwin Ave. (www.facebook.com/Rodeo.General; ✆ **808/572-1868**). At the far end of the store is the oenophile's bonanza, a superior wine selection housed in its own temperature-controlled cave.

   In the more than 6 decades that the **T. Komoda Store and Bakery,** 3674 Baldwin Ave. (✆ **808/572-7261**), has done business in this spot, untold numbers have creaked over the wooden floors to pick up Komoda's famous cream puffs. Old-timers know to come early or they'll be sold out. Then the cinnamon rolls, doughnuts, pies, and chocolate cake take over. Pastries are just the beginning; poi, macadamia-nut candies and cookies, and small bunches of local fruit keep the customers coming back.

East Maui

PAIA

Maui Crafts Guild ★   The old wooden storefront at the gateway to Paia houses crafts of high quality—from pit-fired raku to bowls of Norfolk pine and other Maui woods, fashioned by Maui hands—and in all price ranges. Artist-owned and -operated, the guild claims 25 members who live and work on Maui. Everything can be shipped. 120 Hana Hwy. www.mauicraftsguild.com. ℭ **808/579-9697.**

Maui Hands ★   Maui hands have made 90% of the items in this shop/gallery. Because it's a consignment shop, you'll find Hawaii-made handicrafts and prices that aren't inflated. The selection includes paintings, prints, jewelry, glass marbles, native-wood bowls, and tchotchkes for every budget. This is an ideal stop for made-on-Maui products and crafts of good quality. 84 Hana Hwy. www.mauihands.com. ℭ **808/579-9245.** Additional locations: 3620 Baldwin Ave., Makawao ℭ **808/572-5194;** 612 Front St., Lahaina ℭ **808/667-9898;** and 200 Nohea Kai Dr., Kaanapali ℭ **808/667-7997.**

MAUI AFTER DARK

The island's most prestigious entertainment venue is the $32-million **Maui Arts & Cultural Center** (www.mauiarts.org; ℭ **808/242-7469**). Bonnie Raitt has performed here, as have B. B. King, Hiroshima, Pearl Jam, Ziggy Marley, Lou Rawls, the American Indian Dance Theatre, Jonny Lang, and Tony Bennett. The center is as precious to Maui as the Met is to New York, with a visual-arts gallery, an outdoor amphitheater, offices, rehearsal space, a 300-seat theater for experimental performances, and a 1,200-seat main theater. Whether it's hula, the Iona Pear Dance Company, Willie Nelson, or the Maui Symphony Orchestra, only the best appear here. The center's activities are well publicized locally, so check the "Maui News" or ask your hotel concierge what's going on during your visit.

HAWAIIAN MUSIC   The best of Hawaiian music can be heard most Wednesday nights at the Napili Kai Beach Resort's indoor amphitheater, thanks to the **Masters of Hawaiian Slack Key Guitar Series** (www.slackkey.com; ℭ **808/669-3858**). The weekly shows present a side of Hawaii that few visitors ever get to see. Host George Kahumoku, Jr. introduces a new slack-key master every week. Not to be missed. Check website for dates.

West Maui

The buzz in West Maui is all about **Ulalena ★**, Maui Theatre, 878 Front St. (www.ulalena.com; ℭ **808/856-7900**), a riveting evening of entertainment that weaves Hawaiian mythology with drama, dance, and state-of-the-art multimedia capabilities in a multimillion-dollar theater. Polynesian dance, original music, acrobatics, and chant, performed by a local and international cast, combine to create an evocative experience that often leaves the audience speechless. Performances are given Monday through Friday. Tickets are $60 to $80 for adults, $30 to $50 for children 6 to 12 years. Call for discounts.

THE BEST PLACE IN THE WORLD TO see a movie

Imagine lounging on a comfy beach chair on the island of Maui watching the stars come out in the night sky. As soon as it gets dark enough, the biggest outdoor screen you've ever seen comes to life with a film premiere. This has to be the best place in the entire world to watch movies.

If you're headed to Maui in June, plan your travel dates around the **Maui Film Festival** (𝒞 **808/572-3456** or 579-9244; www.mauifilmfestival.com), which always starts the Wednesday before Father's Day. This is an event you won't want to miss. The 5-day festival features nightly films in the "Celestial Cinema," an under-the-stars, open-air "outdoor theater" on the Wailea Golf Course. The event features premieres and special advance screenings on a 50-foot-wide screen in Dolby Digital Surround Sound. Festival organizer and film producer

Barry Rivers selects "life-affirming" films that often become box-office hits.

In addition to the 5 days and nights of films and filmmaker panels, there's terrific food at many of the events: a Taste of Chocolate night, a Taste of Wailea (with Maui's top chefs creating exquisite culinary masterpieces), a "Starry Night" Dance Party and a host of other foodie events. For the family, there's a Father's Day concert of contemporary Hawaiian music, a sand-sculpture contest, and picnics. And for those interested in Hawaii culture, the festival presents TheStarShow, where live images of celestial objects are projected onto the screen, as experts in Polynesian astronomy and cultural history take the audience on a tour of the night sky and Polynesian navigational lore.

As Rivers puts it: "Rising stars, shooting stars, movie stars, all under the stars."

A very different type of live entertainment is **Warren & Annabelle's,** 900 Front St. (www.warrenandannabelles.com; 𝒞 **808/667-6244**), a magic/comedy cocktail show with illusionist Warren Gibson and "Annabelle," a ghost from the 1800s who plays the grand piano (even taking requests from the audience) as Warren dazzles you with his sleight-of-hand magic. Appetizers, desserts, and cocktails are available (either as a package or a la carte). Two shows Monday through Saturday, check-in is at 5 and 7:30pm. The show-only price is $64; the show plus gourmet appetizers and dessert costs $105. You must be 21 to attend.

The **Kaanapali Beach Hotel** has a wonderful show called **Kupanaha** (www. kupanaha.com; 𝒞 **800/262-8450**) that is perfect for the entire family. It features the renowned magicians Jody and Kathleen Baran and their entire family. The dinner show includes magic, illusions, and the story of the Hawaii fire goddess Pele, presented through hula and chant performed by the Kupanaha Dancers Academy. The shows are Tuesday through Saturday; tickets are $79 to $99 for adults, $65 to $99 for ages 13 to 20, and $49 to $99 for children 6 to 12. Prices include dinner (entree choices include salmon, grilled chicken, short ribs and shrimp, and a vegetarian dish, with a children's menu available).

Upcountry Maui

Upcountry in Makawao, the party never ends at **Casanova,** 1188 Makawao Ave. (𝒞 **808/572-0220**), the popular Italian *ristorante* where the good times

A NIGHT TO REMEMBER: luau, MAUI-STYLE

Most of the larger hotels in Maui's major resorts offer luau on a regular basis. You'll pay about $90 to $125 to attend one. To avoid disappointment, don't expect it to be a homegrown affair prepared in the traditional Hawaiian way. There are, however, commercial luaus that capture the romance and spirit of the occasion with quality food and entertainment in outdoor settings. For information on all of Maui's luaus, go to www.mauihawaiiluau.com.

Maui's best choice is, indisputably, the nightly **Old Lahaina Luau ★★** (www. oldlahainaluau.com; © **800/248-5828** or 808/667-1998). Located just ocean-side of the Lahaina Cannery, the Old Lahaina Luau maintains its high standards in food and entertainment—and enjoys an oceanfront setting that is peerless. Local craftspeople display their wares only a few feet from the ocean. Seating is provided on lauhala mats for those who wish to dine as the traditional Hawaiians did, but there are tables for everyone else.

There's no fire dancing in the program, but you won't miss it (for that, go to the Feast at Lele, p. 159). This luau offers a healthy balance of entertainment, showmanship, authentic high-quality food, educational value, and sheer romantic beauty. (No watered-down Mai Tais, either—these are the real thing.)

The luau begins at sunset and features Tahitian and Hawaiian entertainment, including ancient hula, hula from the missionary era, modern hula, and an intelligent narrative on the dance's rocky course of survival into modern times. The entertainment is riveting, even for jaded locals. The food, which is served from an open-air thatched structure, is as much Pacific Rim as authentically Hawaiian, featuring a whole *imu*-roasted kalua pig along with baked mahimahi in Maui onion cream sauce, guava chicken, teriyaki sirloin steak, lomi salmon, poi, poke, plus a range of traditional vegetables. The cost is $110 for adults, $75 for children 3 to 12 years old.

roll with the pasta. If a big-name mainland band is resting up on Maui following a sold-out concert on Oahu, you may find its members setting up for an impromptu night here. DJs take over on Wednesday (ladies' night). Generally, Friday and Saturday, live entertainment draws fun-lovers from even the most remote reaches of the island. Entertainment starts between 9:30 or 10pm and continues to 1:30am. The cover is usually $10 to $20. First Sunday afternoons, from 2 to 5pm, they have live music, but call ahead to make sure.

Paia & Central Maui

In Central Maui, the **Kahului Ale House,** 355 E. Kamehameha Ave. (www. alehouse.net; © **808/877-0001**), features live music or a DJ most nights; call for schedule.

In Paia, **Charley's Restaurant,** 142 Hana Hwy. (© **808/579-8085**), features an eclectic selection of music from country and western (Willie Nelson has been seen sitting in) to fusion/reggae to rock 'n' roll most nights; call for details or check their website: www.charleysmaui.com. Also in Paia, **Café des Amis,** 42 Baldwin Ave. (www.cdamaui.com; © **808/579-6323**), has live music Monday and Thursday through Saturday nights at 6:30pm.

KAUAI, THE GARDEN ISLE

On any list of the world's most spectacular islands, Kauai, the most remote of the Hawaiian islands, ranks right up there near the top. Here you'll find moody rainforests, majestic cliffs, jagged peaks, emerald valleys, towering palm trees, daily rainbows, and some of the most stunning golden beaches on earth. Soft tropical air, birdsong, the smell of ginger and plumeria, sparkling waterfalls—you don't just go to Kauai, you absorb it with every sense. With quaint villages like Hanalei and impressive geologic phenomena like Waimea Canyon, Kauai appeals equally to families, honeymooners, and nature lovers.

Beaches Snorkelers will love the clear blue waters of the North Shore's **Kee Beach.** For surfing and bodysurfing, **Poipu Beach** provides the right amount of heart-pounding adventure. The picture-perfect setting of **Hanalei Beach** attracts swimmers, snorkelers, body boarders, surfers, and windsurfers.

Things to Do A boat ride up the **Na Pali Coast** affords awe-inspiring views of lush, jagged cliffs plunging into the ocean and waterfalls plummeting to breathtaking depths. Stroll through history in **Old Waimea** town.

Eating & Drinking On excursions across the island, you'll find affordable choices in every town, from hamburger joints to stands dishing up **saimin** (ramenlike noodle soup) to busy neighborhood diners serving **loco moco** (a hamburger patty and fried egg on white rice smothered in gravy). **Ethnic cuisines** including Mexican, Asian, and Central American can also be found on the island. Don't leave Kauai without trying a refreshing **shave ice,** found at roadside stalls and vans.

Nature Catch a technicolor sunset at **Polihale State Park,** which hugs Kauai's western shore for nearly 17 miles. Kayaking **Huleia National Wildlife Refuge** is a fantastic opportunity to combine getting some exercise with seeing Kauai's endangered bird populations.

THE best KAUAI EXPERIENCES

o **Snorkeling on the clear waters of Kee Beach:** Rent a mask, fins, and snorkel, and enter a magical underwater world (p. 243). Facedown, you'll float like a leaf on a pond, watching brilliant fish dart through water clear as day; a slow-moving turtle may even stop by to check you out. Face up, you'll contemplate green-velvet cathedral-like cliffs under a blue sky, with long-tailed tropical birds riding the trade winds.

o **Hiking the Wondrous Waimea Canyon, the "Grand Canyon of the Pacific":** Ansel Adams would have loved this ageless desert canyon (p. 232), carved by an ancient river. Sunlight plays against its rustic red cliffs, burnt-orange pinnacles, and blue-green valleys. There's nothing else like it in the islands.

o **Wandering Through a Tropical Rain Forest:** Kokee State Park (p. 232) is a combination of mystical forest with fog and bog at around 4,000 feet, magical vistas, and exotic birds. The park's 45 miles of trails offer everything from casual nature strolls to hardy camping and hiking adventures among the redwoods.

o **Strolling Through Hawaiian History:** Old Waimea town (p. 211) looks so unassuming that you'd never guess it stood witness to a great many key events in Hawaii's history. This is the place where Captain James Cook "discovered" the Hawaiian Islands, where Russians once built a fort, and where New England missionaries arrived in 1820 to save the heathens. A self-guided walking-tour brochure is available at the West Kauai Visitors' Center in Waimea, the corner of Kaumualii Highway and Hwy. 550 (✆ **808/ 338-1332**). Or sign up for their 3-hour guided tour on Mondays (reservations a must by noon the prior Fri.).

o **Taking a Long Walk on a Short (but Historic) Pier:** First built in 1910, the pier at Hanalei Beach (p. 242) was once a major shipping port for local farmers. Today the rebuilt pier makes a great platform for swimming, fishing, and diving. It's at Black Pot Beach, where, in the olden days, local families would camp out all summer and always have something cooking in a "black pot" on the shore.

o **Watching for Whales:** Mahaulepu Beach (p. 239), in the Poipu area, offers excellent land-based viewing conditions for spotting whales that cruise by from December through April.

o **Journeying into Eden:** For a glimpse of the spectacularly remote Na Pali Coast, all you need do is hike the first 2 miles along the well-maintained Kalalau Trail (p. 252) into the first tropical valley, Hanakapiai. Hardier hikers can venture another 2 miles to the Hanakapiai waterfalls and pools.

o **Catching a Poipu Wave:** Vividly turquoise, curling, and totally tubular, big enough to hang ten, yet small enough to bodysurf, the waves at Poipu are endless in their attraction. Grab a boogie board—you can rent one for just dollars a day—or simply jump in and go with the flow. See p. 241 and 246 for details.

o **Watching the Hula:** The Coconut Market Place, 4–484 Kuhio Hwy. (Hwy. 56), between mile markers 6 and 7, Kapaa (℃ **808/822-3641**), hosts free shows every Wednesday at 5pm and Saturday at 1pm. Arrive early to get a good seat for the hour-long performances of both *kahiko* (ancient) and *auwana* (modern) hula. The real showstoppers are the *keiki* (children) who perform. Don't forget your camera!

o **Bidding the Sun Aloha:** Polihale State Park hugs Kauai's western shore for some 17 miles. It's a great place to bring a picnic dinner, stretch out on the sand, and toast the sun as it sinks into the Pacific, illuminating the island of Niihau in the distance. Queen's Pond has facilities for camping, as well as restrooms, showers, picnic tables, and pavilions.

ORIENTATION

Arriving

United Airlines (www.united.com; ℃ **800/864-8331**) offers direct service to Kauai, with daily flights from Los Angeles and San Francisco. **American Airlines** (www.aa.com; ℃ **800/433-7300**) has direct flights from Los Angeles and Phoenix. **Alaska Airlines** (www.alaskaair.com; ℃ **800/252-7522**) has direct flights from Seattle, Portland and Oakland. **Pleasant Holidays** (www.pleasantholidays.com; ℃ **800/742-9244**), one of Hawaii's largest travel companies, offers low-cost airfare and package deals with nonstop flights from Seattle, Los Angeles, and San Francisco.

All other airlines land in Honolulu (on Oahu), where you'll have to connect to a 30-minute interisland flight on **Hawaiian Airlines** (www.hawaiianair. com; ℃ **800/367-5320**, or 808/838-1555).

You'll land at Kauai's **Lihue Airport,** located 3 miles outside the county seat of Lihue. The final approach to the airport is dramatic; try to sit on the left side of the aircraft, where passengers are treated to an excellent view of the Haupu Ridge, Nawiliwili Bay, and Kilohana Crater. There's a county visitor information kiosk located next to each baggage-claim area. All of the major car-rental companies have branches at Lihue Airport. For tips on insurance and driving rules in Hawaii, see "Getting Around Hawaii" (p. 263). If you're not renting a car (although you should), cabs are available in front of baggage claim at the airport. If you need cab to get to the airport call **Kauai Taxi Company** (℃ **808/246-9554**).

Visitor Information

The **Kauai Visitors Bureau** is located on the first floor of the Watumull Plaza, 4334 Rice St., Ste. 101 (www.gohawaii.com/kauai; ℃ **808/245-3971**). Call ℃ **800/262-1400** or go to their website for a free official "Kauai Vacation Plan." The **Poipu Beach Resort Association,** P.O. Box 730, Koloa, HI 96756 (www.poipubeach.org; ℃ **888/744-0888** or 808/742-7444), has a very helpful website or will also send you a free guide to accommodations, activities, shopping, and dining in the Poipu Beach area.

To learn more about Kauai before you go, contact the **Kauai Historical Society,** 4396 Rice St. (www.kauaihistoricalsociety.org; ℂ **808/245-3373**).

You can now plan your vacation around the island's festivals and local events by checking out the new website, www.kauaifestivals.com.

The Island in Brief

Kauai's three main resort areas, where nearly all the island's accommodations are located, are quite different in climate, price, and type of lodgings offered. On the south shore, dry and sunny **Poipu** is anchored by perfect beaches; it's the place to stay if you like the ocean, watersports, and plenty of sunshine. The **Coconut Coast,** on the east coast of Kauai, has the most condos, shops, and traffic. Hanalei, up on the **North Shore,** is rainy, lush, and quiet, with spectacular beaches and deep wilderness. Because of its remote location, the North Shore is a great place to get away from it all—but not a great place from which to explore the rest of the island.

LIHUE & ENVIRONS

Lihue is where most visitors first set foot on the island. This red-dirt farm town, the county seat, was founded by sugar planters and populated by descendants of Filipino and Japanese cane cutters. It's a plain and simple place, with used-car lots and mom-and-pop shops. It's also the source of bargains: great deals on dining and some terrific shopping buys. One of the island's most beautiful beaches, **Kalapaki Beach ★★**, is just next door at **Nawiliwili,** by the island's main harbor.

The Poipu Beach Resort Area

POIPU BEACH ★★★ On Kauai's sun-soaked south shore, this is a pleasant if sleepy resort destination of low-rise hotels set on gold-sand pocket beaches. Poipu is Kauai's most popular resort, with the widest variety of accommodations, from luxury hotels to B&Bs and condos. It offers 36 holes of golf, 38 tennis courts, and outstanding restaurants. This is a great place for watersports and a good base from which to tour the rest of Kauai. The only drawback is that the North Shore is about 1 to 1½ hours away.

KOLOA This tiny old town of gaily painted sugar shacks, just inland from Poipu Beach, is where the Hawaiian sugar industry was born more than 150 years ago. The mill is closed, but this showcase plantation town lives on as a tourist attraction, with delightful shops, an old general store, and a vintage Texaco gas station with a 1930s Model A truck in place, just like in the good old days.

KALAHEO/LAWAI Just a short 10- to 15-minute drive inland from the beach at Poipu lie the more residential communities of Lawai and Kalaheo. Quiet subdivisions line the streets, restaurants catering to locals dot the area, and life revolves around family and work. Good bargains on B&Bs and a handful of reasonably priced restaurants can be found here.

WESTERN KAUAI

This region, west of Poipu, is more remote than its eastern neighbor and lacks its terrific beaches. But it's home to one of Hawaii's most spectacular natural wonders, **Waimea Canyon ★★★** (the "Grand Canyon of the Pacific"), and, farther upland and inland, **Kokee State Park,** one of its best parks.

HANAPEPE   For a quick trip back in time, turn off Hwy. 50 at Hanapepe, once one of Kauai's biggest towns. Founded by Chinese rice farmers, it's so picturesque that it was used as a backdrop for the miniseries *The Thorn Birds.* Hanapepe makes a good rest stop on the way to or from Waimea Canyon. It has galleries selling antiques as well as local art and crafts. Nearby, at **Salt Pond Beach Park ★** (p. 241), Hawaiians have dried a reddish sea salt in shallow, red-clay pans since the 17th century.

WAIMEA   This little coastal town, the original capital of Kauai, seems to have quit the march of time. Dogs sleep in the street while old pickups rust in front yards. The ambience is definitely laid-back. A stay in Waimea is peaceful and quiet, but the remote location means this isn't the best base if you want to explore the other regions of Kauai, such as the North Shore, without a lot of driving.

On his search for the Northwest Passage in 1778, British explorer Captain James Cook dropped anchor at Waimea and discovered a sleepy village of grass shacks. In 1815, the Russians arrived and built a fort here (now a national historic landmark), but they didn't last long: A scoundrel named George Anton Scheffer tried to claim Kauai for Russia, but he was exposed as an impostor and expelled by King Kamehameha I.

Today even Waimea's historic relics are spare and simple: a statue of Cook alongside a bas-relief of his ships, the rubble foundation of the Russian fort, and the remains of an ancient aqueduct unlike any other in the Pacific. Except for an overabundance of churches for a town this size, there's no sign that Waimea was selected as the first landing site of missionaries in 1820.

THE COCONUT COAST

The eastern shore of Kauai north of Lihue is a jumble of commerce and condos strung along the coast road named for Prince Kuhio, with several small beaches beyond. Almost anything you need, and a lot of stuff you can live without, can be found along this coast, which is known for its hundreds of coconut trees waving in the breeze. It's popular with budget travelers because of the myriad B&Bs and affordable hotels and condos to choose from, and it offers great restaurants and the island's major shopping areas.

KAPAA ★   The center of commerce on the east coast and the capital of the Coconut Coast condo-and-hotel district, this restored plantation town looks just like an antique. False-front wooden stores line both sides of the highway; it looks as though they've been here forever—until you notice the fresh paint and new roofs and realize that everything has been rebuilt since Hurricane Iniki smacked the town flat in 1992. Kapaa has made an amazing comeback without losing its funky charm.

NIIHAU: THE forbidden ISLAND

Just 17 miles across the Kaulakahi Channel from Kauai lies the arid island of Niihau (knee-ee-how), "The Forbidden Island." Visitors are not allowed on this privately owned island, which is a working cattle-and-sheep ranch with about 200 residents living in the single town of Puuwai.

In 1864, after an unusually wet winter that turned the dry scrubland of the small island (18×6 miles) into green pasture, Eliza Sinclair, a Scottish widow, decided to buy Niihau and move her family here. King Kamehameha IV agreed to sell the island for $10,000. The next year, normal weather returned, and the green pastures withered into sparse semi-desert vegetation.

Today Sinclair's great-great-grandson Bruce Robinson continues to run the ranching operation and fiercely protects the privacy of the island residents. Life on Niihau has not changed much in 150 years: There's no running water, indoor plumbing, or electric power. The Hawaiian language is still spoken. Most of the men work for the ranch when there is work, and fish and hunt when there is no work. The women specialize in gathering and stringing *pupu Niihau*, prized tiny white seashells (found only on this island), into Niihau's famous lei, which fetch prices in the thousands of dollars.

THE NORTH SHORE

Kauai's North Shore may be the most beautiful place in Hawaii. Exotic seabirds, a half-moon bay, jagged peaks soaring into the clouds, and a mighty wilderness lie around the bend from the Coconut Coast, just beyond a series of one-lane bridges traversing the tail ends of waterfalls. There's only one road in and out, and only two towns, Hanalei and Kilauea—the former by the sea, the latter on a lighthouse cliff that's home to a bird preserve. Sun seekers may fret about all the rainy days, but Princeville Resort offers elegant shelter and two golf courses where you can play through rainbows.

KILAUEA ★   This village is home to an antique lighthouse, tropical-fruit stands, and Kilauea Point National Wildlife Refuge, a wonderful seabird preserve. The rolling hills and sea cliffs are hideaways for the rich and famous, including Bette Midler and Sylvester Stallone. The village itself has its charms: The 1892 Kong Lung Company, Kauai's oldest general store, sells antiques, art, and crafts; and you can order a jazzy Billie Holiday pizza to-go at Kilauea Bakery and Pau Hana Pizza.

ANINI BEACH ★   This little-known residential district on a 2-mile reef (the biggest on Kauai) offers the safest swimming and snorkeling on the island. A great beach park is open to campers and day-trippers. Several residents host guests in nearby B&Bs.

PRINCEVILLE ★   A little overwhelming for Kauai's wild North Shore, Princeville is Kauai's biggest destination resort, an 11,000-acre development set on a high plain overlooking Hanalei Bay. In addition to the luxury St. Regis Hotel, this resort community also includes about a dozen condo complexes, new timeshare units around two championship golf courses, and cliffside access to pocket beaches.

HANALEI ★★★ Picture-postcard Hanalei is the laid-back center of North Shore life and an escapist's dream; it's also a gateway to the wild Na Pali Coast. Hanalei is the last great place on Kauai yet to face the developer's blade of progress. On either side of two-lane Kuhio Highway, you'll find just enough shops and restaurants to sustain you for your visit—unless you're a hiker, surfer, or sailor, or have some other preoccupation that might keep you here the rest of your life.

HAENA ★★ Emerald-green Haena isn't a town or a beach, but an ancient Hawaiian district, a place of exceptional natural beauty, and another gateway to the Na Pali Coast. This idyllic 4-mile coast has lagoons, bays, great beaches, spectacular snorkeling, a botanical garden, and the only North Shore resort that's right on the sand, the Hanalei Colony Resort (p. 222).

THE NA PALI COAST

The road comes to an end, and now it begins: the Hawaii you've been dreaming about. Kauai's Na Pali Coast (*na pali* means "the cliffs") is a place of extreme beauty and Hawaii's last true wilderness. You can enter this state park only on foot or by sea. Serious hikers—and I mean very serious—tackle the ancient 11-mile-long trail down the forbidding coast to Kalalau Valley (see "Hiking & Camping"). The lone, thin trail that creases these cliffs isn't for the faint of heart or anyone afraid of heights. Those who aren't up to it can explore the wild coast in an inflatable rubber Zodiac, a billowing sailboat, a high-powered catamaran, or a helicopter, which takes you for the ride of your life.

GETTING AROUND

You'll need a car to see and do everything on Kauai. Luckily, driving here is easy. However, there really is only one major road that circles the island, and during rush hour, from about 6 to 9am and 3 to 6pm, this road turns into a giant parking lot. A trip from the airport to Poipu could be as quick as 30 to 45 minutes during non-rush-hour times or as much as 1½ hours during rush hour.

From Lihue Airport, turn right and you'll be on Kapule Highway (Hwy. 51), which eventually merges into Kuhio Highway (Hwy. 56) a mile down. This road will take you to the Coconut Coast and through the North Shore before reaching a dead end at Kee Beach, where the Na Pali Coast begins.

If you turn left from Lihue Airport and follow Kapule Highway (Hwy. 51), you'll pass through Lihue and Nawiliwili. Turning on Nawiliwili Road (Hwy. 58) will bring you to the intersection of Kaumualii Highway (Hwy. 50), which will take you to the south and southwest sections of the island. This road doesn't follow the coast, however, so if you're heading to Poipu (and most people are), take Maluhia Road (Hwy. 520) south.

Kaumualii Highway (Hwy. 50) continues to Waimea, where it then dwindles to a secondary road before reaching a dead end at the other end of the Na Pali Coast.

To get to Waimea Canyon, take either Waimea Canyon Road (Hwy. 550), which follows the western rim of the canyon and affords spectacular views, or Kokee Road (Hwy. 55), which goes up through Waimea Canyon to Kokee State Park (4,000 ft. above sea level); the roads join up about halfway.

CAR RENTALS All of the major car-rental agencies are represented on Kauai (see "Getting Around Hawaii," p. 263). For tips on insurance and driving rules in Hawaii, also see "Getting Around." The rental desks are just across the street from Lihue Airport, but you must go by van to collect your car.

MOTORCYCLE RENTALS The best place to rent a motorcycle is **Kauai Harley-Davidson,** 3–1866 Kaumualii Hwy. (www.kauaiharley-davidson. com; ✆ **888/690-6233** or 808/212-9469). Rates start at $179 for 24 hours.

OTHER TRANSPORTATION OPTIONS Call **Kauai Taxi Company** (✆ **808/246-9554**) for taxi, limousine, or airport shuttle service. **Kauai Bus** (www.kauai.gov, click "Visitors," then "Bus Schedules"; ✆ **808/246-8110**) operates a fleet of 15 buses that serve the entire island. Taking the bus may be practical for day trips if you know your way around the island, but you can't take anything larger than a shopping bag aboard, and the buses don't stop at any of the resort areas—but they do serve more than a dozen coastal towns from Kekaha, on the southwest shore, all the way to Hanalei. Buses run more or less hourly from 5:25am to 10:40pm Monday through Friday and 6:21am to 5:50pm on Saturday. The fare is $2 for adults and $1 for seniors and children ages 7 to 18, as well as passengers with disabilities.

[FastFACTS] KAUAI

Dentists Emergency dental care is available from **Dr. Mark A. Baird,** 4–976 Kuhio Hwy. (✆ **808/ 822-9393**).

Doctors Walk-ins are accepted at **Kauai Urgent Care,** 4484 Pahee St. (✆ **808/245-1532**). You can also try the **North Shore Medical Center,** Kilauea and Oka roads (✆ **808/828-1418**); **Koloa Clinic,** 5371 Koloa Rd. (✆ **808/742-1621**); **Kauai Medical Clinic,** and **Eleele** 4392 Waialo Rd. (✆ **808/335-0499**).

Emergencies Dial ✆ **911** for police, fire, and ambulance service. The **Poison Control Center** can be reached at ✆ **800/222-1222**.

(You will automatically be directed to the Poison Control Center for the area code of the phone you are calling from; they are all available 24/7, and very helpful.)

Hospitals **Wilcox Memorial Hospital,** 3-3420 Kuhio Hwy. (✆ **808/245-1100**), has emergency services available 24 hours a day.

Internet Access All public libraries have Internet access. Libraries are located in Hanapepe (✆ 808/335-8418), Kapaa (✆ 808/821-4422), Koloa (✆ 808/742-8455), Lihue (✆ 808/241-3222), Princeville (✆ 808/826-4310), and Waimea (✆ 808/338-6848). You can

go online to reserve a computer at www.librarieshawaii. org/Serials/databases.html. You must purchase a Hawaii Library Card for $10, which gives you 3 months of access.

Police For nonemergencies, call ✆ **808/241-1711.**

Post Office The main post office is at 4441 Rice St., Lihue. To find the branch office nearest you, visit www.usps.com or call ✆ **800/ASK-USPS** (275-8778).

Weather For current weather and marine conditions, call ✆ **808/245-6001** or 808/245-3564 or go to www.prh.noaa.gov/hnl/.

WHERE TO STAY

You don't want to be stuck with long drives every day, so be sure to review "The Island in Brief," earlier, to choose the location that best fits your vacation needs.

Taxes of 13.42% are added to all hotel bills. Parking is free unless otherwise noted.

Lihue & Environs

INEXPENSIVE

Garden Island Inn ★   This bargain-hunters' delight is located 2 miles from the airport, 1 mile from Lihue, and within walking distance of shops and restaurants. The spacious rooms each have a fridge, microwave, wet bar, TV, coffeemaker, shower-only private bathroom, and ocean view. There's only one caveat: The property sits on a busy street, and some units can be noisy (bring earplugs). Owner Steve Layne offers friendly service and complimentary use of beach gear, golf clubs (a course is nearby, as are tennis courts), and coolers.

3445 Wilcox Rd. (across the street from Kalapaki Beach, near Nawiliwili Harbor). www. gardenislandinn.com. ✆ **800/648-0154** or 808/245-7227. 21 units. $118–$155 double. Extra person $10. **Amenities:** Free watersports equipment; free Wi-Fi.

The Poipu Resort Area

In addition to the accommodations listed below, you can try **Surf Song** (www. surfsong.com; ✆ **877/373-2331**), with four units from $780 to $1,050 per week (plus a cleaning fee of $40–$90; 7-night minimum), and, closer to the beach, **Pua Hale at Poipu** (www.kauai-puahale.com; ✆ **808/742-1700** or 808/742-6523), an intimate cottage within walking distance of the beach for $1,113–$1,300 per week double (plus $85 cleaning fee; 4-night minimum).

THE KING OF condos

One of the easiest ways to find lodging in the Poipu Beach area is to contact **The Parrish Collection Kauai,** 3176 Poipu Rd. (www.parrishkauai.com; ✆ **800/325-5701** or 808/742-2000). Parrish Kauai handles more than 200 "handpicked" rental units for 20 different condo developments, plus dozens of vacation houses, ranging from quaint cottages to elite resort homes. The company has high standards for its rental units and offers extremely fair prices. The condos start at $100 for a spacious one-bedroom, garden-view unit in low season; vacation cottages start at $200.

There's a 3 to 5-night minimum for condos and a 7-night minimum for homes. All rentals are well equipped (full kitchen, washer/dryer, TV/DVD, phone, and high-speed Internet access). Check for specials on the website. Parrish offers a price match guarantee.

If you're staying on Kauai for 5 days or more, ask Parrish about the **Frommer's Preferred Guest Discount** (properties include Nihi Kai Villas, Poipu Kapili Resort, and Waikomo Stream Villas). There's not a better deal on the island. Kudos to Parrish Collection Kauai for these fabulous vacation bargains.

VERY EXPENSIVE

Grand Hyatt Kauai Resort & Spa ★★★   Kauai's largest hotel aims to have one of the smallest carbon footprints. Its 602 luxurious rooms boast not only a fresh gold-and-green palette and pillow-tip beds, but also eco-friendly elements such as low-flow toilets, recycled-yarn carpets, and plush robes made from recycled plastic bottles. Grass-covered roofs and solar panels reduce emissions, food scraps from dining outlets (such as the thatched-roof **Tidepool** restaurant) go to local pig farmers, and used cooking oil becomes biodiesel fuel. But that's just green icing on the cake of this sprawling, family-embracing resort, where the elaborate, multi-tiered fantasy pool and saltwater lagoon more than compensate for the rough waters of Shipwrecks (Keoneloa) Beach, and the 45,000-square-foot indoor/outdoor Anara Spa and adjacent Poipu Bay Golf Course offer excellent adult diversions.

1571 Poipu Rd., Koloa. www.grandhyattkauai.com. ℂ **800/554-9288** or 808/742-1234. 602 units. $449–$639 double; from $629 Grand Club; from $799 suite. $30 resort fee includes self-parking, Wi-Fi, fitness classes, more. Extra person $75. Children 17 and under stay free in parent's room. Packages available. Valet parking $15. **Amenities:** 5 restaurants; 3 bars; babysitting; bike and car rentals; children's program; club lounge; concierge; fitness center; golf course and clubhouse; 3 Jacuzzis; luau; 2 nonchlorinated pools connected by river pool; 1.5-acre saltwater swimming lagoon; room service; spa; 3 tennis courts; watersports equipment rentals; Wi-Fi (included in resort fee).

Ko'a Kea Hotel & Resort ★★   A years-long, multimillion-dollar transformation of the old Poipu Beach Hotel (dormant since 1992's Hurricane Iniki) turned this property into a posh, boutique inn boasting the island's best hotel restaurant, **Red Salt,** as well as a small but expertly staffed spa. *Ko'a kea* means "white coral," which inspires the white and coral accents in the sleek, modern decor; all rooms feature lanais, many with views of the rocky coast (a short walk from sandy beaches). *Note:* At prices this steep, the "garden view" will disappoint—best to spring for at least a partial ocean view.

2251 Poipu Rd., Koloa. www.koakea.com. ℂ **888/898-8958** or 808/828-8888. 121 units. $379–$809 double; from $1,850 suite. Packages available. $25 resort fee includes valet parking, Wi-Fi, fitness center, and more. **Amenities:** Restaurant; 2 bars; concierge; fitness room; Jacuzzi; pool; room service; spa; watersports equipment rentals; Wi-Fi (included in resort fee).

EXPENSIVE

Sheraton Kauai Resort ★★   This modern Sheraton has the feel of old Hawaii and a dynamite location on one of Kauai's best beaches. You have a choice of three buildings: one nestled in tropical gardens with koi-filled ponds; one facing the palm-fringed, white-sand beach (my favorite); or one looking across green grass to the ocean, with great sunset views. Families take note: Kids eat dinner free with a paying adult at the Rumfire Restaurant.

2440 Hoonani Rd. www.sheraton-kauai.com. ℂ **866/716-8109** or 808/742-1661. 394 units. $218–$439 double (maximum 4 in room); from $509 suite for 4. Daily $30 resort fee includes self-parking, Wi-Fi, guest library with newspapers and computers with Internet access, use of fitness center, bicycles, and tennis courts. Extra person $70. Starwood members can get 35% off rack rates for prepaid reservations. Valet parking

$10. **Amenities:** 2 restaurants; bar; babysitting; concierge; fitness room facing the ocean (one of the most scenic places to work out on Kauai); Jacuzzi; 2 outdoor pools (1 w/water playground, 1 for children); room service; small massage-and-skin-care center; 3 tennis courts (2 night-lit); watersports equipment rentals; free Wi-Fi.

MODERATE

Hideaway Cove Villas ★★   Just a block from the beach (and next door to an excellent restaurant) are these gorgeous condominium units in a lush tropical setting at affordable prices. Owner Herb Lee is always on hand to guide you to Kauai's best spots and loan out his collection of beach toys and beach cruiser bicycles. A few of the units have Jacuzzis, so ask when you book.

2307 Nalo Rd. www.hideawaycove.com. ✆ **866/849-2426** or 808/635-8785. 7 units. $185–$264 studio double; $230–$279 1-bedroom double; $275–$422 2-bedroom for 4; $425–$611 3-bedroom for 6; from $725 5-bedroom (discount for 7 nights or more). Cleaning fee $140–$495. 2-night minimum (7 nights during holidays). **Amenities:** Restaurant and bar next door; free beach toys; free Wi-Fi.

INEXPENSIVE

Kauai Cove ★   These immaculate cottages, located just 300 feet from the Koloa Landing, next to the Waikomo Stream, are the perfect private getaway. Each studio has a full kitchen, private lanai (with barbecue grill), and big bamboo four-poster bed. It's close enough that you can walk to sandy beaches, great restaurants, and shopping, yet far enough off the beaten path that privacy and quiet are assured. Don't forget the ubiquitous "cleaning fee" they charge when comparing this property to others.

2672 Puuholo Rd. www.kauaicove.com. ✆ **800/624-9945** or 808/631-9313. 3 units. $129–$239 double. Cleaning fee $75. 3-night minimum preferred. **Amenities:** Use of nearby hot tub, pool, and tennis courts; free Wi-Fi.

Marjorie's Kauai Inn ★   This quiet property, perched on the side of a hill, is just 10 minutes from Poipu Beach and 5 minutes from Old Koloa

MOA BETTER: chickens & roosters

One of the first things visitors notice about Kauai is its unusually large number of *moa* (wild chickens). Kauai has always had a history of having more than its fair share of chickens and roosters running about, but after Hurricane Iniki picked up and scattered the fowl all over the island in 1992, they have been populating at a prodigious rate. Generally, having a few chickens scratching around in the dirt is quaint and downright picturesque. However, the "dark side" of the chicken population explosion is the increase in the number of roosters. In fact, a new industry has cropped up: rooster eradicators. Resorts hire these eradicators to remove the roosters from the well-manicured grounds because the large number of these male birds has led to, well, a sort of crowing contest. Roosters typically crow as the sun comes up. But on Kauai, with the population increase, the roosters crow all day long and throughout the night in some places. Just be warned that part of the "charm" of Kauai is the rooster population, so you might want to consider bringing earplugs.

Town. From its large lanai, it offers stunning views of the rolling pastures and the Lawai Valley. Every unit has a kitchenette, dining table, ceiling fan, and lanai. On the hillside is a huge 50-foot pool, perfect for lap swimming. *Note:* As terrific as this property is, it is not recommended for families with children.

3307 Hailima Rd., adjacent to the National Tropical Botanical Garden. www.marjories kauaiinn.com. © **800/717-8838** or 808/332-8838. 3 units. $200–$240 double. Extra person $20. Rates include continental breakfast. 3- to 5-night minimum preferred. **Amenities:** Jacuzzi; pool; barbecue; free Wi-Fi.

Nihi Kai Villas ★ The Parrish Collection Kauai (see "The King of Condos") is offering the deal of the decade on these well-equipped two-bedroom units, located about 600 feet from the beach. If you stay 7 nights, the rate for these oceanview apartments starts at an unbelievable $150 a night (for up to four people, which works out to just $75 per couple). You may not be getting new carpet, new furniture, new drapes, or a prime beachfront location, but you ARE getting a clean, well-cared-for unit with a full kitchen, washer/dryer, and TV/DVD player; there's also an on-site barbecue and picnic area. The property is a 2-minute walk from world-famous Brennecke's Beach (great for bodysurfing) and a block from Poipu Beach Park. Within a 5-minute drive are two great golf courses, several restaurants, and loads of shopping.

1870 Hoone Rd. www.parrishkauai.com. © **800/325-5701** or 808/742-2000. 70 units. $175–$250 1-bedroom for up 4 guests; $150–$350 2-bedroom for up 6 guests; $315–$450 3-bedroom for 6–8 guests. Cleaning fees $136–$225, processing fee $50. Ask about the Frommer's Preferred Guest Discount. 5-night minimum. From Poipu Rd., turn toward the ocean on Hoowili Rd. and then left on Hoone Rd.; Nihi Kai Villas is just past Nalo Rd. on Hoone Rd. **Amenities:** Concierge; nearby golf course; Jacuzzi; outdoor heated pool; tennis courts; free Wi-Fi.

Western Kauai
MODERATE
Waimea Plantation Cottages ★ This beachfront vacation retreat is like no other in the islands: Among groves of towering coco palms sit clusters of restored sugar-plantation cottages, dating from the 1880s to the 1930s, which have been transformed into cozy, comfortable guest units with period rattan and wicker furniture and fabrics from the 1930s, sugar's heyday on Kauai. Facilities include an oceanfront pool, tennis courts, and laundry. The seclusion of the village makes it a nice place for kids to wander and explore, away from traffic. The only downsides: the black-sand beach, which is lovely but not conducive to swimming (the water is often murky at the Waimea River mouth), and the location, at the foot of Waimea Canyon Drive—its remoteness can be very appealing, but the North Shore is 1½ hours away. Golf courses and tennis courts, however, are much closer.

9400 Kaumualii Hwy. www.waimea-plantation.com. © **800/716-6199** (Coast Hotels) or 808/338-1625. 48 units. $152–$329 1-bedroom double; $203–$389 2-bedroom (sleeps up to 4); $254–$449 3-bedroom (up to 5); from $425 4-bedroom (up to 8); from $740 5-bedroom (up to 10). Resort fee $25, Children 17 and under stay free in parent's room. **Amenities:** Large outdoor pool; free Wi-Fi.

INEXPENSIVE

Kokee Lodge ★   If you want to do some hiking in Waimea Canyon and Kokee State Park, this is an especially excellent choice. There are two types of cabins here: The older ones have dormitory-style sleeping arrangements (and resemble a youth hostel), while the new ones have two separate bedrooms each. Both styles sleep six and come with cooking utensils, bedding, and linens. I recommend the newer units, which have wood floors, cedar walls, and more modern kitchen facilities (some are wheelchair-accessible as well). There are no phones or TVs in the units, but there is a pay phone at the general store. You can purchase firewood for the cabin stove at Kokee Lodge, where there's a restaurant that's open for breakfast and lunch every day. There's also a cocktail lounge, a general store, and a gift shop. Warning for light sleepers: This area is home to lots of roosters, which crow at dawn's first light.

3600 Kokee Rd., Hanapepe. www.westkauailodging.com. © **808/338-0031.** 12 units. From $69–$119. Cleaning fee $39. 2-night minimum. **Amenities:** No phone (and limited cell service).

The Coconut Coast

EXPENSIVE

Kauai Marriott Resort ★★★   This 10-story, multi-wing hotel—the tallest on Kauai since opening in 1986—may be what prompted the local ordinance that no new structures be higher than a coconut tree, but it would be hard to imagine the Garden Island without it. Superlatives include Kauai's largest swimming pool, a sort of Greco-Roman fantasy that would fit in at Hearst Castle; its location on Kalapaki Beach, the best protected beach on the East Side for water sports; and one of the island's most popular restaurants, **Duke's Kauai** (p. 224), among other dining outlets. The long escalator to the central courtyard lagoon, the immense statuary, and the handsome lobby sporting a koa outrigger canoe make you feel like you've arrived somewhere truly unique. Two shopping centers (Harbor Mall and Anchor Cove) and more restaurants are within a short walk; in the opposite direction is the 18-hole championship Kauai Lagoons Golf Club. Rooms tend to be on the smaller side, but feel plush and look chic, with hues of taupe and burnt umber. Try to get at least a partial ocean view—the hoary green Haupu ridge, the bay, and Nawiliwili Harbor provide a mesmerizing backdrop.

3610 Rice St. (at Kalapaki Beach), Lihue. www.marriott.com/lihhi. © **800/220-2925** or 808/245-5050. 356 units. $289–$718 double; check for online packages and discounts. Rollaway $25. $30 resort fee. $10 valet parking (self-parking included in resort fee). **Amenities:** 6 restaurants; 2 bars; free airport shuttle (on request); concierge; fitness center; 5 Jacuzzis; pool; room service; watersports equipment rentals; Wi-Fi (included in resort fee).

MODERATE

Courtyard Kauai at Coconut Beach ★   Located only 10 minutes from Lihue, this property sits on 11 acres between a coconut grove and a white-sand beach. The convenient location is close to shopping and visitor attractions along the Coconut Coast, and also gives you easy access to both the North Shore and the Poipu Beach area on the south shore. The property features a new pool, hot tub, day spa, business center, fitness center, tennis courts, jogging paths, lounge, and expanded restaurant.

650 Aleka Loop. www.courtyardkauai.com. © **800/321-2211** or 808/822-3455. 311 units. $143–$459 double; from $529 suite. Extra person $25. Children 17 and under stay free in parent's room. Resort fee $20, includes parking, Wi-Fi, long-distance calls, and 2 Mai Tais. **Amenities:** Restaurant; bar; fitness center; golf nearby; Jacuzzi; outdoor pool; room service; spa; tennis nearby; jogging path; free Wi-Fi.

Kauai Country Inn ★★ Located on a manicured 2 acres, inland of Kapaa, lies this old-fashioned country inn with four suites and lots of little amenities such as computers in the rooms. Pick as much organic fruit as you want from the abundance of mango, guava, lilikoi, star fruit, orange, and lemon trees on the property. Beatles fans take note: The property also contains the only private Beatles museum in United States. Children over 12 years of age only.

6440 Olohena Rd. www.kauaicountryinn.com. © **808/821-0207.** 4 units. $179–$279 1- and 2-bedroom suite. Extra person $30. Discount car rentals available. 4-night minimum preferred. **Amenities:** Hot tub; continental breakfast; free Wi-Fi.

INEXPENSIVE

Hilton Garden Inn Kauai Wailua Bay ★ A great location on 10-acres oceanside on the Coconut Coast next door to 57-acre Lydgate Beach Park (with the Kamalani Playground for the kids) makes this moderately priced hotel a popular choice with families and vacationers. Hilton took over management in 2016 and conducted major renovations (with big price increases to match); rooms have been updated and now have Serta Perfect Sleeper beds and fresh kitchenettes. Cultural programs, bikes, and daily cocktails are included in the resort fee. It's also close to shopping and restaurants and golf is nearby.

3–5920 Kuhio Hwy. www.hiltongardeninnkauai.com. © **855/410-5694** or 808/441-7789. 216 units. $169–$445 double; from $267 suite; from $257 1-bedroom cottage. Resort fee $22. Extra person $30. Children 18 and under stay free in parent's room. Check website for specials. **Amenities:** Restaurant; bar; Jacuzzi; 2 outdoor pools; complimentary tennis court; free Wi-Fi.

Hotel Coral Reef ★ Once a budget hotel, located right on the white sand beach, this small, unpretentious inn is looking at major renovations (including the addition of a third story when we went to press). It offers friendly service and economical, no-frills rooms in an ideal location, within walking distance of shops, restaurants, golf, and tennis.

1516 Kuhio Hwy. (at the northern end of Kapaa, btw. mile markers 8 and 9). www.hotel coralreefresort.com. © **800/843-4659** or 808/822-4481. 19 units. $159–$359 double. Extra person $25. Children 12 and under stay free in parent's room. Packages available; check for specials. **Amenities:** Pool; continental breakfast; free Wi-Fi.

Rosewood Bed & Breakfast ★ This lovingly restored century-old plantation home, set amid tropical flowers, lily ponds, and waterfalls, has

creeping ACCOMMODATIONS FEES

It's no longer just the airlines that seem to have another fee every time you turn around. We have noticed that a few accommodations on Kauai (Kauai Beach Villas, outside Lihue; and Kalaheo Inn and Kauai Cove, outside Poipu) have started the distasteful practice of charging a "cleaning fee" plus a "booking fee." Isn't cleaning and booking part of the rack rate and part of running an accommodation? Wailea Bay View also has a new "damage insurance." Please! What's next, a fee for clean bedding? An additional fee if you want a blanket? If you find these new fees as appalling as we do, we hope that you will let these accommodations know.

accommodations to suit everyone. There's a Laura Ashley–style room in the main house, along with two private cottages. There's also a bunkhouse with three separate small rooms and a shared shower and toilet. All the beds are "Heavenly Beds," and computers with Internet access are installed in each room. Hostess Rosemary Smith also has a list of other properties she manages.

872 Kamalu Rd. www.rosewoodkauai.com. ✆ **808/822-5216.** 7 units (3 with shared bathroom). $155 double in main house (includes continental breakfast); $85–$125 double in bunkhouse; $155–$225 1-bedroom cottage (sleeps up to 2); $205–$275 2-bedroom cottage (up to 4). Extra person $20. Cleaning fee $95–$145. 3-night minimum. No credit cards. From Kuhio Hwy. (Hwy. 56), turn left at the light at Coco Palms onto Hwy. 580 (Kuamoo Rd.); go 3 miles; turn right at junction of Hwy. 581 (Kamalu Rd.); go 1 mile and look for the yellow house on the right with the long picket fence in front. **Amenities:** Free Internet.

The North Shore

Ocean Front Realty North Shore Rentals (www.oceanfrontrealty.com; ✆ **800/222-5541** or 808/826-6585) handles all kinds of weekly rentals—from beachfront cottages and condos to romantic hideaways and ranch houses. Shopping, restaurants, and nightlife are abundant in nearby Hanalei.

In addition to the B&Bs listed below, you might consider a farm stay at **North Country Farms** (www.northcountryfarms.com; ✆ **808/828-1513**), which has two private, handcrafted cottages on a 4-acre organic farm. It's a great place for families. Each cottage rents for $160 a night plus $95 cleaning fee.

Parrish Collection Kauai (www.parrishkauai.com; ✆ **800/325-5701** or 808/742-2000), which has done such an outstanding job of selecting the best rentals available in the Poipu area, has expanded into the North Shore, and represents 40 properties and counting in Princeville and Hanalei, all meeting the high Parrish standards.

For pure luxury (and an accompanying price tag), check into the area's **St. Regis Princeville** (5520 Ka Haku Rd., Princeville; www.stregisprinceville.com; ✆ **877/787-3447** or 808/826-9644), Hawaii's only St. Regis property.

EXPENSIVE

Hanalei Colony Resort ★   Picture this: a perfect white-sand beach just steps from your door with lush tropical gardens, jagged mountain peaks, and fertile jungle serving as the backdrop. Welcome to Haena, the gateway to the famous Na Pali Coast, with miles of hiking trails, fabulous sunset views, and great beaches. This 5-acre resort offers spacious units—six people could sleep here comfortably—making them great for families. Each has ceiling fans to take advantage of the cooling trade winds (air-conditioning isn't necessary). The atmosphere is quiet and relaxing: no TVs, stereos, or phones. The property has a large pool, laundry facilities, and a barbecue and picnic area. Guests have access to complimentary beach mats and towels, a lending library, and children's toys, puzzles, and games. A full spa and an award-winning restaurant (Mediterranean Gourmet, p. 228) are located next door.

5–7130 Kuhio Hwy., Haena. www.hcr.com. (?) **800/628-3004** or 808/826-6235. 48 units. $289–$609 2-bedroom apt. for 4. Rates include continental breakfast once a week. **Amenities:** Jacuzzi; outdoor pool; no phone; free Wi-Fi.

Hanalei Surf Board House ★★   Book well in advance: This place is fabulous and it sells out fast! Just a block from the beach, these two beautifully decorated studio units are quite a deal. Host Simon Potts is a former record-company executive from England who has "retired" to Hawaii (he's the hardest-working retired guy I've ever met). Potts has collected surfboards from kids he coaches in soccer and lined them all standing up next to one another, creating the most unusual fenced-in yard in Hawaii. His imaginative decor choices extend to the studios, one of which sports a whimsical cowgirl theme and the other, Elvis memorabilia. Both units have kitchenettes, Internet-ready TVs that stream Netflix, DVD players, Bose stereos, iPod docks, barbecues, and backyard lanais. It's just a 2-minute walk to the beach and a 10-minute walk to downtown Hanalei. Note that both units are "smoke-free and child-free zones."

5459 Weke Rd. www.hanaleisurfboardhouse.com. (?) **808/651-1039.** 2 units. $350 double. Cleaning fee $95. 4- to 7-night minimum. **Amenities:** Free Wi-Fi.

MODERATE

Aloha Sunrise Inn/Aloha Sunset Inn ★★   Hidden on the North Shore are these two unique cottages nestled on a quiet 7-acre farm with horses, fruit trees, flowers, and organic vegetables. It's close to activities, restaurants, and shopping, yet far enough away to feel the peace and quiet of a Hawaii of yesteryear. Hosts Allan and Catherine Rietow, who have lived their entire lives on the islands, can help you plan your stay, give money-saving tips, and even hand out complimentary masks, snorkels, and boogie boards and point you to their favorite beaches. *Note:* Cottages are not appropriate for children.

4899-A Waiakalua St., Kapaa. www.kauaisunrise.com. (?) **808/828-1100.** 2 units. $150–$185 double (includes all taxes). Check for internet specials. Cleaning fee $135. 3-night minimum. No credit cards. **Amenities:** Free Wi-Fi.

WHERE TO EAT

Kauai's best dining spots ring the shores: Poipu on the south, Kapaa on the east, and Hanalei on the north. Although Roy's Eating House, Merriman's in Poipu, the Beach House in neighboring Lawai, and Kauai Grill in Princeville remain Kauai's foodie stalwarts, there are some excellent choices at all levels of food pricing. Most of the island's newcomers are moderately priced and have cropped up along Kauai's one main road.

As long as you don't expect filet mignon on a fish-and-chips budget, it shouldn't be difficult to please both your palate and your pocketbook. But if you're looking for lobster, rack of lamb, or risotto to write home about, you'll find those pleasures, too.

For condo dwellers preparing their own meals, I've covered a variety of markets and shops around Kauai—including some wonderful green markets and fruit stands—where you can pick up the island's best foodstuffs. These are listed under "Shops & Galleries" (p. 256).

In the listings below, reservations are not required unless otherwise noted.

Lihue & Environs
EXPENSIVE

Gaylord's ★★ CONTINENTAL/PACIFIC RIM   One of Kauai's most splendid examples of *kamaaina* architecture, Gaylord's is the anchor of a 1930s plantation manager's estate on a 1,700-acre sugar plantation. The main dining room, which winds around a flagstone courtyard overlooking rolling lawns and purple mountains, serves an eclectic menu—from cioppino to burgers to grilled whole fish. There's a pianist Tuesday and Friday evenings and live Hawaiian music Wednedsay and Saturday nights.

At Kilohana, 3–2087 Kaumualii Hwy. www.gaylordskauai.com. ℭ **808/245-9593.** Reservations recommended. Main courses $14–$18 lunch, $21–$36 dinner, Sun brunch $30, $15 children 5–12. Mon–Sat 11am–2:30pm and 5:30–8:30pm; Sun 9am–1:30pm (brunch).

JJ's Broiler ★ AMERICAN   Famous for its Slavonic steak (tenderloin in butter, wine, and garlic), JJ's is a lively spot on Kalapaki Bay, with open-air dining and a menu that covers more than the usual surf and turf. The service ranges from laudable to lamentable, but the quality of the food is consistent.

3416 Rice St. www.jjsbroiler.com. ℭ **808/246-4422.** Reservations recommended for dinner. Lunch sandwiches $12–$18; dinner main courses $12–$39. Daily 11am–9pm.

MODERATE

Cafe Portofino ★★ ITALIAN   This candlelit restaurant offers authentic Italian cuisine at reasonable prices. It's a good pick for a romantic dinner, with a harpist playing softly in the background. The big seller is the pasta. Live music is featured every night. On "club night," Thursday, there is a DJ and dancing ($5 cover after 11pm).

3481 Hoolaulea St. www.cafeportofino.com. ℭ **808/245-2121.** Reservations recommended. Main courses $19–$32. Daily 5–9:30pm.

Duke's Kauai ★ STEAK/SEAFOOD   It's hard to go wrong at Duke's. Part of a highly successful restaurant chain (including Duke's in Waikiki and three similar restaurants on Maui), this oceanfront oasis is the hippest spot in town, with a winning combination of a great view, an affordable menu, popular music, and a very happy happy hour. Hawaiian musicians serenade Wednesday through Monday nights in the Barefoot Bar, adding to the cheerful atmosphere.

At the Kauai Marriott Resort & Beach Club, 3610 Rice St. www.dukeskauai.com. ⓒ **808/246-9599.** Reservations recommended for dinner. Main courses $13–$18 lunch, $24–$33 dinner; "Taco Tuesdays" 4–6pm, with $4.50 fish tacos and $5.50 draft beer. Barefoot Bar daily 11am–11pm; main dining room daily 4:30–10pm.

INEXPENSIVE

Hamura's Saimin Stand ★ SAIMIN   If there were a saimin hall of fame, Hamura's would be in it. It's a cultural experience, a renowned saimin stand where fans line up to take their place over steaming bowls of the ramenlike Island specialty at a few U-shaped counters that haven't changed in decades.

2956 Kress St. ⓒ **808/245-3271.** Most items under $12. No credit cards. Mon–Thurs 10am–10pm; Fri–Sat 10am–midnight; Sun 10am–9:30pm.

Hanalima Baking ★ AMERICAN/HAWAIIAN   A tiny gem located in a small strip center across Kaumualii Highway from the Kauai Community College, it has some of the best breakfast pastries in the islands, everything from ham and cheese rolls to scones. At lunch look for plate lunches, burgers, and sandwiches, all at very reasonable prices. All food is takeout; no seating here.

4495 Puhi Rd. www.hanalimabaking.com. ⓒ **808/246-8816.** Breakfast rolls and pastries $2.35–$2.85; most menu items under $7. Mon–Fri 6am–1pm.

Kalapaki Beach Hut ★ AMERICAN   This tiny eatery has window service and a few tables downstairs, but sit upstairs for an ocean view. It's basic fare, served on paper plates with plastic cutlery at cheap, cheap prices. Breakfasts are hearty omelets, pancakes, and numerous egg dishes. Lunches are heavy on the burgers, sandwiches, a few healthy salads, and fish and chips. This casual restaurant welcomes people in their bathing suits and flip-flops.

3474 Rice St. www.kalapakibeachhut.com. ⓒ **808/246-6330.** Breakfast $7–$10; lunch $7–$11. Daily 7am–8pm.

Tip Top Cafe & Bakery ★ LOCAL   A small cafe/bakery (also the lobby for the Tip Top Motel) that's been serving local customers since 1916. The best deal is breakfast: Most items are $12 or under. Lunch ranges from pork chops to teriyaki chicken, but the specialty is oxtail soup.

3173 Akahi St. ⓒ **808/245-2333.** Breakfast items under $15; lunch entrees $7–$15. Tues–Sun 6:30am–1:45pm.

The Poipu Resort Area

EXPENSIVE

The Beach House ★★★ HAWAII REGIONAL   THE place to go when you want to splurge: Celebrate a birthday, anniversary, or any excuse for a romantic dinner on the beach with delicious food. Come early enough to see the sunset and perhaps a turtle or two bobbing in the waves. Hawaii Regional favorites are featured on the menu, which changes daily.

5022 Lawai Rd. www.the-beach-house.com. *C* **808/742-1424.** Reservations recommended. Main courses $10–$19 lunch, $20–$48 dinner. Daily 11am–9pm (8:30pm mid-Sept to mid-Mar).

Dondero's ★★★ ITALIAN   If you're looking for a romantic dinner either under the stars, overlooking the ocean, or tucked away at an intimate table surrounded by marble floors and Franciscan murals, the Grand Hyatt's stellar Italian restaurant is the place for you. Great, but pricey Italian dishes (worth every penny), include pastas, fresh seafood, tender beef, and thin crust Neapolitan pizzas.

At the Grand Hyatt Kauai Resort and Spa, 1571 Poipu Rd. www.kauai.hyatt.com. *C* **808/240-6456.** Reservations required. Main courses $25–$55. Tues–Sat 6–10pm.

Tapas at Kukuiula ★★★ TAPAS   The food is rustic Asian-Mediterranean tapas, the atmosphere is lively (and sometimes very loud), and the prime location is on the second story of the upscale Shops at Kukuiula. When the sangria cart stops by your table, try the white lychee version—not too sweet—or, for nondrinkers, the strawberry pepper lemonade, while you peruse the eclectic and frequently changing menu.

Kukuiula Village Shopping Center, 2829 Ala Kalanikaumaka St. http://tapaskauai.com. *C* **808/742-7117.** Reservations required. Tapas $10–$36. Sun–Thurs 5:30–9pm; Fri–Sat 5:30–midnight featuring "Late Night" with live music and DJ's 10pm–midnight, plus 25% off the menu.

Merriman's Fish House ★★★ SEAFOOD   A soaring, open, second-floor beauty of a space with distant views of the Pacific and Kauai's jagged peaks houses this perennially popular restaurant. The soft white walls are decorated with photos of the farmers who supply the restaurant. As with all Merriman's restaurants, "farm to table" is the credo here. *Note:* For more casual dining, try Merriman's Pizza & Burgers downstairs.

Kukui'ula Village Mall, 2829 Kalanikaumaka St. #G-149. www.merrimanshawaii.com. *C* **808/742-8385.** Reservations recommended. Main courses $24–$75. Daily 5–9pm.

Roy's Eating House 1849 ★★ HAWAIIAN   The signature touches of Roy Yamaguchi (of Roy's restaurants in Oahu, Big Island, Maui, Tokyo, New York, and Guam) are abundantly present, with fresh local ingredients prepared with a nod to Hawaii's culinary heritage, topped with efficient service. Because appetizers are a major part of the menu, you can sample Roy's legendary fare without breaking the bank. Excellent and affordable wine selections, too.

At the Shops at Kukui'ula, 2829 Kalanimauka St. #A-201. www.eatinghouse1849.com. *C* **808/742-5000.** Reservations highly recommended. Appetizers $9–$18; main courses $13–$42. Daily 5–9:30pm.

Tidepool Restaurant ★★★ SEAFOOD   At this ultraromantic restaurant at the Grand Hyatt, a cluster of thatched bungalows overlooks the lagoon in a dreamy open-aired restaurant with Tiki torches flickering in the moonlight. The restaurant's specialty is fresh fish prepared a number of ways, but it also has juicy steaks and ribs, as well as entrees for vegetarians. Book early, and ask for a table overlooking the water.

At the Grand Hyatt Kauai Resort and Spa, 1571 Poipu Rd. www.kauai.hyatt.com. © **808/240-6456.** Reservations recommended. Main courses $26–$48. Daily 5:30–10pm.

MODERATE

Brennecke's Beach Broiler ★ AMERICAN/SEAFOOD   Cheerful petunias in window boxes and second-floor views of Poipu Beach are pleasing touches at this seafood/burger house. The view alone is worth the price of a drink and pupu, but it helps that the best hamburgers on the south shore are served here, as well as excellent vegetarian selections. It's casual, so drop in before or after the beach.

2100 Hoone Rd. (across from Poipu Beach Park). www.brenneckes.com. © **808/742-7588.** Main courses $14–$19 lunch, $15–$33 dinner. Daily 11am–10pm (street-side deli takeout daily 7am–9pm; bar 10am–10pm).

Keoki's Paradise ★ STEAK/SEAFOOD   A great place to take the kids—they will love the tropical ambience here. The cafe in the bar area serves lighter fare and features live Hawaiian music nightly. The sunset prix-fixe menu, served from 4:45 to 5:45pm, of three courses for $26 is a great deal.

At the Poipu Shopping Village, 2360 Kiahuna Plantation Dr. www.keokisparadise.com. © **808/742-7534.** Reservations recommended. Main courses $12–$17 bar menu, $23–$37 dinner. Daily 4:45–9pm in main dining room; cafe menu daily 11am–10:30pm.

INEXPENSIVE

Joe's on the Green ★ AMERICAN   Breakfasts are a bargain, especially if you go before 8am Monday through Saturday, and get the early bird special for $8.50. You'll enjoy a great setting—outdoors overlooking the golf course—and a menu with everything from fluffy pancakes to biscuits and gravy to healthy tofu scramble. Lunch is popular for its range of sandwiches, salads, and desserts (do not pass up the warm chocolate-chip cookie).

2545 Kiahuna Plantation Dr., at the Kiahuna Golf Club Clubhouse. www.ygli.bluedomino.com. © **808/742-9696.** Breakfast $8.50–$15; lunch $9–$15. Daily 7am–2:30pm; happy hour 3–7pm Sun–Thurs with small-plate menu and live Hawaiian music.

Kalaheo Café & Coffee Co. ★★ COFFEEHOUSE/CAFE   This coffeehouse also serves masterful breakfasts, including breakfast burritos and omelets. At lunch, the fabulous grilled turkey burgers (heaped with grilled onions and mushrooms on a sourdough bun) are the headliner. And finally, by popular demand, the cafe is serving dinner (Tues–Sat only) with a limited menu that changes weekly.

2–2560 Kaumualii Hwy. (Hwy. 50; across the street from Brick Oven Pizza). www.kalaheo. com. © **808/332-5858.** Breakfast $5–$13, lunch $7–$15; dinner $13–$30. Mon–Sat 6:30am–2:30pm; Tues–Thurs 5–8:30pm; Fri–Sat 5–9pm; Sun 11am–2pm.

Western Kauai

Shrimp Station ★ SHRIMP   Looking for a picnic lunch to take up to Waimea Canyon? Stop at this roadside eatery, which is nothing more than a kitchen with a few picnic tables outside—but the shrimp cooking up inside will make up for the lack of ambience. The shrimp is prepared a variety of ways, but the star attractions are the shrimp plates (with choice of garlic shrimp, Cajun, Thai, or sweet chili garlic). If you're taking them out, make sure you grab plenty of napkins; you'll need them after munching these tasty but messy morsels.

9652 Kaumualii Hwy., Waimea. www.theshrimpstation.com. ℂ **808/338-1242.** Shrimp platters $12. Daily 11am–5pm.

The Coconut Coast
MODERATE

Caffè Coco ★★ GOURMET BISTRO   This gets my vote for the most charming ambience on Kauai, with gourmet fare cooked to order—and at cafe prices. Sit outside under tiki torches and listen to live music (hula Fri, jazz Sun) as you peruse the changing menu of excellent vegetarian and other healthful delights. Service can be laid back, so relax, it's Hawaii.

4–369 Kuhio Hwy., Wailua. www.restauranteur.com/caffecoco. ℂ **808/822-7990.** Reservations recommended for parties of 4 or more. Main courses $6–$13 light fare, $15–$21 platters. Tues–Fri 11am–2pm; Tues–Sun 5–9pm.

INEXPENSIVE

Bubba Burgers ★ AMERICAN   Here at the house of Bubba, they dish out humor, great T-shirts, and burgers nonpareil, including Boca and taro burgers for vegetarians. The burger is king, attitude reigns, and lettuce and tomato cost extra. For a burger joint, it's big on fish, too. Other locations: Kukuiula Village, 2829 Ala Kinoiki, Poipu (ℂ **808/742-6900**), and 5-5161 Kuhio Hwy, Hanalei (ℂ **808/826-7839**).

4–1421 Kuhio Hwy. www.bubbaburger.com. ℂ **808/823-0069.** All items under $10. Daily 10:30am–8pm.

Mermaids Cafe ★ ISLAND   A tiny sidewalk cafe with brisk takeout and a handful of tables on Kapaa's main drag. Mermaids uses kaffir lime, lemongrass, local lemons, and organic herbs, when possible, to make the sauces and beverages to go with its toothsome dishes.

4-1384 Kuhio Hwy. www.mermaidskauai.com. ℂ **808/821-2026.** Main courses $9–$14. Daily 11am–9pm.

Monico's Taqueria ★★ MEXICAN   At this popular taqueria, Monico and his team make everything from scratch (that's lard-free) and serve generous portions that come with rice and a small bowl of beans. Add to that an ice cold beer, and you truly are in paradise.

4–356 Kuhio Hwy., Kinipopo Shopping Village. ℂ **808/822-4300.** Plates $13–$24. Tues–Sun 11am–3pm and 5–9pm.

En Route to the North Shore

Duane's Ono-Char Burger ★ BURGER STAND   On the way to the North Shore, stop here for hefty all-beef burgers (with Boca burgers for vegetarians). The broiled fish sandwich (another marvel of the seasoned old grill) and the marionberry ice cream shake, a three-berry combo, are popular as well.

Kuhio Hwy. ℭ **808/822-9181.** Hamburgers $5–$8. Mon–Sat 10am–6pm; Sun 11am–6pm.

The North Shore

VERY EXPENSIVE

Kauai Grill ★★★ CONTINENTAL/PACIFIC RIM   The views of the craggy, Bali Hai–like cliffs and the Pacific Ocean below would be enough to lure you into this romantic, signature restaurant of the St. Regis Princeville, but the food, from award-winning chef Jean-George Vongerichten, makes this place a must try on every foodie's list.

St. Regis Princeville, 5520 Kahaku Rd. www.princevillehotelhawaii.com. ℭ **808/826-9644.** Main courses $44–$95; 5-course tasting $85 ($105 with wine pairings). Tues–Sat 5:30–9:30pm.

MODERATE

Hanalei Gourmet ★ AMERICAN   The wood benches and blackboards of the old Hanalei School, built in 1926, are a haven for today's Hanalei hipsters noshing on cross-cultural tastings, from stir-fried veggies over udon noodles to artichoke hearts fried in beer batter. Informal to the max, the TV over the bar competes with the breathtaking view of the Hanalei mountains and waterfalls, and the wooden floors keep the noise level high (the music can be almost deafening). Live music on Sunday and Wednesday nights adds to the fun.

At the Old Hanalei Schoolhouse, 5–5161 Kuhio Hwy. www.hanaleigourmet.com. ℭ**808/826-2524.** Main courses $8–$13 lunch, $10–$29 dinner. Deli daily 8am–10:30pm; restaurant 11am–9:30pm; bar open until 10:30pm.

Kilauea Bakery & Pau Hana Pizza ★ PIZZA/BAKERY   When owner, baker, and avid diver Tom Pickett spears an ono and smokes it himself, his catch appears on the Billie Holiday pizza. The in-house baked breads go well with the soups and hot lunch specials, and the pastries with the new full-service espresso bar, which serves only the best of the bean. The Picketts have added a small dining room, and the few outdoor picnic tables under umbrellas are as inviting as ever.

At Kong Lung Center, Kilauea Rd. (off Hwy. 56, on the way to the Kilauea Lighthouse). www.kilaueabakery.com ℭ **808/828-2020.** Pizzas $12–$33. Daily 6am–9pm.

Mediterranean Gourmet ★★ MIDDLE EASTERN   This oceanfront, "hidden" restaurant, next door to the Hanalei Colony Resort, is the perfect backdrop for chef/owner Imad Beydoun's Middle Eastern dishes, which he embellishes with an island twist. The menu has traditional Middle Eastern cuisine, as well as more familiar dishes (chicken quesadilla, rack of lamb, New York strip steak). Don't leave until you try the homemade baklava and a cup of Turkish coffee. There's live music Tuesday, Wednesday, Friday, and Sunday.

At the Hanalei Colony Resort, 5–7132 Kuhio Hwy. www.kauaimedgourmet.com. © **808/826-9875.** Main courses $13–$20 lunch, $19–$37 dinner. Tues–Sun noon–8:30pm. Happy hour 3–6pm.

Postcards Cafe ★ GOURMET SEAFOOD/NATURAL FOODS The charming plantation-style building that used to be the Hanalei Museum is now home to Hanalei's gourmet eatery, with healthful ingredients, seafood, and international flavors served in a cheery atmosphere. Gluten-free and vegan also fill the menu.

Kuhio Hwy. (at entrance to Hanalei town). http://postcardscafe.com. © **808/826-1191.** Reservations highly recommended for dinner for groups of 4 or more. Main courses $19–$38. Daily 6–9pm.

INEXPENSIVE

Tropical Taco ★ MEXICAN Stop by this roadside eatery for a tasty assortment of tacos and burritos, plus the signature "fat Jack" (a 10-in. deep-fried tortilla with cheese, beans, and beef or fish). Owner Roger Kennedy offers "anything you want to drink, as long as it's lemonade."

At the Halelea Bldg., 5–5088 Kuhio Hwy. www.tropicaltaco.com. © **808/827-TACO** (8226). Most items under $15. Mon–Fri 8am–8pm; Sat–Sun 11am–5pm.

EXPLORING KAUAI

A Tour of the Island

Four-Wheel-Drive Back-Road Adventure ★ Great for getting off the beaten path and seeing the "hidden" Kauai, this 4-hour tour follows a figure-eight path around Kauai, from Kilohana Crater to the Mahaulepu coastline. The tour, done in a four-wheel-drive van, not only stops at Kauai's well-known scenic spots, but also travels on sugar-cane roads (on private property), taking you to places most people who live on Kauai have never seen.

Aloha Kauai Tours, 1702 Haleukana St. www.alohakauaitours.com. © **866/511-7820** or 808/245-8809. Tours $80 adults, $63 children 12 and under. Daily 8am and 1pm; reservations required.

Lihue & Environs

Grove Farm Homestead Museum ★ HISTORIC SITE/MUSEUM You can experience a day in the life of an 1860s sugar planter on a visit to Grove Farm Homestead, which shows how life was when sugar was king. Founded in 1864 by George N. Wilcox, a Hanalei missionary's son, Grove Farm was one of the earliest of Hawaii's 86 sugar plantations. His estate looks much as it did when he lived here, complete with period furniture, plantation artifacts, and Hawaiiana.

4050 Nawiliwili Rd. (Hwy. 58), at Pikaka St. (2 miles from Waapa Rd.). www.grovefarm. org. © **808/245-3202.** Admission $20 adults, $10 children 11 and under. Open only for tours Mon and Wed–Thurs at 10am and 1pm; reservations required.

Kauai Museum ★ MUSEUM   The history of Kauai is kept safe in an imposing Greco-Roman building that once served as the town library. This great little museum is worth a stop before you set out to explore the island. It contains a wealth of historical artifacts and information tracing the island's history from the beginning of time to when Capt. James Cook landed on Kauai in 1778, to the monarchy period, the plantation era, and the present.

4428 Rice St. www.kauaimuseum.org. © **808/245-6931.** Admission $15 adults, $12 seniors, $10 students 13–17, $2 children 7–12. Mon–Sat 10am–5pm. Guided tours Mon–Fri 10:30am.

The Poipu Resort Area

No Hawaii resort has a better entrance: On Maluhia Road, eucalyptus trees planted in 1911 as a windbreak for sugar-cane fields now form a monumental **tree tunnel.** The cool, leafy-green tunnel starts at Kaumualii Highway and emerges at the golden-red beach.

Allerton Garden of the National Tropical Botanical Garden ★ HISTORIC SITE/GARDEN   Discover an extraordinary collection of tropical fruit and spice trees, rare Hawaiian plants, and hundreds of varieties of flowers at the 186-acre preserve known as **Lawai Gardens,** said to be the largest collection of rare and endangered plants in the world. Adjacent **McBryde Garden,** a royal home site of Queen Emma in the 1860s, is known for its formal gardens, set amid fountains, streams, waterfalls, and European statuary.

Visitor Center, Lawai Rd. (across the street from Spouting Horn). www.ntbg.org. © **808/742-2623.** Self-guided tours of McBryde Garden daily 9:30am–5pm (last shuttle in is 3:30pm), $30 adults and $15 children 6–12 (trams into the valley leave once an hour on the half-hour; last tram 3:30pm); guided tour of Allerton Garden daily 9am, 10am,11am, noon, 1pm, 2pm, and 3pm, $50 adults and $25 children 6–12 (children under 5 are free). Advance reservations required, reserve a week in advance in peak months of July–Sept.

Prince Kuhio Park ★ PARK   This small roadside park is the birthplace of Prince Jonah Kuhio Kalanianaole, the "People's Prince," whose March 26 birthday is a holiday in Hawaii. He opened the beaches of Waikiki to the public in 1918 and served as Hawaii's second territorial delegate to the U.S. Congress. What remains here are the foundations of the family home, a royal fish pond, and a shrine where tributes are still paid in flowers.

Lawai Rd. Just after mile marker 4 on Poipu Rd., veer to the right of the fork in the road; the park is on the right side.

Spouting Horn ★ NATURAL ATTRACTION   This natural phenomenon is second in regularity only to Yellowstone's Old Faithful. It's quite a sight—big waves hit Kauai's south shore with enough force to send a spout of funneled salt water 10 feet or more up in the air; in winter the water can get as high as six stories.

Spouting Horn is different from other blowholes in Hawaii, in that it has an additional hole that blows air that sounds like a loud moaning. According to Hawaiian legend, this coastline was once guarded by a giant female lizard, Mo'o, who would gobble up any intruders. One day, along came Liko, who wanted to fish in this area. Mo'o rushed out to eat Liko. Quickly, Liko threw a spear right into the giant lizard's mouth. Mo'o then chased Liko into a lava tube. Liko escaped, but legend says Mo'o is still in the tube, and the moaning sound at Spouting Horn is her cry for help.

At Kukuiula Bay, beyond Prince Kuhio Park (see above).

Western Kauai
WAIMEA TOWN

If you'd like to take a self-guided tour of this historic town, stop at the **West Hawaii Visitors' Center** (© **808/338-1332**), at the corner of Kaumualii Hwy and Hwy. 50, to pick up a map and guide to the sites. Call ahead for hours.

Kiki a Ola (Menehune Ditch) ★ HISTORIC SITE   Hawaiians were expert rock builders, able to construct elaborate edifices without using mortar. They formed long lines and passed stones hand over hand, and lifted rocks weighing tons with ropes made from native plants. Their feats gave rise to fantastic tales of *menehune,* elflike people hired by Hawaiian kings to create massive stoneworks in a single night—reputedly for the payment of a single shrimp (see "Discover the Legendary Little People," below). An excellent example of ancient Hawaiian construction is Kiki a Ola, the so-called Mene-hune Ditch, with cut and dressed stones that form an ancient aqueduct that still directs water to irrigate taro ponds. Only a 2-foot-high portion of the wall can be seen today; the rest of the marvelous stonework is buried under the roadbed.

From Hwy. 50, go inland on Menehune Rd.; a plaque marks the spot about 1½ miles up.

DISCOVER THE legendary little people

According to ancient Hawaiian legend, among Kauai's earliest settlers were the *menehune,* a race of small people who worked at night to accomplish magnificent feats. Above Nawiliwili Harbor, the **Menehune Fish Pond**—which at one time extended 25 miles—is said to have been built in a single night, with two rows of thousands of menehune passing stones hand to hand. The menehune were promised that no one would watch them work, but one person did; when they discovered the spy, they stopped working immediately, leaving two gaps in the wall. From Nawiliwili Harbor, take Hulemalu Road above Huleia Stream; look for the HAWAII CONVENTION AND VISITORS BUREAU marker at a turnoff in the road, which leads to the legendary fish pond. Kayakers can paddle up Huleia Stream to see it up close.

Russian Fort Elizabeth State Historical Park ★ HISTORIC SITE
To the list of those who tried to conquer Hawaii, add the Russians. In 1815, a
German doctor tried to claim Kauai for Russia. He even supervised the construction of a fort in Waimea, but he and his handful of Russian companions
were expelled by Kamehameha I a couple of years later. Now a state historic
landmark, the Russian Fort Elizabeth (named for the wife of Russia's Czar
Alexander I) is on the eastern headlands overlooking the harbor, across from
Lucy Kapahu Aukai Wright Beach Park. The fort is now mostly in ruins. You
can take a free self-guided tour of the site, which affords a keen view of the
west bank of the Waimea River, where Captain Cook landed, and of the island
of Niihau across the channel.

Hwy. 50 (on the ocean side, just after mile marker 22), east of Waimea.

THE GRAND CANYON OF THE PACIFIC: WAIMEA CANYON ★★★

The great gaping gulch known as Waimea Canyon is quite a sight. This valley,
known for its reddish lava beds, reminds everyone who sees it of the Grand
Canyon. Kauai's version is bursting with ever-changing color, just like its
namesake, but it's smaller—only a mile wide, 3,567 feet deep, and 12 miles
long. A massive earthquake sent all the streams flowing into a single river that
ultimately carved this picturesque canyon. Today, the Waimea River—a silver
thread of water in the gorge that's sometimes a trickle, often a torrent, but
always there—keeps cutting the canyon deeper, and nobody can say what the
result will be 100 million years from now.

You can stop by the road and look at the canyon, hike down into it, or
swoop through it in a helicopter. For more information, see "Hiking & Camping," later in this chapter, and "Helicopter Rides over Waimea Canyon & the
Na Pali Coast," p. 233.

THE DRIVE THROUGH WAIMEA CANYON & UP TO KOKEE

By car, there are two ways to visit Waimea Canyon and reach Kokee State
Park, 20 miles up from Waimea. From the coastal road (Hwy. 50), you can
turn up Waimea Canyon Drive (Hwy. 550) at Waimea town, or you can pass
through Waimea and turn up Kokee Road (Hwy. 55) at Kekaha. The climb is
very steep from Kekaha, but Waimea Canyon Drive, the rim road, is narrower
and rougher. A few miles up, the two merge into Kokee Road.

The first good vantage point is **Waimea Canyon Lookout,** between mile
markers 10 and 11 on Waimea Canyon Road. From here, it's another 6 miles
to Kokee. There are a few more lookout points along the way that also offer
spectacular views, such as **Puu Hina Hina Lookout,** between mile markers
13 and 14, at 3,336 feet; be sure to pull over and spend a few minutes ponder-
ing this natural wonder. (The giant white object that looks like a golf ball and
defaces the natural landscape is a radar station left over from the Cold War.)

KOKEE STATE PARK ★★

It's only 16 miles from Waimea to Kokee, but it's a whole different world,
because the park is 4,345 acres of rainforest. You'll enter a new climate zone,

where the breeze has a bite and trees look quite continental. This is a cloud forest on the edge of the Alakai Swamp, the largest swamp in Hawaii, on the summit plateau of Kauai. Days are cool and wet, with intermittent bright sunshine, not unlike Seattle on a good day. Bring your sweater, and, if you're staying over, be sure you know how to light a fire (overnight lows dip into the 40s Fahrenheit/single digits Celsius).

The forest is full of native plants, such as mokihana berry, ohia lehua tree, *iliau* (similar to Maui's silversword), and imports such as Australia's eucalyptus and California's redwood. Pigs, goats, and black-tailed deer thrive in the forest, but the *moa,* or Polynesian jungle fowl, is the cock of the walk.

Right next to Kokee Lodge (which lies on the only road through the park, about a mile before it ends) is the **Kokee Natural History Museum ★** (www. kokee.org; © **808/335-9975**), open daily from 9am to 4:30pm (admission: at least $1 donation). This is the best place to learn about the forest and Alakai Swamp before you set off hiking in the wild. The museum shop has great trail information as well as local books and maps, including the official park trail map. I recommend getting "The Pocket Guide on Native Plants on the Nature Trail for Kokee State Park" and "The Road Guide to Kokee and Waimea Canyon State Park."

A **nature walk** is the best introduction to this rainforest; it starts behind the museum at the rare Hawaiian koa tree. This easy self-guided walk of about .25 miles takes about 20 minutes if you stop and look at all the plants identified along the way.

Two miles above Kokee Lodge is **Kalalau Lookout ★**, the spectacular climax of your drive through Waimea Canyon and Kokee. When you stand at the lookout, below you is a work in progress that began at least 5 million years ago. It's hard to stop looking: The view is breathtaking, especially when light and cloud shadows play across the red-and-orange cliffs.

There's lots more to see and do up here. Anglers fly-fish for rainbow trout (see p. 246 for info on fishing licenses), while hikers tackle the 45 trails that lace the Alakai Swamp (p. 250). That's a lot of ground to cover, so you might want to plan on staying over. If pitching a tent is too rustic for you, the **Kokee Lodge** (p. 219) has wonderful cabins set in a grove of redwoods—they're one of the best lodging bargains in the islands. The restaurant at Kokee Lodge is open for breakfast and lunch daily from 9am to 4pm.

For advance information, contact the **State Division of Parks,** 3060 Eiwa St., Room 306 (http://dlnr.hawaii.gov/dsp/parks/kauai/; © **808/274-3444**), and the **West Kauai Lodging,** www.westkauailodging.com; 4469 Halepule Rd., Waimea, HI 96796 (© **808/338-0031**). The park is open daily year-round. The best time to go is early in the morning to see the panoramic view of Kalalau Valley from the lookout at 4,000 feet, before clouds obscure the valley and peaks.

HELICOPTER RIDES OVER WAIMEA CANYON & THE NA PALI COAST ★★★

Don't leave Kauai without seeing it from a helicopter. It's expensive, but worth the splurge. You can take home memories of the thrilling ride up and over the Kalalau Valley on Kauai's wild North Shore and into the 5,200-foot

6 | MAKE A PILGRIMAGE TO A hindu temple

Believe it or not, a sacred Hindu temple is being carved out of rocks from India on the banks of the Wailua River. The **San Marga Iraivan Temple** is being built to last "a thousand years or more," on the 458-acre site of the Saiva Siddhanta Church monastery. The Chola-style temple is the result of a vision by the late Satguru Sivaya Subramuniyaswami, known to his followers as Gurudeva, the founder of the church and its monastery. He specifically selected this site in 1970, recognizing that the Hawaiians also felt the spiritual power of this place. The Hawaiians called it *pihanakalani*, "where heaven touches the earth." The concrete foundation is 68×168 square feet and 3 feet thick, designed not to crack under the weight of the 3.2-million-pound temple dedicated to the Hindu god Shiva. The granite for the temple is being hand-quarried by some 70 stonemasons in India, then shipped to Kauai for final shaping and fitting on the site. The center of the temple will hold a 700-pound crystal, known as the Sivalingam, now displayed at the monastery's smaller temple on the grounds.

Hindu pilgrims come from around the globe to study and meditate at the monastery. The public is welcome to the monastery temple, open daily from 9am to noon. There is also a weekly guided tour of the grounds that includes the San Marga Iraivan Temple. The tour time varies depending on the retreat schedule at the monastery. For information, go to www.himalayanacademy.com/monastery or call (✆ **808/822-3012,** ext. 4. You must make reservations to tour the monastery.

A few suggestions if you plan to visit: Carry an umbrella (it's very rainy here). Wear what the Hindus call "modest clothing" (certainly no shorts, short dresses, T-shirts, or tank tops); traditional Hindu dress is ideal. Also, even though this is a monastery, there are lots of people around, so don't leave valuables in your car.

To get here, turn mauka (inland) off Kuhio Highway (Hwy. 56) at the lights, just after crossing the bridge, onto Kuamoo Road (btw. Coco Palms Hotel and the Wailua River). Continue up the hill for just over 4 miles. A quarter-mile past mile marker 4, turn left on Kaholalele Road and go 1 block to the end of the road. The **Information Center** is at 107 Kaholalele Rd. Park on Temple Lane. You must make reservations for a guided tour the monastery and note: The guided tours book up weeks in advance. You can do a self-guided from 9am to noon daily.

vertical temple of Mount Waialeale, the most sacred place on the island and the wettest spot on earth (and, in some cases, you can even take home a video of your ride). All flights leave from Lihue Airport. *Money-saving tip:* You can save 15% to 37% by booking online.

Blue Hawaiian ★★★   Blue Hawaiian has been the Cadillac of helicopter tour companies on Maui and the Big Island for more than a decade, and it has recently expanded its operations to Kauai. I strongly recommend that you try to book with Blue Hawaiian first. The operation is first class and the equipment state-of-the-art. Plus, the craft has individual business class–style seats, two-way communication with the pilot, and expansive glass for incredible views.

Lihue Heliport #8, 3651 Ahukini Rd. www.bluehawaiian.com. (✆ **800/745-2583** or 808/245-5800. 55- to 60-min. tour $247 (check for online discounts).

Jack Harter ★ The pioneer of helicopter flights on Kauai, Jack was the guy who started the sightseeing-via-helicopter trend. The 90-minute tour hovers over the sights a bit longer than the 60-minute flight so you can get a closer look, but I found the shorter tour sufficient.

4231 Ahukini Rd. www.helicopters-kauai.com. ☎ **888/245-2001** or 808/245-3774. 60- to 65-min. tour $289 ($259 if booked online); 90- to 95-min. tour $434.

The Coconut Coast
FERN GROTTO

This is one of Kauai's oldest (since 1946) and most popular tourist attractions. The grotto is the source of many Hawaiian legends. Along the Wailua River is a lush outcrop of tropical ferns, plants, and other vegetation around an open rock formation, known as Fern Grotto. The site of weddings, this is a peek into what Kauai looked like before roads, telephone poles, and all the modern conveniences. You can visit Fern Grotto by going with **Smith's Motor Boats** (www.smithskauai.com; ☎ **808/821-6895**), which operates a 157-passenger motorized barge that takes people up and down the river on an 80-minute cruise, with a hula show on the return trip. Tours depart daily from 9:30am to 3:30pm from Wailua Marine State Park (turn off Kuhio Hwy./Hwy. 56 into the park). The cost is $20 for adults and $10 for children 3 to 12 (book online for 10% off). Reservations are recommended. Book online for a 10% discount.

WAILUA RIVER STATE PARK

Ancients called the Wailua River "the river of the great sacred spirit." Seven temples once stood along this 20-mile river, which is fed by 5,148-foot Mount Waialeale, the wettest spot on earth. You can go up Hawaii's biggest navigable river by boat or kayak (see "Boating" and "Kayaking"), or drive Kuamoo Road (Hwy. 580), sometimes called the King's Highway, which goes inland along the north side of the river from Kuhio Highway (Hwy. 56)—from the northbound lane, turn left at the stoplight just before the ruins of Coco Palms Resort. Kuamoo Road goes past the *heiau* (temple) and historic sites to Opaekaa Falls and Keahua Arboretum, a State Division of Forestry attempt to reforest the watershed with native plants.

The entire district, from the river mouth to the summit of Waialeale, was once a sacred historic site, believed to be founded by Puna, a Tahitian priest who, according to legend, arrived in one of the first double-hulled voyaging canoes to come to Hawaii, established a beachhead, and declared Kauai his kingdom. All of Kauai's *alii* (royalty) are believed to be descended from Puna. Here, in this royal settlement, are remains of the seven temples, including a sacrificial *heiau,* a planetarium (a simple array of rocks in a celestial pattern), the royal birthing stones, and a stone bell to announce a royal birth.

There's a nice overlook view of 40-foot **Opaekaa Falls** ★★ 1½ miles up Hwy. 580. This is probably the best-looking drive-up waterfall on Kauai. With the scenic peaks of the Makaleha Mountains in the background and a restored Hawaiian village on the riverbanks, these falls are what the tourist-bureau folks call an "eye-popping" photo op.

hollywood LOVES KAUAI

More than 50 major Hollywood productions have been shot on Kauai since the studios discovered the island's spectacular natural beauty. Here are just a few:

o Manawaiopu Falls, Mount Waialeale, and other scenic areas around the island appeared in *Jurassic Park.*

o Kauai's lush rainforests formed a fantastic backdrop for Harrison Ford in both *Raiders of the Lost Ark* and *Indiana Jones and the Temple of Doom.*

o Mitzi Gaynor sang "I'm Gonna Wash That Man Right Outta My Hair" on Lumahai Beach in *South Pacific.*

o Elvis Presley married costar Joan Blackman near the Wailua River in the 1961 film *Blue Hawaii.*

o Beautiful Kee Beach, on the North Shore, masqueraded as Australia in the miniseries *The Thorn Birds,* starring Richard Chamberlain and Rachel Ward.

o Kauai appeared as the backdrop for *Outbreak,* the 1994 thriller about the spread of a deadly virus on a remote tropical island, starring Dustin Hoffman.

o Hoffman also appeared with Robin Williams and Julia Roberts in *Hook* (1991), in which Kauai stood in as Never-Never Land.

o James Caan, Nicolas Cage, Sarah Jessica Parker, and Pat Morita shared laughs on Kauai (which appeared as itself) in *Honeymoon in Vegas.*

Now you can visit these and other Kauai locations that made it to the silver screen, plus locations from such TV classics as *Fantasy Island* and *Gilligan's Island,* with **Hawaii Movie Tours** (www.robertshawaii.com/kauai/tours/hawaii-movie-tours; ✆ **800/831-5541** or 808/539-9400). The commentary and sightseeing stops are supplemented by video clips of the location shots (complete with surround sound). You'll see more of Kauai on this tour (including private estates not open to the public) than you would if you explored the island yourself. Tickets are $114 for adults and $61 for children 4-11 (discounts for booking online); lunch is included.

Near the Opaekaa Falls overlook is **Poliahu Heiau,** the large lava-rock temple of Kauai's last king, Kaumualii, who died on Oahu in 1824 after being abducted by King Kamehameha II.

SLEEPING GIANT

If you squint your eyes just so as you pass the 1,241-foot-high Nounou Ridge, which forms a dramatic backdrop to the coastal villages of Wailua and Waipouli, you can see the fabled Sleeping Giant. On Kuhio Highway, just after mile marker 7, around the mini-mall complex Waipouli Town Center, look *mauka* (inland) and you may see what appears to be the legendary giant named Puni, who, as the story goes, fell asleep after a great feast. If you don't see it at first, visualize it this way: His head is Wailua and his feet are Kapaa.

Paradise Found: The North Shore ★★★

No matter how much time you have on Kauai, make it a priority to see the North Shore. No doubt about it—this is Hawaii at its best.

ON THE ROAD TO HANALEI

The first place everyone should go on Kauai is Hanalei. The drive along **Kuhio Highway** (Hwy. 56, which becomes Hwy. 560 after Princeville to the end of the road) displays Kauai's grandeur at its absolute best. Just before Kilauea, the air and the sea change, the light falls in a different way, and the last signs of development are behind you.

Birders might want to stop off at **Kilauea Point National Wildlife Refuge,** a mile north of Kilauea, and the **Hanalei National Wildlife Refuge,** along Ohiki Road, at the west end of the Hanalei River Bridge. (For details, see "Birding" on p. 255.) In the Hanalei Refuge, along a dirt road on a levee, you can see the **Hariguchi Rice Mill,** now a historic treasure.

Now the coastal highway heads due west and the showy ridgelines of Mount Namahana create a grand amphitheater. The two-lane coastal highway rolls through pastures of grazing cattle and past a tiny airport and the luxurious Princeville Resort.

Five miles past Kilauea, just past the Princeville Shopping Center, is **Hanalei Valley Lookout.** Big enough for a dozen cars, this lookout attracts crowds of people who peer over the edge into the 917-acre Hanalei River Valley. Seldom will you see so many shades of green in one place: The green rice, taro, and streams lace a patchwork of green ponds that back up to green-velvet Bali Hai cliffs. Don't be put off by the crowds; this is definitely worth a look. You might even see an endangered Hawaiian black-necked stilt.

Farther along, a hairpin turn offers another scenic look at Hanalei town, and then you cross the **Hanalei Bridge.** The Pratt truss steel bridge, prefabbed in New York City, was erected in 1912; it's now on the National Register of Historic Landmarks. If it ever goes out, the nature of Hanalei will change forever; currently, this rusty one-lane bridge isn't big enough for a tour bus to cross.

You'll drive slowly past the **Hanalei River** banks and Bill Mowry's **Hanalei Buffalo Ranch,** where 200 American bison roam in the tropical sun; you may even see buffalo grazing in the pastures on your right. The herd is often thinned to make buffalo patties. (You wondered why there was a buffalo burger on the Ono Family Restaurant menu, didn't you?)

In Hanalei, Nui, turn right on Aku Road before Ching Young Village and then take a right on Weke Road; **Hanalei Beach** (p. 242), one of Hawaii's most gorgeous, is a half-block ahead on your left. Swimming is excellent here year-round, especially in summer, when Hanalei Bay becomes a big, placid lake.

If this exquisite 2-mile-long beach doesn't meet your expectations, head down the highway, where the next 7 miles of coast yield some of Kauai's other spectacular beaches, including **Lumahai Beach,** of *South Pacific* movie fame, as well as **Tunnels Beach** (p. 243), where the 1960s puka-shell necklace craze began, and **Haena Beach Park** (p. 243), a fabulous place to kick back and enjoy the waves, particularly in summer. Once you've found your beach, stick around until sundown and then head back to one of the North Shore's

BRIDGE ETIQUETTE: SHOWING ALOHA ON KAUAI'S one-lane bridges

Hawaii's drivers are much more laid-back and courteous than most mainland drivers. Hanalei has a series of one-lane bridges where not only is it proper etiquette to be courteous, but it's also the law. When you approach a one-lane bridge, slow down and yield if a vehicle, approaching in the opposite direction, is either on the bridge or just about to enter the bridge. If you are in a long line of vehicles approaching the bridge, don't just join the train crossing the bridge. The local rule of thumb is about seven to eight cars over the bridge, then yield and give the cars waiting on the other side of the bridge a chance to come across. Of course, not everyone will adhere to these rules, but then, not everyone visiting Hawaii truly feels the spirit of aloha.

restaurants for a Mai Tai and a fresh seafood dinner (see "Where to Eat," p. 228). Another perfect day in paradise.

ATTRACTIONS ALONG THE WAY

Limahuli Garden of the National Tropical Botanical Garden ★ GARDEN   Out on Kauai's far North Shore, beyond Hanalei and the last wooden bridge, there's a mighty cleft in the coastal range where ancestral Hawaiians lived in what can only be called paradise. Carved by a waterfall stream known as Limahuli, the lush valley sits at the foot of steepled cliffs that Hollywood portrayed as Bali Hai in the film classic *South Pacific*. This small, almost secret garden is eco-tourism at its best. It appeals not just to green thumbs, but to all who love Hawaii's great outdoors. Here botanists hope to save Kauai's endangered native plants. You can take the self-guided tour to view the plants, which are identified in Hawaiian and English. From taro to sugar cane, the mostly Polynesian imports tell the story of the people who cultivated the plants for food, medicine, clothing, shelter, and decoration. In addition, Limahuli's stream is a sanctuary to the last five species of Hawaiian freshwater fish.

Visitor Center, a half-mile past mile marker 9 on Kuhio Hwy. (Hwy. 560). www.ntbg.org. ©️ **808/826-1053.** Admission $20 self-guided tour, free for children 18 and under; $40 guided tour, $20 children 10–17, only children 10 years and over on tour. Tues–Sat 9:30am–4pm; guided tours start 10am. Advance reservations required for 2½-hr. guided tour. During peak season of July–Sept, book at least a week ahead.

Na Aina Kai Botanical Gardens ★★★ GARDEN   Do not miss this incredible, magical garden on some 240 acres, sprinkled with around 70 life-size (some larger-than-life-size) whimsical bronze statues, hidden off the beaten path of the North Shore. It has something for everyone: waterfalls, pools, arbors, topiaries, colonnades, gazebos, a maze you will never forget, a lagoon with spouting fountains, a Japanese teahouse, and an enchanting path along a bubbling stream to the ocean. A host of different tours are available, from 1½ hours ($35) to 5 hours ($85) long, ranging from casual, guided strolls to rides in the covered CarTram to treks from one end of the gardens to the ocean. Currently, these tours are open to adults and children 13 and older. Book a tour before you leave for Hawaii so you won't be disappointed.

4101 Wailapa Rd. www.naainakai.com. ✆ **808/828-0525.** Tues–Fri 9am–5pm. Tours vary. Advance reservations strongly recommended. To get here from Lihue, drive north past mile marker 21 and turn right on Wailapa Rd. At the road's end, drive through the iron gates. From Princeville, drive south 6½ miles and take the 2nd left past mile marker 22 on Wailapa Rd. At the road's end, drive through the iron gates.

Waioli Mission House Museum ★ MUSEUM This two-story wood-frame house, built in 1836 by Abner and Lucy Wilcox of New Bedford, Massachusetts, is an excellent example of what life was like for the New England missionaries who came to Kauai to convert the "heathens" to Christianity.

Kuhio Hwy. (Hwy. 560), just behind the green Waioli Huia Church. http://grovefarm.org/waiolimissionhouse. ✆ **808/245-3202.** Donation $10 adults, $5 children 5–12. Tours Tues, Thurs, and Sat 9am and 3pm. When you arrive, ring bell for entry.

THE END OF THE ROAD

The real Hawaii begins where the road stops. This is especially true on Kauai—for at the end of Highway 560, the spectacular **Na Pali Coast** begins. To explore it, you have to set out on foot, by boat, or by helicopter. For details on experiencing this region, see p. 252 for hiking and camping, p. 244 for boating, and p. 233 for helicopter rides.

BEACHES

Eons of wind and rain have created this geological masterpiece of an island, with fabulous beaches like Hanalei, Kee, and Kalapaki. All are accessible to the public, as stipulated by Hawaii law, and many have facilities.

Lihue's Best Beach

KALAPAKI BEACH ★

At 150 feet wide and ¼ mile long, this white sand beach is protected by a jetty and patrolled by lifeguards, making it very safe for swimmers. The waves are good for surfing when there's a winter swell, and the view from the sand of the steepled 2,200-foot peaks of the majestic Haupu Ridge that shield Nawiliwili Bay is awesome. From Lihue Airport, turn left onto Kapule Highway (Hwy. 51) to Rice Street, turn left and go to the entrance of the Marriott, pass the hotel's porte-cochere and turn right at the shoreline access sign. Facilities include lifeguards, free parking, restrooms, and showers.

The Poipu Resort Area

MAHAULEPU BEACH ★★

Mahaulepu is the best-looking unspoiled beach in Kauai and possibly in the whole state. Its 2 miles of reddish-gold, grainy sand line the southeastern shore at the foot of 1,500-foot-high Haupu Ridge, just beyond the Grand Hyatt Kauai and sugar-cane fields, which end in sand dunes and a forest of casuarina trees. Almost untouched by modern life, Mahaulepu is a great

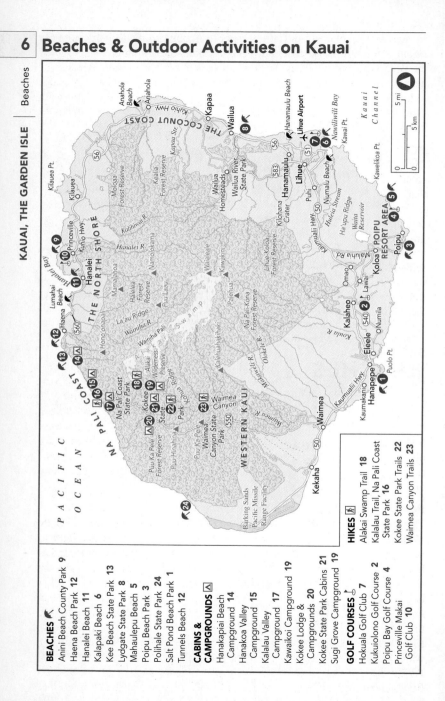

BEACHES ⌇

Anini Beach County Park **9**
Haena Beach Park **11**
Hanalei Beach **11**
Kalapaki Beach **6**
Kee Beach State Park **13**
Lydgate State Park **8**
Mahaulepu Beach **5**
Poipu Beach Park **3**
Polihale State Park **24**
Salt Pond Beach Park **1**
Tunnels Beach **12**

CABINS & CAMPGROUNDS ⌂

Hanakapiai Beach Campground **14**
Hanakoa Valley Campground **15**
Kalalau Valley Campground **17**
Kawaikoi Campground **19**
Kokee Lodge & Campgrounds **20**
Kokee State Park Cabins **21**
Sugi Grove Campground **19**

GOLF COURSES ⛳

Hokuala Golf Club **7**
Kukuiolono Golf Course **2**
Poipu Bay Golf Course **4**
Princeville Makai Golf Club **10**

HIKES 🥾

Alakai Swamp Trail **18**
Kalalau Trail, Na Pali Coast State Park **16**
Kokee State Park Trails **22**
Waimea Canyon Trails **23**

escape from the real world. It's ideal for beachcombing and shell hunting, but swimming can be risky, except in the reef-sheltered shallows 600 feet west of the sandy parking lot. There's no lifeguard, no facilities—just great natural beauty everywhere you look. To get here, drive past the Grand Hyatt Kauai 3 miles east on a red-dirt road, past the golf course and stables. Turn right at the T intersection, go 1 mile to the big sand dune, turn left, and drive a half-mile to a small lot under the trees.

POIPU BEACH PARK ★

Big, wide Poipu is actually two beaches in one; it's divided by a sandbar, called a *tombolo*. On the left, a lava-rock jetty protects a sandy-bottom pool that's perfect for children; on the right, the open bay attracts swimmers, snorkelers, and surfers. And everyone likes to picnic on the grassy lawn graced by coconut trees. You'll find excellent swimming, small tide pools for exploring, great reefs for snorkeling and diving, good fishing, nice waves for surfers, and a steady wind for windsurfers. Poipu attracts a daily crowd, but the density seldom approaches Waikiki levels, except on holidays. Facilities include restrooms, showers, picnic areas, Brennecke's Beach Broiler nearby (p. 226), and free parking in the red-dirt lot. To get here, turn on Poipu Beach Road, and then turn right at Hoowili Road.

Western Kauai

SALT POND BEACH PARK ★

Hawaii's only salt ponds still in production are at Salt Pond Beach, just outside Hanapepe. Generations of locals have come here to swim, fish, and collect salt crystals to dry in sun beds. The tangy salt is used for health purposes and to cure fish and season food. The curved reddish-gold beach lies between two rocky points and features a protected reef, tide pools, and gentle waves. Swimming here is excellent, even for children; this beach is also good for diving, windsurfing, and fishing. Facilities include a lifeguard, showers, restrooms, a camping area, a picnic area, a pavilion, and a parking lot. To get here, take Hwy. 50 past Hanapepe and turn on Lokokai Road.

POLIHALE STATE PARK ★

This mini-Sahara on the western end of the island is Hawaii's biggest beach: 17 miles long and as wide as three football fields. This is a wonderful place to get away from it all, but don't forget your flip-flops—the midday sand is hotter than a lava flow. The golden sands wrap around Kauai's northwestern shore from Kekaha plantation town, just beyond Waimea, to where the ridgebacks of the Na Pali Coast begin. The state park includes ancient Hawaiian *heiau* (temple) and burial sites, a view of the "forbidden" island of Niihau, and the famed **Barking Sands Beach,** where footfalls sound like a barking dog. (Scientists say that the grains of sand are perforated with tiny echo chambers, which emit a barking sound when they rub together.) Polihale also takes in the Pacific Missile Range Facility, a U.S. surveillance center that snooped on Russian subs during the Cold War, and Nohili Dune, which is nearly 3 miles long and 100 feet high in some places.

Be careful in winter, when high surf and rip currents make swimming dangerous. The safest place to swim is **Queen's Pond,** a small, shallow, sandy-bottom inlet protected from waves and shore currents. There are facilities for camping, as well as restrooms, showers, picnic tables, and pavilions. To get here, take Hwy. 50 past Barking Sands Pacific Missile Range and follow the signs through the sugar cane fields to Polihale. Local kids have been known to burgle rental cars out here, so don't leave tempting valuables in your car.

The Coconut Coast

LYDGATE STATE PARK ★

This 1-acre seacoast park has a rock-wall fish pond that blunts the open ocean waves and provides the only safe swimming and the best snorkeling on the eastern shore. A great place for a picnic or for kite flying on the green, the park is 5 miles north of Lihue on Kuhio Highway (Hwy. 56); look for the turnoff just before the Aston Aloha Beach Resort. Facilities include a pavilion, restrooms, outdoor showers, picnic tables, barbecue grills, lifeguards, and parking.

The North Shore

ANINI BEACH COUNTY PARK ★★

Anini is Kauai's safest beach for swimming and windsurfing. It's also one of the island's most beautiful: It sits on a blue lagoon at the foot of emerald cliffs, looking more like Tahiti than almost any other strand in the islands. This 3-mile-long gold-sand beach is shielded from the open ocean by the longest, widest fringing reef in Hawaii. With shallow water 4 to 5 feet deep, it's also the very best snorkel spot on Kauai, even for beginners. Anini has a campground, picnic and barbecue facilities, and a boat-launch ramp; several B&Bs and vacation rentals are nearby. Follow Kuhio Highway (Hwy. 56) to Kilauea; take the second exit, called Kalihiwai Road (the first dead-ends at Kalihiwai Beach), and drive a half-mile toward the sea; then turn left on Anini Beach Road.

HANALEI BEACH ★

Gentle waves roll across the face of half-moon Hanalei Bay, running up to the wide, golden sand; sheer volcanic ridges laced by waterfalls rise to 4,000 feet on the other side, 3 miles inland. Celebrated in song and hula, and featured on travel posters, this beach owes its natural beauty to its age—it's an ancient sunken valley with posterosional cliffs. Hanalei Bay indents the coast a full 1 mile inland and runs 2 miles point to point, with coral reefs on either side and a patch of coral in the middle—plus a sunken ship that belonged to a king, so divers love it. Swimming is excellent year-round, especially in summer, when Hanalei Bay becomes a big, placid lake. The aquamarine water is also great for body boarding, surfing, fishing, windsurfing, canoeing, kayaking, and boating (there's a boat ramp on the west bank of the Hanalei River). The area known as **Black Pot,** near the pier, is particularly good for swimming, snorkeling, and surfing. This beach is always packed with both locals and visitors, but you can usually find your own place in the sun by strolling down the shore; the bay is big enough for everyone. Facilities include a pavilion, restrooms, picnic tables, and parking. To get here, take Kuhio Highway (Hwy. 56), which becomes Hwy. 560 after Princeville. In Hanalei town, make a right on Aku Road just after Tahiti Nui, and then turn right again on Weke Road, which dead-ends at the parking lot for the Black Pot section of the beach; the easiest beach access is on your left.

KEE BEACH STATE PARK ★★

Where the road ends on the North Shore, you'll find a dandy little reddish-gold beach almost too beautiful to be real. (If it looks familiar, it was featured in *The Thorn Birds, Lord of the Flies,* and more.) Kee (*kay*-ay) is on a reef-protected cove at the foot of fluted volcanic cliffs. Swimming and snorkeling are safe inside the reef but dangerous outside; those North Shore waves and currents can be killers. This park has restrooms, showers, and parking—but no lifeguard. To get here, take Kuhio Highway (Hwy. 56), which becomes Hwy. 560 after Princeville; Kee is about 7½ miles past Hanalei.

TUNNELS BEACH & HAENA BEACH PARK ★★

Postcard-perfect gold-sand Tunnels Beach is one of Hawaii's most beautiful. When the sun sinks into the Pacific along the fabled peaks of Bali Hai, there's no better-looking beach in the islands: You're bathed in golden rays that butter up the blue sky, bounce off the steepled ridges, and tint the pale clouds hot pink. Catch the sunset from the pebbly sand beach or while swimming in the emerald-green waters, but do catch it. Tunnels is excellent for swimming nearly year-round and is safe for snorkeling because it's protected by a fringing coral reef (the waters can get rough in winter, though). The long, curvy beach is sheltered by a forest of ironwoods that provides welcome shade from the tropic heat.

Around the corner is grainy-gold-sand Haena Beach Park, which offers excellent swimming in summer and great snorkeling amid clouds of tropical fish. But stay out of the water in winter, when the big waves are dangerous. Haena also has a popular grassy park for camping. Noise-phobes will prefer Tunnels.

Take Kuhio Highway (Hwy. 56), which becomes Hwy. 560 after Princeville. Tunnels is about 6 miles past Hanalei town, after mile marker 8 on the highway (look for the alley with the big wood gate at the end), and Haena is just down the road. Tunnels has no facilities, but Haena has restrooms, outdoor showers, barbecue grills, picnic tables, and free parking (no lifeguard, though).

WATERSPORTS

Several outfitters on Kauai not only offer equipment rentals and tours, but also give out expert information on weather forecasts, sea and trail conditions, and other important matters for hikers, kayakers, sailors, and other backcountry adventurers. For watersports questions and equipment rental, contact **Kayak**

Kauai (www.kayakkauai.com; © **888/596-3853** or 808/826-98440), located on the east coast at the Wailua River Marina, 3–5971 Kuhio Hwy, Kapaa. You can also go with **Snorkel Bob's,** in Kapaa at 4–734 Kuhio Hwy. (Hwy. 56), just north of Coconut MarketPlace (www.snorkelbob.com; © **808/823-9433**), and in Koloa at 3236 Poipu Rd. (just south of Poipu Shopping Village), near Poipu Beach (© **808/742-2206**).

Boating

One of Hawaii's most spectacular natural attractions is Kauai's **Na Pali Coast.** Unless you're willing to make an arduous 22-mile hike (p. 252), there are only two ways to see it: by helicopter (see "Helicopter Rides over Waimea Canyon & the Na Pali Coast," p. 233) or by boat.

When the Pacific humpback whales make their annual visit to Hawaii from December to March, they swim right by Kauai. In season, most boats on Kauai—including sail- and powerboats—combine **whale-watching** with their regular adventures.

Kauai has many freshwater areas that are accessible only by boat, including the Fern Grotto, Wailua State Park, Huleia and Hanalei national wildlife refuges, Menehune Fish Pond, and numerous waterfalls. If you want a tour of these fabulous regions, **Wailua River Guides,** 4–788 Kuhio Hwy., Kapaa (www.wailuariverguides.com; © **866/955-2925** or 808/821-2800), has an excellent tour of the Wailua River with a brief hike to a "secret" waterfall and a swim. The price, which includes lunch, all equipment, and van transportation from its shop to the marina and back, is $85 for adults and $75 for children 5 to 13 (not appropriate for kids under 5).

Captain Andy's Sailing Adventures ★ Captain Andy operates a 55-foot, 49-passenger catamaran out of two locations on the south shore ranging from a snorkel/picnic cruise, a 5½-hour cruise to the Na Pali Coast ($149–$169 adults, $109–$119 children 2–12; includes continental breakfast, deli-style lunch, snorkeling, and drinks) to a 6-hour Na Pali Zodiac cruise on inflatable boats ($159 adults, $119 children 5–12). *Tip:* Book online for a $10 discount.

Kekaha Small Boat Harbor; and Port Allen. www.napali.com. © **800/535-0830** or 808/335-6833. Prices vary depending on trip.

Holoholo Charters ★ Offering a range of boats from swimming/snorkeling sailing to powerboat charters to the Na Pali Coast, Holoholo's tours range in price from $119 adults, $99 for children for the 3½-hour sunset cruise of the Na Pali Coast on a power catamaran to $205 for adults, $139 for children for the 7-hour trip on the 61-foot powerboat *Holoholo* to the forbidden island of Niihau, where you stop for snorkeling with continental breakfast, a buffet lunch, and snorkel equipment included. *Tip:* Book online for $10 to $15 off per person.

Port Allen. www.holoholokauaiboattours.com. © **800/848-6130** or 808/335-0815. Prices and departure points vary depending on trip.

Scuba Diving

Diving on Kauai is dictated by the weather. In winter, when heavy swells and high winds hit the island, it's generally limited to the more protected south shore. Probably the best-known site along the south shore is **Caverns,** located off the Poipu Beach resort area. This site consists of a series of lava tubes interconnected by a chain of archways. A constant parade of fish streams by (even shy lionfish are spotted lurking in crevices), brightly hued Hawaiian lobsters hide in the lava's tiny holes, and turtles sometimes swim past.

In summer, when the north Pacific storms subside, the magnificent North Shore opens up, and you can take a boat dive locally known as the **Oceanarium,** northwest of Hanalei Bay, where you'll find a kaleidoscopic marine world in a horseshoe-shaped cove. From the rare (long-handed spiny lobsters) to the more common (taape, conger eels, and nudibranchs), the resident population is one of the more diverse on the island. The topography, which features pinnacles, ridges, and archways, is covered with cup corals, black-coral trees, and nooks and crannies enough for a dozen dives.

Because the best dives on Kauai are offshore, I recommend booking a two-tank dive off a dive boat. **Bubbles Below Scuba Charters,** 4353 Waialo Rd., Port Allen Small Boat Harbor (www.bubblesbelowkauai.com; © **808/332-7333**), specializes in highly personalized small-group dives, with an emphasis on marine biology. The 36-foot *Kaimanu* is a custom-built Radon dive boat that comes complete with a hot shower. Two-tank boat dives cost $130–$190 (if booked directly); nondivers can pay $90 to come along for the ride. In summer (May–Sept), Bubbles Below offers a three-tank trip for experienced divers only to the "forbidden" island of Niihau, 90 minutes by boat from Kauai. You should be comfortable with vertical drop-offs, huge underwater caverns, possibly choppy surface conditions, and significant currents. You should also be willing to share water space with the resident sharks. The all-day, three-tank trip costs $345 (booked directly), including tanks, weights, dive computer, lunch, drinks, and marine guide (if you need gear, it's $35 more).

On the south side of the island, call **Fathom Five Adventures,** 3450 Poipu Rd. (next to the Chevron), Koloa (www.fathomfive.com; © **808/742-6991**).

Snorkeling

See the introduction to this section (p. 244) for locations of **Snorkel Bob's.**

For great shoreline snorkeling, try the reef off **Kee Beach/Haena Beach Park,** located at the end of Hwy. 560. **Tunnels Beach,** about a mile before the end of Hwy. 560 in Haena, has a wide reef that's great for poking around in search of tropical fish. Be sure to check ocean conditions—don't go if the surf is up or if there's a strong current. **Anini Beach,** located off the northern Kalihiwai Road (btw. mile markers 25 and 26 on Kuhio Hwy., or Hwy. 56), just before the Princeville Airport, has a safe, shallow area with excellent snorkeling. **Poipu Beach Park** has some good snorkeling to the right side of Nukumoi Point—the *tombolo* area, where the narrow strip of sand divides the ocean, is best. If this spot is too crowded, wander down the beach in front of the Koa Kai Resort; if there are no waves, this place is also hopping with marine life. **Salt Pond Beach Park,** off Hwy. 50 near Hanapepe, has good snorkeling around the two rocky points, home to hundreds of tropical fish.

Sport Fishing

DEEP-SEA FISHING Kauai's fishing fleet is smaller and less well recognized than others in the islands, but the fish are still out there. All you need to bring is your lunch and your luck. The best way to arrange a sport-fishing charter is through the experts; the best booking desk in the state is **Sportfish Hawaii** ★ (www.sportfishhawaii.com; ☎ **877/388-1376** or 808/396-2607), which books boats on all the islands. These fishing vessels have been inspected and must meet rigorous criteria to guarantee that you will have a great time. Prices range from $1,300 for a full-day exclusive charter (you and five of your closest friends get the entire boat to yourselves), $1,100 for a 3-quarter day charter, and $750 for a half-day exclusive. Frankly, the fishing is better off the Kona coast, and the prices are more reasonable, too.

FRESHWATER FISHING Freshwater fishing is big on Kauai, thanks to the dozens of man-made reservoirs. They're full of largemouth, smallmouth, and peacock bass (also known as *tucunare*). The **Puu Lua Reservoir,** in Kokee State Park, also has rainbow trout and is stocked by the state every year. Fishing for rainbow trout in the reservoir has a limited season: As we went to press, anglers may fish daily from sunrise to sunset from June 14 until September 28, these dates seem to vary greatly year to year. Check www.dlnr hawaii.gov/dar for current dates.

Before you rush out and get a fishing pole, you must have a **Hawaii Freshwater Fishing License,** available through the **State Department of Land and Natural Resources,** Division of Aquatic Resources, 3060 Eiwa St., Room 306 (http://dlnr.hawaii.gov/dar/fishing/licenses-and-permits/; ☎ **808/587-0109**); Monday to Friday 8am to 3:30pm. You can also get a license through any fishing-supply store; try **Walmart,** 3–3300 Kuhio Hwy. (☎ **808/246-1599**), or **Salt Pond County Store,** Eleele (☎ **808/335-5966**). Or, you can get your license online (www.ehawaii.gov/dlnr/fish/exe/fresh_main_page.cgi); a 7-day tourist license costs $10 (plus a $1 convenience fee if purchased online).

When you get your license, pick up a copy of the booklet "State of Hawaii Freshwater Fishing Regulations."

If you would like a guide, **Sportfish Hawaii** (www.sportfishhawaii.com; ☎ **877/388-1376** or 808/396-2607) offers guided bass-fishing trips starting at $265 for two people for a half-day and $450 for two for a full day.

Surfing

Hanalei Bay's winter surf is the most popular on the island, but it's for experts only. **Poipu Beach** is an excellent spot to learn to surf; the waves are small and—best of all—nobody laughs when you wipe out. Check with the

local surf shops (www.nukumoisurf.com/Surf_Report.html) or call the
Weather Service (© 808/245-3564) to find out where the surf's up.

Poipu is also the site of numerous surfing schools, check with Nukumoi Suf Shop for their current recommended list of surfing instructors.

Equipment is available for rent (ranging from $6 an hour or $25 a day for "soft" beginner boards to $8 an hour or $30 a day for hard boards for experienced surfers) from **Nukumoi Surf Shop,** across from Brennecke's Beach, Poipu Beach Park (www.nukumoisurf.com/surfshophawaii.html; © **808/742-8019**); and **Hanalei Surf Co.,** 5–5161 Kuhio Hwy. (across from Zelo's Beach House Restaurant in Hanalei Center; www.hanaleisurf.com; © **808/826-9000**).

Tubing

Back in the days of the sugar plantations, local kids would grab inner tubes and jump in the irrigation ditches crisscrossing the cane fields to get an exciting ride. Today you can enjoy this (formerly illegal) activity by tubing the flumes and ditches of the old Lihue Plantation with **Kauai Backcountry Adventures** (www.kauaibackcountry.com; © **888/270-0555** or 808/245-2506). Passengers are taken in four-wheel-drive vehicles high into the mountains above Lihue to look at vistas generally off-limits to the public. At the

---

ESPECIALLY FOR kids

Surfing with an Expert (p. 246) If seven-time world champ Margo Oberg, a member of the Surfing Hall of Fame, can't get your kid—or you—up on a board riding a wave, nobody can. She promises same-day results even for klutzes.

Paddling up the Huleia River (p. 244) Indiana Jones ran for his life up this river to his seaplane in *Raiders of the Lost Ark.* You and the kids can venture down it yourself in a kayak. The picturesque Huleia winds through lush Huleia National Wildlife Refuge, where endangered species like great blue herons and Hawaiian gallinules take wing. It's ideal for everyone.

Climbing the Wooden Jungle Gyms at Kamalani Playground (p. 242) Located in Lydgate State Park, Wailua, this unique playground has a maze of jungle gyms for kids of all ages. Spend an afternoon whipping down slides, exploring caves, hanging from bars, and climbing all over.

Cooling Off with a Shave Ice (p. 226) On a hot, hot day, stop by **Brennecke's**

Beach Broiler, across from Poipu Beach Park (© **808/742-7588**), and order a traditional Hawaiian shave ice. This local treat consists of ice shavings stuffed into a paper cone and topped with a tropical-flavored syrup. If you can't decide, go for the "rainbow"—three different flavors in one cone.

Exploring a Magical World (p. 238) **Na Aina Kai Botanical Gardens** (www.naainakai.org) sits on some 240 acres, sprinkled with around 70 life-size (or larger-than-life-size) whimsical bronze statues, hidden off the beaten path of the North Shore. The tropical children's garden has a gecko hedge maze, a tropical jungle gym, a tree house in a rubber tree, and a 16-foot-tall Jack-in-the-Beanstalk giant with a 33-foot wading pool below. It's open Tuesday through Friday, by family tour only (check the website for times), and one Saturday a month for "Keiki Day"; book before you leave home to avoid disappointment.

flumes, you will be outfitted with a giant tube, gloves, and headlamp (for the long passageways through the tunnels). All you do is jump in the water, and the gentle gravity-feed flow will carry you through forests, into tunnels, and finally to a mountain swimming hole, where a picnic lunch is served. The 3-hour tours are $106 and appropriate for anyone ages 5 to 95. Swimming is not necessary, as all you do is relax and drift downstream.

Windsurfing & Kitesurfing

Anini Beach is one of the safest beaches for beginners to learn windsurfing. Lessons and equipment rental are available at **Windsurf Kauai** (www.windsurf-kauai.com; ✆ **808/828-6838**). Owner Celeste Harzel has been teaching windsurfing on Anini Beach for nearly 3 decades; she has special equipment to help beginners learn the sport. A 2-hour lesson is $100 and includes equipment and instruction. If you fall in love with windsurfing and want to keep going, she'll rent the equipment for $25 an hour. Serious windsurfers should head to **Hanalei Bay** or **Tunnels Beach** on the North Shore.

HIKING & CAMPING

Kauai is an adventurer's delight. The island's greatest tropical beauty isn't easily reachable; you've got to head out on foot and find it. For more information on Kauai's hiking trails, contact the **State Division of Parks,** 3060 Eiwa St., Lihue (http://dlnr.hawaii.gov/dsp/hiking/kauai; ✆ **808/274-3446**); the **State Division of Forestry and Wildlife,** 1151 Punchbowl St., Room 325, Honolulu (http://dlnr.hawaii.gov/dofaw/; ✆ **808/587-0166**); **Kauai County Parks and Recreation,** 4444 Rice St., Ste. 105, Lihue (www.kauaiexplorer.com/hiking_kauai/; ✆ **808/241-4460**); or the **Kokee Lodge Manager,** P.O. Box 819, Waimea, HI 96796 (www.kokee.org/; ✆ **808/335-6061**).

Kayak Kauai ★, at the Wailua River Marina just south of Kapaa (www.kayakkauai.com; ✆ **888/596-3853** or 808/826-9844), is the premier all-around outfitter on the island. It's staffed by local experts who keep track of weather forecasts as well as sea and trail conditions. They have a lot of pertinent information that hikers, campers, and other backcountry adventurers need to know. Plus, they have custom guided hiking tours starting at $81 per person for four people. If you don't plan to bring your own gear, you can rent it here or at **Pedal 'n Paddle,** in Hanalei (www.pedalnpaddle.com; ✆ **808/826-9069**). If you want to buy camping equipment, head for **Ace Island Hardware,** at Princeville Shopping Center (✆ **808/826-6980**), or **Walmart,** near the airport in Lihue (✆ **808/246-1599**).

A Warning About Flash Floods

When it rains on Kauai, the waterfalls rage and rivers and streams overflow, causing flash floods on roads and trails. If you're hiking, avoid dry streambeds, which flood quickly and wash out to sea. Before going hiking, camping, or sailing, especially in the rainy season (Nov–Mar), check the weather forecast by calling ✆ **808/245-6001**.

GUIDED HIKES The Kauai chapter of the **Sierra Club** (www.hawaii. sierraclub.org/kauai) offers four to seven different guided hikes every month, varying from an easy family moonlit beach hike to a moderate 4-mile trip up some 1,100 feet, plus 8-mile-plus treks for serious hikers only. The club also does guided hikes of Kokee State Park (see below), usually on weekends. Because there's no staffed office, the best way to contact the chapter is to check the website; outings are usually listed 3 to 6 months in advance, with complete descriptions of the hike, the hike leader's phone number, and what to wear and bring. You can also check Kauai's daily newspaper, *The Garden Island,* for a list of hikes in the "Community Calendar" section. Generally, the club asks for a donation of $5 per person per hike for nonmembers, $1 for children under 18 and Sierra Club members. It also does service work (clearing trails, picking up trash) on the hikes, so you may spend an hour doing service work, and then 2 to 3 hours hiking. Last year, the club took three service-work trips along the Na Pali Coast trail to help maintain it.

Western Kauai
TRAILS IN WAIMEA CANYON
On a wet island like Kauai, a dry hike is hard to find. But in the desert-dry gulch of Waimea Canyon, known as the "Grand Canyon of the Pacific" (once you get here, you'll see why—it's pretty spectacular), you're not likely to slip and slide in the muck as you go.

CANYON TRAIL You want to hike Hawaii's Grand Canyon, but you don't think you have time? Take the Canyon Trail to the east rim for a breathtaking view into the 3,000-foot-deep canyon. Park your car at the top of Halemanu Valley Road (located btw. mile markers 14 and 15 on Waimea Canyon Rd., about a mile down from the museum). The 3.5-mile round-trip takes 2 to 3 hours and leads to Waipoo Falls (as does the hike described below) and back. I suggest going in the afternoon, when the light is best.

HIKE TO WAIPOO FALLS ★ The 3-hour round-trip hike to Waipoo Falls is one of Kauai's best hikes. The two-tiered, 800-foot waterfall that splashes into a natural pool is worth every step it takes to get here. To find the trail, drive up Kokee Road (Hwy. 550) to the Puu Hina Hina Outlook; a quarter-mile past the lookout, near a NASA satellite tracking station on the right, a two-lane dirt road leads to the Waipoo Falls trail head. From here, the trail winds through a jungle dotted with wild yellow orchids and flame-red torch ginger before it leads you out on a descending ridgeback that juts deep into the canyon. At the end of the promontory, take a left and push on through the jungle to the falls. At the end, reward yourself with a refreshing splash in the pool.

TRAILS IN KOKEE STATE PARK ★★
At the end of Hwy. 550, which leads through Waimea Canyon to its summit, lies a 4,640-acre state park of high-mountain forest wilderness (3,600–4,000 ft. above sea level). The rainforest, bogs, and breathtaking views of the Na Pali coastline and Waimea Canyon are the draw at Kokee. This is the place for

hiking—among the 45 miles of maintained trails are some of the best hikes in Hawaii. Official trail maps of all the park's trails are for sale for $2 to $10 at the **Kokee Natural History Museum** (*© 808/335-9975*).

A few words of advice: Always check current trail conditions; up-to-date trail information is available on a bulletin board at the Kokee Natural History Museum. Stay on established trails, as it's easy to get lost here. Plan so you are finished with your hike well before dark. (Remember, Hawaii is close to the equator, so there is practically no twilight, and after sunset it gets dark quickly.) Carry water and rain gear—even if it's perfectly sunny when you set out—and wear sunscreen.

For complete coverage of the state park, see p. 232.

AWAAWAPUHI TRAIL   This 3.25-mile hike (6.5 miles round-trip) takes about 3 hours each way and is considered strenuous by most, but it offers a million-dollar view. Look for the trailhead at the left of the parking lot, at mile marker 17 between the museum and Kalalau Lookout. The well-marked, well-maintained trail now sports .25-mile markers, and you can pick up a free plant guide for the trail at the museum. The trail drops about 1,600 feet through native forests to a thin precipice right at the very edge of the Na Pali cliffs for a dramatic and dizzying view of the tropical valleys and blue Pacific 2,500 feet below. It's not recommended for anyone with vertigo (although a railing will keep you from a major slip and fall). Go early, before clouds obscure the view, or late in the day.

The Awaawapuhi can be a straight-out-and-back trail or a loop that connects with the **Nualolo Trail** (3.75 miles), which provides awesome views and leads back to the main road between the ranger's house and the Kokee cabins, which is about a mile and a half from where you started. So you can hike the remaining 1.5 miles along the road or hitch a ride if you decide to do the entire loop but can't make it all the way.

HALEMANU-KOKEE TRAIL   This trail takes you on a pleasant, easy-to-moderate 2.5-mile round-trip walk through a native koa-and-ohia forest inhabited by native birds. The trailhead is near mile marker 15; pick up the Faye Trail, which leads to this one. The Halemanu-Kokee links Kokee Valley to Halemanu Valley (hence the name); along the way, you'll see a plum orchard, valleys, and ridges.

PIHEA TRAIL   This is the park's flattest trail, but it's still a pretty strenuous 7.5-mile round-trip. A boardwalk that runs along about a third of the trail makes it easier, especially when it's wet. The trail begins at the end of Hwy. 550 at Puu O Kila Lookout, which overlooks Kalalau Valley; it goes down at first and then flattens out as it traces the back ridge of the valley. Once it enters the rainforest, you'll see native plants and trees. It intersects with the Alakai Swamp Trail (see below). If you combine both trails, figure on about 4 hours in and out.

ALAKAI SWAMP TRAIL ★   If you want to see the "real" Hawaii, this is it—a big swamp that's home to rare birds and plants. The trail allows a rare glimpse into a wet, cloud-covered wilderness preserve where 460 inches of rainfall a year is common. This 7-mile hike used to take 5 hours of sloshing through the bog, with mud up to your knees. Now a boardwalk protects you from the shoe-grabbing mud. Come prepared for rain. (The only silver lining is that there are no mosquitoes above 3,000 ft.)

The trailhead is off Mohihi (Camp 10) Road, just beyond the Forest Reserve entrance sign and the Alakai Shelter picnic area. From the parking lot, the trail follows an old World War II four-wheel-drive road. Stick to the boardwalk; this is a fragile eco-area. At the end of the 3.5-mile slog, if you're lucky and the clouds part, you'll have a lovely view of Wainiha Valley and Hanalei from Kilohana Lookout.

CAMPGROUNDS & WILDERNESS CABINS IN KOKEE

CABINS & TENT CAMPGROUNDS Camping facilities include state campgrounds (one next to Kokee Lodge, and four more primitive backcountry sites), one private tent area, and the **Kokee Lodge** (✆ **808/335-9975**), which has 12 cabins for rent through West Kauai Lodging at very reasonable rates (www.westkauailodging.com). At 4,000 feet, the nights are cold, particularly in winter, and no open fires are permitted at Kokee. The best deal is a stay at the cabins, reviewed on p. 219. The **Kokee Lodge Restaurant** (✆ **808/335-6061**) is open daily from 9am to 2:30pm for breakfast and lunch. Groceries and gas aren't available in Kokee, so stock up in advance; it's a long trip back down the mountain.

The **state campground** at Kokee allows tent camping only. Permits can be obtained on their website or from a state parks office on any island; on Kauai, it's at 3060 Eiwa St., Room 306, Lihue (http://dlnr.hawaii.gov/dsp/camping-lodging/kauai; ✆ **808/274-3444**). The permits are $18 per night; the time limit is 5 nights in a single 30-day period. Facilities include showers, drinking water, picnic tables, a pavilion with tables, restrooms, barbecues, sinks for dishwashing, and electric lights.

Tent camping at **Camp Sloggett,** owned by the Kauai YWCA, 3094 Elua St. (www.campingkauai.com/accomodations.html; ✆ **808/245-5959**), is available for $15 per person per night (children under 5 stay free). The sites are on 1½ acres of open field, with a covered pit for fires and a barbecue area, plus volleyball and badminton nets. For a solo traveler or couple, **Caretaker's Cottage** is a one-bedroom cottage with a king-size bed, linens provided, a full kitchen, and a wood-burning stove for just $120 per night on weekdays and $135 to $150 per night on weekends, with a 2-night minimum. To get here, continue on the highway past park headquarters and take the first right after the Kokee Lodge. Follow the dirt road and look for the wooden CAMP SLOGGETT sign; turn right and follow the bumpy road past the state cabins into a large clearing.

BACKCOUNTRY CAMPING The more primitive backcountry campgrounds include **Sugi Grove** and **Kawaikoi,** located about 4 miles from park headquarters on the Camp 10 Road, an often-muddy and steep four-wheel-drive road. Sugi Grove is located across the Kawaikoi Stream from the Kawaikoi campsite. The area is named for the sugi pines, which were planted in 1937 by the Civilian Conservation Corps. This is a shady campsite with a single picnic shelter, a pit toilet, a stream, and space for several tents. The Kawaikoi site is a 3-acre open grass field, surrounded by Kokee plum trees and forests of koa and ohia. Facilities include two picnic shelters, a composting toilet, and a stream that flows next to the camping area. There is no potable water—bring in your own or treat the stream water.

Permits, which are $18 per night, are available online at http://dlnr.hawaii.gov/dsp/camping-lodging/kauai. State Parks Office, 3060 Eiwa St., Room 306 (© **808/274-3444**). You're limited to 5 nights in any 30-day period.

The North Shore: Na Pali Coast State Park

Simply put, the Na Pali Coast is the most beautiful part of the Hawaiian Islands. Hanging valleys open like green-velvet accordions, and waterfalls tumble to the sea from the 4,120-foot-high cliffs; the experience is both exhilarating and humbling. Whether you hike in, fly over, or take a boat cruise past, be sure to see this park.

Established in 1984, Na Pali Coast State Park takes in a 22-mile stretch of fluted cliffs that wrap around the northwest shore of Kauai between Kee Beach and Polihale State Park. Volcanic in origin, carved by wind and sea, "the cliffs" (*na pali* in Hawaiian), which heaved out of the ocean floor 200 million years ago, stand as constant reminders of majesty and endurance. Four major valleys—Kalalau, Honopu, Awaawapuhi, and Nualolo—crease the cliffs.

Unless you boat or fly in (see "Boating" on p. 244, or "Helicopter Rides over Waimea Canyon & the Na Pali Coast," p. 233), the park is accessible only on foot—and it's not easy. An ancient footpath, the **Kalalau Trail,** winds through this remote, spectacular 6,500-acre park, ultimately leading to Kalalau Valley. Of all the green valleys in Hawaii, and there are many, only Kalalau is a true wilderness—probably the last wild valley in the islands. No road goes here, and none ever will. It's home to long-plumed tropical birds, golden monarch butterflies, and many of Kauai's 120 rare and endangered species of plants. The hike into the Kalalau Valley is grueling and takes most people 6 to 8 hours one-way.

Despite its inaccessibility, this journey into Hawaii's wilderness has become increasingly popular since the 1970s. Overrun with hikers, helicopters, and boaters, the Kalalau Valley was in grave danger of being loved to death. Strict rules about access have since been adopted. The park is open to hikers and campers on only a limited basis, and you must have a permit (although you can hike the first 6 miles, to Hanakoa Valley, without a permit). Permits are $20 per night and are issued online at http://dlnr.hawaii.gov/dsp/camping-lodging/kauai. For more information, contact the **Kauai State Parks Office,** 3060 Eiwa St., Room 306 (© **808/274-3444**).

HIKING THE KALALAU TRAIL ★★
The trail head is at Kee Beach, at the end of Hwy. 560. Even if you go only as far as Hanakapiai, bring water.

THE FIRST 2 MILES: TO HANAKAPIAI BEACH   Do not attempt this hike unless you have reasonable footwear (closed-toe shoes at least; hiking shoes are best), water, a sun visor, insect repellent, and adequate hiking clothes (shorts and a T-shirt are fine; your bikini is not). It's only 2 miles to Hanakapiai Beach, but the first mile is all uphill. This tough trail takes about 2 hours one-way and dissuades many, but everyone should attempt at least the first half mile, which gives a good hint of the startling beauty that lies ahead. Day hikers love this initial stretch, so it's usually crowded. The island of Niihau and Lehua Rock are often visible on the horizon. At mile marker 1, you'll have climbed from sea level to 400 feet; now it's all downhill to Hanakapiai Beach. Sandy in summer, the beach becomes rocky when winter waves scour the coast. There are strong currents and no lifeguards, so swim at your own risk. You can also hike another 2 miles inland from the beach to **Hanakapiai Falls,** a 120-foot cascade. Allow 3 hours for that stretch.

THE REST OF THE WAY   Hiking the Kalalau is the most difficult and challenging hike in Hawaii, and one you'll never forget. Even the Sierra Club rates the 22-mile round-trip into Kalalau Valley and back as "strenuous"—this is serious backpacking. Follow the footsteps of ancient Hawaiians along a cliffside path that's a mere 10 inches wide in some places, with sheer 1,000-foot drops to the sea. One misstep, and it's *limu* (seaweed) time. Even the hardy and fit should allow at least 2 days to hike in and out (see below for camping information). Although the trail is usually in good condition, go in summer when it's dry; parts of it vanish in winter. When it rains, the trail becomes very slippery, and flash floods can sweep you away.

A park ranger is now on-site full time at Kalalau Beach to greet visitors, provide information, and oversee campsites.

CAMPING IN KALALAU VALLEY & ALONG THE NA PALI COAST

You must obtain a camping permit; see above for details. The camping season runs roughly from May or June to September (depending on the site). All campsites are booked almost a year in advance, so call or write well ahead of time. Stays are limited to 5 nights. Camping areas along the Kalalau Trail include **Hanakapiai Beach** (facilities are pit toilets, and water is from the stream), **Hanakoa Valley** (no facilities, water from the stream), **Milolii** (no facilities, water from the stream), and **Kalalau Valley** (composting toilets, several pit toilets, and water from the stream). Keep your camping permit with you at all times.

GOLF & OTHER OUTDOOR ACTIVITIES

Golf

For last-minute or future discount tee times, call **Stand-by Golf** (www. hawaiistandbygolf.com; © **888/645-BOOK** [2665]) between 7am and 10pm.

Standby offers discounted (up to 30% off greens fees), guaranteed tee times for same-day or future golfing.

In the listings below, the cart fee is included in the greens fee unless otherwise noted.

LIHUE & ENVIRONS

Hokuala Golf Club ★   The **Ocean Course** ★ (formerly Kiele Championship Course at Kauai Lagoons when it reopened in 2011) back 9 now has 3 new holes, including the longest stretch of continuous ocean holes of any course in Hawaii! The original designer, Jack Nicklaus, headed up the 4-year long renovation work. Facilities include a driving range, lockers, showers, a restaurant, a snack bar, a pro shop, practice greens, a clubhouse, and club and shoe rental.

3351 Hoolaulea Way, Kalapaki Beach (less than a mile from Lihue Airport). www.hokuala kauai.com/golf. ✆ **800/634-6400** or 808/241-6000. Greens fees for Hokuala course $205 ($150 for guests of the Kauai Marriott; $165 for guests of select hotels and condos on Kauai), $115–$135 after noon. From the airport, make a left on Kapule Hwy. (Hwy. 51) and look for the sign on your left.

THE POIPU RESORT AREA

Kukuiolono Golf Course ★   This is a fun 9-hole course in a spectacular location with scenic views of the entire south coast. You can't beat the price— $9 for the day, whether you play 9 holes or 90. The course is in Kukuiolono Park, a beautiful wooded area donated by the family of Walter McBryde. There are plenty of trees to keep you on your game. When you get to the second tee box, check out the coconut tree dotted with yellow, pink, orange, and white golf balls that have been driven into the bark. Don't laugh—your next shot might add to the decor! Facilities include a driving range, practice greens, club rental, a snack bar, and a clubhouse. There are no reserved tee times, and no credit cards are accepted.

Kukuiolono Park, Kalaheo. ✆ **808/332-9151.** Greens fees $10 for the day; optional cart rental $10 for 9 holes, cash only. Take Hwy. 50 into the town of Kalaheo; turn left on Papaluna Rd., drive up the hill for nearly a mile, and watch for the sign on your right; the entrance has huge iron gates and stone pillars.

Poipu Bay Golf Course ★★   This 6,959-yard, par-72 course with a links-style layout was, for years, the home of the PGA Grand Slam of Golf. Designed by Robert Trent Jones, Jr., the challenging course features undulating greens and water hazards on 8 of the holes. Facilities include a restaurant, a locker room, a pro shop, a driving range, and putting greens.

2250 Ainako St. (across from the Grand Hyatt Kauai). www.poipubaygolf.com. ✆ **800/858-6300** or 808/742-8711. Greens fees $250 before noon ($180 for Grand Hyatt guests); $170 after noon; $135 after 1pm plus a $5 resort fee for all tee times. Check website for specials. Take Hwy. 50 to Hwy. 520; bear left into Poipu at the fork in the road; turn right on Ainako St.

THE NORTH SHORE

Princeville Makai Golf Club ★★   Here's your chance to play one of the best courses in Hawaii which recently underwent a multimillion-dollar renovation. This Robert Trent Jones, Jr.–designed devil of a course sits on 390 acres molded to create ocean views from every hole. Some holes have a waterfall backdrop to the greens, others shoot into the hillside, and the famous par-4 12th has a long tee shot off a cliff to a narrow, jungle-lined fairway 100 feet below. "The average vacation golfer may find the Makai Course intimidating, but they don't mind because it's so beautiful," Jones says.

At the Princeville Resort, 5–3900 Kuhio Hwy. www.makaigolf.com. © **808/826-1912.** Greens fees $275 ($195 for resort guests). Check website for specials. Take Hwy. 56 to mile marker 27; the course is on your right.

Biking

There are a couple of great places on Kauai for two-wheeling: the **Poipu** area, which has wide, flat roads and several dirt cane roads (especially around Mahaulepu); and the cane road (a dirt road used for hauling sugar cane) between **Kealia Beach** and **Anahola,** north of Kapaa.

The following places rent bikes, from a low of $15 a day (with big discounts for multiday rentals): **Outfitters Kauai,** 2827A Poipu Rd. (look for the small five-shop mall before the road forks to Poipu/Spouting Horn; www. outfitterskauai.com; © **808/742-9667**), and **Kauai Cycle and Tour,** 1379 Kuhio Hwy. (www.bikehawaii.com/kauaicycle; © **808/821-2115**), where bike rentals start at $15 a day.

GUIDED BIKE TOURS **Outfitters Kauai** ★ (www.outfitterskauai.com; © **808/742-9667**) offers a fabulous downhill bike ride from Waimea Canyon to the ocean. The 12-mile trip (mostly coasting) begins at 6am, when the van leaves the shop in Poipu and heads up to the canyon. By the time you've scarfed down the fresh-baked muffins and coffee, you're at the top of the canyon, just as the sun is rising over the rim—it's a remarkable moment. You'll make a couple of stops on the way down for short, scenic nature hikes. The tour lasts about 4 to 4½ hours. The sunset trip follows the same route. Both tours cost $108 for adults, $88 for children 12 to 14.

Birding

Kauai provides some of Hawaii's last sanctuaries for endangered native birds and oceanic birds, such as the albatross. At **Kokee State Park,** a 4,345-acre wilderness forest at the end of Hwy. 550 in southwest Kauai, you have an excellent chance of seeing some of Hawaii's endangered native birds. You might spot the *apapane,* a red bird with black wings and a curved black bill, or the *iwi,* a red bird with black wings, orange legs, and a salmon-colored bill. Other frequently seen native birds are the honeycreeper, which sings like a canary; the *amakihi,* a plain olive-green bird with a long, straight bill; and the *anianiau,* a tiny yellow bird with a thin, slightly curved bill. The most common native bird at Kokee is the *moa,* or red jungle fowl, brought as domestic stock by ancient Polynesians. Ordinarily shy, they're quite tame in this environment. David Kuhn leads custom hikes, pointing out Hawaii's rarest birds on his **Terran Tours** (© **808/335-0398**), which range from a half-day to 3 days and feature endemic and endangered species.

Kilauea Point National Wildlife Refuge ★, a mile north of Kilauea on the North Shore (www.fws.gov/kilaueapoint; ✆ **808/828-1413**), is a 200-acre headland habitat that juts above the surf and includes cliffs, two rocky wave-lashed bays, and a tiny islet that serves as a jumping-off spot for seabirds. You can easily spot red-footed boobies, which nest in trees, and wedge-tailed shearwaters, which burrow in nests along the cliffs. You may also see the great frigate bird, the Laysan albatross, the red-tailed tropic bird, and the endangered nene. Native plants and the Kilauea Point Lighthouse are other highlights. The refuge is open Tuesday-Saturday from 10am to 4pm (closed on federal holidays); admission is $5. To get here, turn right off Kuhio Highway (Hwy. 56) at Kilauea, just after mile marker 23; follow Kilauea Road to the refuge entrance.

Peaceful Hanalei Valley is home to Hawaii's endangered Koloa duck, gallinule, coot, and stilt. The **Hanalei National Wildlife Refuge** (www.fws.gov/hanalei; ✆ **808/828-1413**) also provides a safe habitat for migratory shorebirds and waterfowl. It's not open to the public, but an interpretive overlook along the highway serves as an impressive vantage point. Along Ohiki Road, which begins at the west end of the Hanalei River Bridge, you'll often see white cattle egrets hunting crayfish in streams.

Tennis

Public tennis courts are managed by the **Kauai County Parks and Recreation Department,** 4444 Rice St., Ste. 150 (www.kauai.gov/Government/Departments-Agencies/Parks-Recreation/Park-Facilities; ✆ **808/241-4460**). Check the website for a list of the 10 county tennis courts around the island, all free and open to the public. Private courts that are open to the public include the **Hanalei Bay Resort,** Princeville (http://hanaleibayresort.com/tennis; ✆ **808/821-8225**), which has eight courts available for $10 per person for 1 to 2 hours. Call to reserve.

SHOPS & GALLERIES

Shopping is a pleasure on this island. Where else can you browse vintage Hawaiiana practically in a cane field, buy exquisite home accessories in an old stone building built in 1942, and get a virtual agricultural tour of the island through city-sponsored green markets that move from town to town throughout the week, like a movable feast? At Kauai's small, tasteful boutiques, you can satisfy your shopping ya-yas in concentrated spurts around the island. This is a bonanza for the boutique shopper—particularly the one who appreciates the thrill of the hunt.

"Downtown" Kapaa continues to flourish, and Hanalei, touristy as it is, is still a shopping destination. (Ola's and Yellowfish more than make up for the hurricane of trinkets and trash in Hanalei.) Kilauea, with Kong Lung Store and the fabulous Lotus Gallery, is the style center of the island. Basically, you can anticipate spending some of your vacation time in the great shops in Hanalei, a few art galleries and boutiques, and a handful of shopping centers—not much to distract you from an afternoon of hiking or snorkeling. The gift items and treasures you'll find in east and north Kauai, however, may be among your best Hawaiian finds.

Green Markets & Fruit Stands

The county of Kauai sponsors regular weekly **Sunshine Markets** (www. realkauai.com/FarmersMarkets) throughout the island, featuring fresh Kauai **Sunrise papayas** (sweeter, juicier, and redder than most), herbs and vegetables used in ethnic cuisines, exotic fruit such as rambutan and atemoya, and the most exciting development in pineapple agriculture, the low-acid white pineapple called **Sugarloaf,** rarer these days but still spottily available. These markets, which sell the full range of fresh local produce and flowers at rock-bottom prices, present the perfect opportunity to see what's best and in season. Farmers sell their bounty from the backs of trucks or at tables set up under tarps. The biggest market is at **Kapaa New Town Park,** in the middle of Kapaa town, on Wednesday at 3pm. The Sunshine Market in **Lihue,** held on Friday at 3pm at the Vidinha Stadium Parking Lot, is close in size and extremely popular. The schedule for the other markets: **Koloa Ball Park,** Monday at noon; **Kalaheo Neighborhood Center,** Papalina Road off Kaumualii, Tuesday at 3:30pm; **Kilauea Neighborhood Center,** Keneke off Lighthouse Road, Thursday at 4:30pm; and **Kekaha Neighborhood Center,** Elepaio Road, Saturday at 9am. Especially at the Koloa market, which draws hundreds of shoppers, go early and shop briskly.

On the North Shore, Kilauea is the agricultural heart of the island, with two weekly green markets: the aforementioned county-sponsored **Sunshine Market** (www.kauai.gov/Kamaaina/SunshineMarkets/tabid/214/Default.aspx), Thursday at 4:30pm at the Kilauea Neighborhood Center. Everything in the wide-ranging selection is grown or made on Kauai, from rambutan and long beans to sweet potatoes, corn, lettuce, and salsas and chutneys.

Also on the North Shore, about a quarter-mile past Hanalei in an area called Waipa, the **Hawaiian Farmers of Hanalei**—anywhere from a dozen to 25 farmers—gather along the main road with their budget-friendly, just-picked produce. This market is held every Tuesday at 2pm. You'll find unbelievably priced papayas (in some seasons, several for a dollar, ready to eat), organic vegetables, inexpensive tropical flowers, avocados and mangoes in season, and, when possible, fresh seafood. The best of the best, in season, are rose apples, mountain apples, and the orange-colored papaya lilikoi.

Closer to the resorts, in **Poipu,** on Wednesday from 3:30 to 6pm, the **Kukui'ula Village** Shopping Center, 2820 Ala Kalanimauka (✆ **808/742-9545**), has a great selection of produce. On Saturday, 9am to 1pm, another farmers market is held at the Kauai Community College, 3–1901 Kaumualii Hwy. (✆ **808/245-8311**), just outside **Lihue.**

Lihue & Environs

DOWNTOWN LIHUE   The gift shop of the **Kauai Museum,** 4428 Rice St. (www.kauaimuseum.org; ✆ **808/245-6931**), is your best bet for made-on-Kauai arts and crafts, from Niihau-shell leis to woodwork, lauhala and coconut products, and more.

KILOHANA PLANTATION   Even if you are not interested in shopping, don't miss this architectural marvel that houses a sprinkling of galleries and shops. Located at 3–2087 Kaumualii Hwy., this 35-acre Tudor-style estate sprawls across the landscape in Puhi, on Hwy. 50 between Lihue and Poipu, and has an eclectic range of interesting boutique shops such as Banana Patch Studio & Aloha Spice, Sea Reflections, The Artisans Room, The Hawaiian Collection Room, and Cane Field Clothing & Gallery.

The Poipu Resort Area

Expect mostly touristy shops in Poipu, the island's resort mecca; here you'll find T-shirts, souvenirs, black pearls, jewelry, and the usual quota of tired marine art and trite hand-painted silks.

Exceptions: The formerly characterless **Poipu Shopping Village,** at 2360 Kiahuna Plantation Dr., is shaping up to be a serious shopping stop. An example of its standout attractions: the tiny **Bamboo Lace** boutique attracting all the fashionistas with resort wear and accessories that can segue from Hawaii to the south of France in a heartbeat. Across the courtyard, **Sand People** is great for understated resort wear (such as Tencel jeans) and Indonesian coconut picture frames, while the newly renovated **Overboard** rides the wave of popularity in aloha wear and surf stuff.

The shopping is surprisingly good at the **Grand Hyatt Kauai,** with the footwear mecca **Sandal Tree, Water Wear Hawaii** for swim stuff, and **Reyn's** for top-drawer aloha shirts and the Kauai Kids line for the children.

In neighboring **Old Koloa Town** (www.oldkoloa.com), you'll find everything from **Koloa Mill Ice Cream & Coffee** and **Island Soap and Candle Works** (where you can watch them make soap and candles) to **Crazy Shirts** on Koloa's main drag, Koloa Road.

The newest addition to the Poipu resort area is **Kukui'ula Village** (www. theshopsatkukuiula.com; © **808/742-0234**). Built around a center court, it is host to a farmers market Wednesday's from 3:30 to 6pm, complete with music and cooking demonstrations. Retailers making Kukui'ula Village home range from **Lappert's Ice Cream** to **Tommy Bahama** (© **808/742-8808**), with its upscale resort wear for men and women, to **Blue Ginger** (© **808/742-2633**), featuring island-inspired ladies' and children's wear, to a handful of galleries like **Halele'a** (© **808/742-9525**), with a focus on works by island artists in different media, to **Living Foods Market & Café** (© **808/742-2323**), opened by Jim Moffat of Bar Acuda fame. The market carries locally grown produce as well as a wide selection of gourmet meats, cheeses, and packaged items, and a well-stocked wine department and nifty cooking tools.

Western Kauai

HANAPEPE   This west Kauai hamlet is becoming a haven for artists, but finding them requires some effort. The center of town is off Hwy. 50; turn right on Hanapepe Road just after Eleele if you're driving from Lihue. Long before you see the sign for the **Taro Ko Chips Factory ★**, 3940 Hanapepe Rd. (✆ **808/335-5586**), located in an old green plantation house, you can smell the chips being cooked in a tiny, modest kitchen at the east end of town. Despite their breakable nature, these chips make great gifts to take home. To really impress them back home, get the lihi mung–flavor.

Farther on, Hanapepe Road is lined with gift shops and galleries, including the **Banana Patch Studio,** 3865 Hanapepe Rd. (www.bananapatchstudio. com; ✆ **808/335-5944**), whose artists create ceramic bowls, tiles, and plates. Nearby, **Kauai Fine Arts** (✆ **808/335-3778**) offers an odd mix that works: antique maps and prints of Hawaii, authentic Polynesian tapa, old Matson liner menus, and a few pieces of contemporary island art. Taking a cue from Maui's Lahaina, where every Friday night is Art Night, Hanapepe's gallery owners and artists recently instituted the **Friday Night Art Walk** every Friday from 6 to 9pm. Gallery owners take turns hosting this informal event along Hanapepe Road.

Another great treat to take home is **Kauai Kookies** (www.kauaikookie. com; ✆ **800/361-1126** or 808/335-5003), with the factory outlet at 1–3529 Hwy. 50 in Hanapepe. Choose from eight delicious kinds of cookies (Kona coffee macadamia-nut, chocolate-chip mac-nut, peanut butter, guava mac-nut, and so on) to ship home, or carry a few around in your car.

KOKEE   Up in Kokee State Park, the gift shop of the **Kokee Natural History Museum** (✆ **808/335-9975**) is THE stop for botanical, geographical, historical, and nature-related books and gifts, not only on Kauai, but on all the islands. Audubon bird books, hiking maps, and practically every book on Kauai ever written line the shelves.

The Coconut Coast

As you make your way from Lihue to the North Shore, you'll pass the Coconut Grove MarketPlace, in Kapaa, as well as the shops lining the street in Kapaa town. This tiny area is a treasure trove of small, ma and pop shops with great prices for savy shoppers.

KAPAA   Moving toward Kapaa on Kuhio Highway (Hwy. 56), don't get your shopping hopes up. Until you hit Kapaa town, quality goods are slim in this neck of the woods. The **Coconut MarketPlace,** 484 Kuhio Hwy. (www. coconutmarketplace.com), features the ubiquitous **Elephant Walk** gift shop, **Hawaiian Music Store,** and various other underwhelming souvenir and clothing shops sprinkled among the sunglass huts. Also in the Coconut Market Place, be sure to check out **Auntie Lynda's Treasures,** which has great finds in Hawaiian jewelry (including a coconut purse), wood carvings, shell jewelry, and vintage surf collectibles (from painted surfboards to surfboard clocks). While you're here, be sure to have a scoop of **Lappert's Ice Cream.** As we went to press, the Coconut MarketPlace was undergoing a major re-model.

In the green-and-white wooden storefronts of nearby **Kauai Village,** 4–831 Kuhio Hwy., you'll find everything from **Long's Drugs** to *yin chiao* Chinese cold pills and organic produce at **Papayas Natural Foods** to **Safeway.** Although its prepared foods are pricey, Papayas carries the full range of health-food products and is your only choice in the area for vitamins, prepared health foods to go, health-conscious cosmetics, and bulk food items.

Kapaa town itself is full of surprises. On the main strip, across the street from the **ABC Store,** you'll find the recently expanded **Kela's Glass Gallery,** 4–1354 Kuhio Hwy. (© **808/822-4527**), the island's showiest showplace for handmade glass in all sizes, shapes, and prices, with the most impressive selection in Hawaii. Go nuts over the vases and studio glass pieces, functional and nonfunctional, and then stroll along this strip of storefronts to **Hula Girl,** 4–1340 Kuhio Hwy. (www.ilovehulagirl.com; © **808/822-1950**), where a wonderful whimsy prevails: aloha shirts (pricey), vintage-looking luggage covered with decals of old Hawaii, zoris, sunglasses, and shells.

The North Shore

Kauai's North Shore is the premier shopping destination on the island. Stylish, sophisticated galleries and shops, such as **Kong Lung Trading,** in a 1942 Kilauea stone building (the last to be built on the Kilauea Plantation) off Hwy. 56 on Kilauea Road (www.konglung.com; © **808/828-1822**), have launched these former hippie villages as top-drawer shopping spots. Save your time, energy, and, most of all, discretionary funds for this end of the island. Kong Lung remains a showcase of design, style, and quality, from top-of-the-line dinnerware and bath products to aloha shirts. The book selection is fabulous.

Directly behind Kong Lung is **Lotus Gallery** (www.jewelofthelotus.com; © **808/828-9898**), a showstopper for lovers of antiques and designer jewelry. There are gems, crystals, Tibetan art, antiques and sari clothing from India, 12th-century Indian bronzes, temple bells, Oriental rugs, pearl bracelets—items from $30 to $50,000.

In Hanalei, at **Ola's,** by the Hanalei River on the Kuhio Highway (Hwy. 560) after the bridge and before the main part of Hanalei town (© **808/826-6937**), Sharon and Doug Britt, an award-winning artist, have amassed a head-turning assortment of American and Island crafts, including Doug's paintings and the one-of-a-kind furniture that he makes out of found objects, driftwood, and used materials.

From health foods to groceries to Bakelite jewelry, the **Ching Young Village Shopping Center,** in the heart of Hanalei, covers a lot of bases. It's more funky than fashionable, but Hanalei, until recently, has never been about fashion. People take their time here, and there are always clusters of folks lingering at the few tables outdoors. **Hot Rocket** (© **808/826-7776**) is ablaze with aloha shirts, T-shirts, and Reyn Spooner and Jams sportswear.

Next door to Ching Young Village is **On the Road to Hanalei** (© **808/826-7360**), worth checking out for the unusual T-shirts (great gifts to take home because they don't take up much suitcase space), scarves, pareu, jewelry, and other unique gifts.

Across the street in the **Hanalei Center,** the standout boutique is the **Yellowfish Trading Company** ★ (✆ **808/826-1227**), where owner Gritt Benton's impeccable eye and zeal for collecting are reflected in the 1920s to 1940s collectibles: menus, hula-girl nodders, hula lamps, and wonderful finds in books and aloha shirts.

ENTERTAINMENT & NIGHTLIFE

Suffice it to say that you don't come to Kauai to trip the light fantastic—this is the island for winding down. But there are a few nightlife options.

For action after sunset, music, dancing, and bars, the hotels and resorts are the primary players. The **Coconut MarketPlace,** 4–484 Kuhio Hwy., Kapaa, has a free hula show every Wednesday at 5pm, and Saturday at 1pm, and Hawaiian music Friday at 5pm. The **Poipu Shopping Village,** 2360 Kiahuna Plantation Dr. (✆ **808/742-2831**), also offers free hula dance performances every Monday and Thursday at 4:30pm.

The **Kauai Marriott Resort & Beach Club,** 3610 Rice St. (✆ **808/245-5050**), offers live music at **Duke's Barefoot Bar** (✆ **808/246-9599**) daily (except Tues) from 4 to 6pm and again from 8:30 to 10:30pm on Friday and Saturday. Generally, the music is Hawaiian, but occasionally they offer other contemporary groups.

The south shore, with its sunset view and miles of white-sand beaches, is a great place for nightlife. At the far end of Poipu, **Seaview Terrace** at the **Grand Hyatt Kauai Resort & Spa,** 1571 Poipu Rd. (www.kauai.hyatt.com; ✆ **808/742-1234**), has live Hawaiian music and entertainment from 6 to 9pm nightly. In Grand Hyatt lounge, Stevenson's Library, also offers music nightly from 8-10pm.

Also in Poipu, **Keoki's Paradise,** in the Poipu Shopping Village, 2360 Kiahuna Plantation Dr. (✆ **808/742-7534**), offers live music Sunday to Wednesday 7 to 9pm; and Thursday to Saturday 5 to 7pm and again 7:30 to 9:30pm, with the cafe menu available from 11am to 10:30pm. Hawaiian, reggae, and contemporary music draw the 21-and-over dancing crowd.

Beyond Poipu, in the old plantation community of Hanapepe, every Friday from 6 to 9pm is Hanapepe's **Friday Night Art Walk** (p. 259).

Hanalei Gourmet, in the Old Hanalei Schoolhouse, 5–5161 Kuhio Hwy. (✆ **808/826-2524**), has live music Friday and Saturday nights from 7:30 to 9:30pm. Down the road, **Tahiti Nui** (✆ **808/826-6277**) is a great place to experience old Hawaii with nightly live music every night from 6:30pm; on Thurs-Saturday nights, dance bands rock from 9:30pm to midnight (cover charge may apply). The restaurant/bar is family-friendly, and there always seems to be someone who drops in and starts singing and playing music, just like in the old days.

The **St. Regis** (✆ **808/826-9644**), in Princeville, has nightly live music in the St. Regis Bar from 6:30 to 9:30pm.

PLANNING YOUR TRIP TO HAWAII

Hawaii has so many places to explore, things to do, sights to see—it can be bewildering to plan your trip with so much vying for your attention. Where to start? That's where I come in. In the pages of this chapter, I've compiled everything you need to know to plan your ideal trip to Hawaii.

The most important thing to do: Decide where you want to go. Read through each chapter (especially each chapter introduction) to see which islands fit the profile and offer the activities you're looking for. I strongly recommend that you **limit your island hopping** to one island per week. If you decide to go to more than one in a week, be warned: You could spend much of your precious vacation time in airports and checking in and out of hotels. Not much fun!

So let's get on with the process of planning your trip. Searching out the best deals and planning your dream vacation to Hawaii should be half the fun.

GETTING THERE
By Plane

Most major U.S. and many international carriers fly to **Honolulu International Airport (HNL),** on Oahu. Some also offer direct flights to **Kona International Airport (KOA),** near Kailua-Kona on the Big Island; **Kahului Airport (OGG),** on Maui; and **Lihue Airport (LIH),** on Kauai. If you can fly directly to the island of your choice, you'll be spared a 2-hour layover in Honolulu and another plane ride. If you're heading to Molokai or Lanai, you'll have the easiest connections if you fly into Honolulu.

ARRIVING AT THE AIRPORT
IMMIGRATION & CUSTOMS CLEARANCE International visitors arriving by air should cultivate patience. U.S. airports have considerable security practices in place. Clearing Customs and Immigration can take as long as 2 hours.

AGRICULTURAL SCREENING AT THE AIRPORTS At Honolulu International and the neighbor-island airports, baggage and passengers bound for the mainland must be screened by agricultural officials. Officials will confiscate local produce such as fresh avocados, bananas, and mangoes in the name of fruit-fly control. Pineapples, coconuts, and papayas inspected and certified for export; boxed flowers; leis without seeds; and processed foods (macadamia nuts, coffee, jams, dried fruit, and the like) will pass.

GETTING AROUND HAWAII

For additional advice on travel within each island, see "Getting Around" in the individual island chapters.

Interisland Flights

Hawaii's major interisland carrier is **Hawaiian Airlines** (www.hawaiianair. com; © **800/367-5320**).

Visitors also have two commuter airlines to choose from: **Island Air** (www. islandair.com; © **800/323-3345**), which flights to Kauai, Oahu, Maui and Lanai and **Mokulele Airlines** (www.mokulele.com; © **866/260-7070**), which flies to Oahu, Maui, Molokai, Lanai and Kona, on the Big island.

By Car

Hawaii has some of the more expensive car-rental rates in the country (the most expensive is the island of Lanai, where the cars are very, very pricey). To rent a car in Hawaii, you must be at least 25 years of age and have a valid driver's license and credit card.

Rental cars have cut back their fleets on all islands. I recommend booking your car rental as soon as you book your airfare, or you could get stuck without a car. This goes double for the tiny islands of Molokai and Lanai, which have a small rental car fleet to begin with.

GASOLINE Gas prices in Hawaii, always much higher than the U.S. mainland, vary from island to island. Check www.gasbuddy.com to find the cheapest gas in your area.

Cruising Through the Islands

If you're looking for a taste of several islands in a single week, consider **Norwegian Cruise Line** (www.ncl.com; © **866/234-7350**), the only cruise line that operates year-round in Hawaii. NCL's 2,186-passenger ship *Pride of America* circles the Hawaiian Islands, stopping on the Big Island, Maui, Kauai, and Oahu; some itineraries even go to Fanning Island in the Republic of Kiribati before returning to Honolulu. The disadvantage of a cruise is that you won't be able to see any of the islands in depth or at leisure; the advantage is that you can spend your days exploring the island where the ship is docked and your nights aboard ship sailing to the next port of call.

INSURANCE Hawaii is a no-fault state, which means that if you don't have collision-damage insurance, you are required to pay for all damages before you leave the state, whether or not the accident was your fault. Your personal car insurance may provide rental-car coverage; check before you leave home. Some credit card companies also provide collision-damage insurance for their customers; check with yours before you rent.

DRIVING RULES Hawaii state law mandates that all car passengers must wear a **seat belt** and all infants must be strapped into a car seat. You'll pay a $112 fine plus fees if you don't buckle up. **Pedestrians** always have the right of way, even if they're not in the crosswalk. You can turn **right on red** after a full and complete stop, unless otherwise posted.

GETTING MARRIED IN THE ISLANDS

Hawaii is a great place for a wedding. The islands exude romance and natural beauty, and after the ceremony, you're already on your honeymoon. More than 20,000 marriages are performed annually on the islands, mostly on Oahu; nearly half are for couples from somewhere else. The booming wedding business has spawned more than 70 companies that can help you organize a long-distance event and stage an unforgettable wedding, Hawaiian style or your style. However, you can also plan your own island wedding, even from afar, and not spend a fortune doing it.

In a special session in 2013, the Hawaii State Legislature approved same-sex marriages.

The Paperwork

The state of Hawaii has some very minimal procedures for obtaining a marriage license. The first thing you should do is contact the **Honolulu Marriage License Office** (for a license, go to http://emrs.ehawaii.gov/emrs/public/home.html; © **808/586-4545**). The application is $60 plus a $5 processing fee and is good for 30 days. Both parties must be 15 years of age or older and not more closely related than first cousins. That's it.

Planning the Wedding
DOING IT YOURSELF

The marriage-licensing agents are usually friendly, helpful people who can steer you to a nondenominational minister or marriage performer who's licensed by the state of Hawaii. These marriage performers are great sources of information for budget weddings. They usually know wonderful places to have the ceremony for free or for a nominal fee. For the names and addresses of marriage-licensing agents on the Big Island, call © **808/974-6008;** on Maui and Lanai, © **808/984-8210;** on Molokai, © **808/553-7870;** and on Kauai, © **808/241-3498;** or on the web at https://emrs.ehawaii.gov/emrs/public/find-performer.html.

USING A WEDDING PLANNER

Wedding planners—many of whom are marriage-licensing agents as well—can arrange everything for you, from a small, private outdoor affair to a full-blown formal ceremony in a tropical setting. They charge anywhere from $95 to a small fortune—it all depends on what you want. On the Big Island, contact **Paradise Weddings Hawaii** (www.paradiseweddingshawaii.com; ℂ **800/240-9336** or 808/883-9067); on Maui, **The Maui Wedding Planner** (www.mauiweddingplanner.com; ℂ **808/268-0796**); on Kauai, try **Coconut Coast Weddings & Honeymoons** (www.kauaiwedding.com; ℂ **808/651-8622**); on Oahu, contact Rev. Toni Baran and Rev. Jerry Le Lesch at **Love Hawaii** (www.lovehawaii.com; ℂ **808/235-6966**), which offers wedding services starting at $95. The Hawaii Visitors & Convention Bureau (www.gohawaii.com; ℂ **800/GO-HAWAII** [464-2924] or 808/923-1811) can provide contact information for other wedding coordinators, and many of the big resorts have their own coordinators on staff as well.

WHEN TO GO

Most visitors don't come to Hawaii when the weather's best in the islands; rather, they come when it's at its worst everywhere else. Thus, the **high season**—when prices are up and resorts are booked to capacity—is generally from mid-December to March or mid-April. The last 2 weeks of December, in particular, are the prime time for travel to Hawaii. If you're planning a holiday trip, make your reservations as early as possible, expect crowds, and prepare to pay top dollar for accommodations, car rentals, and airfare.

The **off season,** when the best rates are available and the islands are less crowded, is spring (mid-Apr to mid-June) and fall (Sept to mid-Dec)—a paradox because these are the best seasons to be in Hawaii, in terms of reliably great weather. If you're looking to save money, or if you just want to avoid the crowds, this is the time to visit. Hotel rates and airfares tend to be significantly lower, and good packages are often available.

> ### Travel Tip
>
> Your best bets for total year-round sun are **Waikiki Beach** and the **Ko Olina** (southwest) coast of Oahu, the Big Island's **Kona-Kohala Coast,** the south **(Kihei/Wailea)** and west **(Lahaina/Kapalua)** coasts of Maui, and **Poipu Beach** and the southwest coast of Kauai.

Note: If you plan to come to Hawaii between the last week in April and early May, be sure you book your accommodations, interisland air reservations, and car rentals in advance. In Japan, the last week of April is called **Golden Week** because three Japanese holidays take place one after the other. Waikiki is especially busy with Japanese tourists during this time, but the neighboring islands also see dramatic increases.

Due to the large number of families traveling in **summer** (June–Aug), you won't get the fantastic bargains of spring and fall. However, you'll still do much better on packages, airfare, and accommodations than you will in the winter months.

Climate

Because Hawaii lies at the edge of the tropical zone, it technically has only two seasons, both of them warm. There's a dry season that corresponds to **summer** (Apr–Oct) and a rainy season in **winter** (Nov–Mar). It rains every day somewhere in the islands any time of the year, but the rainy season sometimes brings enough gray weather to spoil your tanning opportunities. Fortunately, it seldom rains in one spot for more than 3 days straight.

The **year round temperature** doesn't vary much. At the beach, the average daytime high in summer is 85°F (29°C), while the average daytime high in winter is 78°F (26°C); nighttime lows are usually about 10°F cooler. But how warm it is on any given day really depends on *where* you are on the island.

Each island has a *leeward* side (the side sheltered from the wind) and a *windward* side (the side that gets the trade wind's full force). The **leeward** sides (the west and south) are usually hot and dry, while the **windward** sides (east and north) are generally cooler and moist. When you want arid, sun-baked, desertlike weather, go leeward. When you want lush, wet, junglelike weather, go windward.

Hawaii is also full of microclimates, thanks to its interior valleys, coastal plains, and mountain peaks. Kauai's Mount Waialeale is the wettest spot on earth, yet Waimea Canyon, just a few miles away, is almost a desert. On the Big Island, Hilo is one of the wettest cities in the nation, with 180 inches of rainfall a year, but at Puako, only 60 miles away, it rains less than 6 inches a year. If you travel into the mountains, the climate can change from summer to winter in a matter of hours because it's cooler the higher you go. So if the weather doesn't suit you, just go to the other side of the island—or head into the hills.

On rare occasions, the weather can be disastrous, as when Hurricane Iniki crushed Kauai in September 1992 with 225-mph winds. Tsunamis have swept Hilo and the south shore of Oahu. But those are extreme exceptions. Mostly, one day follows another here in glorious, sunny procession, each quite like the other.

Average Temperature & Number of Rainy Days in Waikiki

	JAN	FEB	MAR	APR	MAY	JUNE	JULY	AUG	SEPT	OCT	NOV	DEC
HIGH (°F/°C)	80/27	80/27	81/27	82/28	84/29	86/30	87/31	88/31	88/31	86/30	84/29	81/27
LOW (°F/°C)	70/21	66/19	69/21	66/19	70/21	72/22	73/23	74/23	74/23	72/22	70/21	67/19
RAIN DAYS	10	9	9	9	7	6	7	6	7	9	9	10

Average Temperature & Number of Rainy Days in Hanalei, Kauai

	JAN	FEB	MAR	APR	MAY	JUNE	JULY	AUG	SEPT	OCT	NOV	DEC
HIGH (°F/°C)	79/26	80/27	80/27	82/28	84/29	86/30	88/31	88/31	87/31	86/30	83/28	80/27
LOW (°F/°C)	61/17	61/16	62/17	63/17	65/18	66/19	66/19	67/19	68/20	67/19	65/18	62/17
RAIN DAYS	8	5	6	3	3	2	8	2	3	3	4	7

Holidays

When Hawaii observes holidays (especially those over long weekends), travel between the islands increases, inter-island airline seats are fully booked, rental cars are at a premium, and hotels and restaurants are busy.

Banks, government offices, post offices, and many stores, restaurants, and museums are closed on the following legal national holidays: January 1 (New Year's Day), the third Monday in January (Martin Luther King Jr. Day), the third Monday in February (Presidents' Day), the last Monday in May (Memorial Day), July 4 (Independence Day), the first Monday in September (Labor Day), the second Monday in October (Columbus Day), November 11 (Veterans' Day/Armistice Day), the fourth Thursday in November (Thanksgiving Day), and December 25 (Christmas). The Tuesday after the first Monday in November is Election Day, a federal government holiday in presidential-election years (held every 4 years, and next in 2020).

State and county offices are also closed on local holidays, including Prince Kuhio Day (Mar 26), honoring the birthday of Hawaii's first delegate to the U.S. Congress; King Kamehameha Day (June 11), a statewide holiday commemorating Kamehameha the Great, who united the islands and ruled from 1795 to 1819; and Admissions Day (third Fri in Aug), which honors the admittance of Hawaii as the 50th state on August 21, 1959.

Other special days that are celebrated in Hawaii by many people, but involve no closing of federal, state, and county offices, are the Chinese New Year (which can fall in Jan or Feb), Girls' Day (Mar 3), Buddha's Birthday (Apr 8), Father Damien's Day (Apr 15), Boys' Day (May 5), Samoan Flag Day (in Aug), Aloha Festivals (Sept–Oct), and Pearl Harbor Day (Dec 7).

[FastFACTS] HAWAII

Area Codes Hawaii's area code is 808; it applies to all islands. There is a long-distance charge when calling from one island to another.

Business Hours Most offices are generally open Monday through Friday from 9am to 5pm. Bank hours are Monday through Thursday from 8:30am to 4pm and Friday from 8:30am to 6pm; some banks are open on Saturday. Shopping centers are open Monday through Saturday from 10am to 9pm, and Sunday from 10am to 7pm.

Disabled Travelers Travelers with disabilities are made to feel very welcome in Hawaii. Hotels are usually equipped with wheelchair-accessible rooms, and tour companies provide many special services. The **Hawaii Center for Independent Living** (✆ **808/522-5400**) can provide information.

The only travel agency in Hawaii specializing in needs for travelers with disabilities is **Access Aloha Travel** (www.accessalohatravel. com; ✆ **800/480-1143**), which can book anything, including rental vans (available on Oahu only; for other islands call Wheelers, ✆ 877/735-6365), accommodations, tours, cruises, airfare, and anything else you can think of.

Electricity The United States uses 110 to 120 volts AC (60 cycles).

Family Travel The larger hotels and resorts

offer supervised programs for children and can refer you to qualified babysitters. By state law, hotels can accept only children ages 5 to 12 in supervised activities programs, but they often accommodate younger kids by simply hiring babysitters to watch over them. You can also contact **People Attentive to Children (PATCH),** which can refer you to babysitters who have taken a training course on child care. On Oahu, call ✆ **808/839-1988;** on the Big Island, call ✆ **808/322-3500** in Kona or ✆ **808/238-3463** in Hilo; on Maui, call ✆ **808/242-9232;** on Kauai, call ✆ **808/246-0622;** on Molokai and Lanai, call ✆**800/498-4145;** or visit www.patch hawaii.org.

Baby's Away (www.babysaway.com) rents cribs, strollers, highchairs, playpens, infant seats, and more on Oahu (✆ **800/496-6386** or 808/699-7749), the Big Island (✆ **800/996-9030** or 808/756-5800), and Maui (✆ **800/942-9030** or 808/631-8618).

Gay & Lesbian Travelers
Hawaii is known for its acceptance of all groups. The number of gay- or lesbian-specific accommodations on the islands is limited, but most properties welcome gays and lesbians like any other travelers. **Gay Hawaii** (www.gayhawaii.com) is a website with gay and lesbian news, blogs, features, and other information for the entire state. For the Big Island,

Oahu, Maui, and Kauai, check out the website for **Out in Hawaii** (www.outin hawaii.com).

Health
Centipedes Centipedes can really pack a wallop with their sting. They're generally found in damp, wet places, such as under woodpiles or compost heaps. Wearing closed-toe shoes can help prevent stings. If you're stung, apply ice at once to prevent swelling. See a doctor if you experience extreme pain, swelling, nausea, or any other severe reaction.

Scorpions Rarely seen, scorpions are found in arid, warm regions. Their stings can be serious. Campers in dry areas should always check their boots before putting them on and shake out sleeping bags and bed rolls. Symptoms of a scorpion sting include shortness of breath, hives, swelling, and nausea. In the unlikely event that you're stung, apply diluted household ammonia and cold compresses to the area of the sting and seek medical help immediately.

Hiking Safety In addition to taking the appropriate precautions regarding Hawaii's bug population, hikers should always let someone know where they're heading and when they plan to return. Too many hikers get lost in Hawaii because they don't let others know their basic plans. And make sure you

know how strenuous the route and trail you will follow are—don't overestimate your ability.

Before you head out, always check weather conditions with the **National Weather Service** (www.prh. noaa.gov/hnl; ✆ **808/973-5286** on Oahu; see individual island chapters for local weather information). Do not hike if rain or a storm is predicted; flash floods are common in Hawaii. Hike with a pal, never alone. Plan to finish your hike at least an hour before sunset; because Hawaii is so close to the equator, it doesn't have a twilight period, and thus gets dark quickly after the sun sets. Wear hiking boots, a sun hat, clothes to protect you from the sun and from getting scratches, and high-SPF sunscreen on all exposed skin. Take plenty of water, basic first aid, a snack, and a bag to pack out what you pack in. Many experienced hikers and boaters pack a cellphone in case of emergency; just dial ✆ **911.**

Vog The volcanic haze dubbed "vog" is caused by gases released when molten lava—from the continuous eruption of Kilauea volcano on the Big Island—pours into the ocean. Some people claim that long-term exposure causes bronchial ailments, but it's highly unlikely to cause you any harm in the course of your visit.

There actually is a vog season in Hawaii: the fall

and winter months, when the trade winds that blow the fumes out to sea die down. Then vog is felt not only on the Big Island, but also as far away as Maui and Oahu.

One more word of caution: If you're pregnant or have heart or breathing problems, avoid exposure to the sulfuric fumes in and around the Big Island's Hawaii Volcanoes National Park.

Ocean Safety Note that sharks are not a big problem in Hawaii. Since records have been kept, starting in 1779, there have been only about 100 shark attacks in Hawaii, of which 40% have been fatal. Most attacks occurred after someone fell into the ocean from the shore or from a boat; in these cases, the sharks probably attacked after the person was dead. But here are the general rules for avoiding sharks: Don't swim at sunrise, at sunset, or where the water is murky due to stream runoff—sharks may mistake you for one of their usual meals. And don't swim where there are bloody fish in the water, as sharks become aggressive around blood.

Seasickness The waters in Hawaii can range from as calm as glass (off the Kona Coast on the Big Island) to downright frightening (in storm conditions); they usually fall somewhere in between. In general, expect rougher conditions in winter than summer. If you plan on boating, take whatever seasickness prevention works best for you—medication, acupressure wristband, gingerroot tea or capsules, or any combination. But do it **before you board;** once you set sail, it's generally too late.

Stings The most common stings in Hawaii come from jellyfish, particularly Portuguese man-of-war and box jellyfish. A bluish-purple floating bubble with a long tail, the **Portuguese man-of-war** is responsible for some 6,500 stings a year on Oahu alone. These stings, although painful and a nuisance, are rarely harmful; fewer than 1 in 1,000 requires medical treatment. The best prevention is to watch for these floating bubbles as you snorkel (look for the hanging tentacles below the surface). Get out of the water if anyone near you spots these jellyfish. If you get stung: First, pick off any visible tentacles with a gloved hand, a stick, or anything handy; then rinse the sting with salt- or freshwater, and apply ice to prevent swelling and to help control pain. Avoid folk remedies like vinegar, baking soda, or urinating on the wound, which may actually cause further damage. Most Portuguese man-of-war stings will disappear by themselves within 15 to 20 minutes. Still, be sure to see a doctor if pain persists or a rash or other symptoms develop.

Transparent, square-shaped **box jellyfish** are nearly impossible to see in the water. Fortunately, they seem to follow a monthly cycle: 8 to 10 days after the full moon, they appear in the waters on the leeward side of each island and hang around for about 3 days. Also, they seem to sting more in the morning hours. The stings can cause anything from no visible marks to hivelike welts, blisters, and pain lasting from 10 minutes to 8 hours. If you get stung: First, pour regular household vinegar on the sting; this will stop additional burning. Do not rub the area. Pick off any vinegar-soaked tentacles with a stick. For pain, apply an ice pack. Seek additional medical treatment if you experience shortness of breath, weakness, palpitations, muscle cramps, or any other severe symptoms.

Punctures Most sea-related punctures come from stepping on or brushing against the needlelike spines of sea urchins (known locally as *wana*). Be careful when you're in the water; don't put your foot down (even if you have booties or fins on) if you can't clearly see the bottom. A sea urchin puncture can result in burning, aching, swelling, and discoloration (black or purple) around the area where the spines entered your skin. The best thing to do is to pull out any protruding spines. The body will absorb the spines within

24 hours to 3 weeks, or the remainder of the spines will work themselves out. Again, contrary to popular thought, do not urinate or pour vinegar on the embedded spines—this will not help.

Cuts All cuts obtained in the marine environment must be taken seriously because the high level of bacteria present in the water can quickly cause the cut to become infected. The best way to prevent cuts is to wear a wet suit, gloves, and reef shoes. Never touch coral; not only can you get cut, but you also can damage a living organism that took decades to grow. For a coral cut: Gently pull the edges of the skin open and removing any embedded coral or grains of sand with tweezers. Next, scrub the cut well with fresh water. If pressing a clean cloth against the wound doesn't stop the bleeding, or the edges of the injury are jagged or gaping, seek medical treatment.

Internet & Wi-Fi In every island, branches of the **Hawaii State Public** Library System have free computers with Internet access. To find your closest library, check www.librarieshawaii.org/Serials/databases.html. There is no charge for use of the computers, but you must have a Hawaii library card, which is free to Hawaii residents and members of the military. Visitors have a choice of two types of cards: a $25 nonresident card that is good for 5 years (and may be renewed for an additional $25) or a $10 visitor card ($5 for children 18 and under).

If you have your own laptop, every **Starbucks** in Hawaii has Wi-Fi. For a list of locations, go to **www.starbucks.com/retail/find/default.aspx.**

Most major hotels and interisland airports have **Internet kiosks** that provide basic Web access for a per-minute fee.

Mail At press time, domestic postage rates were 34¢ for a postcard and 49¢ for a letter. For international mail, a first-class letter of up to 1 ounce costs $1.15 to Canada and Mexico); a first-class postcard costs the same as a letter. For more information, go to **www.usps.com.**

Mobile Phones Before you get on the plane to Hawaii, check with your wireless company's coverage map on its website. There are parts of Hawaii (and in some resorts) where coverage is not very good. If you need to stay in touch at a destination where you know your phone won't work, **rent** a phone that does from **InTouch USA** (www.intouchglobal.com; ✆ 800/872-7626), but be aware that you'll pay 89 cents a minute or more for airtime.

If you're not from the U.S., you'll be appalled at the poor reach of our **GSM (Global System for Mobile Communications) wireless network,** which is used by much of the rest of the world. Your phone will probably work in most major U.S. cities; it may not work in many rural areas. And you may or may not be able to send SMS (text messaging) home.

THE VALUE OF US$ VS. OTHER POPULAR CURRENCIES

US$	C$	£	€	A$	NZ$
1	1.31	0.89	0.89	1.32	1.48

Money & Costs The currency conversions quoted above were correct at press time. However, rates fluctuate, so before departing consult a currency exchange website such as www.xe.com to check up-to-the-minute rates.

ATMs (cashpoints) are everywhere in Hawaii—at banks, supermarkets, Longs Drugs, and Honolulu International Airport, and in some resorts and shopping centers.

Visitors from outside the U.S. should also find out whether their bank assesses a 1% to 3% fee on charges incurred abroad.

WHAT THINGS COST IN HAWAII

	US$
Hamburger	6.00–12.00
Movie ticket (adult/child)	10.50/7.50
Taxi from Honolulu Airport to Waikiki	28.00–45.00
Entry to Bishop Museum (adult/child)	23.00/15.00
Entry to Wet 'n' Wild (adult/child)	50.00/38.00
Entry to Honolulu Zoo (adult/child)	14.00/6.00
Entry to Maui Ocean Center (adult/child)	28.00/20.00
Tour of Maui Tropical Plantation (adult/child)	20.00/10.00
Entry to Haleakala National Park (person/car)	8.00/15.00
Old Lahaina Luau (adult/child)	110.00/75.00
20-oz. soft drink at convenience store	2.50
16-oz. apple juice	3.50
Cup of coffee	3.00
Moderately priced three-course dinner without alcohol	50.00
Moderately priced Waikiki hotel room (double)	145.00–195.00

Credit cards are accepted everywhere except TheBus (on Oahu), taxicabs (all islands), and some small restaurants and bed-and-breakfast accommodations.

Packing Hawaii is very informal. Shorts, T-shirts, and tennis shoes will get you by at most restaurants and attractions; a casual dress or a polo shirt and long pants are fine even in the most expensive places. Jackets for men are required only in some of the fine-dining rooms of a very few ultra-exclusive resorts—and they'll cordially provide men with a jacket if they don't bring their own. Aloha wear is acceptable everywhere, so you may want to plan on buying an aloha shirt or a *muumuu* (a Hawaiian-style dress) while you're in the islands.

The tropical sun poses the greatest threat to anyone who ventures into the great outdoors, so be sure to pack **sun protection:** a good pair of sunglasses, strong sunscreen, and a light hat. One last thing: **It can get really cold in Hawaii.** If you plan to see the sunrise from the top of Maui's Haleakala Crater, venture into the Big Island's Hawaii Volcanoes National Park, or spend time in Kokee State Park on Kauai, bring a warm jacket; 40°F (4°C) upcountry temperatures, even in summer when it's 80°F (27°C) at the beach, are not uncommon. It's always a good idea to bring at least a windbreaker, a sweater, or a light jacket. And be sure to toss some **rain gear** into your suitcase if you'll be in Hawaii

between November and March.

Passports Every air traveler entering the U.S. is required to show a passport.

Safety Although tourist areas are generally safe, visitors should always stay alert, even in laid-back Hawaii (and especially in Waikiki). Avoid deserted areas, especially at night. Don't go into any city park at night unless there's an event that attracts crowds. Generally speaking, you can feel safe in areas where there are many people and open establishments.

Avoid carrying valuables with you on the street, and don't display expensive cameras or electronic equipment. Hold on to your pocketbook, and place your billfold in an inside pocket. In theaters, restaurants, and other public places, keep your possessions in sight.

Oahu has seen a series of purse-snatching incidents, in which thieves in slow-moving cars or on foot have snatched handbags from female pedestrians. The Honolulu police department advises women to carry purses on the shoulder away from the street or, better yet, to wear the strap across the chest instead of on one shoulder. Remember also that hotels are open to the public and that in a large property, security may not be able to screen everyone entering. Always lock your room door.

Recently, burglaries of tourists' rental cars in hotel parking structures and at beach parking lots have become more common. Park in well-lighted and well-traveled areas, if possible. Never leave any packages or valuables visible in the car.

Generally, Hawaii has the same laws as the mainland United States. Nudity is illegal in Hawaii. There are NO legal nude beaches (I don't care what you have read). If you are nude on a beach (or anywhere) in Hawaii, you can be arrested.

Smoking marijuana also is illegal. Yes, there is medical marijuana in Hawaii, but. if you attempt to buy it or light up, you can be arrested.

Senior Travel Discounts for seniors are available at almost all of Hawaii's major attractions and occasionally

at hotels and restaurants. The Outrigger hotel chain, for instance, offers travelers ages 50 and older up to 20% discount off regular published rates. Always ask when making hotel reservations or buying tickets. And always carry identification with proof of your age—it can really pay off.

Smoking For both cigarettes and vapor pipes, it's against the law to smoke in public buildings, including airports, shopping malls, grocery stores, retail shops, buses, movie theaters, banks, convention facilities, and all government buildings and facilities. There is no smoking in restaurants, bars, and nightclubs. Also, there is no smoking within 20 feet of a doorway, window, or ventilation intake. Nearly all the beaches on Oahu are no-smoking.

Taxes The United States has no value-added tax (VAT) or other indirect tax at the national level. Every state, county, and city may levy its own local tax on all purchases, including hotel and restaurant checks and airline tickets. These taxes will not appear on price tags.

Hawaii state general excise tax is 4%. Hotel tax is 13.96% on Oahu and 13.42% on all the other islands. Oahu adds an additional .546% surcharge on all items purchased there (including hotel rooms) to pay for the upcoming public rail system, which is still under construction.

Telephones All calls on-island are local calls; calls from one island to another via a land line are long distance and you must dial 1; then the Hawaii area code, 808; and then the phone number. Many convenience groceries and packaging services sell **prepaid calling cards** in denominations up to $50. Many public pay phones at airports now accept American Express, MasterCard, and Visa. **Local calls** made from most pay phones cost 50¢. Most long-distance and international calls can be dialed directly from any phone. **To make calls within the United States and to Canada,** dial 1 followed by the area code and the seven-digit number. **For other international calls,** dial 011 followed by the country code, city code, and the number you are calling. Calls to area codes **800, 888, 877,** and **866** are toll-free.

For **directory assistance** ("Information"), dial 411 for local numbers and national numbers in the U.S. and Canada. For dedicated long-distance information, dial 1, then the appropriate area code plus 555-1212.

Time The continental United States is divided into **four time zones:** Eastern Standard Time (EST), Central Standard Time (CST), Mountain Standard Time (MST), and Pacific Standard Time (PST). Alaska and Hawaii have their own zones. For example, when it's 7am in Honolulu (HST), it's 9am in Los Angeles (PST), 10am in Denver (MST), 11am in Chicago (CST), noon in New York City (EST), 5pm in London (GMT), and 2am the next day in Sydney.

Daylight saving time, in effect in most of the United States from 1am on the second Sunday in March to 1am on the first Sunday in November, is not observed in Hawaii, Arizona, the U.S. Virgin Islands, and Puerto Rico. Daylight saving time moves the clock 1 hour ahead of standard time.

Tipping Tips are a very important part of certain workers' income, and gratuities are the standard way of showing appreciation for services provided. (Tipping is certainly not compulsory if the service is poor!) In hotels, tip **bellhops** at least $1 per bag ($3–$5 if you have a lot of luggage) and tip the **chamber staff** $2 to $3 per person per day (more if you've left a disaster area for him or her to clean up). Tip the **doorman** or **concierge** only if he or she has provided you with some specific service (for example, calling a cab for you or obtaining difficult-to-get theater tickets). Tip the **valet-parking attendant** $1 to $2 every time you get your car.

In restaurants, bars, and nightclubs, tip **service staff** and **bartenders** 15% to 22% of the check, and tip **valet-parking attendants** $1 per vehicle.

As for other service personnel, tip **cab drivers** 15% of the fare; tip **skycaps** at airports at least $1 per bag ($3–$5 if you have a lot of luggage); and tip **hairdressers** and **barbers** 15% to 20%.

Toilets You won't find public toilets or "restrooms" on the streets in Hawaii but they can be found in hotel lobbies, bars, restaurants, museums, department stores, and service stations. Large hotels and fast-food restaurants are often the best bet for clean facilities. Restaurants and bars in resorts or heavily visited areas may reserve their restrooms for patrons.

Visas The U.S. State Department has a **Visa Waiver Program (VWP)** allowing citizens of the following countries to enter the United States without a visa for stays of up to 90 days: Andorra, Australia, Austria, Belgium, Brunei, Czech Republic, Denmark, Estonia, Finland, France, Germany, Greece, Hungary, Iceland, Ireland, Italy, Japan, Latvia, Liechtenstein, Lithuania, Luxembourg, Malta, Monaco, the Netherlands, New Zealand, Norway, Portugal, San Marino, Singapore, Slovakia, Slovenia, South Korea, Spain, Sweden, Switzerland, and the United Kingdom. (**Note:** This list was accurate at press time; for the most up-to-date list of countries in the VWP, consult www. travel.state.gov/content/

visas/english.html.) Even though a visa isn't necessary, in an effort to help U.S. officials check travelers against terror watch lists before they arrive at U.S. borders, visitors from VWP countries must register online through the Electronic System for Travel Authorization (ESTA) before boarding a plane or a boat to the U.S. Travelers must complete an electronic application providing basic personal and travel eligibility information. The Department of Homeland Security recommends filling out the form at least 3 days before traveling. Authorizations will be valid for up to 2 years or until the traveler's passport expires, whichever comes first. Currently, there is a $160 (this is the best information I could find) fee for the online application. Existing ESTA registrations remain valid through their expiration dates. **Note:** Any passport issued on or after October 26, 2006 by a VWP country must be an **e-Passport** for VWP travelers to be eligible to enter the U.S. without a visa. Citizens of these nations also need to present a round-trip air or cruise ticket upon arrival. E-Passports contain computer chips capable of storing biometric information, such as the required digital photograph of the holder. If your passport doesn't have this feature, you can still travel without a visa if the valid passport was issued before October 26, 2005, and includes a machine-readable zone; or if the valid passport was issued between October 26, 2005 and October 25, 2006, and includes a digital photograph. For more information, go to **http://travel.state.gov.** Canadian citizens may enter the United States without visas, but will need to show passports and proof of residence.

Citizens of all other countries must have (1) a valid passport that expires at least 6 months later than the scheduled end of their visit to the U.S.; and (2) a tourist visa.

Index

A

Aaron's Dive Shop (Oahu), 72
Accommodations
  Big Island, 91–98
    Hamakua Coast, 96
    Hawaii Volcanoes
      National Park,
      97–98, 120
    Hilo, 96–97
    Kohala Coast, 93–96
    Kona Coast, 91–93
  fees, 221
  Kauai, 215–222
  Maui, 147–158
    Central Maui, 147–148
    South Maui, 152–157
    Upcountry Maui,
    157–158
    West Maui, 148–152
  Oahu, 30–39
    airport hotels, 30
    Honolulu beyond
      Waikiki, 37
    North Shore, 38–39
    Waikiki, 31–37
    Windward Coast, 37–38
Addiction (Honolulu), 82
Agricultural screening at the
  airports, 263
Ahuena Heiau (Big Island), 105
Air tours
  Big Island, 121
  Oahu, 77
Air travel, 262–263
  Big Island, 86
  Kauai, 209
  Maui, 141–142
  Oahu, 22
Akaka Falls (Big Island), 113
Alakai Swamp Trail (Kauai),
  250–251
Ala Moana (Oahu), 26
  accommodations, 37
Ala Moana Beach Park (Oahu), 68
Ala Moana Center (Oahu), 80
Ala Wai Municipal Golf Course
  (Oahu), 75
Alii Gardens Marketplace (Big
  Island), 133
Alii Kula Lavender (Maui), 177
Aliiolani Hale (Honolulu), 62–63
Allerton Garden of the National
  Tropical Botanical Garden
  (Kauai), 230
Aloha Beach Service (Oahu),
  72, 74
Aloha Kauai Tours, 229
Aloha Stadium Swap Meet
  (Oahu), 80
Aloha Tower (Honolulu), 59
Aloha wear, Oahu, 79
Anaehoomalu Bay (A-Bay; Big
  Island), 122
Anini Beach (Kauai), 212, 245

Anini Beach County Park
  (Kauai), 242
Area codes, 267
Art Night (Maui), 200
As Hawi Turns (Big Island), 135
Atlantis Submarines, 4, 74, 127,
  190, 197
Awaawapuhi Trail (Kauai), 250

B

Bailey House Museum (Maui), 169
Bailey House Museum Shop
  (Maui), 200
Baldwin Home Museum
  (Maui), 171
Ballet, Oahu, 83
Bamboo forest (Maui), 179–180
Bank of Hawaii (Honolulu), 56
Banyan Drive (Big Island), 115
Banyan Tree (Maui), 171
Bargaining, in Chinatown
  (Honolulu), 58
Barking Sands Beach (Kauai), 241
Beach Bar (Waikiki), 82
Beaches, 1. *See also* Watersports;
  and specific beaches
  best, 5
  Big Island, 124–125
  family, 9
  Kauai, 239–243
  Maui, 183–187
  Oahu, 68–71
Bears' Coffee (Big Island), 100
Big Beach (Oneloa Beach;
  Maui), 186
Big Island, 84–138
  accommodations, 91–98
    Hamakua Coast, 96
    Hawaii Volcanoes
      National Park,
      97–98, 120
    Hilo, 96–97
    Kohala Coast, 93–96
    Kona Coast, 91–93
  arriving in, 86
  best experiences, 85–86
  in brief, 87–89
  entertainment and nightlife,
    137–138
  exploring, 105–122
    Hamakua Coast,
      113–115
    Hawaii Volcanoes
      National Park,
      117–121
    Hilo, 115–117
    Holualoa, 106–107
    Kailua-Kona, 105–106
    for kids, 106
    Kohala Coast, 108–109
    The Kohala Coast, 122
    Kona Coast, 105, 122
    Mauna Kea, 110–113
    North Kohala, 109–110
    South Kona, 107–108
    South Point (Land's
      End), 122

Waipio Valley, 114–115
  getting around, 89–90
  golf and other outdoor
    activities, 130–133
  hiking and camping, 128–130
  restaurants, 98–104
  shops and galleries, 133–137
  visitor information, 86
Big Island Candies (Big
  Island), 136
Big Island Mountain Bike
  Association, 132
Big Kahuna Rentals (Oahu), 76
Bike Hawaii (Oahu), 76
Bike Works (Big Island), 132
Biking
  Big Island, 132
  Kauai, 255
  Maui, 197–198
Birding
  Big Island, 132–133
  Kauai, 255–256
Bishop Museum (Oahu), 47
Black Pot (Kauai), 242–243
Blue Dragon (Big Island), 138
Blue Hawaiian Helicopters, 121,
  170, 234
Boating
  Big Island, 125
  Kauai, 244
  Maui, 187–189
  Oahu, 72
Bubbles Below Scuba Charters
  (Kauai), 245
Business hours, 267

C

Café des Amis (Maui), 206
Camping and wilderness cabins
  Big Island, 128–130
  Maui, 192–195
Camp Sloggett (Kauai), 251
Canoe paddling, 7
Canyon Trail (Kauai), 249
Captain Andy's Sailing Adventures
  (Kauai), 244
Captain Dan McSweeney's Whale
  Watch Learning Adventures,
  4, 125
Captain Steve's Rafting Excursions
  (Maui), 189, 191–192
Caretaker's Cottage (Kauai), 251
Car travel and rentals, 263–264
Casanova (Maui), 205–206
Caverns (Kauai), 245
Cellphones, 270
Central Maui, 142
  accommodations, 147–148
  exploring, 169–171
  nightlife, 206
  restaurants, 158–159
  shopping, 199–200
Central Oahu (Ewa Plain), 28,
  66–67
Charley's Restaurant (Maui), 206
Charter Desk at Honokohau
  Marina (Big Island), 127